Financial Fraud and Guerrilla Violence in Missouri's Civil War, 1861–1865

Mark W. Geiger

Yale
UNIVERSITY
PRESS
New Haven & London

Yale University Press books may be purchased in quantity for educational,
business, or promotional use. For information, please e-mail sales.press@yale.edu
(U.S. office) or sales@yaleup.co.uk (U.K. office).

Set in Electra and Trajan types by Tseng Information Systems, Inc.
Printed in the United States of America by Sheridan Books, Ann Arbor, Michigan.

Library of Congress Cataloging-in-Publication Data
Geiger, Mark W.
Financial fraud and guerrilla violence in Missouri's Civil War, 1861–1865 /
Mark W. Geiger.
p. cm.
Includes bibliographical references and index.
ISBN 978-0-300-15151-0 (hardcover : alk. paper) 1. United States—History—Civil War,
1861–1865—Finance. 2. Missouri—History—Civil War, 1861–1865—Finance.
3. Missouri—Economic conditions—19th century. 4. Missouri—Politics and
government—1861–1865. 5. Fraud—Missouri—History—19th century. 6. Bank fraud—
Missouri—History—19th century. 7. Conspiracies—Missouri—History—19th century.
8. Guerrillas—Missouri—History—19th century. 9. Violence—Missouri—History—
19th century. 10. Regionalism—Missouri—History—19th century. I. Title.
E480.G45 2010
977.8′03—dc22
2009047994

A catalogue record for this book is available from the British Library.

This paper meets the requirements of ANSI/NISO Z39.48-1992 (Permanence of Paper).

10 9 8 7 6 5 4 3 2 1

CONTENTS

Illustrations follow p. 54 and p. 114

LIST OF APPENDIXES

Acknowledgments

I would like to take this occasion to gratefully acknowledge the support that the Minnesota Population Center at the University of Minnesota, the Center for Economic History at UCLA, and the United States Studies Centre at the University of Sydney extended to me while I was writing this book. Much of the material in chapter 6 was published as "Indebtedness and the Origins of Guerrilla Violence in Civil War Missouri" in the *Journal of Southern History* 75, no. 1 (2009): 49–82. The readers and staff at the JSH gave me excellent advice on how to improve the article. I also particularly want to thank my wife, Lisa, my dissertation advisor, LeeAnn Whites at the University of Missouri, Naomi Lamoreaux at UCLA, and the staff at the State Historical Society of Missouri in Columbia, Missouri. Readers at Yale University Press and the Press's own staff helped me in many ways. My children, Harley, Uintah, Klaus, and Ellen, have encouraged me and supported me throughout. Finally, I would like to thank George Anderson, who gave me the idea in the first place.

INTRODUCTION

This book describes a previously unknown financial conspiracy that occurred in Missouri at the beginning of the Civil War. In 1861, a small group of pro-secession politicians, bankers, and wealthy men conspired to divert money from Missouri's banks to arm and equip rebel military units then forming through-out the state. The scheme backfired and caused widespread indebtedness among Missouri's planters and their extended families, ending their decades-long domination of the state's economic and political life. The chain of events set off by the failed conspiracy was unique to Missouri, but the records of it give a detailed picture of military mobilization in both sections of the country during the earliest phase of the Civil War. This episode also contributes new data to several larger questions of Civil War history, including the nature of wartime guerrilla violence in the border states, and postwar leadership persistence in the New South.

Missouri's post–Civil War history differed from that of other former slave states. These differences are well known, but historians have previously missed this episode, which helped set the state on its separate path. Traditional documentary sources, such as newspapers and personal papers, contain almost no direct commentary on these events. Also, multiple obstacles, beginning with geography, both mask and impede access to surviving evidence. The most important primary-source data—county circuit court records—are scattered over a region the size of West Virginia. The pattern of military funding, however, emerges only through examining large numbers of defaulted-debt cases, which are buried among other case records. As with these materials, most of the other available evidence is scattered in large pools of data. I noticed the documentary traces of these events because I once managed an audit department that investigated fraud.

What happened was this. In early 1861, pro-Confederate volunteers through-out Missouri began forming militia units to defend the state's expected secession. To provide arms and equipment, a group of senior state politicians and bankers secretly plotted to divert money from Missouri's banks and the state treasury. After secession, this group, led by the newly elected governor, planned to repay the banks through a sale of state bonds. Except that Missouri was a contested border state and the group had to act in secret, the Missourians' plan closely matched measures lately taken by the Alabama state government to arm its own volunteers. In May and June of 1861, however, preemptive Union military strikes overturned Missouri's elected state government and ended the original financing plan.

Missouri's bankers were willing to provide the money, but after mid-June the pro-secession state government was in flight from federal forces. Acting inde-pendently, branch bankers in the interior of the state then mounted what was in effect a giant check-kiting scheme, making thousands of unsecured loans to leading pro-Confederate citizens in their communities. These men, usually the bankers' own relatives, then channeled the money to the rebel forces. These ac-tions amounted to a massive fraud perpetrated against the banks' other deposi-tors, shareholders, and creditors. The bankers granted over twenty-nine hundred such loans in forty counties in central and western Missouri, more than a third of the state. Most of the state's branch banks joined in this lending, which totaled about three million dollars. This was a huge sum of money when the latest mili-tary sidearm, the .44 caliber Colt New Model Army revolver, sold at wholesale for twenty dollars.[1]

Bankers and borrowers alike expected the South to win quickly, and Missouri's Confederate state government-in-exile pledged to underwrite the costs of the war. With this supposed safety net in place, the borrowers signed for far more money than they were eventually able to repay, and the bankers drained their in-stitutions of cash. The costs of this gamble became clear late in 1861 when Union military authorities began purging pro-Confederate bankers, which meant nearly all the bankers in the state. Most of the bankers resigned, some fled, and a few were imprisoned or shot. Union men took control of the banks and filed civil lawsuits to recover on the defaulted loans. Thousands of pro-Confederate Missourians were suddenly liable for personal debts which they had thought the Confederate government would assume.

The defendants in the lawsuits included many of the state's wealthiest and most prominent pro-Confederate citizens and their extended kinfolk. After mid-1862, judgments arising from the lawsuits caused mass insolvency in this elite group, which had dominated the state's business and politics for decades. Eventually, county sheriffs auctioned nearly three hundred and fifty thousand acres of farmland to satisfy the court judgments. Damage from the lawsuits probably extended beyond the original borrowers. There were no bankruptcy laws in force that could have scheduled an orderly payment of debts, and one family's insolvency could touch off a chain of others. The leading families' economic, social, and kinship relations were so intertwined that whole extended family networks went down at once. The litigation created a revolution in landownership that decapitated the state's southern society. Today a subaltern southern culture survives in Missouri, but little remains of a traditional southern aristocracy, unlike in other former border slave states like Kentucky and Maryland. Many of these newly landless families emigrated. Most went west and south, but some scattered as far as Brazil and Mexico.

As a further turn in this story, the indebtedness intensified the guerrilla war that raged in Missouri from mid-1862 on. This was the worst such conflict ever to occur on American soil, and it is an aberration in American history that has never been fully explained. Pro-Confederate Missourians went to the brush for all the same reasons as their counterparts in other districts occupied by Union troops, including conquered parts of the Confederacy proper. But the Missourians had an added grievance, in that thousands of southern families were losing their land in the lawsuits arising from the debts. A disproportionate number of the young men from these dispossessed families joined the guerrilla bands, making common cause with desperate and violent men from the bottom of society. Many guerrillas later turned to banditry, most famously the James-Younger gang. The violence so disrupted civil society that conditions did not settle down for nearly two decades after the war. In the 1870s eastern newspapers called Missouri "the robber state."

Looking beyond this melodramatic story, the financing episode contributes to our understanding of several larger questions of Civil War history. Within Missouri, the fallout from the financing helps explain the puzzling and anomalous level of guerrilla violence, as well as the absence today of an aristocratic tradition in the state. Also, by destroying Missouri's southern leadership, the mass indebtedness contributed to the postwar redrawing of sectional boundaries. Missouri, and recently Maryland, are the only states considered southern in 1861 that are no longer so classified. Meanwhile, the vicious guerrilla conflict and its aftermath have become Missouri's signature contribution to the nation's common knowledge of the Civil War, and a durable and profitable media resource. The first novel about Missouri guerrillas appeared in 1861; the most recent film, and doubtless not the last, came out in 2007.

In the larger history of the war, this citizens' mobilization in Missouri shows a form of Civil War financing used throughout both sections of the country that other scholars have not previously studied. Only in Missouri (and part of Kentucky), however, did such financing backfire on its organizers, owing to Missouri's status as a border state. Historians have written extensively about Civil War military supply and procurement, but such studies focus on the actions of governments. However, through most of 1861, governments North and South lacked the money, the legal authority, and the administrative capacity necessary for military mobilization. Without private financing in this transitional period, the shooting war could not have started until months later.

The ground-up military mobilization of 1861 was also an important milestone in the transformation of the United States from a nation of courts and parties, in Stephen Skowronek's phrase, into a modern administrative state. Before the Civil War, the nation's standing army was minuscule, with a supply capacity to match. Mobilization for all the nation's early wars relied heavily on initial financing from private sources. By law, state militia and volunteers largely equipped themselves. State governments used various means to compensate private citizens for these expenses, treating them as loans made to the state. If a war lasted long enough, the government would provide replacement equipment. This reliance on private credit worked for the nation's early wars, which were low-tech and limited, but was inadequate for the challenge facing the nation in 1861. On December 1, 1860, U.S. forces numbered sixteen thousand. Two months later a half million men in the non-seceding states alone had volunteered for military service. By 1865 the Union Army had a million men under arms. After 1861, the U.S. War Department took responsibility for all matters of military supply, making a permanent change in the nation's means of war.

The events in Missouri bear on another question of nineteenth-century U.S. political economy, that of the market revolution in the antebellum period. This idea has never gained much traction among economic historians, but there is evidence that social attitudes and relations underwent a major change before the Civil War. Here, we can compare the actions of the Missouri bankers with their counterparts in New Orleans. In the crisis of 1861, bankers in the Crescent City insisted on honoring their commitments to northern creditors. The bankers held to this position throughout the war, despite their own political convictions, adverse public opinion, and pressure from the Confederate government. The bankers' actions clearly show the importance they placed on preserving their institutions' capital, reputation, and business relationships. In short, the New Orleans bankers acted like modern managers. The Missouri bankers, faced with the same crisis, handed over all the banks' money to their own relatives.[2]

The different behavior of the two sets of bankers stems, I believe, from the degree of penetration of market culture and values in the two places. New Orleans had been the South's banking center for decades, and the city's bankers had long-term relations with their counterparts in the North and in Europe. The Missouri bankers had no such body of institutional memory or tradition to draw on. In January 1857, Missouri had one chartered (currency-issuing) bank with six branches, counting the parent bank. Four years later there were nine banks with forty-two branches. Such rapid expansion meant that few of the new bankers, who by 1861 were doing business with New Orleans, New York, London, and Liverpool, had prior industry experience. Most of Missouri's bankers had been successful merchants, and they managed the new banks like conventional mercantile partnerships. In this way, Missouri's new banks resembled the banks of thirty years before in industrializing New England. In both places, the banks were extended-family businesses with a core of officers, principal shareholders, and customers with close personal and family ties. But merchants are not trustees and bankers are, in that they have the care of assets they themselves do not own. The New Orleans bankers compartmentalized their business and personal lives, following the modern Wall Street saying that money is thicker than blood. The Missourians were not there yet.

This monograph is both an economic and a social history, exploring economic events that produced important social changes. Also, the events described here tell two different stories, one local and regional, and the other national. The first story was in most respects unique to Missouri and atypical of what was happening in the rest of the country. The turn that events took in Missouri was partly the result of historical accident. Instead of purging disloyal bankers, Union authorities could have closed the banks altogether. In that case, it is unclear who or what would have been around later to sue for recovery on the defaulted promissory notes. If Missouri's antebellum elite had survived the war with their property intact, the later history of this group might have been different. As it was, detailed records now exist in Missouri that show how the American system worked in wartime, right before state and citizenship began to change into more recognizably modern forms. The episode also poses a contemporary question: whether modern rebels have gotten money by similar means. Many parts of the modern world have mixed populations deeply divided in their politics, a broken political system, and powerful interests aligned with the rebels. Aided by modern communications, a group of bankers today could do as Missouri bankers did in 1861, but faster and more efficiently.

The financial conspiracy of 1861 and all that followed from it occurred at a time and place, and to a group of people, that combined to create significant social change. The banks mainly served the richest members of society, and it was this elite group that suffered most from its connection to the banks. Borderlands are inherently unstable regions, and before the Civil War Missouri's Boonslick was the farthest northwestern extension of plantation culture, slavery, and widespread support for the rebellion. If Missouri had been located closer to the Confederate core, the state's plantation system could have withstood the misfortunes of a few thousand people. Missouri's bankers, too, had more power and less governmental restraint on that power in 1861 than at any other time in the state's banking history. Missouri bank officers before the Civil War made up a small group, but their importance went well beyond their numbers. These men, the presidents and cashiers of some forty-two banks, effectively controlled the money supply and most of the available commercial credit in the state. When the bankers supported the losing side in the war, this institutional power caused great damage.

Ironically, therefore, despite the combined leverage of geographic location, elite involvement, and institutional power, the freedom of action of all parties was in many ways restricted. Given the sharply divided loyalties of Missouri's citizens, the state's northern and southern factions inevitably came into conflict. The state's southern men controlled a strategic resource—the banks—and Missouri's Unionists had little choice but to try to block its use. The struggle over the banks led Missouri's southern leaders into a worsening series of alternatives. Missouri's bankers could only use their power in ways that would wreck their own fortunes, those of their extended families, and eventually those of the social class to which they belonged. Even though they had only recently been founded when the war broke out, in important respects Missouri's country banks were anachronistic, and the bankers' family ties and loyalties compromised their institutions.

Chapters in this book advance in chronological order. The first part of the study describes the early plot to get money for the pro-secession Missouri State Guard, changes to these plans, and the resulting developments that created widespread indebtedness in the Boonslick and nearby counties. The second half of the study analyzes the effects of the indebtedness. These outcomes included heightened guerrilla violence in Missouri, a seriously weakened planter class, and, by the end of the war, changes in the state's character, culture, and leadership. The final chapter puts the events in Missouri into national perspective.

Many readers will find the main primary sources, court and financial records, to be inaccessible, tedious, or both. I have tried to confine technical material to endnotes and to Appendixes 1 and 2, so as not to impede the book's flow. Some supporting data, especially the biographical material, are too extensive to include in this book. Readers interested in this material can access it on Yale University Press's website. Besides court papers, the most important primary sources used for this study are financial data, genealogical information, and military and legislative records. Locating and transcribing the data were only the first obstacles to this study. Except for the legislative materials, all the primary sources used in this study were large enough to make data management a problem. Relational database software proved an essential tool for mapping complex connections among individuals, families, military units, and banks. Appendix 1, Research Design and Methodology, describes the research method.

Since the book contains a good deal of local history, including many names, local historians and genealogical researchers may find parts of the book of interest. I have avoided academic jargon and tried to write as clearly as possible, to make the book accessible to nonspecialist readers.

FINANCIAL CONSPIRACY

On November 7, 1860, when Abraham Lincoln was elected sixteenth president of the United States, he faced a serious legitimacy problem. Lincoln was the first president belonging to the six-year-old Republican Party, and he had won election with only 40 percent of the popular vote and without carrying a single southern state. Three days after Lincoln's election, the South Carolina legislature called a special convention to consider the state's relations with the federal Union. On December 20, the convention voted unanimously to dissolve South Carolina's union with the United States of America. Over the next five months ten more southern states left the Union, the last being North Carolina on May 20. In the deepening crisis, no one knew what the slave states of the Upper South and the Middle Border would do. Such concern was well founded. Four of these states—Virginia, North Carolina, Arkansas, and Tennessee—did not secede initially, but did so after Lincoln's first call for troops.[1]

Conditions in the border states were volatile. According to James McPherson, secessionists might easily have prevailed in Maryland, Kentucky, and Missouri. In the presidential election, Missourians had voted overwhelmingly for the two centrist candidates, Stephen A. Douglas and John Bell, who had pledged to preserve equality between the country's sections. But a committed minority of Missouri's voters sympathized strongly with the South. Such men included the rich slave owners and their extended families in the Boonslick and nearby counties, the most powerful special interest group in the state. For this group as in the deeper South, the election of a Republican president, who opposed extending slavery into the territories, was intolerable. Stakes were high. Missouri had the largest white population of any slave state, and more slaves than either Arkansas or Florida. After New Orleans, St. Louis would have been the Confederacy's second-largest city. The largest United States arsenal in any of the slave states was in St. Louis, with sixty thousand muskets and other arms in storage. The state was also a breadbasket for the South, as well as a major supplier of horses and mules. The state's strategic location astride two of the nation's major transport routes, the Mississippi and Missouri Rivers, could block Union access to the West.[2]

The leader of Missouri's southern faction was the state's newly elected governor, Claiborne Fox Jackson. Jackson was a native Kentuckian and a career politician, first elected to the Missouri general assembly in 1836. The new governor came from a modest background and had labored unceasingly to rise in the world, being successively a merchant, banker, farmer, and politician. Jackson's single-minded pursuit of success had earned him a reputation as an inveterate conniver, and he was called "Fox" Jackson by his many political enemies. Besides earning money, Jackson aspired to join the social elite of rural society by becoming a gentleman farmer, a planter. By 1861 he had achieved his goal, and he owned forty-eight slaves and over twelve hundred acres of land.[3]

Consistent with his social ambitions, Jackson was strongly committed to the southern cause. Long before he became governor he was a prominent member of the Central Clique, a close-knit group of planter-politicians from Missouri's Boonslick region who dominated state politics. As sectional politics became increasingly radical through the 1840s and 1850s, so did Jackson. In 1849, he and several other members of the Central Clique engineered the downfall of Missouri's longtime senator Thomas Hart Benton, whom they viewed as an obstacle to a more radical, proslavery agenda. In 1854, Jackson led a proslavery militia into the Kansas Territory to protect southern rights, as they saw it, and to battle abolitionists. In 1860, Jackson campaigned as a Douglas Democrat on a moderate, conciliatory platform, but after his election he immediately began working to engineer Missouri's secession. On January 3, 1861, two weeks after South Carolina's vote, Jackson took office as governor of Missouri in Jefferson City. In his inaugural address, he asked Missouri's newly elected Twenty-First General Assembly to call a state convention to consider secession. "Missouri, then," Jackson said, "will in my opinion best consult her own interest, and the interests of the whole country, by a timely declaration of her determination to stand by her sister slave-holding States, in whose wrongs she participates, and with whose institutions and people she sympathizes."[4]

Missourians were deeply divided, but Jackson had accurately described the sympathies of the new state assembly. For reasons having to do with malapportioned districts and holdover senators, the number of secessionists in the Twenty-First General Assembly exceeded their percentage of the popular vote, though not by so much that they could ignore other parties. John McAfee of Shelby

County, a Breckinridge Democrat, became speaker of the house. Lieutenant Governor Thomas C. Reynolds, a committed secessionist and later the Confederate governor of Missouri, presided over the senate. In early February and with Governor Jackson's backing, the assembly's secessionist members introduced several funding bills to arm and equip the state militia, the Missouri State Guard, and to prepare the state for war. The legislators thought, as did nearly everybody, that the secession crisis would be over within a few weeks. Short-term financing to buy supplies and to pay militia volunteers would seemingly be enough.[5]

Outside Missouri, events were coming to a boil. Mississippi seceded five days after Jackson's inauguration, and five other states of the Lower South followed over the next two weeks. On February 4, delegates from the seven states met in Montgomery, Alabama, to organize the Confederate States of America. Public opinion in Missouri in this period was fluid. In editorial comment in the early months of 1861, major newspapers in both the North and the South predicted that, while Missouri did not then wish to secede, the state would resist federal military action against the South. In January 1861 the *New York Herald* wrote, "The Missouri Legislature is in session, and that State will secede like the rest, unless the full measure of justice be conceded. The State is every moment becoming more and more revolutionary." Two months later, in March, the *Charleston Mercury* wrote, "Missouri is acting coolly and deliberately. She has had no thought of secession, yet entertains a strong sympathy for her Southern sisters. Her convention, now in session, will not pass a secession ordinance, but they will speak out and tell ABRAHAM LINCOLN that when he proposes to coerce the South he must include Missouri in his calculations. Missouri is loyal to Southern institutions, and will prove it when the proper time arrives." In Missouri itself, in Boonville, on April 22, Mrs. Nancy Chapman Jones, the wife of a retired banker, wrote to her daughter in San Antonio that "the people here are in a state of great excitement. The court house was crowded last Saturday, Mr. Vest made a secession speech the palmetto flag [the South Carolina state flag] was waveing over Boonville and the seecession feeling, is gaining ground very rapidly." On May 4 Mrs. Jones added, "The accession [secession] feeling prevails here almoste universally and the flag waves over our town."[6]

Identity is an elusive idea, but it is connected to how other people view you, as well as to how you view yourself. By the first measure, Missouri was a southern state before the Civil War. During the struggle over Kansas statehood in the 1850s, northern newspapers commonly grouped Missourians with other southerners. In August 1856, the *New York Times* reprinted a story from an Iowa paper, reporting that "[the Border Ruffians] are over one thousand strong, are composed of Missourians, South Carolinians, and Georgians, and are fully armed with cannon &c., prepared for war." Newspaper descriptions of Missouri resembled Frederick Law Olmsted's southern travel writing, depicting the state as a wilderness of wasted potential, blighted by slavery. In 1857 a *New York Times* correspondent wrote, "Improvements scarcely deserved the name, although we saw several indisputable evidences of long settlement. In fact, we everywhere discovered indications of the *curse* [slavery]. No villages greeted our longing gaze as we rattled over the road; no thrifty, cheerful homes looked out upon us from surrounding groves. At one stopping place, we found a *Railroad Hotel*, a *horse saw-mill* and a *whisky-shop*, to compose the only important point within fifteen miles of *Jefferson City*. All that looked encouraging in the way of progress, was an occasional glimpse of the Pacific Railroad grade, which is slowly progressing westward, notwithstanding the unmarketable character of the Bonds of the Border-Ruffian States." Here the writer equates progress with railroad construction, to link the state to the Atlantic port cities and industrial New England. (The writer's assertion that Missouri's bonds were unmarketable was not true.)[7]

The African American and abolitionist press was even blunter. Frederick Douglass blasted white Missourians in his newspaper as "the most depraved and desperate villains to be found anywhere." Elsewhere, the African American press excoriated Missouri as a barbarous land of lynch mobs, beheadings, scalpings, burnings at the stake, river pirates, duels, and, on one occasion, a punishment of seven hundred fifty lashes meted out to a slave. The *New York Times* agreed, thundering, "Heaven spare us from the *infection*—not the *bullets*—for in no other civilized land can there be found so obscene, depraved, brutish a race of beings, as inhabit the border counties of Missouri. A visit to their border towns is indeed sickening. Barrooms, saloons, and grog-shops are always filled with a drinking, gambling, swearing, fighting, blaspheming gang of loafers, who talk of nothing sensible or moral,—but, especially for the last few weeks, they talk mostly of killing Abolitionists in Kansas, ravishing the women, and carrying off to their bestial dens the young and beautiful."[8]

These quotations are typical northern newspaper fare on Missouri and Missourians. A few journalists disagreed. In July 1861 an editorialist for the *New York Times* predicted that railroad construction through Missouri would turn the state away from the South. Trade would boom with the Atlantic coastal cities, migrants from the Midwest and the Northeast would come to the state, and eastern investors would pay to develop Missouri's natural resources. All this, according to the *Times* writer, would cause slavery in Missouri eventually to disappear. Few newspapers expressed such views, however. As it happened, many of the writer's predictions came true, but there was nothing peaceful about the transition.[9]

There is no single answer to how Missourians viewed themselves. Located at the crossroads of the nation, Missouri has always been subject to more diverse influences than, say, states of the Deep South. Also, the state's varied internal geography fostered localized subcultures. Booming, free-labor St. Louis, with the largest percentage of immigrants of any U.S. city; the slave-labor plantations of the Boonslick; and the sparsely populated, poor-white Ozarks were worlds apart from one another. Still, in 1850 and 1860 the state had much in common with the South in matters of population, economy, land ownership, and politics. The state's dominant culture and leadership were also clearly southern before the war. The views of Missouri's leaders on sectional issues could be as extreme and bellicose as any in the South. Dr. Benjamin F. Stringfellow, a former Missouri attorney general and the leader of a proslavery Kansas militia, had this to say in an 1856 speech in St. Joseph: "I tell you to mark every scoundrel . . . tainted with free-soilism, or abolitionism, and exterminate him. Neither give nor take quarter from the damned rascals. I propose to mark them in this house, and on the present occasion, so you may crush them out." According to Stringfellow, in such a time of crisis, niceties of law and qualms of conscience only got in the way. Stringfellow urged his audience "one and all to enter into every election district in Kansas . . . and vote at the point of the bowie knife and the revolver."[10]

Most Missouri politicians spoke more temperately than Stringfellow but shared his loyalties. In the ten years before the war, over 85 percent of Missourians elected to statewide office owned slaves and were natives of slave states. In the 1840s and 1850s, except for Thomas Hart Benton, Missouri's congressional delegation staunchly supported southern causes and issues. Benton's views cost him his job at the hands of the Central Clique. Missouri's David R. Atchison, one of the South's most outspoken defenders in the U.S. Senate, was a member of the "F Street Mess," a powerful group of southern senators who boarded together in Washington at a house on F Street. In the 1850s Atchison toured the South canvassing for recruits for the Kansas struggle. In Atchison's speeches and letters he described Missouri as the frontline state in the struggle against abolitionism. Major southern newspapers such as the *Charleston Mercury* saw the state as a natural ally, sharing a common culture, values, and political and economic interests with the South. Many shared these sentiments. During the secession crisis, northern political leaders viewed Missouri's loyalty as shaky at best. When the war came, both of Missouri's U.S. senators and two of the state's seven representatives felt strongly enough about the southern cause to leave Congress, by resignation or expulsion. Southern leaders recognized this political support. In his prewar speeches, no less an authority on the South than Jefferson Davis described Missouri as a southern state. Throughout the war, the Confederate battle flag bore stars representing Missouri and Kentucky.[11]

Missouri voters, however, proved to be more moderate than anyone had anticipated. The drive for secession in Missouri suffered a serious setback in February and March, and it came in danger of failing altogether. Despite the governor's support and that of many members of the assembly, enough moderates sat in that body to stall the bills to arm the state militia. The assembly did, however, call the special convention requested by the governor. On February 18, the day Jefferson Davis took office in Montgomery, Alabama, as the president of the Confederate States of America, Missouri voters chose three delegates to the Missouri State Convention from each of the state's thirty-three senatorial districts. The Unionists won handily, with Conditional Union and Unconditional Union candidates receiving one hundred ten thousand votes. Secessionist candidates garnered only about thirty thousand votes, mostly in the Boonslick counties and in the poor-white counties along the Arkansas border. Not a single Breckinridge Democrat secured a seat in the convention.[12]

The convention met first in Jefferson City at the Cole County courthouse on February 28, before adjourning to better quarters at the Mercantile Library in St. Louis. On March 19, the convention, one vote short of unanimity, voted that "at present there is no adequate cause to impel Missouri to dissolve her connections with the Federal Union, but on the contrary she will labor for such an adjustment of existing troubles as will gain the peace, as well as the rights and equality of all the states." Missouri was the only state to call a secession convention that voted not to secede. The convention adjourned on March 22, its work done, and set the third Monday in December 1861 as the date for a second session. Recalling these events after the war, Thomas L. Snead, Governor Jackson's secretary and personal aide, wrote that the Unionist landslide in the convention election and the delegates' unambiguous vote demoralized the secessionists in the general assembly. The original sponsors of the militia bills declared that they themselves would now vote against these bills, as the people of Missouri so overwhelmingly opposed any warlike measures.[13]

The convention's vote not did not faze Governor Jackson, who had his own ideas about what was good for the state. While searching for funds to arm the militia, the governor received help from an unexpected quarter. The secession crisis had touched off a secondary crisis in the nation's financial markets, and the situation gave the governor leverage over Missouri's banks. In the weeks following the presidential election, the worsening political situation almost paralyzed commerce. At the end of 1860 and the beginning of 1861, trade and industry halted. Receivers of produce at the seaboard could realize nothing from sales, and credit was nearly unobtainable. At some of the southern ports all foreign trade was at a standstill. The export of domestic produce largely stopped.

Merchants and wholesalers canceled existing orders for finished goods and new orders plummeted. Throughout the country, factories closed and workers were let go or put on short hours. Many mercantile houses could not meet payments on their outstanding debts and went under.[14]

Financial markets fared no better. Short-term interest rates shot up around the country, reflecting the fear in the marketplace. Prices of U.S. Treasury bonds fell to 10 percent below par, the lowest point since the War of 1812. The bond market's weakness sparked a sell-off in Europe, depressing prices still further. Banks called in loans and refused merchants their usual credit terms. The stock markets declined almost to the lowest level reached during the Panic of 1857. Everywhere there was a drastic decline in bank deposits, as people withdrew their money. Fearing panic runs on their capital, the South Carolina banks suspended specie payments almost immediately after the presidential election, setting off a chain reaction. In November, the Baltimore and Philadelphia banks suspended. The New York banks, the largest and most important in the country, partially suspended in December. Investors moved money to safe havens wherever possible, ideally to Europe. Gold almost disappeared from the market, vanishing into hoards in wells, gardens, graveyards, and woods. Banks refused to accept each other's paper money.[15]

Missouri banks, with one exception, suspended specie payments in late November, in violation of Missouri's banking act of 1857. By law, banks chartered in Missouri had to accept the currency of other chartered Missouri banks and pay out gold or silver in return. The penalty for refusal was cancellation of the bank's charter to do business. Governor Jackson was better able to deal with the financial crisis than most state governors. Jackson was one of the most sophisticated financiers in the state, with twenty years' experience in banking. The governor's brother Wade was a bank director, and his brother-in-law William Breathitt Sappington was president of the Bank of Missouri branch at Arrow Rock. Before becoming governor, Jackson had been the state bank commissioner, Missouri's chief administrator of banking and currency law, for three years.[16]

At the governor's urging, on March 18 the general assembly voted not to annul the banks' charters and to waive the statutory 20 percent penalty on their circulating banknotes. In return, the banks would lend the state a half million dollars to fund the July 1861 interest payment on outstanding state bonds. The state government would then issue a half million dollars in new bonds, which the banks would then sell to repay the loan. Historians have known these facts but paid scant attention to Missouri's finances, which the unfolding political drama overshadowed. The agreement with the banks has seemed to historians, as it did to Missourians at the time, to have the sole aim of preventing further damage to the state's economy. In fact, the governor's financial plan had everything to do with his larger political agenda.[17]

Missouri's bankers, in common with much of the state's business elite, were almost all southern sympathizers. An exchange of incriminating letters shows that Jackson intended to use the bank loan not to pay the state's bond interest but instead to arm the Missouri State Guard. The letters also make it clear that the bankers cooperated willingly with the governor's plan. The state would then repay the banks as planned with the new bond issue approved by the general assembly. Only minor details remained unsettled: printing the bonds, scheduling the transfer of the money, and appointing state commissioners to receive it. The assembly could not complete these arrangements before adjourning on March 22, and the St. Louis banks had not yet paid out the money when the Jackson government was overturned seven weeks later. The bankers' relations with the secessionists remained close, however. In March 1861 the legislature had created the St. Louis Board of Police Commissioners, in an attempt to go around the regular municipal government and take control of the city. Jackson named four secessionists to the board, including John A. Brownlee, president of the Merchants' Bank of St. Louis, as the Police Board's president.[18]

Outside Missouri the military crisis deepened. On April 12, South Carolina troops under General P. G. T. Beauregard opened fire on Fort Sumter, and the commandant of the fort, Colonel Robert Anderson, surrendered the following day. On the 15th, President Lincoln called for the non-seceding states to provide seventy-five thousand men to put down the rebellion. Missouri's quota was four thousand men. On April 17, the same day that Virginia seceded, Jackson wrote to U.S. Secretary of War Simon Cameron, terming the president's call "illegal, unconstitutional, and revolutionary; in its objects inhuman and diabolical." That same day, Jackson met with leading secessionists in St. Louis, including Major General Daniel M. Frost, the Missouri State Guard commander for the St. Louis district. At this meeting Frost, Jackson, and the rest decided to seize the U.S. Army arsenal at St. Louis, convention vote or no. Jackson sent emissaries to Jefferson Davis and to Virginia seeking siege guns and mortars.[19]

On April 19 Jackson wrote secretly to David Walker, president of the Arkansas convention, stating that public opinion in Missouri was moving in favor of secession and that the state should be ready to secede within thirty days. The next day, on April 20, Jackson called a special session of the general assembly beginning May 2, "to place the State in a proper attitude of defense." At the same time, he ordered the Missouri State Guard to assemble in their respective districts for six days of training and drill, as provided by law. Also on April 20, rebels seized the small U.S. arsenal in Liberty, Missouri, in the first overt act of rebellion against the United States government in the state. By then, in all parts of the state, both sides were feverishly arming themselves. Jackson secretly ordered stockpiles of gunpowder hidden around the state. Still without money, Jackson ordered supplies paid for in scrip, or government IOUs, redeemable after the crisis ended.[20]

The two most prominent Union military leaders in St. Louis were U.S. Army Captain Nathaniel Lyon and Missouri Congressman Francis Preston Blair, Junior. Lyon, a West Point graduate and a career officer, transferred to St. Louis in February. He immediately allied himself with Blair and the most militant pro-Union faction in the city. By March, Lyon was bypassing his commanding officer, U.S. General William S. Harney, in writing to Lincoln, the War Department, and the governors of neighboring states to seek arms, ammunition, and troops. Lyon also recruited twenty-five hundred volunteers in St. Louis and inducted them into the United States Army. On April 27, these troops elected Lyon their general, a rank confirmed by Secretary of War Cameron and the adjutant general's office in Washington on May 18.[21]

Blair, meanwhile, was organizing the pro-Union German-American citizens in St. Louis into the paramilitary Wide Awake clubs, which became the nucleus of a new Unionist militia, the Missouri Home Guard. At the same time in St. Louis, Lieutenant Governor Reynolds was organizing the pro-secession Minute Men. From Jefferson City, Governor Jackson ordered Missouri State Guard General Daniel M. Frost to seize the United States arsenal in St. Louis. On Monday, May 6, the same day Arkansas seceded, Frost ordered the State Guard to encamp at a site he named Camp Jackson, after the governor, close to the arsenal. Unknown to Frost, the Union commanders in St. Louis had sent the arsenal's arms and munitions to Illinois for safekeeping.[22]

Governor Jackson continued to push his financial plans forward. Though pro-southern, the bankers of the Farmers' Bank of Missouri in Lexington balked over the bank's share of the half-million-dollar loan. The governor gave the bankers a stark choice. They could either agree to his demand or expect a visit from the Missouri State Guard, who might, in the governor's words, "make a draft upon the whole vault," that is, to clean the bank out. The bankers chose to deal with the governor. Robert A. Barnes, the president of the parent branch of the Bank of the State of Missouri (hereafter referred to as the Bank of Missouri), the largest bank in the state, raised a more serious concern in a letter to Jackson on May 9. Barnes wrote that he had to "take care how I loaned the Governor money to take the State out of the Union. Now, while I wish to furnish you with the money, I wish to be able to show that we have merely complied with the law." Barnes added that the federal government was demanding a loan from the bank as well, and would not wait much longer. Barnes pressed Jackson to move the money out of St. Louis before martial law was imposed.[23]

After receiving Barnes's letter, Jackson immediately wrote to former Missouri governor Sterling Price. Price had succeeded Jackson as state bank commissioner in the summer of 1860, when Jackson resigned to run for governor. Jackson warned Price that "there is no telling how soon Martial law may be proclaimed in St. Louis, and in such an event our money would be cut off from us at once." Jackson urged Price to help him pressure the bankers to move quickly, to send the money to certain branch banks in the interior of the state, which Jackson named. Historians have known that Jackson was communicating with secessionist leaders in this period, but they have overlooked these letters. U.S. troops found the letters in papers the governor abandoned after the southern defeat at Boonville on June 17, 1861. St. Louis newspapers published the letters, which were then picked up by newspapers around the country.[24]

The danger that Barnes and Jackson foresaw was real, even though martial law was not declared until August 14 (see Chapter 5). On May 8, the day before Jackson wrote to Price, General Nathaniel Lyon learned the siege guns the governor had requested from the Confederacy had arrived in St. Louis, seized from the federal arsenal at Baton Rouge. Lyon decided to attack the Missouri State Guard forces at Camp Jackson, before they could strengthen their position further. On May 10, Lyon surrounded Camp Jackson with his volunteer troops, who were almost all German-American recruits from St. Louis. General Frost had to surrender and allow his men to be arrested. During these proceedings an unruly crowd gathered and threw rocks and brickbats at Lyon's troops, the latter "drunk with beer and reeking of sauerkraut," in the words of one critic. Both sides opened fire, leaving twenty-eight people dead and wounding many more, a higher death toll than in the Baltimore riots of three weeks before. That night rioters filled the streets of St. Louis.[25]

Toward the evening of May 10, Governor Jackson, who was in St. Louis, returned to Jefferson City and reported Lyon's coup to the general assembly. After reconvening on May 2, the different factions in the assembly had deadlocked and accomplished little. Now, outraged by the events in St. Louis, the lawmakers passed a flurry of bills. One gave the governor nearly complete power over the Missouri State Guard, now broadened to include every able-bodied man in Missouri. Other measures set aside all the money in the state treasury to buy arms, and directed Missouri counties to lend money to the state. The assembly further approved a million dollars in state bonds and a new million-dollar defense loan from the state's banks, with the money to go directly to the governor.[26]

A brief, uneasy lull now followed, as both sides continued preparing for war. On May 12, Jackson appointed Sterling Price major general in command of all Missouri State Guard forces. Jackson appointed eight other brigadier generals, one for each military district of the state, and ordered them to enroll all the men of their respective districts at once. At the same time, citizens in the Boonslick counties held meetings to raise money to arm troops. On May 20, North Carolina seceded, the last state to do so before the Jackson government, by that time in exile, passed an ordinance of secession for Missouri in October.[27]

As far as raising money went, Lyon did Jackson a favor in provoking the general assembly to pass these measures. The governor's original plans for the bank loan had leaked to the press, a fact overlooked in previous histories of the state. St. Louis papers demanded the government consult the banks' stockholders before taking any action. Investors in Boston and New York, who had provided much of the Missouri banks' capital, also watched these events nervously. The *New York Times* urged eastern holders of Missouri bank shares to send their proxies to St. Louis, with instructions to have them used to oppose the governor's plans. By this time so much attention was focused on the St. Louis bankers that they were unable to help Governor Jackson, despite their sympathies.[28]

Part of the reason fighting in Missouri didn't begin immediately was that Union commanders were struggling for control over federal military forces in the state. Lyon and Blair urged the removal of General Harney, the ranking U.S. commander, for not putting down secessionist sentiment vigorously enough. Conservatives in the state opposed his removal, fearing that a more aggressive commander would push the state into open civil war. Lincoln left the decision on Harney's status to Blair, who relieved the general of his command on May 30. Lyon succeeded Harney as commander of U.S. forces in Missouri, a command Lyon was to hold one week. On June 6, Missouri was joined to the command of General George B. McClellan, though the news did not reach Lyon or McClellan until June 18.[29]

On Tuesday, June 11, the leaders of both sides—Blair, Lyon, Jackson, and Price—met in a last try for peace at the Planters' House hotel in St. Louis. There was bad blood between Price and Blair; the men had nearly dueled on two earlier occasions. Neither side would yield a thing. For more than four hours the group argued about relations between state and nation, command of the military forces in Missouri, and United States authority. Finally, Lyon broke off negotiations, declaring that he would see everyone in Missouri dead before he would allow the state to dictate terms to the federal government.[30]

With the breakup of the Planters' House meeting, Jackson and Price commandeered a train and headed for Jefferson City, stopping to burn the Gasconade and Osage River bridges. In Jefferson City, Jackson issued a proclamation that was telegraphed to all parts of the state. He reported the failure of the conference with Lyon and Blair and called for fifty thousand volunteers for the Missouri State Guard. The governor also sent orders to the district militia commanders appointed a month earlier. He ordered Missouri State Guard Brigadier General John B. Clark, later Missouri's representative to the Confederate Congress, to report with his men at Boonville. Jackson and his militia commanders considered Boonville, on the Missouri River and in the heart of the Boonslick, more easily defended than the capital. Jackson and Price joined Clark in Boonville with their staffs and a militia company from Jefferson City. The second mustering point for the southern forces was Lexington, west of Boonville along the Missouri River.[31]

General Lyon embarked from St. Louis with about two thousand men on June 14 and occupied Jefferson City without opposition the following day. Fearing arrest, members of Jackson's administration and the general assembly left the city before Lyon's arrival. Lyon left a garrison of three companies in Jefferson City and advanced upriver to Boonville, arriving the morning of June 17. Lyon's forces immediately attacked the hastily assembled Missouri State Guard volunteers and routed them after a brief fight, the first land battle of the Civil War. Governor Jackson and what remained of Missouri's Twenty-First General Assembly fled Boonville with the retreating Guard troops. Jackson and the legislators formed a government in exile in Neosho, Missouri, in the southwest corner of the state. There, Jackson tried one last time to secure the money from the banks as originally planned. In late June, Jackson sent State Treasurer Alfred W. Morrison, a longtime crony married to the governor's second cousin, to St. Louis to make the rounds of the banks. Morrison didn't get far before Lyon learned of Morrison's errand and had him arrested.[32]

William E. Parrish, in *Turbulent Partnership: Missouri and the Union, 1861–1865*, describes Lyon's putsch at Camp Jackson as a huge blunder, driving many conditional Unionists into the Confederate camp, including former governor Price. Jackson's correspondence with Price shows that the latter's Unionism was conditional indeed. Price went on to command all southern forces in Missouri and later became a major general in the Confederate States' army. Also, many contemporary observers, including the eastern newspapers, ordinary Missourians, and Governor Jackson himself, thought public opinion in Missouri was shifting toward secession. This may have been true; public opinion about secession had changed in the Upper South, and it might have in Missouri as well. Northern newspapers had nothing but praise for Lyon, writing that only prompt military action kept Missouri from seceding. The *New York Times* wrote that Missouri's traitorous and duplicitous elected officials had led the state's citizens astray, and that Lyon had saved Missouri from the horrors of civil war. The writer was too sanguine; Missouri would become one of the cockpits of the war. After Lyon's death in August 1861 at the Battle of Wilson's Creek, the U.S. Congress passed a posthumous resolution of thanks to him for saving Missouri for the Union.[33]

After the fight at Boonville, all pretense of peace in Missouri was gone. Though federal forces in central Missouri faced no organized resistance yet, the region swarmed with rebels, and federal authority extended no farther than rifle range. Reconvening in an emergency session, Missouri's onetime secession convention surprised everybody on July 31 by taking control of the government, declaring the governor's and lieutenant governor's positions "vacant," and outlawing the Twenty-First General Assembly. These measures, which are unique in American history, were of dubious legality, but Missouri's Unionists were not about to object. The provisional government, as the convention renamed itself, elected Hamilton Gamble, a distinguished jurist, as provisional governor.[34]

Claiborne Fox Jackson had hoped to stage-manage Missouri into the Confederacy without anyone noticing. The smooth transition the governor had envisioned was impossible after the outbreak of fighting in St. Louis and at Boonville. With the Confederate defeat at Boonville in June 1861, the Jackson government became national news. Major newspapers around the country reported the governor's secret dealings with Jefferson Davis and other Confederate leaders, with acid commentary on the governor's character. The governor's scheme to misappropriate the half-million-dollar bank loan was seen as outright theft, as well as treason, and the bankers' role in the affair as only slightly less guilty than Jackson's. The *Chicago Tribune*, referring to Barnes's incriminating correspondence with Jackson, urged other banks to at once suspend all dealings with the Bank of Missouri, as it was controlled by traitors. Throughout his political career Jackson had been an operator and wire-puller. Now he was caught in the wire-puller's worst nightmare: exposure.[35]

The Jackson government, however, refused to die. From Neosho, the government enacted further military and financial measures, among other things pledging to repay all private expenses incurred to defend the state against foreign invasion. The Confederacy assisted as well. In August, the Confederate Congress set aside a million dollars for Missouri State Guard troops, who were by that time cooperating with Confederate military forces. The Jackson government passed an ordinance of secession on October 28, 1861, and on November 1 approved ten million dollars in war bonds. On November 28, the Confederate Congress admitted Missouri as a full and equal member. On paper, Missouri became the eleventh Confederate state.[36]

A New Orleans firm printed the Missouri bonds approved in November. Governor Jackson himself brought the bonds back to Missouri in January 1862 and used a portion of them to pay the Missouri State Guard troops. Four months later, in May, Jackson traveled to Memphis on the same errand. How the troops reacted to being paid in these bonds is unknown. Also in January 1862, the Confederate Congress voted for a million dollars for the Missouri State Guard, in return for which the Jackson government deposited one million dollars' worth of the new state bonds in the Confederate treasury. Richmond made a further million dollars available on similar terms on February 15. By then, Union troops had forced Missouri's Confederate state government to leave the state, never to return. The government first moved to Arkansas, then to Texas, and finally to Louisiana. Governor Jackson, for his part, spent the rest of his life on the run from federal forces. He moved his family to a squalid settlement of Missouri refugees in Sherman, Texas, and died of stomach cancer in December 1862 in Little Rock, Arkansas. As late as the 1950s, Missouri's Confederate bonds, with some denominations showing Jackson's picture, were still turning up, with some holders seeking to redeem them with the state treasurer.[37]

Jackson's plan to finance the militia was a good one, and it would have worked if federal troops had not overturned the state government. However, even though Jackson was a sophisticated and experienced financier, the plan did not originate with him. Six months before Jackson's exchange of letters with Barnes, Alabama's Governor Andrew B. Moore had raised money for that state's militia forces in the same way. Acting on his own authority and before the state general assembly met, Moore arrived in Montgomery in early December, contacted the banks, and advised them to suspend specie payments to forestall a run on their reserves. A few weeks later, after Alabama's secession convention had gathered on January 7, it legalized the banks' suspension of specie payments, on the governor's recommendation. Without the convention's approval, the banks would have lost their charters.[38]

When it met, the Alabama legislature affirmed the convention's approval of the bank's suspension, provided the banks would buy, at par, $638,350 in Alabama state bonds. The state then used the money to arm the militia forces. In a separate act, the general assembly approved a bond issue for up to two million dollars, to arm the militia for the defense of the state. The state would then redeem the bonds over a period of several years with money from taxes. These were the same steps that Governor Jackson took, down to assigning specific contributions from each bank. The only substantive difference was that in Missouri the governor and the bankers had to conceal their actions from the legislature and the public. Alabama voters had approved of secession by a wide margin, and the state government had a popular mandate to act as it did.[39]

Moore and Jackson had in fact been in communication. In late December, as Moore was advising Alabama's bankers to suspend specie payments, he appointed commissioners to the other fourteen slave states to explain Alabama's position. Alabama's commissioner to Missouri, William Cooper, went to Jefferson City on December 18, where he met with both the outgoing and incoming governors, Robert M. Stewart and Claiborne Fox Jackson. The Missouri general assembly was not yet in session, but Cooper met with those legislators who were in town. These meetings were clearly amicable. On December 29, 1860, Cooper gave what the *St. Louis Missouri Republican* termed a "strong" secession speech in the hall of the Missouri House of Representatives. After he returned to Alabama, Cooper reported that he had no doubt that Missouri would federate with the South rather than the North.[40]

Missouri's Unionists had won the first round, but the fighting in the state was only just beginning. The southern forces rallied after their poor showing at Boonville. During the late summer and fall of 1861 the Missouri State Guard inflicted a series of defeats on the state's Union forces that left the latter reeling. It looked for a time as if Jackson and the Twenty-First General Assembly might return to power in Jefferson City. Also during the fall, from its perch in southwest Missouri, the Jackson government noisily and repeatedly reminded everyone that it was the only legal, elected government of the state. In the confusion it was unclear exactly which government was legal, and which one outlawed. Missouri's voters had rejected secession at the polls twice. In November 1860 they had elected Governor Jackson, who had campaigned as a Unionist and concealed his true intentions. Four months later, in February, Missourians chose delegates for the special convention who overwhelmingly rejected secession. Even so, Union military forces in Missouri in the fall of 1861 found themselves an occupying army in hostile territory. Union forces controlled the rivers, the railroad lines, St. Louis, and the largest towns, but they were spread too thin to police the countryside. Sympathetic civilians provided aid and comfort to the southern forces, which were able to wreak great havoc. Ominously, the *New York Times* first reported guerrilla violence in Missouri as early as July 28.[41]

New Banks

Missouri's branch banks, which played a critical role in financing the secession movement in Missouri, were with few exceptions of recent origin when the war started. Until the law changed in 1857, Missouri's constitution of 1820 allowed only one currency-issuing bank in the state, with a maximum of six branches, counting the parent bank. Since its establishment in 1837, that bank had been the Bank of Missouri. Between 1857 and the end of 1860 the number of chartered banks in the state, counting parents and branches, increased sevenfold. By January 1861, Missouri had nine currency-issuing banks with thirty-three external branches. None of these, except for the Bank of Missouri, had been in business for more than three and a half years. Twenty of the thirty-six new banks had existed for eighteen months or less.[1]

By 1857, when the law changed, Missouri was overdue for banking reform. The Bank of Missouri had supplied a stable paper currency, which circulated at par with specie. The problem was there was too little of it. By October 1854, the bank had $1.7 million in outstanding circulation, when the state's population was about nine hundred and thirty thousand. This gave Missouri under two dollars of circulating currency for each person, the lowest ratio for any state of comparable size. The state bank was in fact an anachronism. Many states, Missouri among them, had created such banks in the 1830s. Most of these banks were gone by the 1850s, leaving behind reputations for corruption and mismanagement. Missouri's state bank survived because of its conservative business policies, which reflected the hard-money views of Missouri's dominant politician of the day, Thomas Hart Benton. Benton was a Jacksonian Democrat and the hardest of hard-money men, known as "Old Bullion" in the United States Senate for his opposition to paper currency. Reflecting the senator's distrust of banks, the state government owned three-quarters of the bank's shares, and the bank's paid-in capital was less than one-quarter of the maximum set by the state constitution. Even with such restricted capital, the bank circulated much less currency than its charter allowed.[2]

In the years preceding the Civil War, three kinds of money circulated in the United States: gold and silver coin, U.S. treasury notes, and private banknotes. The value of specie—in particular gold—set the standard for all other currency, but the gold supply was inadequate to the needs of commerce. Besides coinage, the U.S. Treasury issued small quantities of interest-bearing notes, which banks mainly held as reserves. These notes were not legal tender, except for payment of debts owed the U.S. government, such as excise taxes or tariffs. To supplement the small amount of U.S. coinage, foreign gold and silver coins circulated in the U.S. until abolished as legal tender by act of Congress in 1857. By that time the mines of California had increased the country's gold supply enough to make foreign coinage unnecessary. Banknotes issued either by state banks or by private banking corporations made up the balance of circulating money. In 1861, currency issued by the U.S. government was only 3 percent of all the money in circulation, or M1 (cash plus demand deposits).[3]

Given the relatively small amounts of Missouri money, out-of-state currency circulated widely in the state. In early 1857, the *St. Louis Missouri Democrat* estimated that Missouri merchants received two-thirds of their payments in out-of-state banknotes. Since there were hundreds of such issues, the system favored swindlers and forgers, and it was expensive in other ways. The value of these private banknotes rose and fell with the solvency and reputation of the issuing institutions, and convertibility was difficult. An 1852 report issued by the St. Louis Chamber of Commerce stated that because the state lacked a satisfactory currency of its own, merchants had to buy eastern exchange for premiums ranging as high as 14 to 16 percent. Only the best state banks and big-city banks had currency that served as a circulating medium farther than a few hundred miles from their main offices. A letter written by a Mr. Lowndes to John C. Calhoun in about 1840 shows how costly such currency could be. Lowndes's letter described his experiences after leaving his home in Virginia for a three-state swing through Kentucky, Tennessee, and Maryland. He had to change currency eight times, paying a brokerage fee for each transaction.[4]

Credit availability was a related problem. Besides the state bank, which was the only one that could legally issue currency, two other types of banking institutions did business within Missouri: private banks and savings institutions. Country districts depended on credit since most of the cash in circulation, banknotes and specie alike, was in St. Louis. Commercial credit, which private banks and savings institutions could provide, was especially important for planters and merchants. Planters had no cash except in the autumn after they had sold their harvests. This seasonal income flow meant that agriculturalists had predictable short-term credit needs. Merchants who bought stock in coastal cities also needed short-term loans, though they could also get credit from their suppliers. Both groups needed a means of long-distance funds transfer.

Private banks neither issued currency nor accepted deposits but made loans out of the partners' own capital. Since they did not publish financial statements, it is difficult to gauge how important the private banks were. Statistics are incomplete, but an 1859 Missouri gazetteer listed twenty-nine private banks in Missouri, of which twenty-one were in St. Louis. A year later there were twenty-four such banks, fifteen of them in St. Louis. Some of these banks were large, but others probably amounted to little more than currency exchanges. More important than the private banking partnerships were the savings banks. Savings banks began as associations to pool the savings of working people, to make loans for home purchase or construction. The idea originated in Scotland in 1810, and the Philadelphia Savings Fund Society, founded in 1816, was the first such institution in the United States. Savings banks spread in the settled parts of the United States in the 1830s, and to Missouri, a frontier state, in the 1840s and 1850s. By the middle of the 1850s Missouri had twenty-five savings banks, most of them in St. Louis. The largest of these, Boatmen's Savings Institution in St. Louis, received its original charter in 1847 and a new charter in 1855. By January 1857 the Boatmen's was the Bank of Missouri's most important competitor, with almost $1.3 million in total assets and $350,000 in stockholders' equity.[5]

The savings banks differed in important ways from the state bank, however, and from the other currency-issuing banks founded in 1857 and after. Though savings banks accepted deposits and loaned money, they could not issue currency and had no branches, and they were much smaller than the state bank. Many savings institutions began with no capital at all, and the largest of them, Boatmen's, could increase its stockholders' equity only to four hundred thousand dollars. The Bank of Missouri, by way of comparison, had $1.2 million in stockholders' equity in October 1854 and was authorized to increase this figure to $5 million. Also, savings institutions were subject to no reserve limits or controls on their use of capital, and shareholders could pay for their shares in any manner the directors saw fit to accept. The Missouri state government regulated savings banks only minimally, which made them useful beyond their original purposes. Missouri's laws made little distinction between savings banks and other for-profit corporations. The laws did not restrict savings institutions to real estate loans, and non-depositors could own shares. Many wealthy businessmen, especially in St.

Louis, incorporated savings banks to provide themselves with short-term loans at good rates to buy inventory or materials, and to offer trade credit to their customers. Savings banks could do both, besides enabling the incorporators to share risks and to hire experienced help. Many of the incorporators of the banks chartered under Missouri's 1857 law had already helped found savings institutions.[6]

By the middle of the 1850s, there was a broad consensus among Missourians that the state's banking laws needed reform. The looming expiration of the Bank of Missouri's charter on February 1, 1857, forced the issue. When the Eighteenth General Assembly met in Jefferson City in December 1854, Governor Sterling Price urged the legislators to take up the banking question. Otherwise, he warned, the Bank of Missouri's charter would expire during the next term of the general assembly, and the state would have no currency except out-of-state banknotes. The governor recommended what he felt was the simplest solution, to recharter the state bank and to increase its paid-in capital to the five-million-dollar legal limit.[7]

The Eighteenth General Assembly, however, did not have time to consider banking. Missouri senator David Rice Atchison's term was ending, and the legislators used most of the session to decide on his replacement. Also, Governor Price's recommendation did not go far enough. Missouri's population had increased roughly two and a half times since the bank's founding in 1837, but the bank could not grow because of its restrictive charter. The state either needed more banks, or a much larger state bank than the constitution allowed. But Missouri's state government did not have the money to expand the banking system to the extent needed. Any significant expansion of banking capital would have to come from private investors. The assembly remained stalled on the issue until late in the session, when Senator Alexander Robinson of Missouri's Eighth District proposed a constitutional amendment to allow more banks. After some debate, the assembly approved an amendment to allow up to ten currency-issuing banks with total capital of up to twenty million dollars. Under the state's constitution, one general assembly could propose a constitutional amendment and the next assembly would vote on it, so there the matter rested for the time. Enough unfinished business remained when the assembly adjourned that it scheduled an extra session for November 1855. Then, the legislators renewed the state bank's charter for four more years, until 1861, as a stopgap measure.[8]

The procedure to amend the state constitution allowed a period for public debate. In 1855, when the assembly took up the state's banking laws for consideration, free banking was the most common banking system in the northern states. Fourteen of the nation's thirty-three states had free banking laws, and by 1860 that number had grown to eighteen. Under free banking, a state would grant a banking charter to any group of investors that requested one, provided they would invest at least the minimum capital set by law. Most free banking laws made would-be bankers buy state bonds, usually at least twenty-five thousand dollars' worth, which the state treasurer would hold in trust. Then, the bank could circulate an equal amount of paper money. If the bank did not redeem its notes with specie, the state sold the bonds to compensate the noteholders. Free banking was thus a backhanded way to use state bonds as the basis for a circulating currency, while getting private investors to pay the bill and assume the risk.[9]

Free banking found little support in Missouri, however. Neighboring Illinois and Iowa had free banking, but the banks of Illinois were a bad advertisement for the system. The state's seventy-five banks had almost nine million dollars of banknotes in circulation, backed by less than a quarter of a million dollars in specie reserves—or two cents on the dollar. Many Missourians viewed out-of-state banknotes as a plague, and from the 1830s the state had passed a series of laws against their use. Speeches and newspaper editorials of the day referred to foreign banknotes as "shinplasters," "rags," "worthless paper," and the like, accurate descriptions of the notes of many Illinois banks. Free banking laws set low capital thresholds to attract private investors, an editorial in the *St. Louis Missouri Republican* argued, but the states got what they paid for, and many of the new banks opened with the minimum capital allowed. The ability of these banks, and often their willingness, to redeem their banknotes with specie was questionable. The public was rightly skeptical of such currency, and these notes often circulated at a discount. Also, while the banks did create new credit, too often the major borrowers were the banks' own backers, rather than the larger public. States in effect gave owners of free banks a license to enrich themselves in return for providing the state with an inferior circulating currency.[10]

Since the end of the nineteenth century most economists and banking historians have held a similarly low opinion of free banking, though recent scholarship shows that it worked better than once thought. But free banking or no, Missouri's banking system needed private investment to expand. Faced with this necessity, when Missouri's Nineteenth General Assembly met in December 1856, the legislators were ready to accept the banking amendment. On January 14, 1857, after little debate, the Missouri senate passed the amendment with a vote of 24 to 6; the house followed two days later, voting 97 to 25. The amendment settled the big questions about banking in the state. Currency-issuing banks could operate only with state charters, of which the legislature could grant up to ten. Total capital in these banks could not exceed twenty million dollars, paid in full in specie. There remained, however, many questions about corporate governance, lending practices, and oversight. After the amendment passed, the senate and house merged their two banking committees into a joint committee to draft a banking bill. Applicants for bank charters began to line up immediately. The same day the Missouri house passed the amendment, and nine days before Missouri's new governor, Trusten Polk, signed it into law, Senator Henry Blow of St. Louis introduced the first bill for a bank charter. By the beginning of February, legislators had introduced twenty-seven such bills, all of which the assembly referred to the joint committee.[11]

Despite its unwieldy size, the joint committee completed its work quickly. On February 21, the joint chairs of the committee, Senator Conrad C. Ziegler and Representative John Brooks Henderson, presented the committee's report and a proposed bill to their respective chambers. The Missouri house passed the bill after only three days of debate that consisted mainly of squabbling over where to place branch banks. The senate followed suit the next day. The new law ran to twenty-six pages and covered the state's entire system of chartered (currency-issuing) banks. The law's four major sections covered corporate governance, capital and lending rules, financial reporting, individual charters for the ten new banks, and the powers and duties of the state bank commissioner, a position which the law created.[12]

Though the joint committee had written a complex bill in less than five weeks, they had doubtless received much help in drafting it. During January and early February, both of the state's major newspapers, the *St. Louis Missouri Democrat* and the *St. Louis Missouri Republican*, published editorials with detailed recommendations for the new law. As soon as the constitutional amendment passed, lobbyists descended on the legislators, mostly from St. Louis, but also from other towns that wanted banks. The lobbyists made their arguments in time-honored fashion. During a debate over the bill, one senator remarked that "there had been wine enough brought here from St. Louis and drank, to swim in from here [the senate chamber] to the City Hotel."[13]

The law chartered ten new banking corporations, each consisting of a parent bank with several branches. The law did not follow a single model but incorporated features from many different state laws. The closest model was Virginia's 1837 banking law, but Missouri's law had stricter reserve and capital standards. Virginia's law, on the other hand, had more controls on lending and barred certain people from becoming bank officers. The new Missouri law standardized bank charters for all banks, and all banks received equal privileges. Missouri thus became one of only a handful of states to have a general banking law without free banking. Novel features of the Missouri law were the restricted number of charters, a high minimum capital requirement, and a high specie-to-circulation reserve requirement. No bank could go into business with less than one million dollars in capital stock, paid in full in specie. Most states then allowed banks to open with only fifty thousand dollars in capital, sometimes paid for in questionable ways. Missouri's banks also had to keep specie reserves equal to one-third of their outstanding circulation. Again, this was high by the standards of the day, and copied from Louisiana's banking law.[14]

Newspaper commentary on the new law was uniformly favorable. *Bankers' Magazine and Statistical Register* (hereafter *Bankers' Magazine*), the most important trade journal of the banking industry, pronounced Missouri's law superior to the banking laws of Illinois, New York, and Ohio. The *St. Louis Missouri Republican* and the *St. Louis Missouri Democrat*, on opposite sides of most issues, both approved the law. The *Democrat* reported that the law had surprised them in not favoring any special interest group. Instead, with one or two exceptions, the law would protect all interests, and was admirable. The *Democrat* had misread the law, however, which was thoroughly partisan in its application. Before the law's passage, on December 29, 1856, outgoing governor Sterling Price delivered his final message as governor to the newly seated Nineteenth General Assembly. The governor listed his administration's accomplishments, and then set forth policy objectives that he hoped the legislators would consider after his departure. The governor hoped that banking reform would make credit more freely available to farmers and country merchants, and at better rates. The state also badly needed a stable, circulating currency, convertible to specie at par. The absence of enough currency and credit, Price argued, benefited only a few rich men, retarded the state's economic development, and imposed unnecessary costs on ordinary people. The governor urged the assembly to make sure the people and their government kept control of the state's banks. Ideally, the customers of a local bank would also be its shareholders and officers, rather than a handful of wealthy men in distant cities.[15]

The governor had more than traditional American federalism in mind, however, and he objected to one group of wealthy men in particular. "It cannot be denied," Price wrote, "that a growing spirit of bitter hostility to the time-honored institutions [that is, slavery] of Missouri, has shown itself in the city of St. Louis among a portion of its inhabitants. . . . [The] balance of the State [should be] independent of its metropolis, which chooses to give aid and comfort to our enemies. . . . To extend reasonable banking facilities to our commercial capital it is not necessary to run the slightest risk of converting Missouri into a bank-ridden state, controlled by anti-slavery corporations in St. Louis."[16]

Governor Price did not object to all of St. Louis. The promoters who received charters were all wealthy St. Louisans, who between them had incorporated literally scores of companies. The new banks themselves would become St. Louis corporations, and some of the largest corporations in the state. The key word was "antislavery." Agreeing with the governor's recommendations, the Missouri legislature did not award a bank charter to any investor group that included anti-slavery men, German-Americans in particular. Instead, the law struck a delicate political balance. In the Missouri House, an unlikely alliance of representatives from St. Louis and from the high-slavery counties of the Boonslick passed the law. As Governor Price was well aware, these two places were at opposite ex-tremes of the North-South ideological divide. What united the two factions on the banking issue was, of course, money. The new banks would issue the only legal paper currency in the state, up to three times the banks' paid-in capital. In lending this currency, the banks would earn a rate of return nearly three times higher than that of other lending institutions, after paying taxes and fees to the state. The law protected this currency from competition as well. No new banks could open because the law limited the number of charters, and other laws made it illegal to circulate out-of-state banknotes.[17]

In return for these privileges, the banks had to provide banking services not only in St. Louis, the state's commercial center, but in specific branch locations named in the bank charters. Banks with the minimum one million dollars in capital had to set up two branches, each capitalized at not less than a hundred thousand dollars apiece. Banks with more capital had to set up at least three branches. However, the law ensured that parent banks would not be able to con-trol their branches. Branch stock sold separately, and if not enough local people bought the shares, the parent bank had to contribute the balance of the required minimum capital. The law thus shifted banking capital out of St. Louis and into the high-slavery counties, in effect subsidizing branch banking there with St. Louis money. But even if the branch's entire capital came from the parent bank, the latter could name only four of the branch's nine directors. Branches thus received advantages from their institutional affiliations but had few reciprocal duties.[18]

The new law made branch banking an excellent deal, and legislators competed to locate branch banks within their districts. When the Nineteenth General As-sembly selected members for its standing committees, the number of members of the house banking committee almost doubled from the previous assembly, going from seven members to thirteen. (The size of the senate banking com-mittee did not change.) Except for St. Louis, most of the committee members from both houses came from counties with high slave populations. When the legislators had finished, the branch locations mapped the ley lines of power in the state: more than half of the banks outside St. Louis were within a few miles of the Missouri River.[19]

Besides St. Louis, there were two other principal clusters of banks. One cluster centered around Howard County, the heart of the Boonslick and Missouri's most developed plantation district. The center of the other cluster was the Kansas City–Independence area, on the western edge of the state along the Kansas border. These three areas represented the most vibrant regions in the state's economy, but they also showed the economy's schizophrenic nature. St. Louis was the nation's fifth-largest city, a booming, free-labor trading and manufacturing center with one of the largest foreign-born populations of any American city. The other two regions were rich rural areas of slaves, plantations, and large commercial farms. There, the population was largely homogeneous, of old American stock, with deep roots in the South. In April, acting governor Hancock Jackson appointed Claiborne Fox Jackson (no relation) Missouri's first bank commissioner. Jackson was a polarizing figure in Missouri politics, but even his political foes agreed he was the best man for the job.[20]

Shares in the new banks sold briskly, not only in Missouri but in New York, Boston, and Chicago. Several banks were able to close their subscription books and to open for business sooner than they had anticipated. In St. Louis, the banks' capital came from distinct groups. Steamboat men and manufacturers invested in the Bank of St. Louis, dry goods and grocery merchants in the Merchants' Bank. The Southern Bank got its money from boatyards, manufacturing, and leather goods. Lumber interests invested in the Exchange Bank, and the construction industry in the Mechanics' Bank. Business halted in October, however, when the Panic of 1857 broke over the nation. One of the new banks failed to form at all and returned its charter to the state. The remaining banks were fortunate, in a way, in the timing of the panic. None of the banks had been in business long enough to have large loan portfolios. By the end of the second quarter of 1860 Missouri's banks were past their birthing pains, and this was the last relatively quiet period the nation was to have for some time. Financial markets had recovered from the Panic of 1857, and the fateful election of 1860 was still some months off. By early 1860 Missouri had nine currency-issuing banks doing business in forty-two locations, counting parents and branches. Each bank had at least two branches, the Bank of Missouri having the most with ten. Stock in the branch banks sold well enough that by the end of September 1860, the parent banks only had to provide about 30 percent of the branch banks' capital.[21]

The new banks served both of Missouri's two main industries before the Civil War, the southern trade and the western trade. Missouri's farms and workshops produced support commodities for the plantations of the cotton South, and they supplied the material needs of western settlers passing through the state. The southern trade was the more profitable of the two. Missouri produced horses,

mules, and oxen for draft animals, corn and hogs to feed slaves, hemp for cotton baling, and tobacco for wrapper leaf in making cigars. Overall, Missouri
formed one point of a classic trading triangle. The South sold cotton to the mills
of England and New England and used the money to pay Missouri's farmers
and merchants. The Missourians then bought finished goods from the Northeast. Missouri's overall balance of trade was favorable with the South and West,
and unfavorable with the East. St. Louis and the Missouri River counties west
of the city, where most of the branch banks were, served both the western and
the southern businesses. St. Louis was the great collection point for all this commerce, physical distribution, warehousing, transport, wholesale and retail sales,
and banking, dominating the entire Missouri Valley and the Upper Mississippi
Valley above New Orleans.[22]

Regardless of the direction in which their customers lay, banks in the Boonslick mainly serviced the agricultural economy—both the export of agricultural
commodities and the import of finished items for use on the farms and plantations. Agricultural loans covered farmers' expenses through the harvest sea-
son and until they could sell their crops. Merchants borrowed money to finance
inventory until they could sell it and collect the cash. In addition, the public
expected banks to make unsecured "accommodation loans" to trustworthy citizens, on the strength of their signatures alone. Loans, though renewable, had
short maturities by today's standards, often limited to less than a year by the
bank's charter. This was long enough to cover an agricultural cycle or a trip east
to buy finished goods, and until customers settled their accounts. Outside St.
Louis, the banks mainly served large landowners whose wealth was in illiquid
assets like land and slaves. Rich as these men were, they had little available cash
and relied on the banks for short-term credit.[23]

In the later decades before the Civil War one of the banks' major lines of business was long-distance funds transfer for commercial transactions. If a merchant
in Lexington, Missouri, wished to buy goods in New York, he would first find
out the New York price by letter or telegram. The merchant would then go to a
Lexington bank that had a correspondent or parent bank in St. Louis, which in
turn had a correspondent bank in New York. Using local money, the merchant
would buy a draft, or certified check, drawn on the New York bank. Country
banks in the interior of the United States often kept deposits in major banks in
coastal cities for such transactions. But the banking system also depended on
mutual trust and a fine appreciation of the relative values of the New York and
Missouri currency, which could change daily.[24]

After St. Louis got telegraphic contact with the East via Louisville in 1847, the

Figure 2.1. Parent and branch bank locations, January 1861.

banks' communication lines stretched a long way. Account books of Missouri's chartered banks do not survive, but the University of Missouri Western Manuscripts Collection has the records for 1859–1860 of the private banker Weston F. Birch of Brunswick, Missouri. Brunswick is a town in Chariton County on the Missouri River and was a regular stop for steamboats. From January 1859 to December 1860 Birch recorded six hundred twenty-four transactions in "exchange" (notes discounted and bills of exchange). Three hundred ninety of these transactions, or 63 percent, involved settlement with a St. Louis bank or business firm. New York banks and businesses accounted for one hundred fifty-seven, or

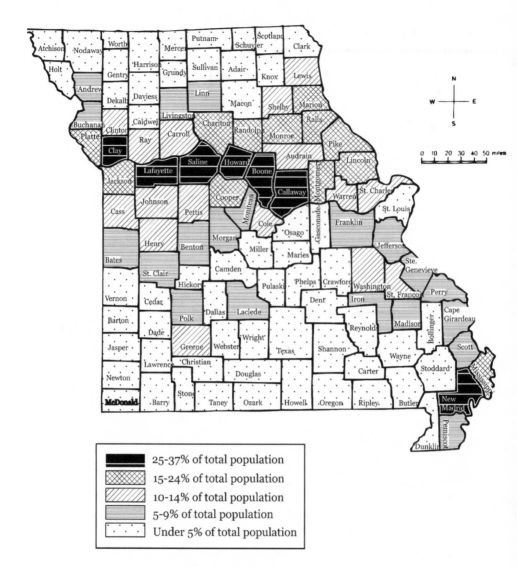

Figure 2.2. Slaves as a percentage of total population, 1860.

25 percent. Most of the rest of Birch's business was with other Missouri banks, but he occasionally discounted notes from Liverpool, London, New Orleans, Baltimore, Richmond, Philadelphia, Cincinnati, Pittsburgh, and Louisville.[25]

Within the limits set for it and for the customers that it served, Missouri's 1857 banking law was a success. The branch bank networks were an innovative form of business organization, with each branch bank running as a semi-independent franchise. This capital structure allowed the banks to tap otherwise inaccessible sources of money, and brought access to credit and circulating currency to parts of the state that had neither. It is difficult to tell how much Missouri's total banking capital increased, since savings institutions, insurance companies, and private banks also loaned money. The dollar amount of currency in circulation, however, increased significantly. On June 30, 1860, Missouri had $6.17 of paper currency in circulation for each person, placing Missouri at the median of all the states. Missouri's banks had fifty-two cents of specie reserves for each dollar in circulation, giving the state some of the strongest currency in the country. By 1860, three years after their founding, the St. Louis banks were the dominant financial institutions in the Upper Mississippi Valley. The nearest banks of comparable size were hundreds of miles away, in New Orleans and Louisville. Arkansas had no banks at all, Kansas had one, and Iowa's banks were small and had little money in circulation. Neighboring Illinois, home to the rising city of Chicago, had no banks with a million dollars of paid-in capital. Instead, fifty-four of the state's seventy-five banks had fifty thousand dollars or less in capital.[26]

Later events were to show, however, that Missouri's 1857 law had two major flaws. The first was the law's overt favoritism, in using the banking industry as an instrument to support slavery; the second was the power of the bank commissioner. As to the law's bias, to be fair to the legislators, no one expected them to create a banking system that served the entire public. Antebellum banks mainly served business rather than retail customers. Even so, the new Missouri banks' locations favored some commercial interests more than others. The difference between counties that got banks and those that did not was slavery. Excluding St. Louis, the Missouri counties that got banks under the 1857 law had an average total slave population of 17 percent, compared to 7 percent for counties without banks. Banking, as it existed in the Boonslick in 1860, was a service extension to slave-based commercial agriculture. Howard County was at the heart of Missouri's plantation economy and had the highest percentage of slaves of any county in the state. There, a citizen standing at the front door of the Bank of Missouri branch at Fayette, the county seat, had another six banks to choose from within a forty-five mile radius. Counting the bank in Fayette, Howard County itself had three of these banks.[27]

Seven banks within a forty-five mile radius will not seem like many to modern readers. It was a large number, however, compared to the parts of the state the 1857 law ignored. Missouri's southeast, the worst-served district, had only three banks, all on the region's far eastern edge along the Mississippi River. The interior counties of this district made up more than a third of the state, larger in geographic extent than eight of the thirty-three states in 1860. There, the southeast's two hundred thousand inhabitants had no banks at all. A citizen of Salem, the county seat of Dent County, would travel a hundred and twenty miles to get to Ste. Genevieve, the nearest town with a bank. Since the chartered banks issued the only legal currency, the southeast also had little money in circulation. Outside St. Louis, the Boonslick was literally where the money was.[28]

Banking and economic development could have moved in other directions besides strengthening the plantation system. Excluding St. Louis, the population of the counties that got no banks under the 1857 law grew nearly twice as fast between 1850 and 1860 as that of the counties that did get banks. By 1860 the state had two major mining districts: the lead mines near Granby, in Missouri's far southwest, and the lead, iron, and copper mines in the southeast. Neither region got a bank. The law also ignored the wine industry. Viticulture first came to Missouri in the late 1840s and was on its way to becoming one of the state's major industries by 1860. By 1870 Missouri was second only to California in total annual wine production, and the state remained one of the nation's leading wine producers until Prohibition. The heart of the industry was in the German-settled counties along the south bank of the Missouri River west of St. Louis. Most Missouri Germans shunned slavery, and when the war came they almost unanimously opposed secession. The Missouri legislature excluded Germans when it handed out bank charters. Only one of the fifty-eight incorporators named in the bank charters granted by the 1857 law was German. By 1860, of eighty-four bank officers and cashiers, only one (in St. Louis) was born in Germany.[29]

Plantation agriculture was a profitable business in antebellum Missouri, and any state banking system would have put banks in the counties with high slave populations. But the slaveholders were a minority interest. In Missouri, one family in eight owned slaves, the lowest ratio of any slave state after Delaware and Maryland. In Mississippi, one family in two owned slaves in 1860. In the 1850s, however, Missouri's slaveholders were the dominant special interest group in the state, and the governor and legislature clearly believed the locations of the branch banks served the best interests of the public. None of the state's major newspapers objected to the bias in the law itself or in its application.[30]

Even so, the state's activist stance in granting banking charters only to proslavery groups effectively divided the industry into political factions. Many Missourians also resented that the state had created a privileged class of banking corporations. Even before the Nineteenth General Assembly adjourned, a fight broke out between insider and outsider groups over control of the banking industry, and the battle took on ideological overtones. The first skirmish was over nominations for directors of the Bank of Missouri. (The state still owned a sizable amount of the bank's stock and got to choose several directors.) Proslavery legislators accused one candidate, Mr. William Palm, of being a Freesoiler, and thus unfit for the position. Palm stood by his politics, and a fight over his nomination followed. Palm eventually received enough votes to become a director, but only after much rancor. The fight quickly broadened into a struggle between pro- and antislavery factions within the banking industry itself, represented by the newly chartered banks and the savings banks. In Governor Price's message to the Nineteenth General Assembly, he had raised the specter of antislavery corporations in St. Louis. Judging by what happened, the governor probably had in mind several of the savings banks, especially the German-controlled ones.[31]

The conflict between the chartered banks and the savings banks was over the former's circulating currency. The framers of the 1857 law had intended to create a convertible currency that would circulate throughout the state. Every parent bank and every branch bank issued its own paper currency, which by law was redeemable at par from the bank that issued it. The chartered banks took advantage of this wording to charge brokerage fees to redeem banknotes issued by other branches of the same bank. Also, when they could, the chartered banks made bills payable at some distant location in the state. The Palmyra branch of the Bank of Missouri, in the northeastern corner of the state, would issue drafts and notes redeemable at the Springfield branch, in the far southwest. Springfield would issue paper redeemable in St. Joseph, in the far northwest, and so on. This practice also allowed the banks to avoid or delay paying out specie.[32]

The savings banks were having none of this. As large depository institutions, the savings banks routinely took in and paid out large sums of money in Missouri banknotes. The Boatmen's Savings Institution, in particular, on several occasions sent its agents to branch banks in distant parts of the state to redeem thousands of dollars of the branch's notes with specie, as the law required. This in turn provoked a newspaper war between the supporters of the savings institutions and those of the chartered banks. The former charged the chartered banks with perpetrating a fraud on the people, and applauded the efforts of the savings institutions to force the chartered banks to redeem their notes at par. The chartered banks' supporters claimed that the savings institutions were trying to panic the depositors and noteholders. Tellingly, the banks' supporters contemptuously referred to the savings institutions as "Austrians," meaning Germans, and code for abolitionist, free-soil sentiments. When agents from Boatmen's visited the Farmers' Bank in Lexington, the latter tried to whip up the townspeople into a mob to run the St. Louisians out of town, or worse.[33]

The chartered banks and the savings institutions could have coexisted peacefully enough. Much of their business did not overlap. Mindful of the risks of land speculation, the 1857 law forbade the chartered banks from investing in real estate, other than the banks' own buildings. Many savings institutions were founded to provide real estate finance, and this remained an important line of business even as the savings institutions diversified. The fight between the savings institutions and the banks spread to the courts and the legislature. In 1858, Boatmen's filed suit in the St. Louis County Circuit Court against the Bank of Missouri to force the latter to redeem the notes of one of its branches in specie. The Twentieth General Assembly, which met in December 1858, passed a law that ordered what were in effect punitive audits of the savings institutions. Reports circulated that the banks had bribed the legislature to pass the law, creating an uproar and calls for an investigation. Meanwhile in 1859, Claiborne Fox Jackson, acting as bank commissioner, filed suit in the Missouri Supreme Court against the Boatmen's Savings Institution for illegal banking practices. This dispute was continuing when the Civil War started in Missouri in May and June of 1861 and focused people's attention elsewhere.[34]

From the start, some observers thought the law gave the bank commissioner too much power. In February 1857, the sponsors of the bank bill cautioned the general assembly that "The success of the present banking system depends in no small degree upon the faithful discharge of the duties imposed upon these officers." A month later the *Liberty Tribune* wrote prophetically that if the wrong person became commissioner, he could "swindle the people to almost any degree." The legislators and the *Tribune* writer voiced no specific concerns, but they were right to worry. As defined in the 1857 law, the job had a serious separation of duties problem: the commissioner controlled both the banks' records and the banks themselves. It was the commissioner's duty to examine the banks' records for correctness and legal compliance. The commissioner also had the power to sign off on the records, making them official, and then to oversee their publication. If the commissioner so chose, he could shut the bank down. There was, therefore, nothing to stop the bank commissioner from closing a bank, simply by declaring that it was in violation of its charter or of state law. Since the commissioner controlled the records, he also controlled the evidence of any alleged wrongdoing. A bank could fight the commissioner's action in court or in the legislature. It would take months to get a hearing, though, and by then the bank would be out of business permanently. The commissioner needed only to threaten such action to intimidate a bank or force a course of action on it. Banking depends on trust, and no one trusts a bank closed by a government regulator.[35]

As it turned out, the two men who served as bank commissioner from 1857 until the start of the war were unfortunate choices indeed. In normal times Claiborne Fox Jackson would have been a good choice for the job. Jackson had much experience in finance, he was not larcenous, and during the time he held the position there is no evidence that he behaved improperly. But he did have an agenda, and the times were not normal; the nation was sliding toward civil war. During the three years that he held the job, Jackson would have gotten to know the state's banking system intimately and personally met every one of the bankers. Jackson would have known the details of the banks' finances, and the bankers' politics, affiliations, and networks. When Jackson resigned in the summer of 1860 to run for governor, Governor Robert M. Stewart gave the job to the man who became Missouri's second most prominent pro-secession leader, former governor Sterling Price. When the war came, both Jackson and Price worked to subvert the banking system to support the rebellion. In 1861 the bankers overwhelmingly favored secession, but the law also provided ways to pressure bankers who questioned the governor's plans.[36]

In the last years of the antebellum period, however, the law seemed to work well. The state's dominant elite had gotten the banks that it wanted. The government's policy of using the banking system to support slavery also achieved some success. The most widely held view among historians today is that plantation agriculture in Missouri was losing ground compared to the rest of the economy. Much evidence supports this view. However, even though the percentage of slaves in Missouri's overall population decreased during the 1850s, the number of large plantations in the Missouri River counties increased. There, the number of owners of twenty or more slaves increased 45 percent from 1850 to 1860, a much faster rate than the counties' overall population growth. Most of this expansion was due to wealthy planters who immigrated from other slave states, chiefly Kentucky and Virginia, attracted by the cheap land and the favorable political climate. On the eve of the Civil War in the Boonslick counties, the percentage of households owning slaves ranged from a low of 30 percent to almost half, higher than the state averages for most of the future Confederacy. When war broke out in 1861, these new arrivals came forward in large numbers to fight for the southern cause in their adopted state.[37]

3

New Bankers

The events recounted in this history hinge on actions taken by the branch bankers in 1861 and 1862. In many ways, this book is their story. After the overthrow of the Jackson government in June 1861, Union troops kept a tight grip on St. Louis, and the bankers there had no room to maneuver. Union control over the countryside was much weaker, and it was only intermittent in much of the state until the end of the war. Unlike the St. Louis bankers, the branch bankers could act on their politics. If Governor Jackson's original financing plan had succeeded, or if one or the other army had taken the banks' vault cash, the worst result would have been an empty state treasury and insolvent banks. Given the state's limited amount of circulating currency and access to commercial credit, Missouri's rebels would have had no other source of financing if the branch bankers had not acted as they did. On May 25, two weeks after the first fighting broke out in the state and five days after North Carolina seceded, the *New York Times* editorialized that Missouri's banks held the key to the state's future. In the *Times*'s view, lack of money was all that stopped Governor Jackson from arming the state and handing it over to the secessionists. "The whole fate of treason in Missouri is . . . dependent upon the banks. If they decline to meet the views of the Governor, there will be [no] rebellion, no hanging for treason, no devastation of the State by marching armies. . . . If they consent, they sign the death warrant of all that makes Missouri great, prosperous and respected."[1]

Missouri's Nineteenth General Assembly sought to create a banking system that would allow Missouri's high-slavery counties to profit from the national economy but that would also protect them from it. The branch bankers had to mediate between these two worlds, and in the crisis of 1861 they had to choose between them. On the one side were the bankers' professional and institutional duties, including duties to antislavery corporations in St. Louis and else-where. On the other side were the primal claims of family and neighborhood. The planters, the bankers' main customers, were also the bankers' neighbors, friends, social betters, aspirational group, and kinfolk. The branch bankers be-lieved strongly in the southern cause, but family connections determined where the banks would channel their money. Many of these family ties will seem re-mote to modern readers, but the court records show how important these con-nections were.

To understand the branch bankers, it is necessary to understand how they came to their positions when the banks formed. As new as the banks of 1857 were, the men who managed them in 1860 and 1861 were not the banks' founders. Instead, a close-knit group of promoters had founded not only the banks but scores of other companies as well—insurance companies, savings institutions, railroads, smelters, manufactories, and more besides. Promoters are a specialized type of entrepreneur; in Joseph Schumpeter's view they are entrepreneurs of the purest type. Hired outsiders can perform every other task except to create the enterprise itself. Promoters do not become part of management but instead receive pay-ment, usually in stock, for helping to launch new businesses. A major difference between promoters and other entrepreneurs is that promoters form many more companies. The faster a promoter sets up a company, the faster he gets paid and can move on.[2]

The corporate charters of the new St. Louis banks altogether named fifty-eight incorporators. Seventeen of the fifty-eight were seemingly passive investors and took no part in any other incorporation. The remaining forty-one men named in the bank charters, however, incorporated eighty-one companies in the eight general assemblies after the 1844 session, when Missouri passed its first com-prehensive law defining the status of corporations, and up to 1859. More than half of these incorporations were of financial institutions—savings institutions, insurance companies, and the banks of 1857. Most active of all within the group of forty-one was a core group of fourteen. On average, these men joined in seven incorporations apiece, for sixty-eight companies, one out of eight of all for-profit incorporations in the state during that time. Most of these companies were also financial institutions. Before they founded the banks, these men were already doing much business together, showing more loyalty to one another than to the companies they helped create. In what we would now view as conflicts of inter-est, these men often joined forces to found multiple companies that would com-pete against each other.[3]

The group's track record was more striking because the corporate form of busi-ness ownership was not yet widely used in all states. The U.S. Supreme Court only decided *Dartmouth College v. Woodward*, the landmark case expanding and securing the rights of corporations, in 1819. Missouri joined the Union in 1821, and the First General Assembly granted the state's first corporate charter, for an instructional academy. The state granted its first for-profit corporate charter in 1826, passed its first law defining the general powers, privileges, and liabilities of corporations in 1844, and passed an amended law in 1855. Between the state's founding and the start of the Civil War, the Missouri legislature granted 511 corporate charters for private, for-profit enterprises.[4]

Promoters have no particular attachments to the companies they help found, beyond wanting the stock to do well. The banks were important to the Missouri state government, though. The state hoped to use the banks to protect slavery and slaveowners in Missouri and selected these particular groups of promoters for their politics. The promoters named in the charters were not radicals, however, although they were all conservative Democrats who owned slaves or had owned slaves. When war came most eventually sided with the Union, although some no doubt did so reluctantly. But in the 1850s they clearly did not object to slavery or to making money from it. Well before the war started, the promoters had already moved on, after they had helped select bank officers with much more radical proslavery politics.[5]

Except for the Bank of Missouri and its original five external branches, all the other banks chartered under the 1857 law were new, and so were the bank officers. Of the six new banking corporations headquartered in St. Louis, only one of the bank presidents in 1861 had any previous banking experience. The new bankers were all men of similar stamp as the promoters—job-changing entrepreneurs, whose work histories were a succession of mercantile partnerships. The bankers' careers were so alike that they probably shared a common personality type, but there is too much disagreement about entrepreneurial typologies to be certain. Unlike the promoters, the bank presidents and cashiers had managed all their previous enterprises. Being a bank president was a part-time occupation in those days, and all but one of the St. Louis bank presidents had other businesses. The most common career path ran from farming to clerking, to opening a store, to wholesale trading in groceries or dry goods, and eventually to finance. The bankers made their money in an economy much poorer than our own, in effect passing through a series of filters to get to where they were. They epitomized the contemporary ideal of the self-made man, but that had nothing to do with liberal values. Every St. Louis banker whose politics could be determined was pro-Confederate, even though the city was the center of Unionist sentiment in Missouri.[6]

The wealthiest and most influential of these men was Robert A. Barnes, president of the Bank of Missouri parent branch in St. Louis. Barnes was one of Governor Jackson's original co-conspirators, and the St. Louis newspapers had published the incriminating correspondence between the two after Jackson's flight. Barnes came from Washington, D.C., born in 1808 to a family long settled in Maryland. Barnes's father died when he was thirteen, after which he lived with an uncle in Louisville. He received only a primary school education, but he read widely and was knowledgeable in several subjects. He clerked for two years in a Louisville dry goods firm before moving to St. Louis in 1830, at the age of twenty-one. There, he clerked for a short time with a firm of factors and wholesale grocers. He took a similar position at a second firm, but the firm dissolved after one of the two senior partners left for New Orleans in 1836. The remaining partner formed a new firm with Barnes, but this lasted only for a year. Then Barnes formed a new partnership, still in the wholesale grocery business, with a prominent steamboat captain. Barnes bought out his partner in 1841 and continued the business as sole owner. At its height, Barnes's business extended from New Orleans to Illinois, Wisconsin, and Iowa Territory. In 1840 he became a director of the Bank of Missouri, and in 1859 he became the bank's president. Barnes withdrew from the grocery business in 1861, after Union forces closed the Mississippi River to civilian traffic. He also helped manage the St. Louis Railroad Company and was a major shareholder in several other companies.[7]

John J. Anderson was another prominent banker in St. Louis, and one of the only new Missouri bankers with significant experience in the industry. Anderson was also the only one of the bank promoters who was a bank officer in 1861, and he was president of the Bank of St. Louis when fighting broke out in the city in May. Anderson came from Cahokia, Illinois, of French Creole ancestry, and he came to St. Louis before 1835. Anderson was a merchant until 1842, when he went out of business. Then, with backing from Joseph S. Morrison of Pennsylvania, Anderson founded the private banking house of John J. Anderson & Company. Anderson had the dubious distinction of being the first Missouri banker arrested by Union forces. On May 10, 1861, Anderson was paymaster of the Missouri State Guard troops called up by Governor Jackson, and General Nathaniel Lyon's troops captured Anderson with the rest of the guard volunteers. He regained his freedom in October in a prisoner exchange for Union soldiers captured at the Battle of Lexington, Missouri, several weeks earlier. Anderson remained under a cloud, however, owing to the discovery of incriminating correspondence between his private banking house and several banks in New Orleans.[8]

The years just before the Civil War were a good time to do business in St. Louis, and to launch new enterprises. St. Louis County's population grew almost tenfold from 1840 to 1860, from 16,469 to 160,773. By 1860 St. Louis was the nation's fifth-largest city, slightly smaller than New Orleans. Before the railroads, the city was the starting point for all western travel and commerce. Even by U.S. standards, the population of St. Louis was transient and diverse. More than half the people in St. Louis County were foreign-born, a greater proportion than in New York City. Consistent with the character of their city, in 1861 only one of the fourteen St. Louis bank presidents and cashiers was a Missouri native, and five came from nonslave states. Though the St. Louis bank presidents had been in Missouri for an average of fourteen years, this figure masks a wide variation. When the war broke out in 1861, three of the seven St. Louis bank presidents had been in St. Louis for five years or less. Most had moved more than once before coming to St. Louis; Ezekiel B. Kimball, president of the Southern Bank, moved five times after leaving his home in upstate New York, before he finally settled in St. Louis. Though they supported the Confederacy, the St. Louis bankers took little active role in politics. None of them held political office before the Civil War.[9]

To find backers for the branch banks, the promoters and officers of the parent banks had to reach out to men like themselves, which is to say successful, pro-southern entrepreneurs. But the countryside was a far different place from St. Louis. Ninety percent of Missourians lived on farms or in villages of fewer than two thousand people. After St. Louis the largest town was St. Joseph, with a total population just under nine thousand. Boonville and Lexington, the largest towns along the Missouri River in the interior of the state, had populations of twenty-five hundred and forty-one hundred, respectively. Some towns with branch banks, such as Glasgow in Howard County, had populations of a thousand or less. The St. Louisians were able to create an extensive branch network quickly by adapting a preexisting traditional kinship network of merchants and planters that extended through the Boonslick counties.[10]

In the interior of the state, country merchants were the logical choices to manage the new branch banks, indeed the only choices. Country merchants did business with everybody, including many people on the fringes of the market economy. From the earliest days of settlement, merchants performed banking services for their customers, such as extending credit, getting financing in distant cities, and transferring funds. Often no money changed hands, but instead was used to impute relative prices to goods exchanged, such as bushels of corn for coffee. In long-term commercial relations, such as those between merchants and farmers, many sales were by book-entry. A farmer would build up an account receivable with a storekeeper and settle once or twice a year, when the farmer had sold his harvest. In Missouri, as in most of the South, January 1 was the day to settle accounts from the past year and to enter new arrangements. Merchants also did business using barter, scrip, and IOUs. Even in 1860 a greater dollar volume of payments settled by check than by cash.[11]

The country merchants who became branch bankers had much in common with their counterparts in St. Louis. The two groups were demographically indistinguishable, except that a higher proportion of the branch bankers came from slave states, especially the Old South and the Middle Border. They were native-born, of British or Scotch-Irish ancestry, and in their middle forties, in a time and place where the average life expectancy was about fifty. Nearly all came from humble rural origins and immigrated to Missouri at a young age. The branch bankers, too, had founded and managed a series of successful enterprises. Two-thirds of the branch bank presidents and cashiers were either wholesale or retail merchants. They were Democrats and Masons, and they were among the wealthiest men and the largest slaveowners in their home counties. Besides banking and their other enterprises, many of the branch bankers had large farms as well.[12]

Most of the branch bankers' careers resembled that of Robert W. Donnell, president of the Bank of Missouri branch at St. Joseph. Donnell came originally from Guilford County, North Carolina. In 1838, at the age of twenty-one, he moved to Rock House Prairie in Buchanan County, Missouri, then on the far edge of western settlement. There, he became a junior partner in a general store. Over the next twenty years Donnell entered successive mercantile partnerships and moved from retail to wholesale trade, and eventually to banking. In 1848, Donnell married into the rich and influential Thornton family of Clay County. In 1857, after the passage of the new banking law, Donnell sold his mercantile interests and with his former partner, Albe Saxton, started the new St. Joseph branch of the Bank of Missouri. Donnell and Saxton became president and cashier of the bank, and Donnell's brother-in-law, John C. Calhoun Thornton, became the bank's attorney. In the 1860 census Donnell reported real and personal property worth forty thousand dollars, the median for the branch bank presidents, and ownership of three slaves.[13]

Another bank president was Captain William David Swinney, president of the Glasgow branch of the St. Joseph–based Western Bank of Missouri. Swinney made his money in agriculture, which was a less common career path than Donnell's. Captain Swinney was a native of Campbell County, Virginia, and brought his family to Missouri from Lynchburg in 1832. He settled a large plantation, Sylvan Villa, in Howard County, three miles east of Glasgow, of which he was one of the original founders. By 1860, Swinney owned a thousand acres, seventy-nine slaves, and total property worth over a half million dollars. Here he grew and processed tobacco, as he had done in Virginia. At one time he owned four tobacco factories located in the nearby towns of Glasgow, Fayette, Salisbury, and Huntsville, and shipped his products all over the world. He was a devout Methodist, and, besides commerce and religion, education was his chief interest. He was a founder of Central College in Fayette, and the college's first president, Dr. William A. Smith, was an old friend of Swinney's from his Lynchburg days.[14]

Merchants such as Donnell and large-scale agriculturalists like Swinney were often the only people in their communities to have regular contact with the broader world. Donnell's store customers were the same people who would later be his banking clients: slaveholding planters selling their products outside Missouri, and smaller storekeepers. For many merchants, becoming a banker simply meant specializing in certain services which they already performed. Swinney, as a tobacco grower, had been party to such transactions for his entire career. In becoming bankers, Donnell and Swinney moved from the known to the known.[15]

There were, however, important differences between the St. Louis bankers and the men who became branch bankers. During the four years between the banks' founding and the start of the Civil War, the St. Louis bankers involved themselves more deeply in financial projects, especially railroad development. John J. Anderson promoted and helped finance four different railroads. The country bankers instead worked to transform themselves into landed gentlemen. Ambitious and upwardly mobile as they were, the branch bankers wanted to be more than service providers for the great men of their neighborhoods. They wanted to be those great men, and many set themselves up as planters as soon as they could afford to. In 1860, Major Daniel Berry, president of the Bank of Missouri's Springfield branch, owned forty-three slaves; Alfred Lacey, president of the bank's Cape Girardeau branch, owned eighteen. Dabney C. Garth, president of the Exchange Bank's Glasgow branch, owned twenty-two. Except for Swinney, all of these men began as merchants. Claiborne Fox Jackson himself started as a merchant when he came to Missouri, before entering banking. Captain Swinney was an exception, in starting as a planter and becoming a banker. Usually it was the other way around.[16]

The career of Caleb Jones, of Boonville in Cooper County, shows this pattern of occupational change and upward mobility. Jones came originally from Baltimore, and when he was ten his family moved to Cynthiana County, Kentucky. In 1826, when he was twenty-one, Jones came to Missouri on horseback, swimming his horse across the Missouri River at Franklin. Buying stock on credit, he opened a store at the landing at Arrow Rock, upriver from Franklin and Boonville. His affairs prospered, and in doing business he routinely extended medium-term credit to his customers. In time this led to banking, and Jones became one of the Boonslick's early private bankers. He also bought real estate and eventually owned six thousand acres in Cooper County. By 1861, Jones had sold his banking and mercantile interests and become a gentleman farmer. Despite his strong southern sympathies, he took no part in raising money for the southern volunteers in 1861 and 1862, or at least not to the extent of risking his own property. He died in 1883, said to be the richest man in Cooper County. For such men as Claiborne Fox Jackson and Caleb Jones, to become a planter was to have arrived.[17]

Bankers were not alone in aspiring to be planters. Colonel William Hill Field practiced law for twenty years in Louisville, Kentucky, before retiring and moving to Pettis County, Missouri, in the 1850s. There he set up Eldon, a plantation of two thousand acres and forty slaves. Colonel Field's neighbor in Pettis County, John Stycks Jones, made his money in western freighting enterprises, including the Pony Express. Continuing to run his other businesses, Jones founded Deer Park plantation, named for the plantation he had managed in Mississippi twenty years before. Young men starting out in life sometimes staked their claims early. George Mason Brown, a young Kentuckian living in Saline County, owned only eight slaves when he described himself as a planter in an 1860 state gazetteer.[18]

There is more to joining a social group than simply having the right amount of money. Candidates for membership are always in a sense hostage to the group they wish to join. Whether he qualified as a planter or not, Brown was willing to die for the social order to which he aspired. In May 1861 volunteers elected Brown captain of the Saline Mounted Rifles, a pro-southern military company. In September Brown and his brother, Colonel William Breckenridge Brown, both died while leading an attack on Union militia at Boonville. The ambitions of people like Brown, and others who ran unrelated businesses to meet the expenses of plantation life, suggest more was at stake than profit. For men such as Caleb Jones, William Hill Field, and John Stycks Jones, planting was not only a way to make money but also a way to spend it. Caleb Jones's wife, Nancy Chapman Jones, clearly understood this. Her family remembers her as saying, "It took Caleb Jones, the merchant, to keep up Caleb Jones, the farmer."[19]

The branch bankers were almost unanimously pro-southern, and some were real activists. Colonel Edward Cresap McCarty was president of the Kansas Law and Order Party when he became cashier of the Mechanics' Bank branch at Kansas City. The Kansas Law and Order Party was a paramilitary group that fought to make Kansas a slave state and helped slaveholders immigrate there.

Colonel McCarty published fiery newspaper broadsides with such declarations as "We are determined to clean up the territory [of abolitionists] or fail in the attempt. To arms! At once and come to the rescue! We are all under arms here to-night, and will be ready to-morrow." Other Kansas City bankers who shared his views were Jesse Riddlesbarger, president of the Mechanics' Bank branch, and the Reverend Thomas Johnson, president of the Union Bank branch. Riddles-barger and Johnson co-owned a strongly proslavery newspaper, the *Kansas City Enterprise*, whose masthead motto was "The World Is Governed Too Much." Reverend Johnson was especially prominent in proslavery politics in Kansas, and eastern newspapers reported on him. Frederick Douglass, in particular, blasted Johnson as an outrageous hypocrite. Douglass charged that Johnson used slave labor to run a supposedly Christian mission (Shawnee Mission, Kansas Territory) while he amassed a fortune at the expense of the Indians and the government.[20]

Another important difference between the St. Louis bankers and the branch bankers was kinship. Almost none of the St. Louis bankers were kin to other bankers, perhaps because of the city's size. Upwardly mobile people often con-solidate their positions through marriage, and St. Louis was large enough to have many wealthy families from which to choose a spouse. Only one of the fourteen St. Louis bank presidents and cashiers married into the family of another banker. In comparison, the branch bankers almost look like one large extended family. Surviving data show that ties of marriage or blood related one-third of the branch presidents and almost half of the branch cashiers with the families of other bank officers. In his May 9 letter to Sterling Price (see Chapter 1), Governor Jackson named six banks to which Barnes and the other St. Louis bankers should send money. Jackson and Price themselves had family connections to four of these six banks, as well as to one more nearby bank, in Columbia. Family ties connecting officers and directors within the banks were no less dense. Three out of ten offi-cers and directors of the Arrow Rock branch of the Bank of Missouri in June 1860 were kin to one another. At the Bank of St. Louis branch at Boonville, four out of nine were. Many of the branch bankers were kin to officers and directors of other banks as well. The connections among banking, politics, and family ran all the way to the state capitol. Jackson and Price both held the office of state bank commissioner, and were thus responsible for monitoring the business affairs of their own near relatives to protect the public interest. No one in the Missouri legislature or press even brought up the issue of conflict of interest, suggesting that such situations were commonplace.[21]

Twenty-first-century Americans view banks not only as profit-seeking enter-prises but as public goods that should help promote the general welfare. Judged by that standard, Missouri's 1857 banks and their political connections look third world, if not downright corrupt. In fact, the new banks resembled those of industrializing New England thirty years before. In both places, corporations controlled by extended family groups sold stock to raise money, which they loaned to family members and other insiders. These publicly held banks, though dominated by an extended-family network of insiders, tapped the savings of outsiders who wanted to share in the banks' investment income. Naomi Lamoreaux describes this brand of family capitalism in *Insider Lending: Banks, Personal Connections, and Economic Development in Industrial New England.* According to Lamoreaux, the New England banks in this period resembled investment clubs, and shares of stock were like mutual fund shares in the banks' investment portfolio.[22]

The new Missouri branch banks were similar extended-family businesses, judging by the closeness of the family connections that bound officers, directors, and customers. Lamoreaux found that Massachusetts banks got much more of their loanable capital from shareholders than from depositors. This was true in Missouri as well. While these banks had outside shareholders and customers, the in-group took priority. Equal opportunity aside, this was a rational way to do business when third-party credit reporting was in its infancy. Lenders overcame the problem of asymmetric information by combining business relations with family, neighborhood, and social connections. Also, lending commitments buttressed by personal ties meant that a defaulter could face social ostracism as well as legal sanctions. Market embeddedness, the formal term for this bundling of social and family relations with business, remains a common feature of traditional banking in much of the world, especially in Islamic countries and the Indian subcontinent.[23]

The Civil War created a radical break between Missouri's past and its future, sweeping away both the banks of 1857 and the elite group that controlled them. Had the antebellum regime survived, though, Missouri's industrialization probably would not have followed the same path as did New England's. The critical difference between banking in the two places was barriers to entry. Here, Missouri's 1857 banks more closely resembled Mexican banks during the presidencies of Porfirio Díaz from 1877 to 1911. Missouri's antebellum banks have little obvious connection with the Mexican banks of several decades later. However, Noel Maurer's history of Mexican banking, *The Power and the Money: The Mexican Financial System, 1876–1932,* shows that banks in the two places shared important characteristics.

When General José de la Cruz Porfirio Díaz Mori became president of Mexico in 1877, his government needed money to consolidate its position. Previous Mexican governments had solved this problem by periodically confiscating

private property and looting the country's banks. Díaz and his advisers realized
the banks could serve more strategic ends and help ease the government's money
problems permanently. Banks could provide a stable currency and liquidity, thus
improving the government's ability to tax. Banks could also lend the government
money and act as the government's fiscal agent. Since the Díaz government
had little money of its own, the banks' capital would have to come from private
sources. Here the government faced a credibility problem. Díaz came to power
after a long period of political instability and lawlessness in Mexico, and citizens
rightly distrusted any government-sponsored financial plan. The government
would also have to make banking an attractive investment. The government's
approach to these problems resembled important features of Missouri's 1857 law.
First, the government restricted entry into the industry and awarded banking
monopolies to local power groups in the provinces. Then, the government selec-
tively enforced the property rights of these local elites, defending their power and
business interests against would-be competitors. Thus, the government extended
its authority into remote parts of the country in an essentially feudal power-
sharing arrangement, giving local power groups a stake in the system in return
for their support.[24]

The new system worked, and the banks survived and prospered through the
next three decades of Díaz's largely peaceful, if not democratic, rule. Throughout this time, the overall character of the banking system remained the same —
insider-controlled institutions with close ties to local political elites. Maurer
finds the same pattern of insider lending in these banks as Lamoreaux did in
the New England banks of the 1830s. In both places wealthy families founded
the banks, contributed much of their capital, and dominated their management.
Such families commonly lent money to family members, and in the early history of the banks there was little distance between borrowers and lenders. Maurer also finds, as did Lamoreaux, that even though insiders received preferential
treatment in getting loans, the banks' overall lending record was good. The banks
made prudent loans and did not throw their money away on unfit family members. Mexican banks also invested significantly in industry.[25]

Industry in New England and in Mexico developed differently, however, with
ownership much more closely held in Mexico than in New England. The laws
of most New England states made it easy to get bank charters, and any investor
group that had the minimum capital could start a bank. The region's total banking capital could expand to meet demand, and in time more and more families founded banks. With capital relatively plentiful in New England, banks had
to compete for investment opportunities. In Porfirian Mexico, however, capital

availability constrained new business formation. There, the number of banks and total banking capital grew only modestly. The government's barriers to entry into the banking industry kept out newcomers. Banks continued to loan to the same narrow groups of insiders, and local elites controlled new industries that developed on their turf. The revolution of 1910 ended Díaz's rule, but the underlying political economy remained unchanged until the 1980s. As Maurer writes, the problem with Mexican banking wasn't insider lending, but not enough insider lending.[26]

Missouri's 1857 banks were too short-lived to have much influence on the state's industrialization. But as in Mexico, the Missouri state government limited the number of available bank charters, demanded a high startup investment, and imposed a political litmus. Both places created regional banking monopolies controlled by local elites allied with the government. In both places the state's protection for the banks extended beyond the advantages granted in the banks' charters. In Missouri, when the savings institutions mounted a legal challenge against the chartered banks, both the bank commissioner and the legislature intervened to defend the banks. Both the Mexican and the Missouri governments wanted strong banks for all the usual reasons, but both governments also used banking as part of a larger strategy to counter external threats. In Missouri in 1857 the threat was ideological rather than military, but that would change.

The Díaz government could award its local clients much more control over banking than Missouri's state government could. Still, the state's banking and industrial policy mattered. Throughout U.S. history individual states' policies have strongly influenced their later economic development and their ability to attract investment. The fact that wealthy slaveholders moved to Missouri's Boonslick just before the war shows the state was an attractive destination for these particular economic immigrants. During this same time, the *New York Times* published travelers' reports describing Missouri's business climate as hostile to outside investors, principally because of the state's alliance with the slavery interests (see Chapters 1 and 2). Once Missouri's banking system was in place, the dense web of family connections that underlay the banks' formal organization was a further defense against unwanted outsiders. Later events in Missouri showed how far the entrenched rural elites were willing to go to defend their privileges.

Because Missouri's 1857 banks did not survive the Civil War, the banks' future industrial policy was a potential problem that never became a real one. During the war, however, the bankers' almost total lack of banking experience had much more immediate and serious results. Only four of the sixty-six branch presidents and cashiers had prior banking experience, and then only in small private banking partnerships in their hometowns. Missouri's new branch bankers may not have realized it at the time, but their new roles created a serious conflict of interest for them. A critical difference between bankers and merchants is that bankers have broad fiduciary duties that merchants do not, in that bankers are responsible for assets that they themselves do not own. Missouri's banks were joint-stock companies with publicly traded shares, but the men who managed the banks had spent their working lives thinking of the assets they controlled as their own property and that of their partners.[27]

Outside St. Louis, the leading citizens of the country districts made up a patchwork of local elites, each one a handful of powerful men who knew each other personally and shared multiple kinship, business, and social ties. Besides their own enterprises, many of the branch bankers had also founded towns, counties, colleges, churches, and newspapers. They had literally made the world in which they lived. Their influence extended to the political realm; 62 percent of the branch presidents and 37 percent of the branch cashiers held or had held political office. The big men in these country neighborhoods were the rich farmers, and, in the high slavery counties, the planters. Genteel country life has a seemingly primal appeal, and nothing in the branch bankers' experience would have prompted them to look beyond that. They had almost universally grown up on farms in the older slave states to the east, where the local gentry would have been just the same.[28]

This was a narrow world, and it became narrower for the merchants who became bankers. A merchant lived in a customer democracy, but the branch bankers did business with a single economic stratum, and a particular ethnicity within that stratum. One historian has described the average Missourian in this period as a Methodist farmer from Kentucky with a hundred acres of land and no slaves. There were many such Missourians, but in fact the state's population consisted of multiple groups that had little mutual contact. Blacks and immigrants were for different reasons outside the political and economic mainstream. Blacks took no part in civic life at all. Immigrants, mostly German-Americans, remained largely separate in this period and did business through German-owned savings institutions. The branch bankers of the new 1857 banks did most of their business with people like themselves, and of the same small social set to which they themselves belonged. Less well-off farmers marketed their surplus produce locally, and few others ever had reason to even enter a bank.[29]

As to the planters, even the larger operators had limited experience outside their own neighborhoods. Instead they dealt with bankers and commission merchants, the local term for factors, as intermediaries. Captain Swinney's granddaughter, Berenice Morrison-Fuller, in her reminiscences of plantation life (her own phrase) at Sylvan Villa, some seventy-five years later, wrote, "These large farms were almost self-sufficing. Everything that could be raised or made for home consumption was brought to a fine art." Except for areas close to the navigable rivers, travel and transport were expensive and slow. By 1860 the telegraph, invented fifteen years earlier, linked Missouri's major towns but little else. Except for merchants and factors, and now bankers, most rural Missourians lived in a local world of farming, kinship, and neighborhood.[30]

But the money-center banks were changing in the years just before the Civil War. In Lamoreaux's New England, by the post–Civil War period the banks still had their family ties, but had become more impersonal and bureaucratic institutions. These later banks engaged more in arm's-length transactions with a wider range of clients, and profit-and-loss considerations weighed more against personal connections. Personal relations gradually lost ground to codes of conduct mutually accepted by relative strangers. Salaried professional managers became more common, replacing part-time officers drawn from the ranks of the largest shareholders.

The growing body of professional literature clearly shows the trend toward more legalistic, impersonal business practices. *Bankers' Magazine*, published in Boston from 1845, devoted its pages to explaining how to handle problems arising from secured transactions, individual liability, assignments, crop liens, and other complex issues. For the money-center banks, consensual interpretations of difficult issues were indispensable when thousands of miles might separate the different parties to transactions. St. Louis was an emerging financial center, and the bankers there would have seen how the financial market was changing. Much more than was true for the branch bankers, the St. Louis bankers' life histories suited them for this transformation. The St. Louis bankers had migrated from farms or small towns to a growing city. The branch presidents and cashiers emigrated from farm to frontier, or from frontier to frontier. As far as is known, none of the branch bankers had ever lived in a city.[31]

Except in Kansas Territory, violent conflict between North and South was yet to come. Missouri's 1857 banking law was one small move in a still peaceful but intensifying competition between the two sections. Missouri's economy had diversified significantly by the late 1850s, and the state offered broader investment alternatives than just plantation agriculture. The law, however, ensured that Missouri's banks would serve the plantation interests, as banks did elsewhere in the South. But the state's efforts to bolster slavery within its borders were doomed from the start. Missouri was the farthest northwestern salient of the plantation economy, bounded on three sides by free states. The 1857 banking law helped strengthen the Boonslick planter aristocracy that already dominated the state's business and politics, but the Boonslick itself was an indefensible location. Even so, it took the Civil War to dislodge Missouri's ruling elite, and then only after an interlude of violence unprecedented in American history for its ferocity.

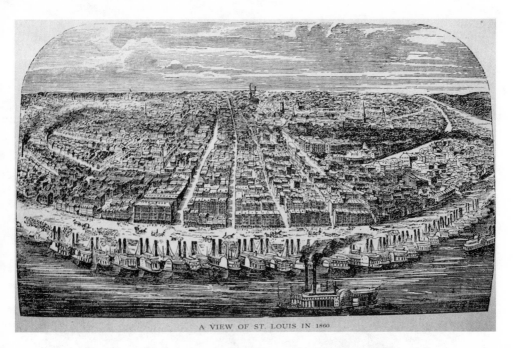

A VIEW OF ST. LOUIS IN 1860

Figure 3.1. City life. St. Louis, 1860. Frontispiece, Edwards and Hopewell, *Edwards' Great West.*

Figure 3.2. Village life. Glasgow, Missouri, 1860s. Collection of the author.

Figure 3.3. Social aspirations: banker/planter homes. Sylvan Villa, Glasgow, Missouri. Home of Captain William David Swinney, President, Western Bank of Missouri branch at Glasgow. Used by permission of the State Historical Society of Missouri, Columbia.

Figure 3.4. Prairie Park, Arrow Rock, Missouri. Home of William Breathitt Sappington, President, Bank of the State of Missouri branch at Arrow Rock. Photograph by Jeff Yelton.

Figures 3.5, 3.6, 3.7, 3.8. Slavery and plantation imagery, Missouri banknotes, ca. 1860.
Images courtesy of Heritage Auction Galleries, HA.com.

Figure 3.9. Missouri Confederate State Government Bond, 1862.
Image courtesy of Heritage Auction Galleries, HA.com.

Figure 3.10. Reverend Thomas Johnson
(1802–65), President, Union Bank of
Missouri branch at Kansas City, 1850s.
Used by permission of the Kansas State
Historical Society.

Figure 3.11. Former Missouri State Bank
Commissioner, Governor Claiborne
Fox Jackson (1806–62), 1861. Used by
permission of the State Historical
Society of Missouri, Columbia.

Figure 3.12. John J. Anderson, President, Bank of
St. Louis parent branch, St. Louis, ca. 1859.
Edwards and Hopewell, *Edwards' Great West.*

Figure 3.13. Robert Barnes (1808–92), President,
Bank of the State of Missouri parent branch,
St. Louis, ca. 1859. Edwards and Hopewell,
Edwards' Great West.

Figure 3.14. Brigadier General Nathaniel Lyon, USA (1818–61). Cover illustration, *Harper's Weekly*, July 13, 1861.

Figure 3.15. Former Governor and Missouri Bank
Commissioner, Major General Sterling Price, CSA
(1809–67), ca. 1863. Used by permission of the State
Historical Society of Missouri, Columbia.

Figure 3.16. United States arsenal at St. Louis. *Harper's Weekly*, May 11, 1861.

Figure 3.17. "The Rebel Ex-Governor, Jackson, of Missouri, Addressing Colonel Mulligan's Troops after the Surrender at Lexington." Cover illustration, *Harper's Weekly*, October 19, 1861.

4

INSIDER LENDING

After the clampdown on the St. Louis bankers, southern fundraising experienced a leadership vacuum that was filled by local initiatives. Despite their military reverses, Missouri's southern men were in some ways better organized than the Unionists, and early on they gained control of most of the banks' money. Missouri's southerners were the earliest permanent white settlers in the state, and the longest established in the Boonslick. Among them were many of each community's richest men—planters, bankers, and leading merchants, men of mature years and long residence. Such men had many personal and commercial connections, and many of them did business by telegraph. Missouri's Unionists had numbers and the superior power of the federal government on their side. The Union men could not, however, stop pro-southern business and community leaders from communicating with one another. When Union forces gained control of the banks, the money was already gone.

Claiborne Fox Jackson had planned to move money from the banks and the state treasury to the Missouri State Guards. The southern defeat at Boonville displaced rather than thwarted this funds transfer. The branch bankers in the interior of the state still had great freedom of action. Court documents from later in the war show that, starting in mid-May 1861, in the areas beyond the reach of federal authority, pro-southern bankers lent large sums to rebel military organizations. Acting independently, the branch bankers eventually transferred more money to the rebels than Jackson had originally sought.

David Pinger, a twenty-nine-year-old German-American merchant in St. Joseph, described the role the banks played during the 1862 military trial of the banker Robert W. Donnell (see Chapter 3). Rebel troops had occupied St. Joseph the previous September, and Pinger feared they would requisition the stock of his store without paying him. Pinger asked Donnell, president of the St. Joseph branch of the Bank of Missouri and a well-known secessionist, to intercede. As Pinger recalled the conversation, Donnell told him that "in case [the troops] should press our stock, [Donnell] thought it would be better for the monied men in the county who sympathized with the secession movement, to make a note with their signatures, for such amount as might be taken from us, which note could be placed in the Bank, of which he is president, to make the money." Donnell's bank would thus credit Pinger's account for the note amount, paying for the goods taken from Pinger's store.[1]

Despite the calm tone of the conversation as related by Pinger, this was testimony before a military tribunal in which Donnell was on trial for treason. In effect, Donnell was using his bank to lend money to the exiled Jackson government to further the rebellion. A month after Pinger's testimony, General Benjamin F. Loan, the (Union) Missouri State Militia commander of the Western District of Missouri, wrote from St. Joseph to General John M. Schofield in St. Louis about Donnell. Loan was holding Donnell in prison, and he requested permission to banish Donnell from Missouri until the end of the war. Speaking of the rebels in St. Joseph, Loan wrote that "we have none more potent for evil than [Robert W. Donnell]."[2]

The "note with their signatures" to which Donnell referred was a promissory note, a common nineteenth-century financial instrument, essentially an IOU or postdated check. After accepting such a note in payment for a sale, a merchant could get payment from the signer on the note's maturity. More commonly, the merchant would discount, or sell, the note to a bank, which would charge a fee for the service. The bank would then receive payment from the note's original signer on the note's maturity. In this way the note became a short-term loan to the note's signer, repayable to the bank. A typical commercial transaction might begin with a farmer, A, who wishes to buy one hundred dollars' worth of groceries. However, A will have no cash for another four months, when he will harvest and sell his crops. In exchange for the groceries, A signs a promissory note to storekeeper B for $110 payable in a hundred and twenty days. A and B have done business together for many years, and they trust each other. The ten dollars represents an interest payment to B, for waiting for his money for one hundred and twenty days. Storekeeper B has his own cash flow to consider. He discounts the note to banker C for $102. C holds the note until maturity and collects $110 from A.

At least while he was testifying before a Union military tribunal, Pinger was a Unionist. If so, he was an exception. Almost all the storekeepers, millers, saddlers, stockmen, tinsmiths, and others who accepted such promissory notes as payment

Figure 4.1. Promissory note signed June 8, 1861, in Boonville, payable to William Jamison by Nathaniel Sutherlin and Walker H. Finley on October 8, 1861, at the banking house of William H. Trigg in Boonville. *William H. Trigg & Co. v. Nathaniel Sutherlin, Walker H. Finley, William E. Jamison* [case CO633069]. March, 1863 session, Cooper County Circuit Court papers, Boonville, Missouri.

were pro-southern, as were the bankers who discounted the notes. A handful of branch bankers were Union men. One was John Brooks Henderson, one of the coauthors of the 1857 banking law. When the war broke out Henderson was president of the Bank of Missouri branch at Louisiana, Missouri, on the Mississippi River close to Mark Twain's boyhood home of Hannibal. Henderson was a Virginian, a slaveholder, and a Democrat, but strongly pro-Union. Pike County voters elected Henderson to the state convention called by Governor Jackson to consider secession; there Henderson became a leader of the Unionist delegates. Later, he raised two regiments of Union troops and became a brigadier general of volunteers. In January 1862, when the U.S. Senate expelled Missouri Senators Waldo P. Johnson and Trusten Polk for treason, Henderson filled Polk's seat. Henderson later won election to the full term. Court records show that the banks managed by men such as Henderson discounted few, if any, of these promissory notes. Except for a few such standouts, however, the events Pinger described in St. Joseph occurred throughout the state, wherever there were branch banks. When the war came, over three-quarters of the presidents and cashiers of these institutions were pro-southern.[3]

Thirty of the state's forty-two parent and branch banks took part in this lending. Union troops occupied St. Louis for the entire war, and the parent branches of the seven banks headquartered there could do little to help the South. Nor could the banks in Ste. Genevieve and Cape Girardeau, where Union forces kept a strong military presence to control the Mississippi River. Most of the thirty

banks that engaged in the lending were in the state's central and western counties, Missouri's main slaveholding district. There, beginning in mid-1861 and continuing through the first year of the war, pro-southern Missourians wrote thousands of unsecured promissory notes to buy military supplies from merchants
like Pinger. The record of the promissory notes survives today in circuit court
papers in the banks' home and nearby counties. As the war progressed, the Union
forces purged pro-southern bankers as part of a drive to expel southern sympathizers from powerful positions. The Union men who took over the banks filed
lawsuits in the civil courts to recover on the promissory notes, by then defaulted.
Figure 4.2 shows the statewide distribution of the banks' lawsuits to recover on
defaulted promissory notes such as Pinger described.[4]

Surviving court records show that Missouri's southern men signed at least
twenty-nine hundred such notes for a total face amount of almost three million
dollars, much more than Claiborne Fox Jackson had originally sought from the
banks (see Appendix 2). The branch cashiers probably acted as the point men for
this wealth transfer to the rebels, but the bank presidents and directors doubtless
took part. The banks were small enough that directors met weekly to review every
request to discount a note that the bank received. The total number of promissory
notes eventually litigated by the banks remains unknown. Thirty courthouses
burned during the Civil War; counting these and later courthouse fires, and
other instances where the records are simply missing, 36 counties out of 114 have
no circuit court records for this period. Of the remaining 78 counties, 40 have
records of 10 or more promissory note cases. On average, each county had 73
cases for the same number of promissory notes, and 87 separate signers of these
notes. (See Appendix 4 for promissory note cases per county, Appendix 2 for
calculations.) Johnson County, Missouri, had the most with 365 cases. Lafayette
and Ray Counties were second and third, with 284 and 254 cases, respectively.
Statewide there were about 3,500 separate signers of these notes.[5]

The Confederates' money transfer was remarkable in several respects, not least
because of the amount involved. Three million dollars was a huge sum in 1861,
equivalent to about $77 million in 2008 dollars (see Appendix 2). In 1860, the
last year before the war, the Missouri state government collected $1.7 million in
taxes, or just over half of what Missouri's rebels raised via the promissory notes.
Later, the Union-controlled banks contributed about two million dollars to the
Union effort over the remaining course of the war. There is no way to tell how
the bankers paid out the promissory notes. However, both bankers and borrowers
would have wanted to get the banks' money out before federal troops could seize
it. The bankers may have chosen to pay the promissory notes in gold and silver,
when they could, as they probably viewed their communities' leading citizens

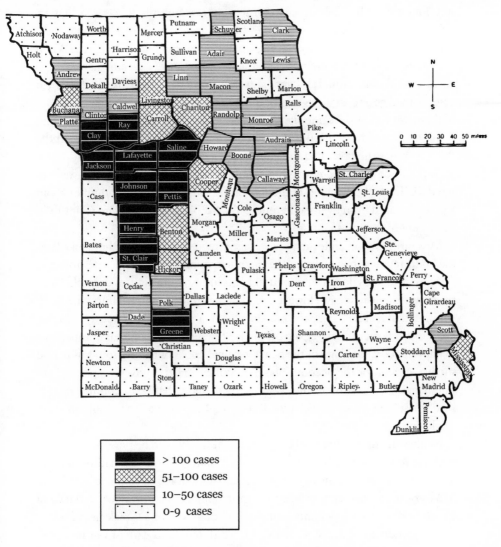

Figure 4.2. Distribution of promissory note lawsuits.

as more likely to repay the money than occupying troops. On July 1, 1861, the thirty banks that lent the money had about three million dollars in specie in their vaults.[6]

The main features of the lending were the same throughout the forty counties where records of the promissory note cases survive. A close look at three adjoining counties in the Boonslick—Cooper, Pettis, and Saline—on the south bank of the Missouri River shows what happened. In these three counties, after excluding suits for ordinary bad debts, 310 promissory notes were written between May 15, 1861, and June 30, 1862, to raise money for the southern forces. Each note had a single payee; most notes had on average between two and three cosigners. When the banks discounted these notes, all the notes' endorsers became liable for repayment and were named as defendants in the civil suits the banks filed. The 310 cases named 369 separate signers of these notes as defendants. A typical feature of the notes is that the same signers' names appear again and again in different combinations, acting variously as maker, co-maker, payee, and assignee. In the three counties the note with the largest face amount was for $8,100; the smallest was for $61. Most were for amounts between $300 and $1,000, repayable in 120 days. The notes litigated in these counties had a total face amount of about $315,000, raised from twelve different banks. Six of these banks were plaintiffs in 91 percent of the cases.[7]

Missouri's Confederates may have raised more money from the banks than the court records show. Besides the unknown number of case files destroyed in fires, court records do not show outright gifts in cash or in kind, or debts that borrowers were able to repay. However, most of the courthouses that burned were in counties that had no banks, and probably few, if any, promissory note cases. Also, the borrowers may not have paid off many of these loans, though it is impossible to know for certain. None of the banks' original books of record from this period survive, except for the account books of William H. Trigg & Company, a private banking firm in Boonville. Trigg's records show that he discounted eighty-six of these promissory notes in the three counties, and had to file suit on every single one.[8]

Neither the signers nor the bankers thought they would be personally responsible for repayment. Missouri's Confederate state government had pledged to assume the debts once the fighting was over. Through 1861 a Confederate victory in Missouri still seemed possible. In August Confederate forces defeated federal troops under Franz Sigel and Nathaniel Lyon at Wilson's Creek near Springfield. Lyon died in this battle, giving the North one of its earliest war heroes. A month later, Missouri State Guard troops under Sterling Price won the Battle of Lexington and captured thirty-five hundred Union troops. Also, though circumstances would have varied from person to person, the notes' signers would not have believed that they were putting their own property at risk. The $315,000 raised in the three counties only equaled about 5 percent of the total value of the signers' property, and 9 percent of the value of their real estate.[9]

The victories at Wilson's Creek and Lexington, however, marked the high point of Confederate military fortunes in the state. The war, also, lasted much longer than anyone expected. Most of the notes' signers were agriculturalists, and the worsening violence and lawlessness made farming impossible. The region was also cut off from the South, the major market for the Boonslick's products. In 1861 the government of the Confederate States closed the lower Mississippi and confiscated Northern assets. In April of that year President Lincoln proclaimed a blockade against Confederate ports and forbade all commerce with the rebels. The war shrank the value of the signers' capital, too. Most of their personal property was tied up in slaves, who ran away as the war progressed. By 1863 and 1864, when the promissory note cases were in court, the signers' debt burden was crushing.[10]

A close look at the notes signed in Cooper and Saline Counties shows that the time distribution of these transactions varied according to the local experience of the war. (In Pettis County only the circuit court minute books, and not the original court papers, are available, and it is only possible to discover the approximate dates that promissory notes were signed there.) The same was true of when the courts heard and settled the cases. The Cooper County circuit court records show that the promissory notes started to be written as early as January 1861, after Governor Jackson's inauguration. Starting with a few notes written in January, the numbers peaked from May through August, especially in June around the time of the First Battle of Boonville. Most of these notes were written over a three-week period, between Camp Jackson on May 10 and the Battle of Boonville on June 17. In September the number of promissory notes written dropped off sharply and continued to decline after that. On September 14, the town's Unionist militia repelled an attack on the town by the Saline Mounted Rifles, a rebel militia unit raised in neighboring Saline County. After that, Unionists kept intermittent control over Boonville, though Confederate forces captured the town twice before the end of the war. Elsewhere in the state, however, depending on when Union forces could regain control, banks funded the rebels for much longer. The last bank to remain under Confederate control was the Farmers' Bank of Missouri parent branch in Lexington, Lafayette County. Union troops did not arrest officers of the Farmers' bank until November 1862.[11]

Cooper County was one of the few Boonslick counties where court sessions continued uninterrupted during the war. Still, it took years to settle the sixty-eight promissory note cases the court eventually heard. The Cooper County Circuit Court met for the September 1861 session but adjourned after only a few days until the following March. Then, the judge continued all noncritical cases, including the earliest bad-debt filings, until September. The first judgments in the Cooper County debt cases came in March 1863. The county sheriffs did not finish auctioning the defendants' property until March 1864, for suits initially filed in late 1861. In many counties, judgments took even longer.[12]

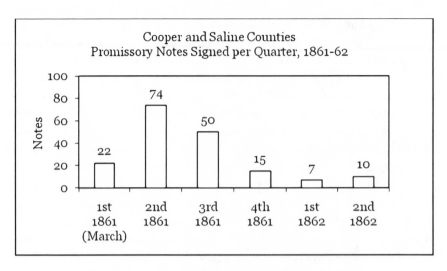

Figure 4.3. Cooper and Saline Counties: Promissory notes
signed per quarter, 1861–1862.

Court records identify all the promissory note signers in each case. Other contemporary sources—the manuscript census, military records, newspapers, county histories, and tombstone inscriptions, to name a few—give further information about the signers. One typical signer was Judge Walker H. Finley of Saline County. Finley was a forty-one-year-old native Kentuckian, a county judge, and a stock dealer; before the war he owned thirteen slaves and 1,160 acres of land. Between mid-1861 and early 1862 Finley signed twenty different notes with twenty-three cosigners. The face amount of these notes totaled about thirty-eight thousand dollars, and they were probably used to buy livestock for the southern forces. Five different Boonslick banks discounted the notes. In 1862, Unionist militia caught Finley with incriminating documents while he was driving ninety-five head of cattle down to the rebel lines. He was charged with being in secret communication with the enemy and narrowly avoided imprisonment, or worse. The banks sued on all twenty of the promissory notes Finley signed, gaining judgments against the defendants for principal, interest, and court costs totaling over forty thousand dollars. None of the defendants had that much money, or credit, in 1863 and 1864, and the Saline County sheriff sold their farms at auction. The 1870 census lists Finley as a tenant farmer owning no real property and with personal property worth four hundred dollars, less than 1 percent of his 1860 holdings.[13]

Except that he was better off than most people, Finley presents as an ordinary pro-Confederate citizen of that time and place. Most of the notes' signers were men of the same stamp. Men like Finley were typical of the bankers' main prewar customers: countrymen rather than townsmen, large-scale commercial farmers and slaveholders, and of old American stock. The notes' signers were born, after Missouri, overwhelmingly in Kentucky, Tennessee, Virginia, and North Carolina. These people were not the foot soldiers of the Confederacy but were long-established citizens, in the upper tier of property ownership in their communities.[14]

Given the thousands of notes signed and the number of counties involved, the lending looks at first like a broad-based, community action. However, a closer look at the 369 promissory note signers in the three sample counties gives a different picture. In this group, among more ordinary men such as Finley, is a virtual Who's Who of Missouri Confederacy in these counties, including two sons of former Governor Meredith Miles Marmaduke and many rich men. In neighboring Lafayette County Sterling Price's son, Edwin Price, was a signer. Other signers were close relatives of Confederate generals, both in Missouri and outside, especially Virginia generals. At the opposite end of the social scale, 12 percent of the signers owned no land, and 10 percent owned land and personal property worth one thousand dollars or less.[15]

The second striking feature about the promissory notes was that most of the hundreds of bankers and borrowers were related to one another by multiple ties of blood and marriage. The pattern of extended family members writing notes back and forth to each other is the same in all counties where the courts have records of these debts. In Cooper County, there were three major extended family groups writing promissory notes in 1861. There is some crossing of county boundaries, but people were usually defendants in their home counties. Walker H. Finley, who lived in Saline County, was a defendant in five Cooper County cases, always with the same codefendants. In each county, bankers and borrowers had ties to specific Confederate military units. In Saline County, the main beneficiaries were the Saline Mounted Rifles and the Jackson Guards; in Cooper and Pettis Counties, the First and Second Missouri Volunteer Infantry and the First and Second Missouri Volunteer Cavalry. At least in these counties, Jo Shelby's command received much of the money raised. Besides noncombatant defendants, nine Confederate regimental colonels signed notes in these counties.[16]

To research how far these family connections extended, I examined family kin relationships at three different degrees of closeness, labeled nuclear, extended$_1$, and extended$_2$. Nuclear and extended$_1$ groups include relatives for which most twenty-first-century Americans would recognize a family connection. The extended$_2$ group is more distant. Nuclear families included parents and children. Extended$_1$ families included these persons plus brothers and sisters, aunts and

uncles, in-laws and their nuclear families of origin, nieces and nephews, grandparents and grandchildren, and first cousins (parents were siblings). Extended$_2$
kinfolk included everyone in extended$_1$, plus second cousins (grandparents were
siblings), and first cousins once removed (child of a parent's first cousin). Surviving genealogical sources show that of the 369 borrowers in the three counties
studied, 88 percent had an extended$_2$ family connection with least one other
signer or banker. Since records and memory of some relationships no longer survive, the actual figure would be higher. The family character of this borrowing
was restrictive as well as inclusive. Only a small minority of southern sympathizers in the sample counties signed promissory notes, and less than 5 percent of
the counties' adult white males, and 6 percent of the household heads (see Appendix 2). The counties' planters arguably had the most to gain from a southern
victory, since that would have assured the future of slavery. However, only one-
quarter of the local planters signed a note (see Chapter 7).[17]

These far-reaching family connections among the notes' signers are consistent with other researchers' findings about southern white society in this period.
"Family," as the term was understood in that time and place, included a much
larger group of kinfolk than is true for most twenty-first-century Americans. In
his study of Orange County, North Carolina, Robert Kenzer found that by the
Civil War the county had divided into eight separate, more or less isolated and
self-contained neighborhoods, each dominated by a particular extended family.
Most of these families, Scotch-Irish Protestants, had immigrated in the 1740s and
1750s. Many of these families had lived together in the same villages in Ireland
and crossed the Atlantic aboard the same vessels. Remaining together, they left the
Atlantic seaboard and migrated west, eventually settling in Orange County.[18]

In Missouri the situation was the same. Agricultural immigrants typically
moved latitudinally, and most of Missouri's early settlers came from Kentucky,
Tennessee, Virginia, and North Carolina. In 1816, John Mason Peck, a Baptist
minister traveling through the first two of these states, noted, "It seemed as though
Kentucky and Tennessee were breaking up and moving to the 'Far West.'" Entire
families, congregations, and neighborhoods often moved together. In the Boonslick, the bankers and signers were bound by family alliances already generations
old in 1861, often dating to the pre-Revolutionary southern Tidewater region.
In the three counties, among signers with documented kinship connections,
each individual was closely related (extended$_1$) on average to four other signers
or bankers, in an average total of two different nuclear families. On average, this
related group of five persons signed fifteen different notes. Counting extended-
family (extended$_2$) connections instead, each borrower was on the average re-

Table 4.1. William Breathitt Sappington kinship connections

Name	Relationship
Levin Breathitt Harwood	niece's husband; first cousin; wife's first cousin
Claiborne Fox Jackson	brother-in-law; wife's cousin's husband
Thomas Jackson	brother-in-law's brother
Darwin William Marmaduke	nephew; wife's first cousin once removed
Vincent Marmaduke	nephew; wife's first cousin once removed

lated, near and far, to seventeen other borrowers in nine different nuclear families. Each of these extended-family groups signed their names to an average of fifty-seven different promissory notes.[19]

The figures given for extended-family connections among signers and bankers are averages only. Some kinfolk groups were larger. Three generations of the Miller family wrote promissory notes back and forth to one another; four brothers in the Shy family did the same. In the counties studied, the three Wallace brothers had the largest number of extended family members who signed notes. In all, the Wallaces' relatives included 131 different signers from 71 different nuclear families, more than one-third of all defendants in the three-county sample. These numbers of kinfolk may seem improbably high, but nuclear families were large, and families lived near one another for generations and usually married close to home.[20]

An example of one extended family of bankers and signers shows the complexity of these kinship ties. In 1861 and early 1862, the Bank of Missouri branch in Arrow Rock accepted forty-seven promissory notes for military supplies. The bank's president, William Breathitt Sappington, was related to the Harwood, Jackson, and Marmaduke families, all living nearby. These four families intermarried eleven times between 1804 and 1860, across three different states. By 1862 every member of these families had multiple kinship connections with every other. Besides ties of blood and marriage, members of these allied families joined in various business ventures at least back to 1828. Nor does this exhaustively describe Sappington's kinship connections with other bankers and defendants. Besides the Harwoods, Jacksons, and Marmadukes, Sappington had another eighteen relatives who either signed promissory notes in the three counties or were bankers there. Table 4.1 shows Sappington's connection to his Harwood, Jackson, and Marmaduke relatives who were bankers, signers, or both in the three-county sample. Many languages have words to describe such relationships. English does not, except for a few obsolete fragments, such as Levitical degrees, morganatic marriage, and distaff cousins. However, the frequency of intermarriage, the generation-spanning durability of these family alliances, and the promissory notes themselves all show how important these family connections were.[21]

The bankers' and borrowers' genealogies and biographies not only reveal their kinship ties to one another, but also suggest individual roles in the promissory note transactions. The borrowers make up a three-tier pyramid, with leaders at the tip underpinned by subordinate groups of followers. This classification is imprecise, because signers of several notes might act in different capacities. At the base of the pyramid were the soldiers and their immediate families, borrowers who signed notes to buy military kit from storekeepers or tradesmen. These borrowers usually signed only one or two promissory notes. The soldiers' group was the largest of the three, accounting for about 66 percent of all signers. The young men of little or no property, noted above, fall into this group.[22]

A closer examination shows that such men usually were related to a banker or another signer of far greater means, sometimes serving in the same military unit. Also in this bottom tier of low-incidence signers were military officers, including the eleven Confederate regimental colonels, who were responsible for supplying their men. The middle tier of the pyramid consisted of storekeepers and tradespeople who accepted notes as payment from the first group and subsequently discounted the notes to a bank. David Pinger, the St. Joseph merchant, was a member of this group. The merchants' names may appear on many promissory notes, and as defendants in as many cases. Merchants and other suppliers make up about 23 percent of all signers.[23]

The story of these first two groups is straightforward. All the signers believed in the southern cause, but the men at the base of the pyramid needed arms, and the issue was survival. Going poorly armed into battle was far riskier than accepting a loan, whether the borrower could pay it back or not. There was also the overwhelming weight of social and family duty. Each of these men had many relatives, friends, and neighbors signing such notes. Nor are the military officers or the storekeepers difficult to understand. For officers, responsibility for equipping the soldiers in their commands came with the rank. Merchants like David Pinger could either accept promissory notes or have their stock requisitioned and receive no compensation at all.

The third and last group, at the top of the pyramid and composed of about 11 percent of borrowers, is more complex. The men in this group were older and richer, and they included twelve of the forty-five rich planters who lived in the three counties sampled. These men were the social equals, or betters, of the bankers. Members of this third group sometimes signed as many as twenty or thirty notes. William S. Brown of Saline County signed thirty-six. These men, working with the bankers, moved the lending forward. These men acted as loan sureties, committing to repayment if the original signers did not pay or if the government rejected a later claim. No one, however, thought they would be personally liable. The Jackson government-in-exile had pledged to repay all private debts incurred for military purposes to defend the state, and the Confederate government stood behind the Jackson government. Given the signers' political connections there is little doubt that the state would have repaid these debts, had the state itself survived. The promissory notes served as receipts for the loans, for which either the banks or the signers themselves could claim repayment once the South had won.[24]

The sample data from the three counties thus show that within a population of hundreds of signers, a much smaller group underwrote the borrowing. The early impetus for the borrowing came from Governor Claiborne Fox Jackson and a small group of senior St. Louis bankers. These men next involved the six branch banks in the Boonslick that would hold the money beyond the reach of Union forces. After the flight of the Jackson government, there was seemingly little, if any, centralized control of the lending. However, the pyramidal hierarchy of borrowers, the family connections that linked them, and the wide disparities in status and social position all point toward some local control. With a careful reading of the available data on the individual signers in the three counties, it is possible to infer who the local leaders were.

Some commonsense assumptions can be made about levels of personal influence in family councils. In general, older, richer men will trump younger, poorer men; fathers will trump sons. Governor Jackson's own family in Saline County shows these differentials. Out of the three hundred sixty-nine defendants in the three-county sample, eleven were members of Jackson's extended$_1$ kin group. These relatives signed some twenty-two promissory notes in the three counties, or about 6 percent of all the notes signed there. Jackson's extended$_2$ family members signed eighty-eight different promissory notes, over one-quarter of the three-county total. One of these extended$_1$ family members was Jeremiah Liggett, who in 1860 was a thirty-one-year-old Saline County merchant with two slaves and no land. Liggett's brother Stephen was married to Jackson's sister-in-law, whose own brother was William B. Sappington, planter, owner of thirty-eight slaves and twenty-three hundred acres, and a bank president.[25]

It is clear whose opinions count in such relationships, and where authority lies. Economic power was not the only disparity. The rich men whose names appear on the promissory notes also headed large extended families. In this smaller group of rich and powerful men, Governor Jackson's plans and policy would have strongly influenced his brother, brother-in-law, nephew, and cousins who were bank officers and directors. In the three-county sample, one family overtops the rest in wealth and prestige and is at the center of the family links connecting bankers and defendants: the extended family of the Sappingtons and Marmadukes, Governor Jackson's in-laws. In this family, two men stand out as the probable leaders of the lending in the three counties: Jackson's brother-in-law William Breathitt Sappington, and the nephew of both men, Vincent Marmaduke.

The patriarch of this clan and the founder of the fortunes of all three men was Doctor John Sappington, William B. Sappington's father, Vincent Marmaduke's grandfather, and Governor Jackson's father-in-law. The elder Sappington pioneered the use of quinine to treat malaria, a scourge of the Mississippi valley in the early nineteenth century. Sappington's Anti-Fever Pills worked, unlike most patent medicines. Sappington sold the pills all the way from Ohio to South Carolina to Texas, and he became one of the richest men in Missouri. Doctor Sappington had a strong sense of family duty and employed his sons, sons-in-law, and as many other relatives as he could in the pill business. The family was also politically connected. One of Doctor Sappington's brothers-in-law, John Breathitt, became governor of Kentucky, and another, George Breathitt, was private secretary to Andrew Jackson. Two of Sappington's sons-in-law, Meredith Miles Marmaduke and Claiborne Fox Jackson, became governors of Missouri.[26]

After the doctor's death in 1856, his son William B. Sappington was one of the two or three senior family members. By that time the family, besides selling anti-malaria pills nationwide, had diversified into farming, stock raising, land speculation, the Santa Fe trade, retailing, politics, saw and grist milling, salt production, coal mining, and money lending. Collectively, the family owned over three hundred slaves in Saline County alone. Besides being the richest man in a county with many rich men, William B. Sappington was Governor Jackson's brother-in-law, brother-in-law to former governor Meredith Miles Marmaduke, and uncle to John Sappington Marmaduke, a future Confederate general and governor of Missouri. In 1857 the family formalized its lending business, putting up much of the money to form the new branch of the Bank of Missouri in Arrow Rock. William B. Sappington became the bank's president, and several other relatives served as directors.[27]

Sappington's nephew, Vincent Marmaduke, was a son of a former governor and brother of a Confederate general, and a lawyer, planter, and stock raiser. After graduating from Yale in 1852, where he was a member of Skull and Bones, Marmaduke read for the law and joined the Saline County bar. Instead of practicing law, however, he principally occupied himself with growing hemp on his plantation of fourteen hundred acres and twenty-nine slaves. In the late 1850s, Marmaduke was a rising star in the state Democratic Party. Elected a delegate to the secession convention of 1861, he initially voted against secession. However, he later spoke out against the Union and was imprisoned in St. Louis, and then banished south. Commissioned a colonel in the Confederate army, he served under generals Bragg and Hindman. Subsequently, Marmaduke went to Europe in the Confederate consular service to negotiate arms buys. On his return to Richmond, he became a colonel in the Confederate Secret Service. In December 1864 he was arrested in the Northwest Conspiracy, a plot to free thousands of Confederate POWs held near Chicago and to form them into an army to open a second, northern front. After a military trial and a narrow escape from hanging, Marmaduke returned to Missouri after the war, shorn of his land, slaves, and money. There he passed the rest of his life quietly, involving himself in newspaper publishing and Confederate veterans' organizations. He died in 1904.[28]

The Sappingtons and Marmadukes were exceptional chiefly in having family connections straight to the governor's mansion. Similar rural magnates lived throughout the Boonslick and nearby counties. They were all rich, long-established men, heads of large families, and dominated the commerce, finance, politics, and social life of their neighborhoods. On their home turf, such men usually get their way. Most had local rather than statewide influence, but local influence mattered in dealing with the local bankers. That such men as Sappington and Marmaduke were the leading men in their home counties does not mean that they personally influenced each of the hundreds of signers of the promissory notes. Their word, however, would have carried great weight with the other rich men in their neighborhoods, who would in turn have communicated with their own kinsmen.

The third noteworthy feature about the lending was its complete uniformity across a wide stretch of territory. Except for the names of the signers, promissory notes written in late 1861 in Andrew County, in far northwestern Missouri, look exactly like promissory notes written in New Madrid County, the farthest southeast county—a distance of some 566 miles. At least three days' journey separated these two locations, traveling by rail and steamboat along the fastest routes. Viewed another way, this is more than half the distance between St. Louis and New Orleans. There is no evidence that borrowers in distant parts of the state communicated with one another. Geographically, people who signed these notes lived close to one of the branch banks, in a scatter diagram with a bank at the center. The uniformity of these notes over such a large area suggests that information was shared. However, the distances involved and the poor communication links make centralized control unlikely. Early in the war Union forces chased Missouri's Confederate leadership, the Jackson government, out of the state, and no other authority replaced it.[29]

The absence of a single leadership group and the relationships between signers and bankers suggest a pattern known in sociology as a small-world network. Sociologists define a network as a group of individuals connected through some means, whether for social, kinship, business, or any other reasons. Networks can be hierarchical, such as a government, a corporation, or a military command. By contrast, a small-world network consists of regional clusters loosely linked to a central authority. Clusters consist of individuals—nodes, in network terminology—connected through multiple relationships. In small-world networks, relations between members within clusters are much closer than in hierarchical networks. Thus, information flows more freely and news spreads faster than in most hierarchical networks. Though decentralized, leadership still exists in small-world networks, but it usually extends only to the boundary of the cluster. Some individuals, called hubs, are more "popular" than others, in the sense of having a greater number of affiliations. The hubs are leaders, who draw their power from their personal influence with members of the group.[30]

Of all the individuals involved with the promissory notes, the bankers and their major customers, the planters, were the likely hubs. That is, bankers and planters had the most personal connections of all the borrowers and lenders. Most of Missouri's bankers in this period built large mercantile businesses before entering banking. Successful merchants, like bankers, know many people. Writing in 1849, the journalist John Beauchamp Jones described the western merchant as "a general *locum tenens*, the agent of everybody! And familiar with every transaction in his neighborhood. He is a counselor without license, and yet invariably consulted, not only in matters of business, but in domestic affairs. . . . Every item of news, not only local, but from a distance,—as he is frequently the postmaster, and the only subscriber to the newspaper—has general dissemination from his establishment, as from a common center; and thither all resort, at least once a week, both for goods and for intelligence."[31]

Besides the bankers, other possible lines of communication existed. Missouri politics had become increasingly polarized since the Kansas crisis in the middle of the 1850s. Missouri's slaveholders had met on several occasions to discuss ways to defend their common interests, notably at the Lexington Proslavery Convention in 1855. The Blue Lodge, a clandestine organization to support slavery in Kansas, also formed during these years, and it offered a ready-made communication network. Many of the bankers were Masons, and the lodges could serve the same purpose.[32]

But more than through anyone else, all community relationships—kinship, business, social, and class—came together through bankers and planters. Bankers brought control of the money and access to modern telecommunications to these wide networks of mingled business and personal connections. Planters lent social prestige and extended-family leadership. An important feature of a small-world network is that clusters have much more autonomy than sublevels of a hierarchical network. Unlike a hierarchical network, removing a regional or even the central hub will not disable a small-world network. In the present instance, the central hub and prime mover in the lending was Governor Claiborne Fox Jackson. Tellingly, when Union forces chased Governor Jackson down to Arkansas, the money did not stop flowing from the banks. Like the rebellion itself, the lending continued without him.[33]

Given the difficulty of travel and the limited availability of the telegraph in 1860, a high concentration of promissory note cases probably marks a small-world network cluster. Individuals composing a cluster would need to be geographically close to one another to communicate easily. Figure 4.2 shows several unconnected concentrations of bank cases. By far the largest is the cluster made up of the Boonslick and adjoining counties, including Cooper, Pettis, and Saline Counties. This central-west region really may be several overlapping clusters. Other, smaller clusters include a two-county northeast region, of which Lewis County is seemingly the center; a region in the Bootheel of southeast Missouri, centering on Mississippi County; and an isolated pocket in St. Charles County outside St. Louis.[34]

The social division of the promissory note signers, and their different degrees of community influence and power, raises questions of agency. The bankers and planters did not necessarily drive events because they controlled the money flow. In 1861, young men on both sides formed military units by volunteering at public meetings and then electing officers from their number. These new military units had immediate and pressing needs for money and equipment. Some volunteers could supply their own horses, guns, and other gear. Others would need some outside help. Somehow, the officers of the new volunteer units and the men too poor to equip themselves met with the local bankers and other rich men. The commitments and agreements made at these meetings probably varied widely and depended on the personalities involved. There is no reason to doubt the commitment and willingness to fight of either the old men or the young men. But each group likely felt pressure from the other to act as it did.

In this way, Missouri Confederates gained control of most of the banks' money, leaving behind a mountain of paper promises. The bankers went further still, handing out so much money to their relatives that they brought their institutions to the brink of insolvency. The St. Joseph banker, Robert W. Donnell, seemingly treated David Pinger, the merchant, with courtesy and consideration. But regardless of Donnell's manners, Pinger was acting under duress. Courteous and considerate or no, the bankers defrauded the people who had money tied up in the banks—depositors, shareowners, and holders of the banks' currency, southern men and Unionists alike.[35]

Clearly, some people felt robbed. On October 1, 1861, in Osceola, St. Clair County, a depositor named Marcellus Harris demanded the return of gold he had placed in the local branch of the Merchants' Bank. When the bank's president, William L. Vaughan, refused, Harris shot and killed him on the spot. Harris was no Unionist. He was a Virginian and a slaveholder, and his brother Edwin was a surgeon with the Confederate army. Nevertheless, the bank had clearly stolen Harris's money. Four months later Harris himself died in an ambush a quarter mile from Osceola, possibly in retaliation for shooting Vaughan. Reporting these events to R. G. Dun & Company, the New York credit rating agency, the local Dun's correspondent wrote tartly, "WLV [William L. Vaughan, the bank president] dead. [Waldo P.] Johnson [one of the bank's principal investors, the former U.S. senator from Missouri, expelled from the Senate for treason] absconded and his immense domains attached. . . . [A]bsconded rebs JW [John Weidemeyer, another bank director] in Texas son in the rebel army property attached for more than it will bring."[36]

5

THE UNIONISTS REGAIN CONTROL

In early 1861, Missouri's secessionist elected government was the state's public face. Nevertheless, in the gubernatorial and national elections of 1860 and in the election to Missouri's special convention of 1861, Unionist candidates received over 75 percent of the vote. During the war, the numbers of Missourians in military service on the two sides presented a more mixed picture of white political sentiment. About thirty thousand Missourians served in the southern forces, plus an unknown number of guerrillas, compared with over a hundred thousand Missourians in the Union army, but this number included about thirty-nine thousand African American soldiers. Another ninety thousand men served in the more-or-less Unionist state militia, but many units would only fight to protect their own neighborhoods from armed raiding parties of either side. Still, in the state's major battles, Union forces were always able to field more local troops than the Confederates.[1]

After the flight of the Jackson government in June 1861, Union power in the state was split between the military command and the civilian provisional government, originally the secession convention called by Governor Jackson. Union forces controlled St. Louis and most of the northern half of the state, as well as the railroads, the Missouri River, and the larger towns. Despite Union military superiority, stopping the flow of the money from Missouri's banks to the rebels proved difficult. Union commanders need most of their troops to guard strategic locations, such as the navigable rivers. Union control over the countryside was intermittent until late in the war, and the country banks were able to actively support the rebellion for some time. Union authorities first tried to rein in the banks by seizing the banks' funds outright. This policy did more harm than good and was abandoned. A second Union strategy targeted the bankers, which took time but eventually worked. But when the Unionists took over the banks there was often little left except bricks and mortar.

A report by Assistant State Bank Commissioner George Penn late in 1861 shows the extent of the problem the banks posed. Penn had remained at his post and replaced his chief, Sterling Price, by that time a major general in the rebel Missouri State Guard. Penn's report divided the St. Louis banks according to their politics. Penn classed the Bank of Missouri, the Merchants' Bank, and the Exchange Bank as pro-Union, and the Bank of St. Louis, the Southern Bank, the Mechanics' Bank, and the Union Bank as pro-southern. Total monetary circulation of Penn's pro-Union banks was $3.4 million, compared with $3.1 million for the pro-southern banks.[2]

Later historians have cited Penn's report uncritically, but it understates the banks' support of the southern cause. Penn classified the Bank of Missouri as Unionist, but Robert Barnes, the president of the parent branch, was one of Jackson's original co-conspirators. Nearly all the officers of the bank's branches were pro-southern. Penn correctly classified the Exchange Bank parent branch as pro-Union, but the officers of the bank's Glasgow branch, Dabney C. Garth and William C. Boon, were red-hot Confederates. Penn's report also omitted the two major banks headquartered outside St. Louis, the Farmers' Bank of Missouri in Lexington and the Western Bank of Missouri in St. Joseph. The Farmers' Bank and all its branches were pro-southern. The Western Bank's parent branch was (probably) pro-Union, but its branches were firmly pro-southern.[3]

The banks' disloyalty was a serious problem, but there were even more pressing concerns. The provisional government had no troops and no money. The state's militia force, the Missouri State Guard, was pro-secession, and when the Jackson government fled Jefferson City it left behind an empty treasury. There was only a small federal force in the state, made up mostly of volunteers recently mustered into United States service by General Nathaniel Lyon. The countryside swarmed with rebels and roving bands of armed men with little loyalty to either side. Besides the provisional government, there were two other competing state governments, one military and one civil. In August 1861 General John C. Fremont declared martial law throughout the state, which remained in force until the end of the war. The military government was the only one that extended into the interior of the state, but civilian justice was not the soldiers' priority. There was also the Jackson government, which stubbornly refused to die. Union fortunes in the state reached their low point with the Confederate victories at Wilson's Creek and at Lexington in August and September. Governor Jackson came to Lexington after the town's capture and lectured the Union prisoners on their folly.[4]

The Union weakness was only temporary, however. As soon as the provisional

government formed, President Lincoln immediately recognized it as the legiti-
mate authority in the state. On August 24, Hamilton Gamble, the provisional
governor, laid the foundation of a new military force when he called for forty-
two thousand six-month militia volunteers. Gamble traveled to Washington a
few days later and secured a promise of arms and a loan of two hundred thousand dollars for the troops. In November, the Lincoln administration agreed to
let the provisional government raise a more permanent force, the Missouri State
Militia, which would remain within the state but be paid and equipped by the
United States. The chain of command remained unclear for most of the war,
however. Besides U.S. forces and different militia organizations, at various times
the governors of Kansas, Iowa, Illinois, Indiana, and Colorado sent troops to Missouri. Several times fighting nearly broke out between rival Union commands. In
particular there was bad blood between Missouri and Kansas troops, going back
to the border war of the 1850s.[5]

As it became clear the conflict would be a long one, the state's military and
civilian authorities had to consider issues of citizens' rights, including rights
of property. During his presidential campaign, Abraham Lincoln repeatedly
pledged to respect private property, meaning slaves, but including other types
of property as well. Lincoln reiterated his position in his first inaugural address,
saying that "the property, peace, and security of no section are to be in any
wise endangered by the now incoming Administration." Far from Washington,
in Boonville, General Nathaniel Lyon on June 18, 1861, issued a proclamation
echoing Lincoln's pledge. Speaking the day after the first significant land action
of the war, Lyon stated, "I hereby give notice to the people of this State that I
shall scrupulously avoid all interference with the business rights and property
of every description recognized by the laws of this State, and belonging to law-
abiding citizens." Lyon was as good as his word; he did not touch the money at
Boonville's branch of the Bank of St. Louis. But Lyon no longer commanded all
federal forces in Missouri. When Lyon issued his proclamation his writ extended
only to the western portion of the state. Nor did he have long to live: Lyon died
on August 10 at the Battle of Wilson's Creek.[6]

General Fremont, appointed in July by President Lincoln as commander of
Union forces in Missouri, had different ideas about property. Fremont arrived
in St. Louis on July 25, 1861, and declared martial law in the city three weeks
later, on August 14. Part of the general's proclamation included orders to seize
all private property used to further the rebellion. On August 30, the general extended martial law to the whole state, including the property provisions. Fremont's proclamation stated that "the property, real and personal, of all persons
in the State of Missouri who shall take up arms against the United States, or who

shall be directly proven to have taken active part with their enemies in the field, is declared to be confiscated to the public use, and their slaves, if any they have, are hereby declared free men." This was one of the first U.S. war measures to confiscate rebel property, and it is remembered today as an early step toward Lincoln's Emancipation Proclamation of September 22, 1862. At the time, however, the president thought Fremont's order too radical and rescinded most of it. Had Lincoln allowed Fremont's order to stand, it would have been a clear directive to Union commanders to seize the funds of any bank suspected of cooperating with the enemy.[7]

Fremont clearly intended his order to apply to the banks. Also in August, Fremont took the first actual steps against the banks, ordering troops to seize all the coin from the parent branch of the Bank of Missouri. Fremont also ordered the bank's branches to send their coin to St. Louis. Colonel Ulysses S. Grant, then stationed in Missouri, took part in this collection effort, which he described in his memoirs. "[In August or September 1861] I had been at Jefferson City but a few days," Grant wrote, "when I was directed from department headquarters to fit out an expedition to [the towns of] Lexington, Booneville and Chillicothe, in order to take from the banks in those cities all the funds they had and send them to St. Louis." In the same period, on August 13, Union forces retreating after their defeat at Wilson's Creek seized the cash of the Springfield branch of the Bank of Missouri. The following day, at the other end of the state, federal troops also seized the funds of the Merchants' Bank branch in Ste. Genevieve and sent the money to St. Louis. From Boonville, one of Nancy Chapman Jones's letters to her daughter in San Antonio gives a citizen's-eye view of these actions. On August 27, 1861, she wrote, "We expected they would rob the banks, as they have done at other places. We heard this morning one of the Banks gaurded [*sic*] against that by burning their paper [currency] and hiding the gold."[8]

Fremont has been widely viewed, at the time and since, as an inept commander. But he was right about the threat the banks posed. However, Union troops disastrously bungled attempts to seize the banks' money in the towns of Lexington and Osceola. Lexington, after Boonville, was the second mustering point for the rebel volunteers called out by Governor Jackson in June. The town was the most important place on the Missouri River between Boonville and Kansas City, and the southern sympathies of the citizenry ran deep. On September 11 a thirty-five-hundred-man Union force commanded by Colonel James A. Mulligan occupied Lexington to safeguard Missouri River traffic and to seize a rebel strong point. The parent branch of the Farmers' Bank of Missouri, one of the state's nine chartered banks, was in Lexington, and Colonel Mulligan impounded the bank's cash, variously estimated between $750,000 and $1.5 million. The same day Mulligan's troops arrived, advance units of Sterling Price's Missouri State Guard forces took up positions on the town's outskirts. Fearing an imminent attack, Mulligan appealed to Fremont in St. Louis for reinforcements, but Fremont waited too long to respond. On September 13, Price's troops sealed off the town, and they attacked the next day. On the 20th, after a spirited defense, Mulligan surrendered.[9]

Northern newspapers reported the loss of Mulligan's command and Price's capture of the money as disasters, and as further evidence (after Wilson's Creek) of the egregious incompetence of Missouri's Union generals. Lexington was the second major southern victory in the state, after Wilson's Creek. While his troops occupied Lexington, General Price, with the captive Colonel Mulligan at his side, with much public fanfare returned the money to the Farmers' Bank. Fifteen thousand dollars remained missing, but two deserters from Mulligan's Brigade later turned up in Chicago with the money. Newspapers all over the country reported this episode, which became an enduring public relations embarrassment for the federal forces. Years later, in 1881, Jefferson Davis recounted the Farmers' Bank incident in *The Rise and Fall of the Confederate Government*, putting the money in the vaults at nine hundred thousand dollars. Handling the matter as he did, General Price made the rebel forces look like the defenders of law and order and of private property.[10]

Union forces appeared in an equally poor light in the clash at Osceola, south of the Missouri River, which occurred about the same time that Mulligan was battling Price. The Union commander at Osceola was Brigadier General James H. Lane, at the head of a force of fifteen hundred Kansas volunteers. Lane had been a leader of antislavery militia forces during the fight over Kansas statehood in the 1850s. Now he was a United States senator as well as a general. Missourians hated Lane and viewed him and his troops as looters and murderers. Now, Lane's force was following southern troops commanded by Brigadier General James S. Rains and Colonel Dewitt Clinton Hunter. Lane's immediate target was the army's supply train, which he tracked to Osceola, southeast of Kansas City at the headwaters of navigation on the Osage River.[11]

The county seat of St. Clair County, Osceola is today a village of eight hundred. In 1861, though, it was an important strategic objective, the major trading center for that portion of the state and for northern Arkansas. The town had two major wholesale merchants who also controlled the local bank, a branch of the Merchants' Bank of St. Louis. To the south were the Granby lead mines, about twenty-five miles southeast of Joplin. The mines were then in full production and a fleet of wagons hauled lead from Granby to Osceola. Business between the two locations flourished in the last year before the war. In 1861, both armies knew that Osceola's warehouses would be full of groceries, whiskey, clothing, hardware, and probably lead from the mines. Also, the bank vault was rumored to be full of cash.[12]

Lane expected that after Lexington, Price's army would resupply at Osceola. The town was strongly pro-southern and had raised three companies of Missouri State Guard volunteers. On September 20, the same day Mulligan surrendered at Lexington, Lane's brigade reached the west bank of the Osage River opposite Osceola. The men of the town were mostly gone, except for a small detachment of inexperienced volunteers. On the twenty-third, after several feints by both sides, Lane's forces shelled the town and set it on fire. Entering the town, Lane and his men took all the military stores they could carry, destroyed the rest, and then burned Osceola to the ground. Reporting these events, a Leavenworth, Kansas, newspaper falsely stated that Lane had captured one hundred thousand dollars from the Osceola bank. When this report reached St. Louis it spooked the financial markets, which were still reacting to the events in Lexington. The Merchants' Bank in St. Louis denied the report, stating the bank officers had removed the funds before Lane's arrival.[13]

The truth, when it became known, was not reassuring. After the Kansas troops left, from the end of September until the middle of November, the bank's money disappeared into promissory notes. In 1863 the parent bank, by then controlled by Unionists, described the events in Osceola in a petition to the state's newly elected Twenty-Second General Assembly. Seeking authorization to close the bank's Osceola branch, the petition charged that the branch officers and directors "[did] squander, waste, and misapply the coin and assets of said branch bank, [accepting] in pretended satisfaction of their debts to the [bank], a great quantity of land, amounting to many thousands of acres of land, at prices greatly exceeding the cash value thereof, the aggregate of which, at the estimate placed upon them by the said Board of Directors, exceeds the sum of one hundred and seventy thousand dollars." Following this, according to the petition, the Osceola bank's directors destroyed the record books and then scattered, making it impossible to continue the business.[14]

Newspapers around the country reported the battles of Lexington and Osceola, which were only a few days apart. The spectacle of Lane and his hated Kansans sacking a largely undefended town did nothing to help the Union cause. Viewing these events from nearby Boonville, Nancy Chapman Jones wrote to her daughter in San Antonio on October 3 that "the Boonville Banks and nearly all the others in the State have been robed [sic], and the money deposited in the mother bank in St. Louis, to be convenient I presume to Gen Fremont." Mrs. Jones was right about General Fremont's aims, but wrong in describing the seizure of the banks' funds as a robbery. The banks got their money back at the end of the war, though there was no way to know that in 1861. Meanwhile, stories of looting, murder, and cruelty at Osceola have circulated from that day to this. During their attack on Lawrence, Kansas, two years later, Quantrill's raiders reportedly shouted "Remember Osceola!"[15]

Faced with this mayhem, bankers moved their cash to safe locations whenever they could. The Arrow Rock branch of the Bank of Missouri first buried its coin and then secretly deposited it in a St. Louis bank, where it remained until the close of the war. The Exchange Bank branch in Columbia buried its gold under fence posts. Both banks were staunchly pro-Confederate. The Unionist cashier of the Southern Bank branch at Independence, David Waldo, disguised himself as a woman and took the money out of the bank hidden under his skirts. He was wise to do so. On August 11, 1862, Confederate forces under Colonel John T. Hughes and William Quantrill attacked Independence, and besieged the Union military headquarters in the Southern Bank building. Driving the Union defenders out by firing the adjoining store (the bank building was stone), the Confederates sacked the town, coming away with twenty wagons of loot. This sort of thing went on in Missouri for four years. It wasn't Shiloh or Gettysburg, but it probably wasn't a day the townspeople of Independence soon forgot.[16]

The chaos in Missouri made it unclear how best to deal with the money. Howard County, on the north bank of the Missouri River, was—and largely still is—one of the most pro-Confederate counties in the state. Claiborne Fox Jackson himself began his banking career in Howard County and lived there for years before moving to adjoining Saline County. Two Confederate generals came from Howard, John Bullock Clark Senior and Junior. The elder Clark also served as senator from Missouri in the First Confederate Congress and representative from Missouri in the Second Confederate Congress. As it happened, two of the county's few Unionists were officers of one of Howard County's three banks, the Fayette branch of the Bank of Missouri. In August 1861, these two, Colonel Adam Hendrix, the bank's cashier, and Robert T. Prewitt, a director, removed the bank's cash to keep it out of the hands of the Confederates. Hendrix and Prewitt then set out for Illinois, intending to deposit the money in another bank. Rebel soldiers commanded by Captain John Poindexter stopped them in Randolph County, however. Poindexter was going to turn the money over to Sterling Price, but Hendrix was able to change Poindexter's mind. Hendrix argued the money belonged to southern men, and that he (Poindexter) would do the southern cause more harm than good by taking the money. Poindexter let them go, and Hendrix and Prewitt continued to Illinois without further incident.[17]

In this way, Hendrix and Prewitt prevented the Fayette bank from accepting promissory notes. The Howard County Circuit Court records show that this bank was plaintiff in only seven such cases. The county's other two banks, once they were Union controlled, filed suits for forty-three defaulted notes. This bizarre incident—Unionists, aided by a Confederate officer, taking Confederate money to Union territory for safekeeping against Confederates—shows how tangled the money issue could become. After Osceola, Union policy toward the banks was more cautious. On one final occasion, on November 5, 1861, soldiers seized one hundred thirty-four thousand dollars from the Bank of St. Louis branch in Boonville. Trusting the parent bank in St. Louis no more than they did the branch, the Union commander had the money deposited with an express company. After that, federal forces stayed out of the bank vaults.[18]

It was, anyway, too late. By November the southerners already had secured most of the money. In hindsight, if federal forces had been able to seize control of the banks in late June 1861, the damage to Missouri's economy could have been avoided, and perhaps the war in the state shortened. The continuing struggle for leadership of Missouri's federal forces hampered Union effectiveness in this and many other areas. From May to November 1861, six different generals commanded U.S. forces in the state. It also took time for Missouri's Unionist politicians and soldiers to decide what to do about the banks. If, as all believed, the fighting would be over within weeks or months, there was no need for any long-term policy toward the banks. These hopes faded after the southern victories in August and September.[19]

Besides trying to seize the banks' coin, Union troops also seized the bankers, as part of a larger strategy to remove disloyal men from powerful positions. The policy included, besides bankers, judges and any other public officials either appointed or elected, and corporate directors and officers. Fremont launched this strategy as well, and the policy outlasted the general. Even before this, in May 1861, General Lyon's troops arrested John J. Anderson, president of the parent branch of the Bank of St. Louis (see Chapter 2). Anderson's arrest, however, was a fluke, occurring months earlier than other arrests of pro-southern bankers. Some of these arrests went bad. On July 30, 1861, a Union soldier shot James S. Lightner, a director of the Farmers' Bank of Missouri at Lexington. The Union account stated that Lightner had attacked the soldier guarding him with a chair. Lightner was originally from Staunton, Virginia, and the newspaper there, the *Spectator*, reported on September 3 that federal troops had murdered Lightner in cold blood while holding him prisoner. Judge Thomas S. Richardson, president of the LaGrange branch of the Union Bank of Missouri, was under military arrest in November 1861 when a soldier shot him, thinking that Richardson was trying to escape. Southerners viewed these incidents as blatant murders of unarmed men. Alfred T. Lacey, president of the Bank of Missouri at Cape Girardeau, feared a similar fate and moved with his family to Memphis, where they remained after the war.[20]

Union authorities took other steps against the bankers as well. In December 1861, General Henry Halleck, Fremont's successor, began a new policy of forcing rebel sympathizers to pay monetary assessments or to post bond, forfeitable for disloyalty. Such bonds could run to several thousand dollars. William H. Trigg, president of the private banking firm in Boonville, had to post a bond of eight thousand dollars. In St. Louis, Robert A. Barnes and John W. Wills, presidents of the parent branches of the Bank of Missouri and the Mechanics' Bank, also had to pay assessments. Union authorities also forced pro-Confederate citizens to take a series of progressively stricter loyalty oaths, and sometimes banished them from the state altogether. The provisional government mandated the first loyalty oath in October 1861, required of anyone holding or seeking public office, serving on a jury, voting, practicing law, or serving as a corporate officer. Often these measures were employed together. In August 1861, Union authorities arrested John A. Brownlee, president of the Merchants' Bank of St. Louis parent branch and Governor Jackson's appointee to the St. Louis Board of Police Commissioners. Brownlee was released but ordered to leave St. Louis and not return without official permission. Brownlee died on October 10, possibly by suicide, before the order took effect and while the bank's Osceola branch was being looted. Others left Missouri of their own accord. After paying his assessment William H. Trigg left Boonville for Courtland, New York, and did not return to Missouri until 1866. The St. Joseph banker Robert Donnell left for Montana Territory after his release from jail and never returned to Missouri.[21]

It took time, but such policies either removed or effectively intimidated pro-Confederate bankers. But some banks continued to aid the rebels through 1862, the last being the Farmers' Bank parent branch in Lexington. There, in November 1862, General Benjamin F. Loan jailed the bank's president and cashier and installed new banking officers more to the general's liking. Loan, who was a lawyer in St. Joseph before the war and who was no fool, accused the bank of laundering money and trafficking in stolen goods. After he jailed the bankers, Loan wrote to General Curtis in St. Louis that the bank and the traders in Lexington knowingly resold livestock to Union military forces that guerrillas previously had stolen from Union men. Thus, Loan charged, rebels amassed fortunes in federal money, while loyal Union men were away fighting. By that time the purge of disloyal bank officers was largely complete, though there never was a clean sweep. Some bankers were careful and lucky enough to remain unmolested throughout the war, though they were the exception. By late 1862, however, the banks were mere shells, and little remained for the Union men to take over. Having paid out nearly all their money to the rebels in 1861, the banks in the interior of the state had little left in the way of liquid assets. By the last half of 1862, most of these banks existed on paper only, and many closed their doors for good.[22]

The banks in St. Louis remained open through all this. St. Louis was the headquarters of the Union forces in the West, and the Confederates never seriously threatened the city. But the handful of pro-Union officers and directors who took over the banks had to deal with a seemingly unending series of financial crises. The first was posed by the promissory notes the rebel-controlled branch banks continued to accept. Southern sympathizers had started writing large numbers of these notes during the second quarter of 1861, most of them payable in one hundred and twenty days. The short maturity reflected common commercial practice of the day, but also the bankers' and borrowers' expectations of a brief conflict. Instead, these notes began defaulting in July, and the number of defaults shot up from there.

As the St. Louis business community learned of the banks' troubles, commercial credit dried up and businesspeople tried to collect outstanding debts, fearing a financial panic. Union military setbacks in the state and General Fremont's poor performance made the markets even shakier. Some of the banks' depositors withdrew their money, weakening the banks further. The banks' suspension of specie payments the previous November, however, forestalled an all-out stampede. Depositors who withdrew their money would have received depreciated or worthless banknotes. Faced with this choice, most depositors left their money where it was. But the banks themselves were afraid of holding deposits, which were the most volatile item on the banks' balance sheets. In August 1861 the Exchange Bank of St. Louis parent branch announced it would no longer accept deposits, not wishing to hold money in such times. The *St. Louis Missouri Republican* reported that several other banks were refusing to open new accounts.[23]

By the beginning of the fourth quarter of 1861, the banks had dangerous levels of bad debt and were faced with a liquidity crisis. The banks were also seriously overexposed to each other in their clearinghouse accounts and as holders of each other's notes. Since there was no national currency, the St. Louis banks routinely received and paid out each other's banknotes. The failure of an issuing bank would make its currency worthless as well and could set off a chain reaction of further bank failures. Fearing such an outcome, in October 1861 one bank after another refused to accept other banks' checks or banknotes. As a result, the state's currency became unusable or worth only a fraction of its face value. By midmonth, only two state banks of nine, the Bank of Missouri and the Merchants' Bank, continued to accept each other's checks and banknotes. The other seven banks did such business as they could in their own notes. By October 15 the *St. Louis Daily Missouri Democrat* reported the Union Bank's notes discredited, the Farmers' Bank in Lexington and the Western Bank in St. Joseph broke, and trade in St. Louis conducted for specie only. This often meant no trade at all, since by that time little gold remained in the state.[24]

By December 1861, the banks' nonperforming debt had doubled from the previous June, to 12 percent of the banks' total loan portfolio, more than a five-fold increase from December 1860. In response to the crisis, the banks quickly reduced the current liabilities they directly controlled: circulating banknotes and indebtedness to other banks. As the banks received their own banknotes in the course of business, they either destroyed them or else did not re-release them into circulation. Since specie was already being hoarded or taken out of the state, the loss of paper currency as well created a sudden shortage of money in Missouri. But the St. Louis banks remained solvent, at the cost of suddenly becoming much smaller institutions. Nonperforming debt continued to climb, peaking at 21 percent of the banks' aggregate loan portfolio in December 1863. By comparison, in the fourth quarter of 2007, financial institutions insured by the Federal Deposit Insurance Corporation had an industry average noncurrent loan rate of 1.39 percent of total loans.[25]

The financial crisis in Missouri eased after February 1862, when Congress passed and President Lincoln signed the Legal Tender Act. The law created, for the first time since the American Revolution, a national currency issued by the federal government. In St. Louis, the new U.S. Treasury notes, known as green-backs, entered circulation as payments on federal military contracts. After the first quarter of 1862, greenbacks increasingly replaced state banknotes as circulat-ing currency. Specie payments remained suspended, however, as they had been since November 1860. For the rest of the war the greenbacks, government bonds, military contracts, and wartime inflation kept the St. Louis banks on life support, but the banks remained illiquid and unstable. The army's business benefited only areas firmly under federal control, which chiefly meant St. Louis. The country banks were in far worse shape. By the end of 1862 their capital was gone, and they had killing levels of bad debt in their portfolios. In the interior of the state the branch banks were nearly dormant during the second half of the war.[26]

The banks badly needed new capital, and there weren't many places to look for it. Federal bailouts did not exist, and the state's provisional government spent any money it had to keep the state militia forces in the field. The banks would have to help themselves. The banks owned the rights to collect a mountain of defaulted debts, which was potentially worth something, and the way to recovery led through the civil courts. The banks' legal efforts at debt collection advanced county by county, depending on when Union forces could oust pro-secession judges and effectively guard the courts. The breakdown of civil administration in the interior of the state between late 1861 and early 1862 meant there were often no courts in which to bring suit. Few circuit courts in the interior of the state continued uninterrupted sessions throughout the war. In some fiercely pro-southern counties that were far from the nearest Union military garrison, regular court sessions did not resume until 1864. Even the shorter court suspensions increased the time between filing and adjudication. Circuit courts held semiannual sessions in each county, so suspending even a single session meant that a year passed between one meeting of the court and the next.

It took years to close out all the cases. In Cooper, Pettis, and Saline Counties, the courts did not close most promissory note cases until 1865, with one case lasting until 1867. Some appeals dragged on into the 1870s. One by one, though, the circuit courts resumed regular sessions. Once the courts were open, the banks' lawyers could start moving the defaulted loan cases forward. By late 1862, it was clear the signers of the promissory notes faced certain legal action on the defaulted debts. The first line of defense was delay. The defendants' attorneys petitioned for continuances until the next session of the court, requested alias writs to other counties for more witnesses, entered defendants' answers and amended answers to the charges, and challenged the legality of the proceedings. But such tactics worked only for so long.

Missouri's debtors, including the signers of promissory notes, were in a much worse position than they would be today. There were no bankruptcy laws, state or federal, in force that would have governed an orderly distribution of assets and payment of debts. Congress passed the last United States bankruptcy act in 1841 and repealed it in 1843; the next act passed in 1867. In Missouri, anyone who signed one of these promissory notes was a defendant on average in three to four cases at once, with between nine and ten codefendants. Each codefendant was liable for the full amount of the note, so any shortfall in repayment came out of the assets of any one of the notes' signers. Nor was there any general law for relief of insolvents, or any orderly way to divide an insolvent debtor's assets. The only Missouri law on insolvents waived court fees arising from criminal charges against insolvent defendants. In the Civil War era, Missouri courts had complete discretion to prioritize judgments. In practice, courts awarded judgments on a first-come, first-served basis, so the last creditor in line would likely receive nothing. To avoid this outcome, if one creditor filed suit against a debtor, other creditors would immediately sue as well. In effect, all of an individual's outstanding debts became immediately payable. In the end, the promissory note cases forced the sale of nearly three hundred and fifty thousand acres of land, at a time when two hundred acres was a large farm. In St. Clair, Hickory, and Johnson Counties, the judgment totals equaled 13, 9, and 8 percent, respectively, of the total value of the counties' real estate in 1860.[27]

The litigation probably triggered further property sales. As in much of the South and West, little cash circulated in many parts of Missouri. Indebtedness was unavoidable, and it also cemented social connections and patronage relations. Complicating matters further, debtors often gave security to their creditors by assigning debts owed to them by a third party. The promissory notes of 1861, therefore, were only part of a larger complex of "friendly" debts between family members, neighbors, landowners, and tenants. One objective of bankruptcy law is to forestall a chain reaction of further bankruptcies. Otherwise, anyone facing a sheriff's auction would mercilessly hound his own debtors, if he had any. In Missouri, thousands of people went bankrupt at the same time. The absence of a bankruptcy law combined with the complex tangle of mutual indebtedness meant that insolvency could spread from house to house, like a fire.[28]

The earliest litigation against the promissory note signers began in late 1861 and gathered momentum in early 1862. It was clear, by that time, that whatever future the Confederacy had did not include Missouri. Even if the South fought its way to independence, not enough Missourians wanted to be part of it. It was equally clear to the promissory note signers that they would receive scant sympathy from the Unionist judges presiding in the courts. Legal details and questions of procedure in the lower courts might delay an adverse judgment, but they would not affect the result. As distasteful as it was, the men who had raised money for the southern cause in 1861 and 1862 had to petition the Unionist government for help. The forum available to them was the state's new Twenty-Second General Assembly, which met in November 1862.

The provisional government had debated whether to hold elections at all, given the conditions in the state, but went ahead because the government needed a greater measure of legitimacy. Missouri's voters had not elected the provisional government, which had taken power after U.S. troops chased the Jackson government out of Jefferson City. Even though Union forces had prevailed in the field, the Jackson government could rightly claim to be the state's only legally elected government. The election in the fall of 1862 was a fraught affair and probably satisfied no one. Thousands of men could not vote because they were serving in one or the other army. The press was censored, and sympathy for the South was considered treason. Citizens could not vote until they had taken an oath of loyalty to the Union before voting, swearing that they had not supported the rebellion in any way since December 17, 1861. The governor's position was not on the ballot, and voters could not vote on the legitimacy of the provisional government itself, nor on any of its measures since it assumed power.[29]

For all these reasons, Missourians cast only fifty-two thousand votes for the Twenty-Second General Assembly, about 33 percent of the 1860 figure. In eighteen counties conditions were so violent the polls did not open at all. Even considering only those counties where polls were open, voter turnout was still only about 35 percent of the 1860 figure. Given that in 1860 there were about two hundred forty thousand eligible voters in the state, the 1862 figure represented an overall turnout of only 22 percent. Even where polls were open, in some counties voter turnout was negligible. The representative from Newton County, Thomas O. Wood, received thirteen votes, which were enough to elect him. Thomas J. O. Morrison represented New Madrid County in the Twenty-Second General Assembly after having received sixteen votes.[30]

When the smoke cleared, the two dominant blocs in the new assembly were the Democrats, also known as the Conservatives, and the Emancipationists. The Democrats were the Douglas wing of the party in 1860, the Breckenridge (secessionist) wing having been suppressed. Even with most of their potential supporters disenfranchised, the Democrats represented the largest single voting bloc in both houses of the assembly, although they did not command a majority. The Emancipationists corresponded to the more moderate wing of the Republican Party. "Republican" was a charged word in Missouri in 1862, one which Emancipationists took care not to use. The Emancipationists favored gradual emancipation of the slaves with compensation to their former owners.[31]

The two smaller factions in the assembly were the Radicals and the Unconditional Unionists. The Radicals, short for Radical Union Party, dominated state politics after the war, and they corresponded to the radical wing of the Republican Party. The Radicals, who made their first appearance in Missouri politics in this election, voted with the Emancipationists most of the time, because they had nowhere else to go. The Unconditional Unionists corresponded to the Constitutional Union Party in the 1860 election. This party favored slavery, peace, and the status quo, and it occupied a disappearing middle ground in politics. When the Twenty-Third General Assembly met in November 1864, the Unconditional Unionists had vanished from the political map. Labels aside, party groupings were in flux and there was much crossover voting. Despite their numerical superiority the Democrats lost on most major issues, being usually on one side of the political divide, with the other three groups opposing them.[32]

The Twenty-Second General Assembly met on December 29, 1862, in Jefferson City and remained in session until March 23, 1863, a span of fourteen weeks.

The time proved inadequate for the assembly to complete its work. The new assembly had to find money to pay the state militia troops, elect U.S. senators, and decide on a railroad policy. Also, the interrupted Twenty-First General Assembly had left behind a backlog of public and private bills. The new assembly reconvened in adjourned session for an extra three weeks, from November 10 until December 3, 1863, to complete its business. Over these two sessions, the house and the senate between them considered over seventeen hundred bills, on average about one every forty minutes.[33]

Missouri's pro-southern citizens, even those who could still vote, had every reason to view this legislature as illegitimate. It was the only show in town, though, and it was at least possible the assembly would pass some debt-relief legislation. The worst indebtedness problems were in counties with large numbers of promissory note cases, but thousands of other people across the state, including many Unionists, fared little better. The war's destruction and disruption of the economy had burdened many more people besides the signers of the promissory notes with debts, and deeply indebted voters formed a sizable constituency. The representatives of the worst indebted counties, almost all of them Democrats, introduced twenty different bills for debt relief. Some measures proposed excluding certain property from debt judgments; others proposed allowing the original owner to repurchase the property within a stated time after satisfying the judgment. Still others would stipulate that any real property sold for debt must be for fair market value.[34]

Debates could become heated. On one occasion, Emancipationist senator Abner L. Gilstrap of Missouri's Seventh District suggested renaming the bill under consideration the "Rebel Debt Relief Act." This flip remark stung the bill's sponsor, Democratic Senator John Doniphan of Missouri's Thirteenth District. Senator Doniphan shot back angrily that Senator Gilstrap's patriotism consisted of forcing men to sell their land at distressed prices so Senator Gilstrap and his friends could buy it. Senator Doniphan thanked God he was no such patriot as Senator Gilstrap. Senator Doniphan also took offense at what he considered an insult to the loyalty of his district. The senator pointed out that men from Platte County (in Senator Doniphan's district) had saved Macon County (in Senator Gilstrap's district) from guerrillas the previous summer. Senator Doniphan typified the dilemma in which many of Missouri's southern men found themselves. A nephew of Alexander Doniphan, a hero of the Mexican War, Senator Doniphan owned twenty slaves in 1860 and was the brother-in-law of the Confederate officer and partisan leader Colonel John C. Calhoun Thornton (himself brother-in-law to the St. Joseph banker Robert W. Donnell). Senator Doniphan was a staunch defender of slavery and of the Union alike, and when elected to the

Missouri senate he was lieutenant colonel of the Unionist Thirty-Ninth Missouri State Militia.[35]

By the end of the legislative session, though, the Twenty-Second General Assembly had given no relief whatever to Missouri's debtors. Of the many bills the legislature considered for debt relief, not a single one passed. And that was the end of it. The next general assembly, the twenty-third, elected in November 1864, scarcely mentioned indebtedness. Partly this reflected the makeup of the assembly, by then controlled by Radicals and Emancipationists. Only a handful of incumbents, all of them Democrats, survived from prewar legislative sessions. Also, by that time the lower courts had settled most of the debt cases already, and the county sheriffs had auctioned the defendants' property. There was little point in contesting the issue further.[36]

The defendants in the promissory note cases also made four separate appeals to the Missouri Supreme Court against the lower-court decisions. The court heard the first appeal in 1864 and the last in 1872, long after the lower courts had closed out the last promissory note debt cases. Two arguments concerned the banks' standing to sue. The first appeal argued the banks were dealing in denominations of currency banned by state law, for which the penalty was the loss of the banks' charters. Without charters, the banks themselves had no legal existence, and therefore no standing to bring suit. The justices denied the appeal, ruling that while the law provided remedies for anyone injured by illegal banking, other existing state laws on banking remained in force. Also, those injured by the illegal banking could not seek relief in unrelated matters. The second appeal challenging the banks' legal standing argued the 1857 banking law chartered only the parent banks, not the branches. Therefore, the branch banks lacked standing to bring suit; only the parent banks could do so. The court denied this petition as well.[37]

The third appeal concerned the legality of the loan contracts. In accepting the promissory notes, the argument ran, the banks at times charged excessive interest, capped at 8 percent a year by a Missouri law of 1861. Thus, the loan contracts were illegal and unenforceable. The court agreed that interest charges over the statutory limit were void and uncollectible, but the contracts themselves were legal and so were interest charges up to the 8 percent limit. Banks, rather than defendants, brought the last and weakest argument, to affirm decisions made by the lower courts. In these cases, several defendants who had signed the notes as sureties argued that they had only signed as an accommodation so the original signers could borrow money. Since the sureties had received no benefit, they should not be liable. The justices denied this appeal as well. In Missouri law, as in U.S. law, all parties to a defaulted debt instrument are jointly and severally liable. It was, and is, the plaintiff's right to sue any of the notes' signers. After the Missouri Supreme Court upheld the lower courts' judgments in these cases, the signers of the promissory notes had exhausted their legal options.[38]

By late 1863 the banks and the defendants were, in different ways, trapped. To survive, the banks had to collect their bad debts. Lawsuits filed by the banks clogged the dockets of the state's civil courts in the final two years of the war, but eventually all cases were settled. Missouri's southern men could only use this interval to play a rigged game in the enemy's courts and legislature. When it was all over, most of the defendants had no property left. Not everyone was willing to accept this brand of justice, however. Political repression, the bitterness of military defeat, and, finally, the forced land sales all made further violence certain.

6

GUERRILLAS

After the collapse of Governor Jackson's plans, only force of arms would achieve Missouri's secession. But this was never even remotely possible. Southern forces never regained the advantage in Missouri after the Battle of Lexington in September 1861. In the end democratic politics, political skullduggery, and military force all failed to take Missouri out of the Union. Still, the conventional war lasted another three years in Missouri, before Confederate forces were decisively defeated at the Battle of Westport in 1864. The guerrilla violence, however, kept right on going.[1]

By most measures, the Confederate guerrilla insurgency in Missouri during the Civil War was the worst such conflict ever to occur on American soil. By one calculation, nearly twenty-seven thousand Missourians died in the violence. Owing to these conditions, the state's population dropped by a third during the war, although an unknown number of people later returned. Counterinsurgency measures tied up tens of thousands of Union troops in garrison and guard duty, search-and-destroy missions, and patrols. The relative level of guerrilla violence in the different states can be gauged by comparing the states' total recorded numbers of clashes between guerrillas and regular troops over the course of the war. Missouri had by far the highest number. This anomalously high level of guerrilla violence in pro-Confederate parts of Missouri compared with other districts that were occupied by Union troops, including conquered parts of the Confederacy proper, has never been satisfactorily explained. Pro-Confederate Missourians had all the same reasons for "going to the brush" as did their counterparts elsewhere. But the Missourians had one additional grievance against Unionists. Guerrillas from the counties with the heaviest land sales belonged disproportionately to the dispossessed families.[2]

That forced sales of thousands of family farms would lead to communal vio-lence and insurrection is a commonsense outcome. Also, this indebtedness was specific to Missouri, except for some limited property sales in Kentucky. The character of the guerrilla violence in Missouri does suggest that the state some-how differed from other occupied areas of mixed loyalties. First, the violence in Missouri was more extensive than other places. Second, the violence continued at a high level long after there was any chance that Missouri could fight its way into the Confederacy. The simplest explanation for both these conditions is that Missouri had more guerrillas than elsewhere, rather than that each Missouri guerrilla engaged in more violence than did his counterparts in other states.

No statistics were gathered at the time on the total number of guerrilla attacks on civilians during the Civil War, in Missouri or elsewhere. The best proxy mea-sure is the number of military engagements in each state, which includes fights between regular military forces and guerrillas. This measure does give a good idea of the relative level of violence in each state, as troops conducted more search-and-destroy missions where the guerrillas were most active. Frederick Dyer's list of military encounters drawn from the *Official Records of the War of the Rebel-lion* shows that Missouri ranked third among the states in the number of military engagements within its borders. Only Virginia and Tennessee had more. In those two other states, the regular armies did most of the fighting in bloody set-piece battles. But in Missouri most of the confrontations were clashes between Union militia and free-floating bands of armed men, only loosely allied with regular Confederate forces. One can make a comparison with Kentucky, the state that most resembled Missouri in 1860. Both were border slave states with populations of comparable size drawn mainly from the South and of the same mixed loyal-ties. The two states had ties of family as well. Before the war, Missouri received more settlers from Kentucky than from any other state. Yet Kentucky, ranking ninth overall, had fewer than half as many military affrays as Missouri.[3]

Wartime conditions in Missouri were infamous and drew national and interna-tional attention.[4] Over the course of the war, the *New York Times* alone reported on the violence in Missouri more than two hundred times. On September 22, 1863, the *Times* had this to say: "Missouri is to-day more dangerously disturbed, if not more dangerously disloyal, than Mississippi. More contempt for the army and the Government is daily poured forth there—more turbulence in talk and in action is indulged in—and human life is less safe than anywhere else within all the military lines of the United States. In this latter respect, the condition of Missouri is fearful. Not a day passes that does not chronicle house-burnings and murders."[5] One month before this story appeared, Confederate guerrillas from Missouri committed the bloodiest civilian massacre of the entire war. On Au-

gust 21, 1863, combined guerrilla bands under William Clarke Quantrill, George
Todd, and William T. "Bloody Bill" Anderson descended on Lawrence, Kansas,
and murdered at least a hundred and fifty unarmed men and boys. Ulysses S.
Grant wrote that he considered Missouri (and Kentucky) more difficult to control than Mississippi.[6]

Both the forced sale of thousands of family farms and the extent of the guerrilla violence set Missouri's war experience apart from what was happening elsewhere. It seems likely the land sales and the violence were linked, and enough
contemporary source material survives to perform evidentiary tests as well. Missouri's guerrillas themselves, however, left few personal accounts. During the war
the guerrillas' families, too, kept silent about what their young men were up to.
Unionist militia routinely targeted guerrillas' families for revenge. After the war,
feelings ran high for years, and too much talk could lead to a murder indictment
or a lynching.

Three guerrillas from Missouri's central-west counties, which had been the
epicenter of the indebtedness, did publish memoirs after the war. These accounts,
however, mainly describe thrilling exploits and explain little beyond the writers'
own experiences. These ex-guerrillas, Hampton Boone Watts, Cole Younger, and
John McCorkle, only briefly mention why they became guerrillas and say almost
nothing about why others did. Watts was only sixteen when he joined Bloody
Bill Anderson's band for a few months in 1864. Watts briefly mentions the strong
southern sentiments in his native Howard County. However, he gives a better sig-
nal of his reasons for joining when he discusses, at length, how well-mannered,
well-dressed, and well-mounted Anderson and his men were—gentlemen all.
Watts plainly adored these daring, dangerous men, many of them little older
than Watts himself. At eighteen, Cole Younger was slightly more mature when
he joined Quantrill's guerrillas in 1862. Younger had had a clearer reason for
joining the guerrillas than did Watts: he wanted revenge for his father's murder.
McCorkle, for his part, joined the guerrillas for protection from Unionist militia
who were harassing and threatening him for having served in the Confederate
Army.[7]

Despite the lack of certain kinds of narrative primary-source materials, the
connection between the guerrillas and the debts can still be ascertained quanti-
tatively. But before going to this analysis, the current scholarship on the causes of
Civil War guerrilla violence needs to be summarized. Historians have researched
the guerrillas for decades. The existing studies, taken together, explain most of
the guerrilla activity that occurred during the war, and they describe what motivated the guerrillas, in Missouri and beyond. This scholarship does not fully explain, however, why the violence in Missouri was so much worse than in other

places. This monograph is concerned solely with that difference and hopes to take existing scholarship as a point of departure and to add something new.

Missouri's guerrillas have always received much attention from the media, and the first available sources on them are from the Civil War era. The earliest reference to the state's guerrillas in the *New York Times* appeared in July 1861; the first novel about them was published, also in New York, the same year. Most of this material is sensational, however, and of little use in understanding the guerrillas' motives. Some of the coverage was positive. After the war, the Missouri Confederate veteran John Newman Edwards wrote prolifically about the guerrillas. But Edwards was a popular journalist and gave his readers what sold, namely gunfights and Three-Musketeers-style bravery against dastardly enemies. Though Edwards had known many of the guerrillas personally, he gave no individual particulars or details about their reasons for joining, instead referring darkly to "unnumbered wrongs." Union spokespeople were as slanted as Edwards, though in the other direction. In public pronouncements, military men, politicians, and journalists excoriated the guerrillas as bushwhackers. This pejorative term probably first came into use in western Virginia in 1861, referring to depraved thieves and cutthroats whose sole objectives were plunder and mayhem. This was not just propaganda. The breakdown of the normal civilian constraints in the war zones, including Missouri, does appear to have unleashed a crime wave, with roving bands of armed men preying on civilians regardless of their politics.[8]

But besides bandits, there were politically motivated guerrillas as well, and the military men were the first to treat the irregulars as worthy of serious study. Despite the anger and frustration that senior Union military commanders publicly expressed, they took a more sophisticated view of the guerrillas than the name-calling implied. Irregular warfare is the oldest warfare there is, and many military theorists have written on the subject. By the mid-nineteenth century the ideas of Carl von Clausewitz and Henri de Jomini dominated U.S. and European military thinking, including on guerrilla warfare. Drawing on their writings, in 1862 the American jurist Francis Lieber summed up contemporary thought on the topic in his pamphlet *Guerrilla Parties Considered with Reference to the Laws and Usages of War*. The Union high command made Lieber's ideas on irregular warfare into official policy, disseminated throughout the Union army in 1863 as General Orders, Number 100.[9]

Lieber evaluated irregulars by their aims, as paramilitary forces contributing to a larger war effort. He drew a sharp distinction between guerrillas and partisans, the latter being small, elite conventional forces given an unconventional military role. Nathan Bedford Forrest, John Hunt Morgan, and John Singleton Mosby were partisan leaders, commanding disciplined military units that raided

Union-held territory and then retired behind Confederate lines. Partisan forces such as these were part of the regular Confederate army and coordinated with conventional troops. By contrast, Lieber defined guerrillas as "self-constituted sets of armed men, in times of war, who form no integrant part of the organized army, do not stand on the regular pay-roll of the army, or are not paid at all, take up arms and lay them down at intervals, and carry on petty war (guerrilla) chiefly by raids, extortion, destruction, and massacre, and who cannot encumber themselves with many prisoners, and will therefore generally give no quarter." Unlike partisans, captured guerrillas were not considered prisoners of war. Guerrillas, according to Lieber, should "be treated summarily as highway robbers or pirates." In other words, captured guerrillas were subject to immediate execution.[10]

Confederate military leaders had attended the same service academies as their Union counterparts, and they all studied the same theory. The Confederate Congress's Partisan Ranger Act of April 21, 1862, however, did not distinguish between partisans and guerrillas. In vague language, the law empowered President Jefferson Davis to commission officers who would recruit irregular forces. Then these units, "after being regularly received into service, shall be entitled to the same pay, rations, and quarters during their term of service, and be subject to the same regulations as other soldiers." The language of the law suggested that such troops would act independently but still report to the regular army command. In practice, although officers commissioned under the act included some famous partisan leaders such as John Singleton Mosby, most such officers and the units they recruited were guerrillas by Lieber's definition. That is, they lived behind enemy lines and moved in and out of uniform and civilian life between raids.[11]

Many Confederate leaders, including Robert E. Lee, feared they would be unable to control the partisan ranger units, and these fears proved justified. In Missouri, Bloody Bill Anderson claimed to fight for the South, and no one was about to argue with him. Nevertheless, in late 1861 Anderson said to a neighbor whom he hoped to recruit, "I don't care any more than you for the South, [Charles] Strieby, but there is a lot of money in this [bushwhacking] business." In the South the Partisan Ranger Act was controversial from the start, and the Confederate Congress repealed it in February 1864.[12]

Both partisans and guerrillas fought in Missouri's war. Confederate general Joseph Orville Shelby, before the war a hemp planter in Waverly, Lafayette County, Missouri, led what was clearly a partisan unit. Shelby's Iron Brigade raided behind enemy lines but also formed the cavalry arm of forces led by Confederate generals Sterling Price and John Sappington Marmaduke. But it was guerrillas, not partisans, who made the war in Missouri an appalling spectacle. Some of Missouri's guerrilla leaders, such as Quantrill, held commissions in the

Confederate army. Others, such as Bill Anderson, did not. It made no difference. Missouri's guerrilla commanders were never subject to military discipline or integrated into the regular Confederate command. The guerrilla bands of Quantrill, Anderson, George Todd, John Thrailkill, Andy Blunt, John T. Coffee, and many others, though they cooperated at times with regular Confederate forces, acted on their own and as they saw fit. General Henry W. Halleck, the ranking Union military commander in Missouri from November 1861 to July 1862, understood the distinction between partisans and guerrillas. To make sure that his entire command understood as well, Halleck issued several general orders on the subject during his tenure in Missouri.[13]

That people will react violently when their property is taken from them may be a commonsense outcome, but proving it is another matter. A quantitative strategy to test for links between the indebtedness and the violence faces two big, but not insurmountable, difficulties. First, while the court records contain the names of all the debtors, there is no comparable source for guerrillas' names. Federal troops shot guerrillas on sight, often without knowing who they were or bothering to find out. In the *Official Records*, a typical report might read "Went on patrol—killed three bushwhackers." (The officers who wrote these reports typically ignored finer distinctions when describing their enemies.) Also, no one knows how many guerrillas there were in Missouri, a number that presumably varied over time, so it is impossible to tell how many names are missing. Perhaps 20 percent of the guerrillas' names have been lost, or 50 percent, or 80 percent. There is no way to tell.[14]

The second problem is that available sources are too imprecise to identify a large control group of pro-Confederate white males who did not become guerrillas. "Supported the rebellion" is a vague phrase that includes lukewarm, conditional Confederate supporters as well as red-hot secessionists. Also, people's political commitment varied over the course of the war. Some switched sides altogether. With a control group, it would be possible to compare the likelihood that a member of an indebted family would join the guerrillas with the likelihood that a member of a nonindebted family would. But even though a large sample of nonguerrilla Confederate supporters cannot be assembled, it is possible, as described below, to set up a small control group.[15]

When dealing with incomplete data, the most promising research strategy is to use several different analytical approaches and look for a preponderance of evidence. The following analysis will explore for a possible linkage in three ways and will use data culled from the circuit court records, the military and provost-marshal records, and Joanne Chiles Eakin and Donald R. Hale's compilation on Missouri guerrillas, *Branded as Rebels*. The first approach will be to compare geographical concentrations of indebtedness and of guerrilla violence in the state as a whole. The second approach will be to look for personal connections between specific known guerrillas and debtors. Finally, guerrillas from indebted families can be compared on various demographic measures with guerrillas from nonindebted families to see if patterns emerge.[16]

If one considers first the summary data available, the facts of geography and timing are consistent with linkage. Though other regions of Missouri experienced guerrilla violence, most incidents occurred in the indebted counties. More than 90 percent of the heavily indebted counties also turn out to have had severe problems with guerrillas (over twenty-five reported incidents, as shown in Figure 6.1). Over the course of the war, indebted counties had on average twice as many reported guerrilla incidents as nonindebted counties, 11.7 incidents versus 5.9 incidents. Geographic coincidence, however, only takes us so far. Guerrillas and debtors may have had nothing to do with one another.[17]

The second research strategy is to look for connections between specific guerrillas and debtors. To do this, five sample counties were selected within the region of overlapping indebtedness and high guerrilla violence. Between March 1, 1861, and June 30, 1862, Confederate sympathizers signed 679 promissory notes that were later litigated in Chariton, Cooper, Lafayette, Pettis, and Saline Counties, in the state's central-west region along the Missouri River. In these same counties, Dyer's *Compendium* lists 112 military engagements, almost all of them guerrilla incidents. (Dyer's count understates the violence by excluding depredations against civilians. These counties were dangerous places.) Circuit court papers for the debt cases preserve the names of the defendants, and the 1860 manuscript census identifies which ones lived in the five counties before the war. The census also contains details on the defendants' families and households.[18]

Study of the guerrillas, too, depends on detailed family and household data. Since the debts affected entire families, the fortunes of the family as a whole are the key concern. Don R. Bowen, in his 1977 study, faced a version of the same issue. The guerrillas he studied were too young to own much property. What mattered was how much property their families owned. Bowen pointed out that earlier researchers had overlooked this problem and reached a false conclusion— namely, that since the guerrillas themselves owned little or no property, they must have come from poor families. Bowen showed that, in fact, the opposite was true. The sample used here, therefore, contains only the fifty-three guerrillas whose families could be identified and who lived within the five counties before the war. Their family data are clearly important for more than showing guerrilla families' wealth. Twenty-three of the fifty-three, or more than 40 percent, were seventeen years old or younger in 1861; the youngest was nine. Boys this young

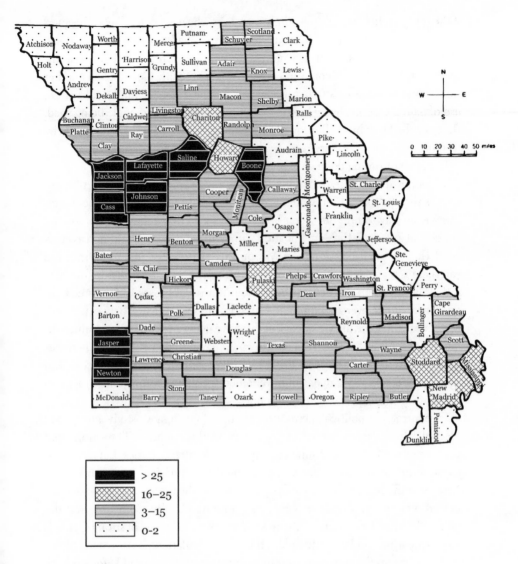

Figure 6.1. Military engagements fought in Missouri, 1861–1865.

would not have signed promissory notes, though older family members might have.[19]

Analyzing these two sample groups reveals that most of the guerrillas had close family connections to the debtors. Of the fifty-three guerrillas, six were defendants in one or more of the promissory note cases. Another thirty-eight had at least one extended$_1$ family member (see Chapter 4) who was a defendant. Most of the thirty-eight had multiple family members who were defendants. The guerrilla Tom Woodson of Pettis County, for example, had a brother and an uncle who were defendants, both of whom were fighting in the Confederate army. Two guerrilla brothers, George and Isaac Cruzen of Saline County, had another brother and the brother's father-in-law being sued. The guerrilla David Ferrell, also of Saline County, had a brother, a brother-in-law, and an uncle being sued. The guerrilla Dr. John W. Benson of Saline County, who was an orphan raised by his mother's family, had three cousins being sued.[20]

The issue of timing deserves a brief comment here. Except for leaders, guerrillas' names usually survive in one, or at most two, primary sources. All these sources show is that an individual was a guerrilla at the date of the document. There is no way to find out when he became a guerrilla. However, no primary source that antedates the debt litigation names any of the forty-four men as guerrillas. Though guerrilla warfare in Missouri dates from the first months of the war, there is no evidence that any of these men joined the guerrillas before they or their family members became defendants in the debt cases. These three findings—geographic overlap, family, and timing—all suggest a link between the indebtedness and guerrilla violence. But these are necessary, rather than sufficient, conditions for linkage. Different results would have strongly suggested there was no connection. But even with these findings, Confederate sympathizers who signed promissory notes may still have joined the guerrillas for some other reason, namely strong political commitment.

To control for political commitment, therefore, a new study group was selected. This group consisted of volunteers to three rebel military units that were organized in May and June 1861, in two adjoining counties, Lafayette and Saline. Pro-Confederate citizens signed about four hundred promissory notes there, with the highest incidence occurring during the months when these units formed. Volunteers to Bledsoe's Battery, Gordon's Cavalry Company, and the Saline Mounted Rifles were young men of prime military age, of strong Confederate sympathies, and eager to fight—the same population pool, presumably, as the guerrillas. In the three units, seventy-four recruits were eligible for study by virtue of being prewar residents of the two counties and having identifiable families. Of the seventy-four, ten signed promissory notes that were later litigated; another twenty-six had extended[1] family members who were sued. The remaining thirty-eight recruits had no connection to the promissory notes. In the first group of thirty-six recruits who signed notes or whose close family members did, four became guerrillas. In the group of thirty-eight recruits with no connection to the debts, one became a guerrilla. It would be a mistake to treat so small a sample as definitive. Still, this test suggests that recruits with a personal connection to the indebtedness became guerrillas more often than did recruits with no connection. With regard to timing, once again no records show a turn to guerrilla fighting before the start of litigation.[21]

A third test for linkage is to compare demographic characteristics of guerrillas from indebted and nonindebted families. My core argument is that indebtedness and attendant loss of land drove larger numbers of young men into the guerrilla bands than would otherwise have been the case. If this is true, these "extra" guerrillas might differ somehow from "ordinary" guerrillas. This proves to be so, in looking at the household property of the fifty-three guerrillas in the five-county sample. As stated, forty-four of the fifty-three known guerrillas in the five-county sample either had signed promissory notes or had close family members who did. The forty-four indebted families had on average significantly more real and personal property than did the remaining nine families with no connection to the debts, $12,544 versus $3,953. This is unsurprising, since a disproportionate number of the counties' wealthier citizens signed the promissory notes. More significant, sorting the families according to the value of their household property shows that none of the nonindebted guerrilla families were wealthy. This is noteworthy because the five counties sampled were home to many rich men who were passionate secessionists, going on to become Confederate generals, members of Congress, and diplomats. Yet in this entire elite group, not a single known individual unconnected to the debts became a guerrilla. Table 6.1 summarizes the results of this comparison.[22]

There is one final way to test for differences between guerrillas from indebted and nonindebted families. The socioeconomic profile of guerrillas from the indebted group in the five central-west counties can be compared with another, separate sample of guerrillas from counties where there were no such debt cases. Support for the Confederate cause was strong in southwest Missouri, but there were no banks there and no promissory notes or resulting property sales. Analysis of a sample of forty-five guerrillas from Jasper and Newton Counties in Missouri's southwest reveals that the socioeconomic profile of the guerrillas there matches that of the central-west guerrillas who came from nonindebted families. As shown in Table 6.1, the southwesterners, like the nonindebted central-west guerrillas, came from families with at best modest property. Many were poor.[23]

Combining all the guerrillas from both geographic samples into a single group underlines the wealth distinction between the indebted and nonindebted groups. Of ninety-eight guerrillas, the only elite men who became guerrillas were either defendants in the debt cases or near relatives of defendants. The other, non-

Table 6.1. Guerrillas—Geographic Sample Comparison

	Central-West all families	Central-West indebted families	Central-West nonindebted families	Southwest all families
Guerrillas				
Individuals	53	44	9	45
Household heads	10 (19%)	9 (20%)	1 (11%)	26 (58%)
Age (1862)				
Oldest	42	42	32	58
Youngest	9	12	9	16
Median	19	20	17	26
Mean	21	21	21	28
≤ 18 years old	23 (43%)	18 (41%)	5 (56%)	7 (16%)
Household Property				
High	$120,500	$120,500	$11,800	$10,000
Low	$0	$0	$0	$0
Median	$6,500	$8,500	$1,300	$1,400
Mean	$11,085	$12,544	$3,953	$2,360
Poorest ⅓	≤ $2,000	≤ $5,500	≤ $500	≤ $700
Wealthiest ⅓	≥ $12,120	≥ $13,600	≥ $1,200	≥ $2,536

indebted guerrilla families in both areas were much further down the socioeconomic ladder. Southwest Missouri was poorer overall than the central-west counties, but the region had, by its own standards, a local elite of better-off farmers
and a few merchants. There are no young men even from these families in the
southwestern group of guerrillas. Unless their families were caught up in the debt
business, sons of upper-class families steered clear of guerrilla warfare.[24]

In short, using different analytical approaches, the available tests all point to
a link between indebtedness and guerrilla violence. Twice as many recorded
guerrilla incidents occurred within indebted counties as elsewhere. Four-fifths
of the presently identifiable guerrillas from the five sampled counties either were
defendants in the debt cases or had close family members who were. A sample
of military volunteers from two indebted counties shows that volunteers from
indebted families were more likely to become guerrillas than were members of
nonindebted families. Finally, no young men from upper-class families became

guerrillas unless their families were indebted. It seems likely that without the indebtedness, the incidence of guerrilla violence in Missouri would have been closer to that experienced in other border states.

Historians of this period have missed the indebtedness because the civilian court records are a largely underutilized primary source. Richard S. Brownlee, for instance, devotes an entire chapter in *Gray Ghosts of the Confederacy* to martial law in Missouri, but refers only cursorily to civil law. In fact, Union commanders in Missouri tried hard to protect the courts and civilian administration. Writing from Jefferson City in January 1863, General Benjamin F. Loan briefed his superior, General Samuel R. Curtis in St. Louis, on the state of civilian justice in Missouri's Central District. Loan stated that "in several counties in the district no courts of record of any kind have held a session for several terms past, say, for more than eighteen months. The records have been stolen, perhaps destroyed, and the civil officers driven from the country. . . . [In Lafayette County, which had 284 debt cases] it was impossible for the sheriff to serve a writ without a guard stronger than 50 men." But the sheriff was serving writs, and Loan was providing troops to protect him. General Loan was not exaggerating about the assault on the justice system. In November 1863 citizens of Jackson County petitioned the state legislature to move the county seat from Independence to Kansas City, to protect the court records from being destroyed by guerrillas. Federal forces kept Missouri's county courthouses under constant guard, and even so thirty Missouri courthouses burned during the war. There are, however, plenty of surviving records from courts that were functioning.[25]

Other scattered evidence also suggests a connection between the debts and the violence. The court records in Chariton County were burned twice, the first time in November 1861, and had to be painstakingly reconstructed by county officials. In the April 1864 court session, the docket contained a two-year backlog of some forty-five promissory note cases. Impatient with what he considered pettifoggery, the presiding judge demanded that the defendants' attorneys present all their witnesses and their entire defense *instanter*—meaning immediately. When the attorneys could not comply, the judge ruled in favor of the banks. In September, acting under orders of the court, fifty-five-year-old Sheriff Robert Carmon was auctioning the defendants' farms when guerrillas under Thrailkill and Todd rode into Keytesville, the county seat. The guerrillas burned down the courthouse and murdered Carmon, who left behind a widow and nine children.[26]

At times, some of the surviving wartime accounts of central Missouri look like Unionist and rebel versions of the debt story. Neither the Missouri guerrillas' postwar memoirs nor the writings of their publicist ally, John Newman Edwards, name loyalty to the South or commitment to slavery, secession, or states' rights among the reasons for taking part in irregular warfare. The narrators do, however, often speak of defending their homes and their honor and seeking to avenge northern "outrages." Modern readers usually assume that such statements refer to war atrocities, as is doubtless often the case. But then as now, "outrage" can also refer to gross or malicious wrongs or injury done to feelings, principles, justice, or morals. A southern man in Missouri's Boonslick needed to look no further than the circuit judge or the county sheriff for this kind of outrage and a reason to pick up a gun.

The history of James Waller of Lafayette County shows how one family constructed its memory of a particular outrage. In 1861 Waller was a prosperous thirty-one-year-old farmer, married with six children and owning six slaves and a thousand acres of land. When the war broke out, Waller and two other men cosigned two promissory notes. By early 1863 the suits were in court; by mid-1864 the Lafayette County sheriff auctioned the defendants' property. In mid-1863 Waller, described in a newspaper article after his death as previously having been a well-respected citizen, joined Andy Blunt's guerrillas. In March 1864 a detachment of the (Union) First Missouri State Militia Cavalry, while chasing Blunt and his men, shot Waller. In his report, Captain James B. Moore noted much sympathy for Waller among the local citizens but described Waller as a "notorious" bushwhacker who took part in the murder of two unarmed Union men and the storming of a jail. Waller had also been involved with the infamous raid on Lawrence, and he bragged of having killed fourteen men there. By 1870 Waller's widow and surviving children had left the area.[27]

Waller's descendants, however, remember his story differently. In the family version, Waller owned a large plantation in Lafayette County (which he did not), and Union troops murdered him when he refused to reveal where he had hidden his "fortune." The soldiers then burned Waller's house and set his slaves free, over their objections. The family version thus preserves the outline of the true events: Union authorities took Waller's property and killed him. Lawsuits are not the stuff of legend, however, and as the family tells it, it was not the courts but the soldiers who took Waller's property. The family account omits any mention of Waller's bushwhacking or any reason for his death other than the Union soldiers' cold-blooded robbery.[28]

The history of the Warren family of Lafayette County is also suggestive. The Warrens originally came there from Virginia via Kentucky, and by the outbreak of the Civil War they had been in Missouri for decades. In 1860 they were a thriving clan in Lafayette County, with fifty-one family members in eight households and ties of blood and marriage to a dozen other families. Together, the Warren households owned seventy-nine slaves and over twenty-five hundred acres of land. After the outbreak of fighting in Missouri in May and June 1861, most of the young Warren men joined the Confederate forces. At the same time, eight Warrens—fathers, sons, brothers, uncles, and cousins—from four different households cosigned eleven different promissory notes, which defaulted in late 1861 and early 1862.[29]

In November 1862 in Lafayette County, General Loan arrested the officers of the Farmers' Bank of Missouri and replaced them with Union men. By early 1863 the bank, under new management, filed lawsuits in the Lafayette County Circuit Court against the Warrens and more than four hundred other defendants who had signed promissory notes between late 1861 and early 1862. Each of the eight Warrens was sued on average twice and each household four times. In 1863, while these suits were in court, the newspapers and military records name three young Warren men from the indebted households as members of a guerrilla band led by Dave Poole, one of William C. Quantrill's lieutenants. In July of that year the Warrens shot their way through a German community in their old neighborhood, indiscriminately killing four people and wounding six or seven more. A month later Poole and the Warrens joined in the Lawrence massacre. The legal outcome, of course, remained unchanged. Judgments in the eleven cases totaled more than thirty-six hundred dollars, forcing the sale of the four households' entire property in 1864. By 1870, of the eight Warrens who were defendants, two had left the state, two had disappeared, one was dead, and three remained in Lafayette County, owning only modest property. Three of the four households were gone.[30]

Missouri's war did not end with the peace in 1865. The state took nearly twenty more years to settle down. The guerrilla fighting left behind a self-perpetuating cycle of violence that was hard to stop. Michael Fellman writes that in the region most ravaged by guerrilla war, violence permeated society and degenerated into a war of all against all. The poet Eugene Field, returning in 1871 to his native Missouri after a long absence, wrote that "life and property were held of slight consequence, violence obtained to a preposterous degree, crime actually ran riot." Field found violent crime worst in those areas that had suffered most from the guerrillas. The nation had viewed Missouri as a southern state before the war. In the years after the war, Missouri became the unique and disgraceful "Robber State." In the U.S. Senate in the 1870s, Missouri Senator Carl Schurz's colleagues needled him repeatedly with accounts of Missouri robberies. During this time eastern newspapers depicted the continuing violence as something that

set Missouri apart from the rest of the country. In 1873 the *New York Times* reported a train robbery in which the passengers, proving better armed and more
dangerous than the bandits, attacked the latter and killed two of their number.
The *Times* commented, "Even for Missouri, paradise of horse-thieves, of lynch-
ers, of railway-wreckers, of all ruffianism and lawlessness, as it is, an outrage such
as this, at this stage of the world's progress, seems bad enough."[31]

Figure 6.2. William Breathitt Sappington
(1811–88), ca. 1845. Painting by George Caleb
Bingham, formerly (1986) in the collection of
Mr. Arthur Cardwell Sappington, Kansas City,
Missouri. Present whereabouts unknown.

Figure 6.3. Marmaduke brothers, ca. 1870. General John Sappington Marmaduke, CSA (1833–87), seated center. Colonel Vincent Marmaduke CSA (1831–1904), seated far right. Courtesy of Friends of Arrow Rock, Arrow Rock, Missouri.

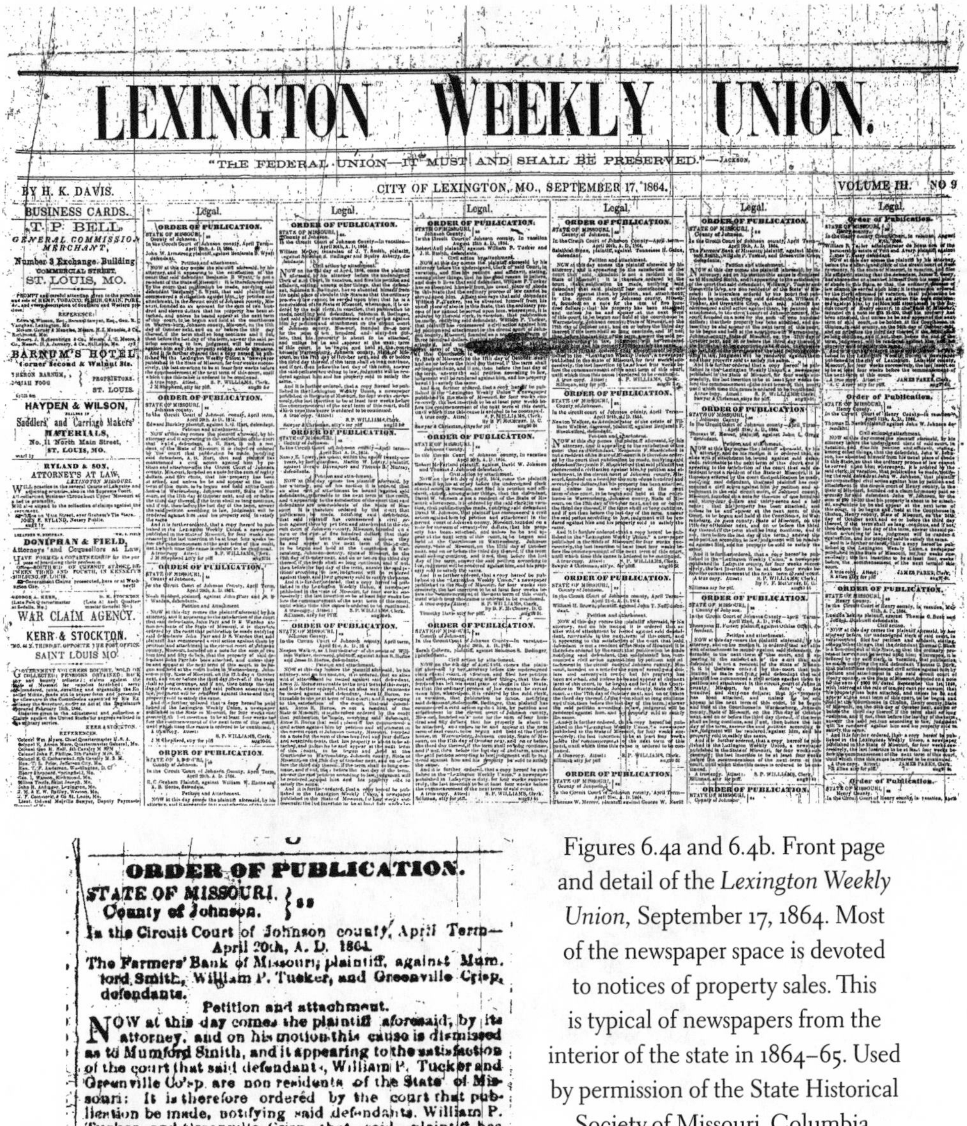

LEXINGTON WEEKLY UNION.

"THE FEDERAL UNION—IT MUST AND SHALL BE PRESERVED."—Jackson.

BY H. K. DAVIS.   CITY OF LEXINGTON, MO., SEPTEMBER 17, 1864.   VOLUME III. NO 9

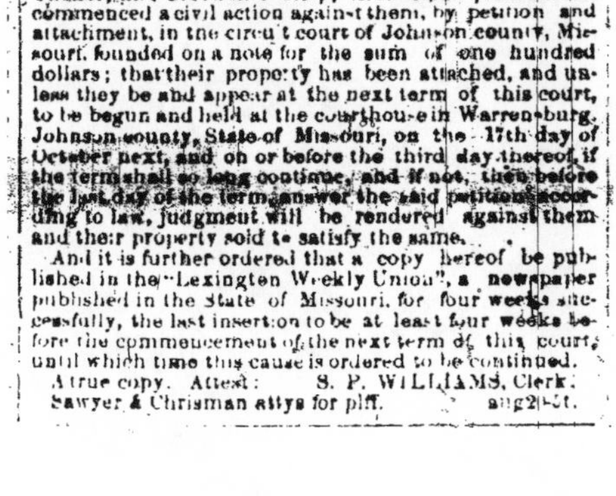

ORDER OF PUBLICATION.

STATE OF MISSOURI, } ss.
County of Johnson. }

In the Circuit Court of Johnson county, April Term—April 20th, A. D. 1864.

The Farmers' Bank of Missouri, plaintiff, against Mumford Smith, William P. Tucker, and Greenville Crisp, defendants.

Petition and attachment.

NOW at this day comes the plaintiff aforesaid, by its attorney, and on his motion this cause is dismissed as to Mumford Smith, and it appearing to the satisfaction of the court that said defendants, William P. Tucker and Greenville Crisp, are non residents of the State of Missouri: It is therefore ordered by the court that publication be made, notifying said defendants, William P. Tucker, and Greenville Crisp, that said plaintiff has commenced a civil action against them, by petition and attachment, in the circuit court of Johnson county, Missouri, founded on a note for the sum of one hundred dollars; that their property has been attached, and unless they be and appear at the next term of this court, to be begun and held at the courthouse in Warrensburg, Johnson county, State of Missouri, on the 17th day of October next, and on or before the third day thereof, if the term shall so long continue, and if not, then before the last day of the term, answer the said petition according to law, judgment will be rendered against them and their property sold to satisfy the same.

And it is further ordered that a copy hereof be published in the "Lexington Weekly Union", a newspaper published in the State of Missouri, for four weeks successfully, the last insertion to be at least four weeks before the commencement of the next term of this court, until which time this cause is ordered to be continued.

A true copy. Attest: S. P. WILLIAMS, Clerk.
Sawyer & Chrisman attys for plff.   aug23-4t.

Figures 6.4a and 6.4b. Front page and detail of the *Lexington Weekly Union*, September 17, 1864. Most of the newspaper space is devoted to notices of property sales. This is typical of newspapers from the interior of the state in 1864–65. Used by permission of the State Historical Society of Missouri, Columbia.

Figure 6.5. John Brooks Henderson (1826–1913),
ca. 1863. Library of Congress.

Figure 6.6. Congressman and General
James H. Lane, USA (1814–66), ca. 1862.
Library of Congress.

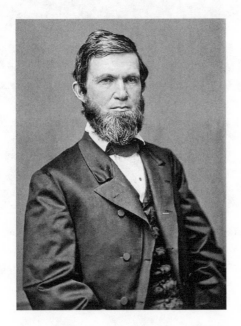

Figure 6.7. General Benjamin F. Loan, U.S.
(1819–81), ca. 1864. Library of Congress.

Figure 6.8. Going to Lawrence: Guerrillas Arch Clement,
Dave Poole, and Dave Hendricks, New Year's Day, 1863,
in Sherman, Texas. Used by permission of the State
Historical Society of Missouri, Columbia.

Figure 6.9. "The Destruction of the City of Lawrence, Kansas and
the Massacre of its Inhabitants by the Rebel Guerrillas, August 21, 1863,"
Harper's Weekly, September 5, 1863.

THE TRANSFORMATION OF
REGIONAL IDENTITY

Most historians now agree that in the South as a whole, planters suffered heavy losses of slaves and other personal property during the war and Reconstruction but preserved most of their real property. The legacy of the war in the South—hyperinflation and debt repudiation—was a disaster for southern creditors, including banks, but left former debtors whole. Southern planters remained the largest landowners in their home counties, even though everyone was poorer than before the war. From this foundation of economic leadership, the antebellum elite regained political control after Reconstruction. In Missouri, because of the forced land sales, planters persisted in the postwar era at lower rates than they would have otherwise. The arrival of thousands of non-southern settlers diluted the planters' influence further. Over the decade ending in 1870, Missouri's population increased almost as much as the combined total for all ten former Confederate states. Almost all Missouri's immigration came from outside the South. In the decades following the war, plantations almost disappeared from the Boonslick, as did nearly the entire African American population. Missouri increasingly differed from the former Confederate states in population, demography, agriculture, land ownership, and politics. In Missouri the combination of the forced land sales and northern immigration achieved what the Radical Republicans could not in the Confederacy proper.[1]

The term "planter" has no universally accepted definition. Southerners themselves used the term loosely. In the Black Belt counties of Alabama and Mississippi, the terms "planter" and "farmer" were often synonymous. Historians nowadays agree that planters in this period were farmers with large landholdings and many slaves. But there consensus ends. Robert Fogel and Stanley Engerman define large planters as owning over fifty slaves, and medium planters as owning between sixteen and fifty slaves. In his study of Black Belt counties in Alabama, Jonathan Wiener defines planters solely by ownership of real property, rather than of slaves. A planter, for Wiener, owned at least ten thousand dollars' worth of real estate in 1850 and thirty-two thousand dollars' worth in 1860, equivalent to about the top 8 percent of landowners. In his study of southwest Georgia, Lee Formwalt also defines planters in size of land holdings rather than slaves. Formwalt's planters are in the top 4.5 percent of landowners, translating into real estate worth six thousand dollars or more in 1850, twenty-four thousand dollars or more in 1860, and eleven thousand dollars or more in 1870. In his study of Harrison County, Texas, Randolph B. Campbell classifies large planters as owners of twenty slaves, and small planters as owners of between ten and nineteen slaves. In Chicot and Phillips Counties, Arkansas, Carl H. Moneyhon defines large planters as owners of twenty or more slaves, and six hundred or more acres.[2]

"Planter" was not a common term in Missouri. In the state's 1860 census, only four respondents identified themselves as planters, whereas almost a hundred and twenty-five thousand identified themselves as farmers. In Mississippi, thirty-one hundred respondents identified themselves as planters and forty-six thousand as farmers. However, close to six hundred Missouri farmers owned five hundred acres or more, and five hundred and forty of the census respondents owned twenty or more slaves. Thirty-eight of these owners had fifty slaves or more. In Missouri, planters were not as thick on the ground as in Mississippi, but they were a definite presence. Although most Missouri slaveholders owned small numbers of slaves, the rich slaveowners in the Boonslick would have been viewed as planters anywhere the South. The Missourians could not compete with the Natchez nabobs, but they were rich men. As in other slave states, they occupied the top rung of the social ladder in their home counties.[3]

Except to a few state and local historians, Missouri's planters are virtually forgotten. To preempt any doubts about identification, the following analysis uses a deliberately conservative and restrictive definition of "planter elite." For this study, a member of the planter elite in the three sample counties, Cooper, Pettis, and Saline, owned at least twenty slaves and land of either acreage or value in the top 3 percent of the county's landowners. In Cooper County in 1860, this meant a farm of at least 800 acres or worth at least $16,000; in Pettis County, 1,000 acres or $22,320; in Saline County, 1,200 acres or $20,000. Defined thus, there were twenty-two planters in Cooper, Pettis, and Saline Counties in 1850, and forty-five in 1860. For 1870, the top 3 percent of landowners by acreage or value is defined as the "landed elite." In these counties, rich planters who remained rich

Table 7.1. Missouri Planter Persistence Rates, 1850–70

Decade	Total planters	Persist	Non-note signers	Persist	Note-signers	Persist
1850–60	22	14 (64%)	22	14 (64%)	N/A	N/A
1860–70	45	20 (44%)	26	16 (62%)	19	4 (21%)

planters from 1850 to 1860, or whose sons or widows did so, persisted at a rate of 64 percent. For the 1860 to 1870 decade, the comparable figure was 44 percent. Table 7.1 summarizes these results.[4]

This chapter compares planter persistence in Missouri to persistence in the states studied by Wiener, Formwalt, Campbell, Moneyhon, and Townes. Each of the other five studies uses its own definition of planters, but the studies by Wiener, Formwalt, and Campbell of Alabama, Georgia, and Texas, respectively, are most comparable to one another in how they define persistence. All three studies measure family rather than individual persistence: a planter persisted if either he (usually), his wife, or his eldest son were still in the elite group ten years later. Also, "persistence" in these studies means social as well as geographical persistence. In other words, the question these studies ask is not how many rich planters or their families remained in the same county ten years later, but how many rich planters were still rich planters. The three studies arrive at findings that are similar in many respects. Missouri, however, is different. Table 7.2 compares planter persistence in Alabama, Georgia, Texas, and Missouri. The 1860–70 persistence rates in the first three states were close to the rates for the preceding decade, whereas in Missouri the rate dropped sharply. Also, except in Missouri, the richest planters in each study persisted at significantly higher rates than did the group as a whole.[5]

The remaining two studies, by Carl Moneyhon and Jane Townes, calculate planter persistence in ways that are more difficult to compare to the other studies. Moneyhon calculates planter persistence rates for individuals, rather than families, in Phillips and Chicot Counties, Arkansas, for the period from 1860 to 1866. There, he finds persistence rates of 88 percent for Phillips County and 77 percent for Chicot County, for individual planters with real property worth over twenty-five thousand dollars in 1860. Townes, who studies Nelson and Goochland Counties, Virginia, in 1860 and 1870, also considers real property ownership and not slaveholdings. Townes looks at individuals, rather than families, that owned five hundred acres or more. She finds that 67 percent of these landowners persisted

Table 7.2. Planter Persistence Compared, 1850–70

Study	Persistence 1850–60	Persistence 1860–70	Wealthy Core, 1860–70
Alabama (Wiener)	47%	43%	50%
Georgia (Formwalt)	30%	34%	72%
Texas (Campbell)	55%	53%	N/A
Missouri (Geiger)	64%	44%	33%

in Nelson County and 75 percent in Goochland County. Townes notes that these are conservative figures that exclude transfers within the same family. The available primary sources make it impossible to do Moneyhon's calculation for Missouri. However, using Townes's method to calculate landowner persistence in the three Missouri counties shows persistence at much lower rates. Ignoring slavery, residents of these counties who owned five hundred or more acres in 1860 persisted in 1870 at a rate of 19 percent. Using the top 3 percent of value instead yields an almost identical result of 21 percent.[6]

Missouri's planters differ from their counterparts in Alabama, Georgia, and Texas in other ways as well. In those three states, most of the non-persistent planters moved out of the study area. Only a few non-persistent planters "skidded," to use Jonathan Wiener's term: that is, remained in the area but were downwardly mobile. This is significant, because as most of the non-persistent planters left the area, some of their number would have been rich planters elsewhere. That is, ignoring geographic persistence, figures for the planters' social persistence would have been higher still. Also in Alabama, Georgia, and Texas, the non-persistent planters who remained in their home counties in 1870 usually remained big landowners, though they were no longer members of the elite. The opposite happened in Missouri, as shown in Table 7.3. There most of the non-persistent planters remained in their home counties in 1870, so their later status is known. In Missouri, a much larger percentage of the non-persistent planters dropped out of the elite altogether than did so elsewhere. In Missouri, fourteen of the twenty-five planters who did not persist into 1870, or 56 percent, remained in their home counties but skidded socially. Also, persistent planters in Missouri owned a smaller percentage of the sampled counties' real property in 1870 than in 1860.[7]

In all these respects, Missouri differed from the other states. In Missouri, planter persistence dropped significantly from 1860 to 1870 compared to the

Table 7.3. Non-persistent Planters, 1860–70

Study	Moved	Skidded
Alabama (Wiener)	91%	9%
Georgia (Formwalt)	72%	28%
Texas (Campbell)	82%	18%
Missouri (Geiger)	44%	56%

previous decade, and Missouri planters also had a much higher rate of downward social mobility than did their counterparts elsewhere. The indebtedness arising from the promissory notes contributed to all of these outcomes. Twenty-six of the forty-five total planters in 1860 had no connection with the promissory notes signed in 1861 and 1862 (see Table 7.1). This group has a 62 percent persistence rate from 1860 to 1870, close to the previous decade's 64 percent. The nineteen remaining planters in the 1860 group were bankers, or else they or their sons signed promissory notes. In this group, only four of nineteen, or their widows or sons, remained in the top 3 percent of landowners in 1870, a persistence rate of 21 percent. Figure 7.1 summarizes these results.

Some of these planters fell a long way. William T. Harrison and John S. Deaderick of Saline County each lost 90 percent of their property, although each still owned something. Major James S. Hopkins of Pettis County owned thirty-five slaves and land worth eighty-three thousand dollars in 1860. Major Hopkins remained in Pettis County after the war, but he owned no land at all in 1870. However, persistence rates for Missouri's planters understate the decline in their postwar influence, which was further diluted by immigration. By 1864 and 1865, surviving newspapers in central Missouri had entire pages filled with notices of sheriffs' auctions of real estate. In 1867 a thirty-five-year-old Pennsylvanian named Dan Fogle toured south Missouri, looking for a new home for his family. Fogle reported that farmland was cheap, plentiful, and for sale, but with no buyers. There was a general fear the former owners might violently reclaim possession.[8]

Dangerous or not, the cheap land attracted many settlers, and Missouri's population grew rapidly after the war. Between 1860 and 1870, Missouri ranked third in overall population increase, after Illinois and Pennsylvania. Of the twenty-three states with a population of one-half million or greater in 1860, Missouri grew at the third-fastest rate, after Michigan and Iowa. Of all the former slave states, Missouri grew fastest, both in nominal and in percentage terms. Missouri's

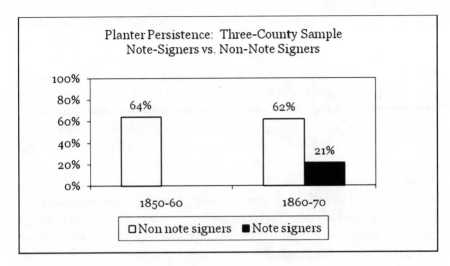

Figure 7.1. Planter persistence: three-county sample. Note signers vs. non–note signers.

U.S.-born white population increased 52 percent over the decade, going from nine hundred thousand to 1.4 million. By comparison, Dixie's combined population increase in the same period was 611,704, excluding Texas. The population growth meant that Missouri's planters, their families, and other big landowners who persisted into the 1870 census, while a low enough percentage of the 1860 group, made up an even smaller percentage of the 1870 landed elite. Looking at large land holdings only, in 1860 there were 108 individuals in the top 3 percent of landowners in the three counties. Of this group, 22 individuals were still in the top 3 percent of landowners in 1870. By that time, however, the total population of the three counties had increased by 47 percent, and there were 176 individuals in the top 3 percent of landowners. Only 13 percent of the landowners in this new, expanded group were holdovers from 1860.[9]

Elsewhere in the South, as shown in the studies by Wiener, Campbell, and Formwalt as well as in Townes's study of Virginia, there was no significant redistribution of property between 1860 and 1870. Indeed, Wiener, Campbell, and Formwalt found that although land values declined steeply over the decade, the elite group owned a larger share of the counties' land in 1870 than in 1860. Moneyhon did not address this question in his Arkansas study. In all five of the studies of planters in other former slave states, the plantation system itself survived the war. Most newcomers to the propertied elite in these states either were already residents of the area in 1860, or came from elsewhere in the South.

These outcomes also were different in Missouri. There, besides population, the number of farms increased as well. The great acreages sold at auction depressed real estate prices, but the buyers' market benefited few Missourians. The war ravaged Missouri's economy and few people had any extra money, and the state's banks were in no condition to extend credit. Instead, immigrants from regions untouched by the war bought the land, arriving from the Midwest, the Northeast, and abroad. From 1860 to 1870 the number of farms in Missouri grew by two-thirds, while the size of the average farm declined by one-third. These trends were even more marked in the three sample counties. There, the total number of farms nearly doubled between 1860 and 1870, and the size of the average farm dropped by almost half, from 288 to 157 acres. The new State Board of Agriculture approved of these developments. In 1866, in the Board's first annual report to the state general assembly, the corresponding secretary stated, "Our farms are too large. This is one of the evils accompanying slavery." The secretary added that smaller farms would result in "increasing the density of population, value of land, facilities of education, creating better society, small towns, reducing taxation, and in fact making the country better and more wealthy."[10]

Looking only at non-native Missourians, almost all the postwar population growth came from settlers not born in slave states. The number of foreign-born Missourians, mainly German-Americans, increased by more than one-third from 1860 to 1870, and the number of Missourians born in free states nearly doubled. In the same period, the number of Missourians born in slave states other than Missouri declined by 3 percent. In 1860, of all U.S.-born whites in Missouri, 38 percent came from slave states (excluding the percentage born in Missouri). Of the U.S.-born whites who were not native to the state, nearly twice as many came from slave states as from free states. In 1850 and 1860 Kentucky and Tennessee headed the list of states whose native sons were living in Missouri. Illinois passed Tennessee in 1870 and Kentucky in 1880; by 1890 Ohio and Indiana had reached second and third place, respectively, ahead of Kentucky. Again, excluding the percentage of the population born in Missouri, in no census after 1860 did respondents born in southern states exceed those born in northern states. Figure 7.2 shows free- versus slave-state nativity of U.S.-born white Missourians born outside the state.[11]

The changed population density, nativity, and farm size made a different agricultural economy. The region speedily adopted midwestern farming practices in the immediate postwar years. In his study of the seven Boonslick counties known after the war as Little Dixie, Robert Frizzell found that the prewar cash crops, tobacco and hemp, declined precipitously. The Mississippi River reopened to civilian traffic after the capture of Vicksburg on July 4, 1863, but trade with the South was a fraction of its former volume. Missouri's hemp industry almost

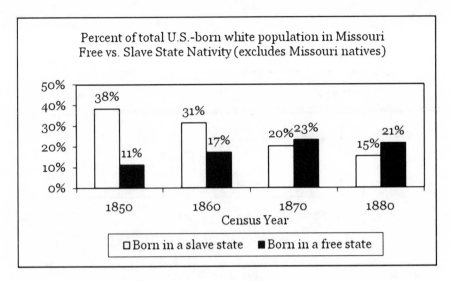

Figure 7.2. Percent of total U.S.-born white population in Missouri:
free vs. slave state nativity (excluding Missouri natives).

disappeared. The market for hemp had chiefly been in the southern states, as baling for harvested cotton. After the war hemp never revived as a money crop in Missouri or Kentucky, the main prewar producers.[12]

Instead, Missouri farmers switched to less labor-intensive crops such as wheat and oats, bought more machinery, and broke up larger tracts of land for sale to farmers who, with their families, performed most of their own labor. After the war, the Boonslick became an important wheat-growing region for the first time. In 1860, Missouri had ranked fifteenth in wheat production. In 1869 the state was in tenth place and by 1889 in seventh place. One feature of Missouri's postwar agriculture that was more typical of the South than of the Midwest was the state's mule breeding industry. After a dip following the war, Missouri led the nation in mules from 1870 to 1890, before being overtaken by Texas in 1900. Corn, cattle, and hogs remained a constant in the region, important before and after the war.[13]

The smaller, family-managed farms required less labor than the plantations. In the seven Boonslick counties studied by Frizzell, the black population declined by 25 percent from 1860 to 1870. The black population increased again during the 1870s, but then decreased through every succeeding decade. Missouri's former rural slave-majority areas gradually became nearly empty of African Americans. In 1860, Saline and Lafayette Counties had three black-majority townships; in the rural portions of these townships, blacks outnumbered whites 3,967 to 3,455.

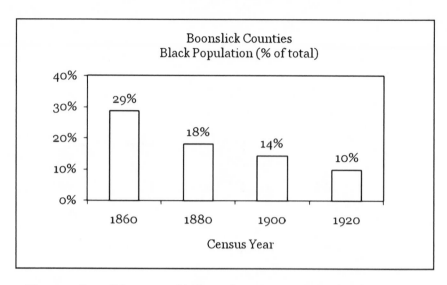

Figure 7.3. Boonslick counties: black population as percentage of total population.

By 2000, whites outnumbered blacks in these same areas by 3,911 to 45. The changes in farm size and the departure of the blacks meant that southern-style sharecropping did not take root in the Boonslick, another feature distinguishing the region from the South. Figure 7.3 shows the decline in the black population of the seven Boonslick counties.[14]

The indebtedness dragged down not only the planters but their extended families as well. Many of these people left the area for good. The Civil War was hard enough on pro-southern Missourians, who had to cope not only with the omnipresent physical danger but also with confiscation, fines, bonds, and abridgments to their civil rights, including disenfranchisement. Loss of all their property added another reason to emigrate to this already formidable list. At the time indebtedness in the United States was governed by a crazy quilt of state laws, and cooperation between different jurisdictions was patchy. Insolvent debtors often simply left for parts unknown. In the three-county sample, eighty-three of the defendants who survived the war, 25 percent of the total, left the state. Texas and Kentucky topped the list of preferred destinations. Next in order of preference were Colorado's Front Range counties and California's Central Valley. Others migrated within Missouri, heading mostly for the southwest counties and the Kansas City area.[15]

The destinations of thirty-seven of the eighty-three former defendants who left the state are unknown, but some probably went to Brazil and Mexico. Dr. John H. Blue of neighboring Chariton County, a defendant in roughly twenty promissory note cases there, joined the Confederate colony in Brazil. Alfred Lewis, brother of the defendant Abram H. Lewis, lived in Durango, Mexico, after the war. There he was the distribution agent for the Confederate expatriate newspaper *The Two Republics*. Many of the defendants, or their sons, fought in Shelby's Iron Brigade. Refusing to surrender in 1865, Shelby and his entire command crossed the Rio Grande into Mexico, where they offered their services to the Emperor Maximilian. Other prominent ex-Confederate Missourians who went to Mexico after the war included former Missouri secretary of state General Mosby Monroe Parsons, former U.S. Senator Trusten Polk, and Sterling Price.[16]

People lost more than property. The defendants Richard E. Snelling of Saline County and Isaac McKee of Cooper County committed suicide because of their debts. The banker John A. Brownlee of St. Louis may have died by suicide as well. In Osceola, the enraged depositor Marcellus Harris shot the president of the local bank, William L. Vaughan, in September 1861 (see Chapter 4). Some disputes between codefendants lasted long after the war and could be bitter and violent. In Cooper County, Nathaniel T. Allison sued Nathaniel Sutherlin, whom Allison had known for more than twenty years, for damages arising from six promissory notes the two had signed in 1861. The Missouri Supreme Court finally decided the case in 1873. After the war, in a dispute over a debt between two defendants, Thomas Allen shot and killed William Maupin in Chariton County.[17]

Missouri's banking industry changed almost beyond recognition. The parent banks in St. Louis were unable to help the Confederate cause much, and they did not suffer the same losses the branch banks experienced. But the war all but halted regular commerce in St. Louis. Before the war, St. Louis had been the major midcountry hub connecting the South, East, and West, via the river network. With the closure of the Lower Mississippi River in 1861, most of the city's trade with the Upper Mississippi Valley shifted to Chicago. A new Chicago–New York trading axis replaced the older St. Louis–New Orleans one. After the river reopened in 1863 St. Louis's trade approached its prewar volume, but it was an artificial prosperity, buoyed by military contracts. The army business ended in 1865, and trade volume at St. Louis dropped to well below prewar levels.[18]

The military business kept the city banks afloat, but the promissory note fiasco drained capital from the branch banks and left them virtual shells—possessing charters to do business but little else. Two of Missouri's nine 1857 banking corporations, the Union Bank and the Farmers' Bank, liquidated in 1866. The remaining seven banks were able to attract new capital by rechartering as national banks under the National Banking Act of 1863. Under this law, a bank could apply for a national charter rather than a state one and sell new stock as it reorganized. Together, the National Banking Act, the several legal tender acts, and the Internal Revenue Act radically changed the U.S. banking industry. These laws created a new federal paper currency that replaced that of the state banks, wiped out the latter's funds transfer business, and increased competition by chartering new banks. The National Banking Act also forbade branch banking, forcing the reorganized St. Louis banks to sell their former branches. Most branch banks closed, but a few reopened as small, independent country banks.[19]

The banks' customers, industries, and profit centers also changed. By 1865 the South, once Missouri's main customer, was bankrupt. One of Missouri's major prewar industries, hemp production, was gone. But the banks developed new lines of business in farm and residential mortgages and short-term financing for postwar industries such as railroads, mining, light manufacturing, and construction. The wartime closure of southern markets served to strengthen Missouri's ties with the Northeast, and by 1869 a spur line connected Missouri to the newly completed transcontinental railroad. Missouri's railroads and banking corporations were the only major antebellum firms to survive the war and become part of the postwar big-business complex. But the banks resembled the two-hundred-year-old ax with the handle replaced three times and the blade twice.[20]

This new world had no room for the prewar bankers. In the later years of the war, Missouri's two Unionist governments—civilian and military—treated the state's pro-southern citizens with increasing harshness. In the November 1864 state elections to the Twenty-Third General Assembly, martial law, the restricted franchise, and the wartime polarization of opinion brought the Radical Union Party to power. This assembly saw a major turnover in membership from previous sessions. Only a quarter of the legislators from the Twenty-Second General Assembly remained, and only 8 members out of 172 had served in any other session of the general assembly. By 1864 and 1865, the victorious Radicals had largely disenfranchised the Democrats and pushed members of the old regime out of the government. The Radical Union Party capped its 1864 election victory by pushing through a new state constitution the following year. The Drake Constitution, named for its main architect, institutionalized discrimination against Missouri's former rebels. To regain the vote, they had to swear the so-called Ironclad Oath, in which they denied having committed eighty-six separate acts. Between them, the Drake Constitution and the Ironclad Oath barred former rebels from public office, many professions, and corporate directorships, including directorships of banks.[21]

These controls did not last long, and Missouri's antebellum southern leadership had a limited restoration after the peace. Hanging on to power through the restricted franchise, for eight years the Radicals carried out their own version of Reconstruction, thoroughly alienating everybody. The state general assembly revoked the Ironclad Oath in 1871, and the U.S. Supreme Court challenged the Drake Constitution's limits on the franchise. When former rebels regained the franchise in 1872, voters elected an entire slate of prominent ex-Confederates to state and national office. The so-called Confederate brigadiers proved to be conciliatory rather than ideological, and willing to cooperate across party lines on matters of common interest. They most often made common cause with other states on populist measures such as railroad and insurance reform, support of farming interests, and restraint of the banks, rather than on strictly southern issues. In 1884 the former Confederate General John Sappington Marmaduke, Claiborne Fox Jackson's nephew and Vincent Marmaduke's brother, won the governorship.[22]

This cohort of southern politicians proved to be the last. As the wartime leaders retired, no younger generation of elite southerners arose in their place. The huge land sales in Missouri in the last two years of the war cut off southern elite culture at the taproot. Noting the disappearance of the plantations and of the tobacco and hemp crops, Robert Frizzell writes that the economic basis for the Boonslick's southern identity vanished within a few years after 1865. Of the seven Missouri governors who took part in the Civil War and who held office after former rebels regained the franchise, six were Union men. The one ex-Confederate elected to the governorship, General John Sappington Marmaduke, may have owed his victory to his opponent. The previous governor, former Union general Thomas Crittenden, had posted a twenty-five-thousand-dollar reward for the capture of Jesse James, dead or alive. Many Missourians viewed James's shooting in 1881 as murder for hire, ending Crittenden's political career.[23]

The influx of non-southern immigrants set the stage for a further turning away from the South, with the long-term decline of Missouri's Democratic Party. Though the Democrats regained political control of the state once the restrictions on the franchise ended, in 1884 General Marmaduke beat his Republican opponent by fewer than five hundred votes. In 1894 the Republicans dominated the election. In that year they elected a majority in the lower house of the state general assembly, all their candidates for state administrative offices, and ten of the state's fifteen members of Congress. Theodore Roosevelt carried the state in 1904, and Missouri elected its first Republican governor, Herbert Spencer Hadley, in 1909. Since then Missouri has been a swing state, a fact that itself sets Missouri apart from the South. Of the twenty different Missouri governors since Hadley, seven have been Republicans. Today the state is something of a unique mix. Analyzing the political culture of each of the fifty states in 1984, Daniel Elazar found Missouri different not only from the other former slave states but from the rest of the country as well.[24]

The period of southern restoration came too late for many of the ex-bankers. Some died during the war, and there were other human costs. John W. Wills, former president of the parent branch of the Mechanics' Bank of St. Louis, disappeared after defaulting on large personal debts. Jesse Riddlesbarger, former president of the Kansas City branch of the Mechanics' Bank and once the town's richest man, died on the Howard County poor farm. Parties unknown shot Reverend Thomas Johnson, the bank president, missionary, newspaper owner, and proslavery activist, in his home in 1865. Relatives of David Waldo, the Independence bank cashier, land speculator, Santa Fe trader, and physician, committed him to the state lunatic asylum. After his release, Waldo helped form another bank in Independence before dying of an overdose of morphine.[25]

In the former branch banks that reopened after the war, the turnover of the bank officers of 1861 was over 80 percent. The Union men who took over the banks during the war got their jobs because of their politics, but they were not mere hacks. The new bankers were themselves successful and capable, and they were in their new positions to stay. Major Henry Smith Turner, after 1863 the president of the Union Bank of St. Louis, was a graduate of West Point and of the elite Cavalry School of Saumur, France. Before the war he held posts in government and finance, including assistant United States treasurer in St. Louis and representative in the Missouri general assembly. Oliver Garrison, a native of New York City and after 1864 the president of the Mechanics' Bank of St. Louis, was previously the president of an iron foundry in the city and had made a fortune in real estate speculation. The Unionist bankers, men to reckon with anyway, had an extra advantage because of the various penalties and limits on civil rights imposed on ex-rebels.[26]

Of the handful of prewar bankers who had been pro-Union, many went on to do well after the war. Milton Tootle, president of the Western Bank parent branch in St. Joseph, became a great power in that city and the founder of a family fortune. He was the main benefactor of the St. Joseph opera house, which is named after him. Robert E. Carr, in 1861 the cashier of the Exchange Bank of St. Louis parent branch, was president of three different railroads after the war. Some bankers whose politics had been of the weather-vane variety during the war also made their way. General Bela Metcalf Hughes, formerly cashier of the Western Bank in St. Joseph, became a prominent attorney of the Denver bar. James Britton, in 1861 the cashier of the Southern Bank of St. Louis's parent branch, became the bank's president in 1864. Later, he continued as president of the bank's successor, the Third National Bank of St. Louis. In 1875 he won election as mayor of St. Louis on a Democratic ticket. John Brooks Henderson, one of the original architects of the 1857 banking law and the U.S. senator appointed to replace the ousted Trusten Polk, remained in the Senate until 1869. He co-sponsored the Thirteenth Amendment to the United States Constitution, abolishing slavery, and introduced it to the Senate. He was also prominent in the adoption of the Fifteenth Amendment. Though Henderson was a Republican, he disagreed with the Radicals in Jefferson City and supported Lincoln's policy of leniency toward the South. Henderson effectively ended his career in elective politics when he voted not to impeach Andrew Johnson in 1866. Johnson's impeachment failed by one vote.[27]

The bankers who left Missouri scattered from Mississippi to Canada, and several prospered. The bank director Thomas H. Price, who during the war served on the staff of his kinsman, General Sterling Price, moved to Mobile, Alabama, where he practiced law and served in the state legislature. A surprising number of ex-Missouri bankers moved to the citadel of Yankeedom, New York. The St. Louis bankers John J. Anderson and Junius Brutus Alexander, respectively presidents of the parent branches of the Bank of St. Louis and the Exchange Bank of St. Louis, both went to New York. Alexander named his Staten Island estate Effingham House, after his family's Virginia plantation. Hiram Northrup, president of the Union Bank of St. Louis branch at Kansas City, and Robert W. Donnell, president of the Bank of Missouri branch in St. Joseph, went to New York as well.[28]

The all-important kinship network took new root in some of these locations. Banished from Missouri in 1863, Robert W. Donnell went to the newly discovered goldfields in Montana Territory. The area was a friendly haven for Missouri's ex-Confederates. In 1865 Donnell's brother-in-law, Colonel John C. Calhoun Thornton, a former Confederate officer, recruiter, and guerrilla captain, joined Donnell and settled in Deer Lodge County. Jesse James joined them there for a time in 1873. In Butte, Donnell opened a grocery and outfitting firm with another ex-Missourian, William S. Tutt, whose brother Thomas was a wholesale grocer in St. Louis and later himself a bank president. Donnell knew the Tutts through another of his brothers-in-law, Leonidas Lawson, who had grown up with the Tutts in Boonville. The store charged frontier prices, three dollars for a dozen eggs when miners' wages were four dollars a month. In about 1868 Donnell and his partners founded a bank, accepting shares in mining ventures as collateral for store purchases and other loans. Miners often paid these loans in tons of ore, which Donnell and his partners shipped by rail to Baltimore for smelting.[29]

Banking and groceries paid better than mining. In 1870, Donnell moved to New York to handle the firm's affairs there, going from a frontier mining camp of two hundred forty people to the country's largest city and financial center. In New York, Donnell banked with the émigré Missourians at Northrup & Chick before he formed a second, New York–based banking partnership linked to the Montana business. Again, Donnell's partners were ex-Missourians he knew before the war, including his brother-in-law Leonidas Lawson. The new firm joined the New York Stock Exchange and became the New York correspondent for small banks throughout the West. Donnell's bank became the fiscal agent for several western states, dealt in municipal bonds of western cities, and speculated in Texas and New Mexico mining properties. Donnell died in 1892 at his home on East Sixty-Seventh Street off Central Park, a world away from Missouri.[30]

Most of the ex-Confederate bankers who remained in Missouri did not get a seat at the postwar table. An exception was William E. Burr, who was in 1861 cashier of the Boonville branch of the Bank of St. Louis. Burr was a committed southern man, and in September 1861 Unionist Home Guard militia took him hostage to forestall an attack by the Saline Mounted Rifles. (They attacked anyway.) But by the war's end Burr was president of the Bank of St. Louis's parent branch and of its successor, the St. Louis National Bank, and later of the St. Louis Clearing House Association. Burr has left little trace of himself behind, except a few bare facts on the public record. This may have been intentional. One of the few histories of St. Louis that mentions his name states that he "financed many of the operations of the Confederate Army." Edward A. Lewis, a branch bank president in 1861 and a presidential elector for John C. Breckenridge, became a Missouri Supreme Court justice in 1874, and in 1876 became presiding judge of the St. Louis Court of Appeals.[31]

Most of the ex-bankers who stayed in Missouri never regained their former standing, and passed the rest of their lives in modest obscurity. County histories have little to say about them. Most lost their money during the war, but a few managed to preserve some capital. When the war began Captain Swinney sent fifty of his slaves from his Howard County plantation to Texas, to be able to keep them if the South won the war. Swinney lost his slaves but still left an estate of four hundred thousand dollars on his death in June 1863. The Swinney family home, Sylvan Villa, was still standing in 1940, though much neglected. The family has since vanished from the area. All these men lost more than money. They were no longer the best men in the counties where they lived. Other men, the war's victors—Germans, Republicans, and the new settlers from the northern states—held the reins of power. The bankers lost their social capital as well. The debts, the property auctions, and the emigration of many of the landless families disrupted the generations-old family networks that had knit prewar society together. Excluded from power and increasingly outnumbered by the newcomers, the remaining planters and bankers were more and more strangers in their own land.[32]

Today a minority of Missourians are of southern origin. Yet the South is still present in Missouri. In October 2005, the United Daughters of the Confederacy counted more members in Missouri than in any of the other non-seceding slave states. A traveler along the Boonslick's back roads sees "Johnny Reb" hood ornaments on pickup trucks, tee shirts silk-screened "American by Birth, Southern by the Grace of God," and Confederate-flag bumper stickers, tattoos, and window decals. Noticeably absent, however, are the trappings of southern elite culture: big country houses, tobacco cultivation, blooded stock, and genteel farming. Missouri's former sister state, Kentucky, had a more typically southern postwar history. There, a rural aristocracy with deep southern roots still figures prominently in the state's social life and cultural identity. Writing in 1855, Frederick Douglass described the Boonslick as the most prosperous, powerful, and vital slaveholding region in the state, concluding that "in no part of the Union [was] Slavery more profitable." Today in the Boonslick only the old houses remain, often owned by commuting urban professionals or converted into bed and breakfasts.[33]

The promissory note episode weakened part of Missouri's southern tradition but reinforced it in another way, more important outside the state than in. The indebtedness and land sales intensified Missouri's wartime guerrilla violence to a level unmatched in the country before or since. Today, Missouri's guerrillas are one of the most widely recognized features of the entire war for the public. In some ways, Missouri has never gotten over the guerrillas. Old Boonslick families pass stories of the bushwhackers, as they are known, from generation to generation, and there is a common notion that many western desperadoes after the war were "bad men out of Missouri." Tellingly, this is also the title of a film. The first novel about Missouri guerrillas appeared in 1861. One historian counted sixty-two Civil War novels set in Missouri, as of 1990. The first book on the Lawrence massacre appeared in 1864, only a year after the event. Jesse James, the most famous guerrilla of all, has been a media celebrity since his train-robbing days, appearing in newspapers, dime novels, films, television programs, comic books, and video games. The first film about the James gang appeared in 1908, seven years before *Birth of a Nation*. The first film about William Clarke Quantrill appeared in 1914.[34]

Interest is still strong. T. J. Stiles's 2002 book *Jesse James: Last Rebel of the Civil War* received a cover review in the *New York Times* Book Review and became a bestseller. Films about Missouri guerrillas have won academy awards, and have often been box office hits. Well-known actors who have played guerrillas include James Stewart; Clint Eastwood; David, Keith, and Robert Carradine; James and Stacy Keach; Dennis and Randy Quaid; Nicholas and Christopher Guest; and Brad Pitt. Now, when a minority of Missourians have southern roots, Missouri's southern identity has passed beyond the borders of the state and become a part of the nation's collective consciousness of the Civil War.[35]

WAR AND THE ADMINISTRATIVE STATE

Pro-Confederate Missourians were not the only private citizens paying to arm their young men in 1861. North and South, people everywhere were doing the same, in effect loaning money to their state governments to go to war. Most histories of Civil War procurement and supply begin with actions taken by state governments to raise troops after the fall of Fort Sumter in April 1861. But there was a prehistory to that phase of mobilization. In the earliest period, troops were equipped at the end of a chain of buck-passing. The United States and Confederate States presidents called for troops, and their secretaries of war had to carry out the presidential orders. These officials turned to the state governors, but they could not respond immediately either. In the end, private citizens and associations, businesses, and local communities armed the volunteers.

The American Civil War was the first time in history a nation mobilized all its material and human resources for a war effort, and was in this sense the first modern war. In proportion to its population and the size of its economy, the Civil War remains the greatest national effort the United States has ever undertaken. About six hundred and twenty thousand soldiers died between Fort Sumter in April 1861 and Palmetto Ranch in May 1865, more than in all the rest of the nation's wars combined until the middle of the Vietnam conflict. More than three million soldiers, 10 percent of the U.S. population in 1860, took part in the Civil War. Yet during the critical months after Lincoln's election in November 1860 and through mid-1861, the enormous military buildup for the war took place under governments that, by modern standards, scarcely existed. For the first half of 1861, no government—North or South, federal or state—had the money, the legal authority, or the administrative capacity to carry out a mass military mobilization. In his July 5, 1861, message to Congress, President Lincoln noted that "one of the greatest perplexities of the government is to avoid receiving troops faster than it can provide for them."[1]

For most of the secession crisis the U.S. government did nothing to prepare for war. President Lincoln, inaugurated on March 4, took the first step to mobilize U.S. forces on April 15, 1861, the day after the surrender of Fort Sumter. That day, the president called for seventy-five thousand volunteers from the non-seceding states to suppress the rebellion. Lincoln relied on two separate acts of Congress for legal authority. The first was a 1795 law empowering the president to call out the state militias for three months' service whenever the laws of the United States "should be opposed or the operation thereof obstructed in any state by combinations too powerful to be suppressed." The second law, from 1803, provided for calling out the militia to preserve law and order in the District of Columbia.[2]

The state militias the president called on were governed by the Militia Act of 1792. On paper the militia totaled more than three million men, although seven hundred thousand of these were from the seceding states. These numbers were almost meaningless, however, as many states had not filed militia reports with the federal government for years, and sometimes decades. Also, the militiamen were soldiers in name only. The militia law required a certain number of muster and drill days each year, but the practice was unenforced and largely ignored. Equipment often consisted of gaudy uniforms worn during Independence Day parades. When these troops began to gather in Washington in May and June of 1861, they were, in the words of one historian, little more than glittering mobs. The United States had a small standing army, which formed the nucleus of both hostile armies in the Civil War. On January 1, 1861, however, U.S. forces were tiny—the total number of officers and enlisted men barely exceeded sixteen thousand. The South started 1861 with no organized armed forces at all, although about one-quarter of the total U.S. officer corps resigned their commissions and went south.[3]

After Fort Sumter, U.S. troop strength ramped up quickly. Lincoln's next call for troops came less than three weeks after the first, on May 3. Then, the president asked the non-seceding states for another forty regiments of volunteers, and increased the size of the regular army by eight regiments and the navy by eighteen thousand sailors. This call-up plus the one of April 15 would bring total U.S. military strength to two hundred thousand. A few days before Congress reconvened on July 4, Secretary of War Simon Cameron reported the War Department had accepted 208 regiments from the states, making a total force of two hundred and thirty thousand men. In his July 5th message to Congress, Lincoln requested authority to raise an army of up to four hundred thousand. On July 22, Congress legalized all the actions the president had taken while Congress was not in session—sending a relief expedition to Fort Sumter, calling out the militia, creating a volunteer army, and enlarging the regular army. Congress also authorized the president to expand the military forces to half a million men. The War Department assigned state quotas totaling a little more than six hundred thousand men, and the states responded by providing seven hundred thousand. By 1865 the Union Army had a million men under arms.[4]

In April 1861, however, the U.S. government could not equip even the first seventy-five thousand volunteers. Instead, Secretary Cameron advised state governors to arm their troops themselves and to bill the War Department. More than money was lacking, though. During the Revolutionary War, the Continental Army had a formal quartermaster's department, headed by a quartermaster general. Congress abolished the office after peace with Great Britain but reestablished it in 1812 when war again loomed. From that time forward U.S. military forces had a quartermaster's department, but by 1861 it was understaffed and neglected. In September 1859 the War Department had, besides the office of the Secretary of War, eleven bureaus and departments with ninety-three staff in Washington, D.C., counting laborers and messengers. Of these, the Quartermaster General's Office of the War Department had fourteen employees working without so much as a typewriter. Outside Washington, the quartermaster's office had another 155 employees scattered around the three-million-square-mile expanse of the continental United States, counting everyone down to commissary clerks and acting wagonmasters. Small as this military establishment was, nine days before South Carolina seceded the U.S. Senate directed the Committee on Military Affairs, Jefferson Davis, chairman, to find ways to further reduce military expenses.[5]

Many of the states, however, had begun to arm themselves well before the federal government did anything. Massachusetts started to arm itself in early January. Also in January, Michigan's governor elect offered the state's militia to the federal government in his inaugural speech. The southern states started even earlier. The South Carolina legislature passed a new military law on November 13, three days after calling the secession convention and more than a month before the state seceded. Five days later, the Georgia legislature set aside a million dollars to arm the state. Volunteers everywhere formed military companies independently of any government's actions. According to Kenneth Stamp, by the end of January 1861, two and a half months before Lincoln's first call for troops, five hundred thousand men in the non-seceding states alone had volunteered for military service. Estimates vary on how many men, other than career officers, volunteered in the Confederate States in early 1861. All sources agree, however, that the number of volunteers swamped military recruiters. But the states faced the same supply problems as the national governments. In March 1861, Indiana, which eventually supplied more than two hundred thousand Union troops, had fewer than five hundred stand of small arms in the entire state, plus eight disassembled cannon and an unknown number of flintlock muskets. Governor Morton's first step to prepare for war was to try to find these arms—many of which proved to be useless—which were scattered around the state among various disbanded militia companies.[6]

Everywhere, governments worked around their early supply problems by relying on private initiatives. State legislatures from Massachusetts to Mississippi harnessed public enthusiasm through laws that encouraged citizens and communities to raise troops on their own and claim compensation for expenses from the state. Existing laws already required state militia and volunteers to largely equip themselves. State governments used various means to compensate private citizens for these expenses, treating them as loans made to the state. By long-established custom and legal precedent, the federal government would then repay the states. Citizens could also send claims directly to Congress. If a war lasted long enough, the U.S. government would provide replacement equipment. This system also accorded with an important principle of American government at the time, the objection to standing armies. Citizen militia armed using short-term loans to the state from private individuals avoided both a standing army and its supporting institutions.

During the early months of the Civil War, private sources raised thousands of troops and millions of dollars. In January 1861, the South Carolina legislature granted corporate charters to early volunteer companies. Legally, these companies were then corporations, able to borrow money in their own names (and to be sued for repayment, if necessary). In April, Virginia's secession convention created a review board to pay military expenses incurred by private citizens. Illinois and Iowa passed similar laws in May. Also in May, North Carolina retroactively legalized measures the counties had taken to equip volunteers who responded to the state adjutant general's call for troops. The same North Carolina law allowed counties to levy taxes to repay private outlays for supplies. Moving more slowly, Georgia's law allowing volunteer companies to organize and make a financial claim on the state passed in December 1861. The U.S. government, for its part, allowed individuals to raise their own commands, in expectation of such compensation. By August 1861, the U.S. War Department was mustering more independent regiments into service than it was receiving from the state governments. By August, also, the administration began allowing generals to recruit their own commands. Just so, Missouri's secessionist state government, elected November 1860 and forcibly overturned the following June, passed such laws of its own.

On May 11, 1861, the same day that saw the passage of the North Carolina law, the Missouri general assembly authorized Governor Jackson to accept military loans from banks, savings institutions, and individuals. Another Missouri law passed the same day created a board to review all other claims for compensation, and allowed counties to advance money for military expenses on the state's behalf.[7]

Unfamiliar as these practices seem, all the United States' early wars relied on private finance. In North America, private finance for public armament dates from the earliest English settlement, and the practice was of much more ancient pedigree in Europe. There, rich men had raised private armies at least since Roman times. In England a variant of this tradition was the sale of officers' commissions, a practice not abolished until 1868. The duty of certain citizens to bear arms and to hold themselves ready for the common defense dates to an 1181 proclamation of King Henry II of England, the Assize of Arms. More recently, the 1689 English Bill of Rights set forth the right of citizens to bear arms for their defense, later incorporated into the U.S. Constitution as the Second Amendment. According to Alexander Hamilton, American opposition to standing armies also dated from the English Bill of Rights. The right of the people to petition Congress, guaranteed to U.S. citizens in the First Amendment to the Constitution, arises from the English common-law principle of sovereign immunity and the exceptions to it, which date from the thirteenth century.[8]

Private military finance worked after a fashion for the nation's early wars, which were small and low-tech. The system worked poorly, however. The citizen soldiers lacked training and were ineffective, and the military claims system was so tangled and inefficient that it invited fraud. Claimants could go through military channels, either by getting a voucher from the commanding officer of the troops who received the supplies, or by filing a claim with the quartermaster general of the state militia. A claimant could also seek compensation through his state representative or senator, his U.S. representative or senator, the U.S. Treasury, or the U.S. Court of Claims. In some places, civilians could also file claims with justices of the peace in their home counties. The U.S. Congress received more private claims than any other government body but had a terrible record in processing them. Congressmen typically considered claims in ex parte hearings, without the claimant or any supporting witnesses present. Claimants often presented their cases through influential friends, who appeared before committees or visited members in private. Congressmen had no time to examine claims properly, and fraudulent or excessive claims slipped through. Congress often found it safest not to act at all. From 1838 to 1848, out of 17,573 private claims that it received, Congress took no action on 8,625 and eventually approved only 910.[9] South Carolina received compensation in 1900 for some of the state's expenses during the War of 1812. Understandably, citizens usually sent claims to Congress only after the claim had been rejected elsewhere.[10]

This bootstrap military mobilization was inadequate for a conflict the size of the Civil War. The lack of standardized equipment, including uniforms, caused many problems. Early Civil War military engagements were often confused affairs, because neither side could distinguish friend from foe. Nor could private sources resupply armies in the field. Mindful of these problems, as well as of rampant corruption in army contracting, when Congress met in called session in July 1861 it almost immediately began to investigate military procurement. In September 1861 the War Department stopped accepting independent military organizations directly into U.S. service, first in New York, then in Pennsylvania and Ohio. The War Department then extended this policy to all the states. In February 1862, under General Orders, No. 18, the War Department named state governors the only legal authorities to raise volunteer troops and commission their officers within their respective states. Many governors, however, continued to accept independent commands. As late as September 1862 in Philadelphia alone eleven colonels were recruiting regiments.[11]

General Orders, No. 18 also centralized military supply under the control of the War Department. The order required officers of volunteer units to get equipment only from the U.S. Quartermaster's Department, and not from the governors of their respective states. In taking this step the War Department made itself responsible for more than it could deliver, and soldiers often had to supplement, legally or illegally, what the government issued. But in time, the new system worked. Centralized supply, as it developed during the war, was a larger and more elaborated version of the supply system used during the Mexican War. For the fiscal year that ended June 30, 1861, total U.S. military outlays were $35 million. The following year the figure jumped to $437 million and during 1864–65 to $1,154 million—almost thirty-three times the prewar amount.[12]

It is impossible to say what proportion of the Civil War's total costs was paid by nongovernmental sources. Except for the Missouri data, total private contributions in the United States and the Confederate States will likely remain unknown. Many patriotic citizens gave money or supplies and never sought repayment. An accurate estimate of total private claims received by the different governments is also beyond reach. In the Confederacy, no one at the time even tried to calculate total government military spending, much less private spending. The Confederacy was fighting—and losing—a war of national survival, and it likely placed a low priority on record-keeping. While it existed, the Confederate government passed legislation to repay states and private citizens for military expenses. No known records exist, however, on how much the government ever paid out for such claims. In the latter part of the war, filing claims with the Confederate government would have been pointless anyway. Prices in the South rose an estimated 9,000 percent from secession until the fall of the Confederacy, and claims for expenses incurred early in the war were worthless by the war's end. For the same reason, private southern creditors would not have bothered to sue debtors. Also, when the war was over, the victorious North forced the southern states to renounce all debts incurred to further the rebellion. Former rebels did not get to file war claims.[13]

The Confederate government did pay some of Missouri's claims, however. In a law of August 30, 1861, the Confederacy assumed responsibility for the expenses of the Missouri State Guard between May 10, 1861, the date of its mobilization, and November 28, when the Guard mustered into Confederate service. After Claiborne Fox Jackson's death in December 1862, his successor, former Lieutenant Governor Thomas C. Reynolds, discovered that Jackson had filed no claims with the Confederate government. Reynolds filed the first such claim in May 1863, for military equipment that Missouri forces had transferred to the Confederacy. Reynolds then began to review the claims made against the state by her creditors, many of whom were former members of the Missouri State Guard. Reynolds drew up a payment schedule that gave priority to Missouri soldiers mustered out because of wounds, second and third priorities to serving enlisted men and officers, and last priority to other creditors. For the balance of the war, Reynolds made a good-faith effort to pay war claims against the state. However, the only means of repayment at his disposal were Confederate treasury notes or Missouri defense bonds. Both were worthless by the end of the war.[14]

U.S. records are better, and the federal and state governments eventually did pay private war claims. In a law of July 27, 1861, the federal government pledged to repay the states' military expenses, including "the costs, charges, and expenses properly incurred by such state(s) for enrolling, subsisting, clothing, supplying, arming, equipping, paying, and transporting its troops." Also, an 1871 federal law allowed citizens of former Confederate states who could prove unbroken loyalty to the U.S. to claim compensation for property seized by federal troops. But any accurate estimate of private military contributions in the North will probably remain out of reach as well, though for different reasons than for the South. U.S. citizens had so many ways to file claims that surviving records are scattered. Also, claims filtered in to federal and state governments for decades after the war ended. Under the U.S. laws, acceptance of a claim depended partly on when the expense occurred, which made documentation important. To discourage fraud, the government set a high standard of documentary proof, and even valid claims sometimes remained unpaid for decades. Such delays meant that petitioners often resubmitted their claims year after year. The U.S. Court of Claims, which was only one payment channel, was still reviewing Civil War claims in the 1920s.[15]

The data for Missouri are complete enough to make a rough estimate of how much money Missouri's Confederates raised from private sources. There is, however, nothing to compare this figure to. No records exist to calculate Confederate government outlays—national or state—for the war in Missouri. Nor can such a figure be calculated for the Union side, though again Union records are better. The most definitive modern calculation of the total direct and indirect costs in the Civil War is by Goldin and Lewis, in "The Economic Cost of the American Civil War." However, available primary sources do not break down the costs of the war—government or private—for each state (see Appendix 1). The most thorough contemporary tabulation of what the federal government owed the states was an 1866 U.S. House of Representatives report written by Congressman James G. Blaine. Blaine did not include all the states' costs, however, and private claims were beyond the scope of his analysis. He noted that his figures did not include "any of that vast sum so generously contributed throughout the loyal States by individuals and by associations for the support of the Union cause."[16]

Plentiful anecdotal evidence, however, supports Blaine's statement about the vast sum raised by private sources. Postwar state and county histories commonly list patriotic citizens who contributed especially generously to the war effort. New Yorkers founded the Union Defence Committee to raise money, and similar organizations sprang up in Boston, Philadelphia, St. Louis, and Chicago. In an 1888 Iowa history, the author wrote that Governor Samuel J. Kirkwood pledged his own property "many times over" to feed and clothe Iowa volunteers in the early days after Sumter. Confederate secretary of the treasury George A. Trenholm alone gave a hundred thousand dollars in currency and the same amount in Confederate securities for the southern troops. One New York colonel listed thousands of dollars of private donations to his regiment alone.[17]

Private war finance, however, affected not only postwar cost estimates, but the progress of the war itself. If people had waited for the different governments to create effective supply chains, widespread fighting could not have started until months later than it did. Private supply might have been inefficient, but for a time there was no alternative. Missouri's rebels probably received more help from private sources than from anywhere else. The Confederacy appropriated money for the war in the West, but because of the distances involved most of the Confederate Department of the Trans-Mississippi was on its own. Also, the shift to centralized military procurement, when it occurred, made the armies more effective. Both governments realized that inadequate logistics might cost them the war, and they took over procurement as quickly as they could. The United States succeeded better at this than the Confederacy, in part because of the latter's states' rights principles, but also because Lincoln was better able to control the state governors than was Jefferson Davis.

The Civil War was not a phony war during its first six months. By midsummer of 1861, the two sides were fighting along a front that stretched almost halfway across the continent, from tidewater Virginia and Maryland to the Kansas border. Frederick Dyer's *Compendium of the War of the Rebellion* listed 1,288 engagements in which Union troops died in combat between July 1, 1861, and March 31, 1865. Eighty-three of these engagements occurred during 1861. More restrictively, the National Park Service's Civil War Battlefield Commission identified 384 significant actions during the Civil War, of which 35 occurred in 1861. Out of these 384 actions, the Commission identified 45 "class A" battles that had a decisive influence on a campaign and a direct impact on the course of the war. Three class A battles occurred in 1861—Fort Sumter, First Manassas, and Wilson's Creek. These battles were not large, compared to what was to come in 1862. The largest battle fought in 1861, and the second class A battle chronologically (the first was Fort Sumter), was First Manassas. The two sides had nearly sixty-one thousand troops engaged there, and combined casualties (killed, wounded, captured, or missing overall) totaled 4,878. The second-largest battle of 1861 was at Wilson's Creek, near Springfield, Missouri, on August 10. Eighteen thousand troops fought there and suffered twenty-three hundred casualties, including General Nathaniel Lyon.[18]

Eight months later, in April 1862, the Battle of Shiloh showed the war had entered a new phase. Over a hundred thousand troops fought at Shiloh, with combined casualties of nearly twenty-four thousand. After that, the largest battles of the war routinely engaged over a hundred thousand troops. In September 1862, about a hundred and forty thousand troops fought at Antietam. The same intensification of the war seen in the famous battles of 1862 was true of the many smaller engagements as well. On average, about 12,600 soldiers died each month over the forty-nine months of the Civil War, from Fort Sumter in April 1861 to Palmetto Ranch in May 1865. By comparison, World War II, the war with the second-highest death toll in the nation's history, had an average monthly death toll of 9,009 over its forty-five-month duration. Civil War casualties were distributed unequally, however. Union battlefield deaths (killed or mortally wounded) give a good measure of the intensity of the fighting. Union casualties were much lower during the second half of 1861 compared with what came later. Part of the higher death toll in 1862 and after reflected the increased

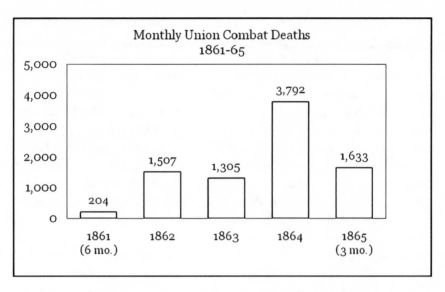

Figure 8.1. Monthly Union combat deaths, 1861–65.

combat experience of the two armies. But also, both sides had built reasonably efficient logistical systems and could bring more troops to bear in battle, and to deadlier effect. A monthly death toll for 1861 equal to that for 1862 would have meant another 7,800 Union battlefield deaths—the equivalent of three and a half more Antietams, the bloodiest single day's battle in American history.[19]

The American Civil War, the nation's largest war, began with the largest grassroots military mobilization in the nation's history. But the Civil War was the last time the United States raised an army in this way. The Civil War produced many administrative innovations, most of which ended when the war did. Centralized military procurement, however, remained in place. Many scholars, most famously Stephen Skowronek, have written on the broad expansion of U.S. government power during the latter part of the nineteenth century. Skowronek, however, argues the critical period was 1877 to 1920, when rapid industrialization spurred such government innovations as business regulation and civil service reform. The change in military procurement was another important and permanent accretion of power to the U.S. government. This change occurred earlier, however, and for different reasons than the developments studied by Skowronek and others working on this topic. The change in military procurement may be an anomaly, but there may be a broader story to the growth of U.S. government power than the one told so far.[20]

The change in military procurement had local implications as well. Philip

Paludan and Reid Mitchell have written about Civil War soldiers' strong ties to their home communities, and grassroots military mobilization was another part of this personal connection. Local financing also reinforced community power relations. If the rich men of a neighborhood pooled their money to outfit troops, it was clear whose sons would be officers. The system could be coercive as well. In both the North and the South communities threatened and intimidated people who did not contribute voluntarily. Men who failed to join the new military units might also face trouble. Soldiers sometimes seized malingerers and paraded them through town, stripped to their underwear, as the military band played the Rogues' March. Crowds gathered to watch and take part in these spectacles.[21]

The professionalization of the army was a broad and long-term process, but centralized supply was an important step in weakening this local connection. It also removed one of the means by which antebellum U.S. communities exerted control over their members. The old-fashioned army combined standard military discipline with a certain measure of community scrutiny and control. Before 1862 the U.S. army in wartime, unlike the much smaller peacetime army, was a collective extension of thousands of local communities. Soldiers in the field remained subject to the judgment of people they knew in civilian life. A man's fellow soldiers might report his behavior to the people back home; worse, the story might appear in the local newspaper. The wartime army had no traditions or mystique of its own to counter the community's authority. Almost all the military units raised during the Civil War disbanded after 1865. There was also less distance between officers and men in these volunteer units. Officers were not professionals and did not come from a hereditary caste. They, too, were often men the soldiers had known all their lives, and the survivors all went home together after the war. As the army evolved after 1862, community accountability gradually lost ground to institutional standards of job performance and responsibility.[22]

The long-term changes in the army, to which centralized supply contributed, in some respects paralleled the shift toward professionalism in the banks. There, too, the older institutional form was a decentralized organization, blurring public and private responsibilities and controlled by cliques and cronies for their own benefit. Wealthy and well-connected individuals and families have always bent public agendas to suit themselves, and doubtless they always will. But the long-term trends in banking and the military led away from weak, decentralized aristocratic control and toward strengthened, centralized, impersonal authority. For disempowered groups, a more rule-driven, impersonal public sphere affords a chance, at least, of greater participation and more equal treatment. But for local notables such as antebellum Missouri's planters and bankers, such a change meant a loss of influence.

In other times and places, the changes in the banking industry and in military supply would have been unremarkable. That Missouri's southern elite suffered such disastrous outcomes from these changes was a chance result of geography and a lost gamble. During the secession crisis and the early part of the war, Missouri's pro-southern citizens sent their young men off to fight the same way that Americans did elsewhere. But Missouri was a border state that remained in the Union, and Missouri's Confederates backed the losing side. These people were caught between two wheels, and wound up worse off than other, similarly placed civilians in either section. Because of this historical accident, the records of their great misfortune reveal a previously hidden aspect of the Civil War.

The papers from the thousands of court cases, tied up in yellowing bundles and stored in attics and cellars of rural county courthouses, record the downfall of a class, and they are now the last traces of these people. The legal jargon and the old-fashioned, formulaic language record a calamity that fell on these communities and produced a vicious reaction. It is, in the end, difficult to grasp the full measure of rage experienced by the people trapped in this way. The failed financial conspiracy of 1861 economically destroyed a part of Missouri's southern population that was already in crisis. No one who has been party to a lawsuit wishes to repeat the experience, and each of these families was in several suits at once. All around them, their friends and relatives were caught up in similar litigation, inevitably ending in the forced sale of all their property. In the insular small towns and rural neighborhoods of the Boonslick, these people would have seen an implacable, punitive justice system taking apart the whole social order, at the point of federal bayonets.

Today Missouri's planters are scarcely remembered. But the state's guerrillas have always been in view, as news, scholarship, or entertainment. Yet planters and guerrillas were linked, not only by events, but in their individual members. Part of the history of Missouri's planters is the story of young men of wealth and prospects descending into a life of terrorism and violent criminality. There they allied with people they would never have met before the war, except for one to preside over the other's hanging. Today these young men, raised to high expectations and a sense of their own importance, survive in public memory only as killers. Many of them probably would have preferred oblivion.

APPENDIX 1:
RESEARCH DESIGN AND METHODOLOGY

HISTORIOGRAPHICAL OUTLINE

There are several excellent surveys of antebellum state banking, notably those by Howard Bodenhorn, Bray Hammond, and Larry Schweikart. However, while these books provided valuable background information on the United States' antebellum banking industry, they were of limited use for interpreting Missouri's post-1857 banks. Missouri's 1857 law was not patterned on the law of any other state, but instead used the Bank of Missouri as a template for the new banks the state chartered. John Ray Cable's study, *The Bank of the State of Missouri*, published in 1923, is a useful, but limited, secondary source. Cable surveys and analyzes the major events in the bank's history, but he also omits much. The two books most useful for interpreting Missouri's post-1857 banks are Naomi Lamoreaux's and Noel Maurer's studies of banking in New England and in Mexico, respectively. Both books deal at length with insider control and lending, and Maurer's book also analyzes the Mexican banks' connections with local power groups. The two authors' discussions of the banks' role in financing industry in their respective regions are especially clarifying. Overall, though, antebellum Missouri banks have received little attention, compared to other topics considered in this monograph. To even establish a basic chronology of the banks' history in this period called for a fair amount of primary research.

There is no such shortage of material on Missouri's guerrillas. Unfortunately, much of the guerrilla literature consists of voyeuristic accounts of violent and lurid incidents, such as the massacres at Lawrence and Centralia. The starting point for serious study of the guerrillas is Francis Lieber's *Guerrilla Parties Considered with Reference to the Laws and Usages of War*. Lieber's ideas not only are of historical interest, but also influenced military policy at the time. Lieber identifies guerrillas as one of several types of irregular fighters, which he classifies according to their war aims. Modern historians mainly use Lieber's work as a primary source and bypass his classifications of irregulars. Many historians do, however, agree with Lieber that in some parts of the occupied South the guerrilla violence formed an insurrection. Lieber defined insurrection as "the rising of people in arms against their Government or a portion of it, or against one or more of its laws, or against an officer or officers of the Government. It may be confined to mere armed resistance or it may have greater ends in view." Lieber's definition certainly applies to conditions in Missouri, but it does not help to distinguish the state's guerrilla violence from that in other border states at the time.[1]

Writing about the occupied South in general, Stephen V. Ash describes conditions that fit Lieber's definition of an insurrection as well. In *When the Yankees Came: Conflict and Chaos in the Occupied South, 1861–1865,* Ash argues that guerrillas who harassed Union troops were not soldiers, but citizens. The guerrillas were thus an arm of their communities rather than of the Confederate military. Ash writes, "Though they saw themselves in a general way as part of the Confederate war effort, their war was really a personal and communal one. They rarely traveled far from their home county and were unresponsive to Confederate authority." In Ash's view, the invading Union army was itself a causal agent that created guerrilla warfare. The guerrillas shared a widely held southern ethos of ennoblement through violence, and they acted to defend their honor against a degrading military occupation.[2]

The Confederacy had its own problems with disloyal citizens in its border regions, as described by Noel C. Fisher in *War at Every Door: Partisan Politics and Guerrilla Violence in East Tennessee, 1860–1869.* Once again the pattern is of a civilian insurgency, or uprising against occupying troops, and not an organized resistance coordinated with a conventional military force. During its two-year tenure in East Tennessee, the Confederate government faced spiraling guerrilla violence, growing frustration among regular troops charged with keeping the peace, and blurred distinctions between civilians, guerrillas, and robbers. The arrival of Union forces in 1863 did not bring peace. Instead, the balance of power shifted to the east Tennessee Unionists in their struggles against their pro-southern neighbors, many of whom fled the area.[3]

Most modern works on Civil War guerrilla warfare focus on commonalities across regions and do not address the aberrant features of Missouri's violence, namely its intensity and extent. Two authors who write specifically about the violence in Missouri are Richard S. Brownlee and Michael Fellman. In his classic *Gray Ghosts of the Confederacy: Guerrilla Warfare in the West, 1861–1865,* Brownlee also finds that Union military forces provoked the "great insurrection" on Missouri's western border after 1861. Much evidence supports this view. Responding to a mass outcry against the behavior of Unionist militia, the Missouri General Assembly in 1863 investigated the conduct of the troops. The legislators found problems everywhere, from simple thievery and officers exceeding their authority to rogue units and outright murder. The assembly's report also condemned the behavior of troops brought in from outside the state, especially the Kansans. Brownlee's conclusions, which are similar to those of Ash and Fisher, help explain why there was guerrilla violence in Missouri. Brownlee does not, however, adequately explain why Missouri was different. Union troops occupied vast sections of the South as well, where the population was overwhelmingly pro-Confederate, rather than of mixed loyalties as in Missouri. Yet Missouri experienced more irregular war and higher levels of violence.[4]

Michael Fellman, in his influential work *Inside War: The Guerrilla Conflict in Missouri during the American Civil War,* does address Missouri's singularity. Fellman finds, as do Ash, Fisher, and Brownlee, that occupying military forces in a hostile civilian population contributed to the violence. Southern prejudice against the German-American militia units sent into "English" areas also contributed to the guerrilla attacks. But Fellman also argues that the struggle over Kansas statehood in the 1850s gave Missourians a head start on the guerrilla war. In the Kansas Territory, the brushfire conflict between pro- and antislavery militias created an intensifying cycle of reprisals and counter-reprisals that was well under way by 1861. After the outbreak of the war, the Kansas troops sent to Missouri victimized civilians, and the Missourians responded in kind. Fellman's argument is reasonable and compelling, but surviving evidence is largely anecdotal and inadequate to either prove or disprove his thesis. For instance, as far as I know, surviving sources are too incomplete to trace specific individuals, families, or communities from the Kansas conflict through the Civil War. Except for a few prominent men, including Claiborne Fox Jackson and Joseph O. Shelby, contemporary sources do not name individual Missourians who joined the Kansas proslavery militias.[5]

Brownlee and Fellman are surely correct about the influence of the Kansas legacy. At the time, many well-placed people believed the Kansas-Missouri feud contributed to the guerrilla war. In January 1862 General Halleck directed his subordinate General John Pope to drive the Kansas troops out of the state or, failing that, to disarm them and hold them prisoner. Four months later, in May, Halleck's successor Brigadier General John M. Schofield wrote to Secretary of War Edwin M. Stanton to urge the removal of all Kansas troops from Missouri. After mid-1862, military and civilian authorities largely kept Kansas troops out of Missouri, except for the tier of counties on the states' common border. There, Colorado troops replaced the Kansans in mid-1864. But ill will between Kansans and Missourians was a major issue mainly in these counties and in the next tier of counties to the east. The guerrilla conflict, however, also raged in parts of Missouri where the Kansans had never set foot, a pattern that calls for explanation.[6]

Besides the overall consensus that guerrilla warfare along the Middle Border represented part of a civilian insurrection, most Civil War historians agree that social attitudes, rather than economic issues, were behind the guerrilla violence. Ash, for instance, discounts class warfare as an important issue for the guerrillas, even though poor people in occupied zones sometimes turned against the middle and upper classes, absent the usual peacetime restraints. Instead, Ash views guerrilla warfare as one expression of a larger pattern of extralegal violence directed not only at the invaders but also at other southerners. Ash notes that guerrillas came from every social class and that rich and poor alike in the occupied areas cooperated to intimidate the freedpeople and keep them in their place.[7]

A significant exception to the consensus on the primacy of social attitudes is the work of Don R. Bowen, which anticipates my own findings. Bowen, who also viewed Missouri's irregular war as a civilian insurrection, found that economic causes played an important role in the violence. In a well-known 1977 article, Bowen noted that some guerrillas from Jackson County, Missouri, came from prosperous, even leading, families. Bowen argued that Missouri's guerrilla violence was consistent with the political-science theory of relative deprivation. According to this theory, when people cannot achieve the goals they seek or face the loss of a way of life already attained, then violence can be expected—political violence in particular. Bowen wrote, "If relative deprivation is a plausible explanation of participation in the [Missouri guerrilla] uprising, then something must have happened to the participants in 1861–1865 so that values which they expected to attain became unattainable. Moreover, what occurred cannot have fallen with equal weight upon those who didn't participate or it cannot be the explanatory factor." According to Bowen, it was the prospect of permanent loss of fortune and social position that drove some of these families' young men into guerrilla bands.[8]

Historians and political scientists often reference Bowen's article, but his ideas have inspired little follow-up work. Also, Bowen did not address the question of why the sons of some well-off slaveholding families became guerrillas, while the sons of other such families—in Missouri and in the other slaveholding elites farther south—did not. However, Bowen's research findings and conclusions about guerrillas from Jackson County are fully consistent with my own discovery of the extensive indebtedness. The indebtedness in central and western Missouri (including Jackson County, which had 123 debt cases) created precisely the condition of *selective* relative deprivation that Bowen deduced. Pro-Confederate citizens there had indeed suffered a loss, which did not fall with equal weight even within their own communities.

Besides the violence, the widespread loss of property contributed to other severe social and economic dislocations affecting Missouri's postwar planter persistence, landownership, agricultural practices, and migration patterns. While historians have studied the fate of the planter class in the former Confederate states for decades, Missouri's planters have received little attention. R. Douglas Hurt's *Agriculture and Slavery in Missouri's Little Dixie* presents a detailed picture of Missouri's planter society before the war but says nothing about the post-1865 fortunes of this group. The classic work on the southern planter class in the postwar period is C. Vann Woodward's *Origins of the New South, 1877–1913*. After Reconstruction ended in 1877, Woodward shows that a new class, which he names the "Redeemers," rose to power throughout the South. The Redeemers were not former planters, and their families had not owned slaves before the war. Instead, the Redeemers were a new business class of capitalist entrepreneurs, with bourgeois values and an interest in northeastern-style industrialization and economic progress. These were the men, Woodward argues, who made the New South.[9]

Jonathan Wiener challenged Woodward's thesis in *Social Origins of the New South*, and Wiener's view is now the prevailing one. Wiener studied planters from five Black Belt counties in Alabama and found that few new families came forward after the war. On the contrary, the richest families between 1850 and 1860 were the same as in the following decade. After the war, the plantation families managed to keep control over the newly free black labor force through a mix of gang labor, tenant farming, sharecropping, and debt peonage. In Wiener's Marxist analysis, however, the old elite became a new class by investing in and managing the eventual industrialization of the South. This so-called "Prussian road" to development thus involved the same people acting in new roles in a new relationship to the means of production. Dwight Billings's book *Planters and the Making of the "New South": Class, Politics and Development in North Carolina, 1865–1900* also challenges Woodward's argument of planter decline. Billings finds evidence that North Carolinian planters managed to keep their social and economic primacy after 1865. Unlike Wiener, however, who finds conflict between planters and merchants with the former winning, Billings finds upper-class consensus in North Carolina.[10]

The present monograph uses a method similar to Wiener's, tracking samples of planter families through multiple censuses. In Wiener's and Billings's works, the planter-class persistence in Alabama and North Carolina depended on these families' land ownership after 1865. Many of Missouri's planters lost their land in the mass indebtedness. What happened to Missouri's planters happens to support Woodward's position, but Missouri may be a special case. A second development that did not occur in other southern and border states also affected Missouri's planters. Unlike those states, Missouri received large numbers of immigrants from the Midwest, New England, and abroad after the war. Despite the reputation of the carpetbaggers, most of the heirs to social primacy in the former Confederacy were native-born southerners and locals, rather than newcomers. This was not true in Missouri.

Because of the war-related indebtedness among Missouri's pro-southern population, the later history of the state's planter class is atypical. It is not clear, however, how indebtedness affected planters in other parts of the South during the war. To my knowledge, the present work is the first panel study of a group of planters through the war years that considers indebtedness. In *The Reconstruction of Southern Debtors*, Elizabeth Lee Thompson assesses the impact of the federal Bankruptcy Act of 1867 and the federal courts on the Reconstruction-era South. While Thompson discusses the characteristics of southerners who petitioned for bankruptcy, her analysis does not extend to the source of their debts. Larry Schweikart, in *Banking in the American South from the Age of Jackson to Reconstruction*, gives a general history of southern banking in this period, but scarcely touches on postwar indebtedness. In *Masters Without Slaves*, James Roark recognizes that southern planters after 1865 suffered heavy debt burdens. However, Roark does not consider the origin of these debts or their effect on planter persistence.

Historians have widely varying views about the nature, and even the existence, of Missouri's southern identity. While most historians grant that a cultural transformation occurred in Missouri in the years after the Civil War, there is little agreement about its nature and extent. Christopher Phillips in *Missouri's Confederate: Claiborne Fox Jackson and the Creation of Southern Identity in the Border West* argues that Missourians thought of themselves chiefly as westerners until the Civil War. In Phillips's view, the fight over secession, and especially over slavery, converted Missourians into southerners. After the war, however, Phillips views Missouri's southern identity as problematic. Phillips argues, as did Wilbur J. Cash, that the Civil War and Reconstruction formed southern identity, as "a frontier the Yankees made." C. Vann Woodward makes the same point, arguing that southern identity came from a postwar culture of "frustration, failure, and defeat." In this view, southern identity amounts to a white grudge over the hard experience of invasion and conquest, victors' justice, and occupation during the war and reconstruction years. Such a definition largely precludes a southern identity for Missouri, since the state stayed in the Union and never experienced Reconstruction.[11]

Gary R. Kremer and Lawrence O. Christensen, in *A History of Missouri, 1875 to 1919*, argue there was no single "Missouri character" in the late nineteenth century. Instead, there was then greater loyalty to the state's regions and to local neighborhoods than to the state as a whole. David Thelen in *Paths of Resistance: Tradition and Dignity in Industrializing Missouri* also views the state as made up of separate regional cultures that commanded local loyalty. Thelen argues the state's regional identity changed owing to a confrontation between the traditional values of family and community and a newer culture of individualism and business competition. Thelen describes various kinds of resistance, beginning with "primitive resistance" but including broader and more sophisticated efforts to restore local control. Michael Cassity in *Defending a Way of Life: An American Community in the Nineteenth Century* finds the same attachment to localism in his study of the town of Sedalia in Pettis County, Missouri. In Cassity's view, when the railroad came to Sedalia in 1861 it overturned traditional, nonmarket ways of living and introduced a conflict between precapitalist and capitalist forces. Both Thelen and Cassity use contemporary sources to show that postwar industrialization caused resentment and rear-guard resistance from a mainly agricultural old order.[12]

The present study arrives at a different conclusion. I take no position on what makes up southern character. I believe that any opinion on that question will, as Abraham Lincoln once wrote in another connection, merely furnish a nest full of eggs for hatching new disputes. But regardless of what southern character is, every documentary source that I examined showed that people inside the state and out considered Missouri a southern state in 1861. Today this southern identification no longer prevails, and the turning point for this change was the Civil War. This change did not occur because eastern capitalism destroyed some rural idyll. The pro-southern Missourians who became indebted came disproportionately from the upper strata of Missouri rural society, and for years had been engaging in for-profit commercial agriculture. These men wanted more connection to the national market, not less. Many had been in the forefront of the railroad agitation of the 1850s. The Missourians hurt by the indebtedness violently resisted what they viewed as a tyrannical government, but nothing suggests they were hostile to the capitalist market.[13]

Two other scholars, Michael Fellman and T. J. Stiles, consider the effects of the guerrilla violence on the state's postwar identity. All the border regions saw guerrilla violence, and Missouri shared this legacy of suffering with the Confederacy. Michael Fellman argues that the character of this fighting, combined with the James gang's celebrity and the energetic publicist John Newman Edwards, produced a Missouri variant of the Noble Lost Cause: the Noble Guerrilla. Stiles, also, argues the Noble Guerrilla became a founding myth for a diehard pro-Confederate political faction in the state. I agree, but with some qualifications. After the war, Missouri received more immigrants than any other southern state, and most came from outside the South. The newcomers had different memories of the war than the longer-term residents, and the Noble Lost Cause has long since faded as a topic of public interest in the state. The guerrillas, however, have been the focus of so much media attention, and for so long, that they now form part of the nation's collective consciousness of the Civil War. The guerrillas have left Missouri and moved to Hollywood.[14]

Finally, this study addresses a topic that has so far received almost no attention, private and local financing for military mobilization during the war's early period. Douglas Ball's *Financial Failure and Confederate Defeat* considers military procurement and payment, but takes a top-down, macroeconomic view of the Confederacy's finances and how Richmond handled such issues as taxation, bond issues, and monetary circulation. On the northern side, books on mobilization and military procurement also focus on government action. Mark R. Wilson's *The Business of Civil War: Military Mobilization and the State* considers the relations between the U.S. federal government and private contractors, and the growth of a federal supply bureaucracy. Phillip Paludan's *A People's Contest: The Union and Civil War 1861–1865* and Reid Mitchell's *The Vacant Chair: The Northern Soldier Leaves Home* are histories of the home front in the North and have a more local focus. None of the works mentioned, however, say much about private contributions to the military effort.

Among modern histories, the book that comes closest to my own focus is William B. Hesseltine's *Lincoln and the War Governors*. The first part of Hesseltine's book contains a useful discussion of how state governments in the North responded to the secession crisis during a period when the federal government did nothing. Hesseltine notes that after Lincoln's election and for the following several months, most state governments faced the same problems as the federal government with funding, administrative capacity, and legal authority. However, this is as far back as Hesseltine goes in his coverage of the states' mobilizations. Though the evidence they provide is anecdotal, older state histories often mention the private and local side of military financing. Examples are Byers's *Iowa in War Times*, published in 1888, and Terrell's *Indiana in the War of the Rebellion*, published in 1869. However, the present monograph is the first detailed study of how communities armed and equipped troops.[15]

Modern estimates of the war's total costs also omit private contributions, though through no fault of the authors. For the reasons given in Chapter 8, except for Missouri there are no data sources on which to base a credible calculation. Excluding private contributions, the most thorough accounting of total direct and indirect costs in the Civil War is by Goldin and Lewis, in "The Economic Cost of the American Civil War." The authors calculate a total direct cost to the North of $3,365,846,000 and to the South of $3,285,900,000.[16] Most modern calculations of the war's costs to the states, including that of Goldin and Lewis, rely on U.S. Representative James G. Blaine's 1866 report, "War Debts of the Loyal States, to Accompany H. R. Bill 282." Sinisi, in *Sacred Debts*, the most thorough study so far of U.S. Civil War military claims, also cites Blaine's report for total U.S. state government outlays.[17]

Blaine, however, did not attempt to calculate the total costs of the war to each state. Instead, Blaine prepared his report to document what the U.S. government owed the states for their war spending, under the act of July 27, 1861. Blaine calculated the federal government owed $467,954,364 to the non-seceding states for their military expenses, enough to raise fears of federal bankruptcy. Even so, Blaine's report covered only a fraction of the war's total direct costs, even for the North. Blaine's report excluded expenses the states paid out of current revenue rather than through bond sales and all money paid directly by the federal government, which dwarfed state spending. Nor did Blaine's report include any indirect costs, such as capital destruction, lost productivity, pensions, or bond interest.[18]

For the South's war outlays, Goldin's main source for direct costs is Todd's *Confederate Finance*. However, Todd calculates state outlays only as war tax assessments the Confederate government levied against the states. Todd omits the states' own war spending and claims the states presented to the Confederate government under its two acts of August 30, 1861. Todd estimates the Confederate treasury received two million dollars in private donations for the war effort, but he states that this is a guess and that it is impossible to know the true figure. Available evidence, though scattered (for example, George A. Trenholm's contributions, which Todd cites), suggests that two million dollars is improbably low. Also,

Todd considers only contributions to the Confederate treasury and not contributions made directly to the troops.[19]

Looking at Missouri only, Blaine calculated that the federal government owed $9,446,575 to the state for its military outlays. Missouri evidently agreed; after the war the state claimed nine million dollars from the United States, of which the state eventually received a little over seven million dollars. This figure, however, significantly understates the total cost of the war to the Union side in the state. On August 24, 1861, Missouri's provisional governor, Hamilton Gamble, took the first steps to create a new Unionist military force, which became the Missouri State Militia. The Lincoln administration underwrote all expenses for these troops, which would remain within the state to defend the state's Unionist government. The U.S. government also supplied Missouri State Militia troops out of U.S. army quartermasters' depots. Since these expenses were paid directly by the U.S. War Department, they do not appear on any accounting of war outlays made by the Missouri state government. Other source documents on U.S. government military outlays only give total figures for different items, for instance uniforms, but do not show which military commands received them. Finally, Missouri's provisional government initially paid the expenses of another military organization, the Enrolled Missouri Militia, out of assessments and confiscations of rebel property. No surviving sources show how much money was collected by such means. Too many unknowns exist to push this analysis further. Even if precise figures for military outlays could be calculated, Missouri was far from typical. Citizens of border states such as Missouri probably spent much more on armament than did citizens elsewhere. The war in the border states was right outside—and sometimes inside—people's doors, and it was a matter of self-defense as well as politics. Also, the state governments' war spending varied enormously, from $800,000 for Kansas to $111 million for New York.[20]

PRIMARY RESEARCH — STUDY DESIGN

This study grew out of an archival find, and the events recounted here were either previously unknown or else thought unconnected. Though many historians find financial sources off-putting, the main reason that researchers have overlooked this story is that many obstacles impede access to the data. The most important primary source, the circuit court records, are scattered over forty rural counties, a region the size of West Virginia. Also, traditional primary sources, such as newspapers, make almost no direct reference to the indebtedness. (Surviving newspapers refer indirectly to the indebtedness, in the form of legal notices for property sales.) After mid-1861, Union authorities in Missouri closed prosouthern newspapers and censored the rest. For much of the interior of the state no complete runs of newspaper issues exist before 1867 or 1868, long after the debt business was over. Union military records contain no obvious references to the indebtedness. The indebtedness did not result from a coordinated plot, but probably spread by word of mouth among the branch bankers. The bankers were prominent southern sympathizers, but Union military commanders handled each situation locally, as part of their efforts to cut off all assistance to the rebels.

For these reasons, data for this study had to be gathered piecemeal. Archives, newspaper accounts, and government documents contained the necessary material on Governor Jackson's intrigues in 1861. However, most of the critical evidence and the main outlines of the story came from large data pools that needed much analysis. The problem was not too little data but rather too much, and too widely scattered. The best line of inquiry was seldom obvious. To avoid wild-goose chases, I would make an early guess and then do exploratory research with a limited number of cases. If the results looked promising, I would draw a larger sample. What worked, finally, was a combination of microhistorical and quantitative research techniques.

PRIMARY SOURCES AND DATA COLLECTION

Three main types of primary-source data formed the basis of this study: circuit court records of defaulted debt cases, quarterly financial-performance data on the banks, and records of Missouri general assembly and state supreme court proceedings. The county circuit court records were the most important single source of data and the basis for everything that followed. A fourth important category of data was biographical, demographic, and genealogical information on defendants and bankers. These data came from a mix of primary and secondary sources.

Circuit clerks summarized the results of each case heard during the court sessions, and the minute books were the starting point for investigation. In the 1860s, however, the clerks recorded civil, criminal, chancery, and petty claims cases in a common journal. Entries on a mass of other proceedings ranging from treason and murder to unlicensed dram shops obscured the debt cases. Courts heard each debt case multiple times before judgment, resulting in multiple entries in the minute books. Owing to the legal shorthand used by the clerks and poor or nonexistent indexing, it was often difficult to tell which entries belonged together. The entries for "*William H. Trigg v. Nathaniel Sutherlin, et al.*" in the Cooper County Circuit Court minute books referred to five separate suits, with different groups of defendants, brought for defaulted notes written in 1861. Entries summarized cases in formulaic, nineteenth-century legal jargon, and entries usually differed only in the names of plaintiffs and defendants, and the monetary amount. The following is an example:

Bank of St. Louis
against
Walker H. Finley Geo Anderson
Wm A. Finley Franklin Plummer
Now on this day comes the plaintiff by her attorney and the defendants though legally served and Solemnly called come not but make default and this cause is taken up and submitted to the Court and the Court finds that said defendants are indebted to said plaintiff in the sum of thirty two hundred eighteen 45/100 dollars the same being founded on a note for the direct payment of money at 10 per cent interest
It is therefore adjudged by the Court that said plaintiff recover against said defendants the said sum of thirty-two hundred and eighteen 45/100 dollars together with his costs in this behalf expended and that she have therefor execution.[21]

As this example shows, entries in the minute books contain raw data on monetary amounts, names of plaintiffs and defendants, and timing of different steps in the court proceedings. The court papers, as distinct from the minute books, filed for each case contained many important details, including the names of all defendants and often either the original promissory note or a copy. The Missouri State Archives in Jefferson City has microfilms of the court records, but many of the films are of poor quality and unreadable. Often the only alternative was to go to the courthouse holding the original records. These materials were often in bad condition, crumbling at the touch, recorded in faded ink, jumbled, and sometimes incomplete. Many documents were barely legible, and had to be scanned and digitally enhanced. Fortunately, the calligraphy was usually good, and sometimes wonderful.

Since the circuit court papers recorded the names of the defendants and the banks, these records were also the starting point for finding biographical information on individuals. Knowing the name of the bank made it possible to discover the names of bank officers and directors, usually from St. Louis newspapers. The population schedules in the manuscript census returns for 1860 gave a basic profile on individuals named, as well as data on other members of their households. The agricultural and slave schedules of the census provided more information, as did marriage records, tombstone inscriptions, county histories, wills, obituaries, genealogical databases, and military and provost-marshal records. Research on individual St. Louis bank promoters, planters, and guerrillas progressed in much the same way.

The banks' reconstructed financial records for the period 1861–65 showed when the banks discounted the notes, when the notes defaulted, the total amount of money involved, and the impact on the banks' financial condition. The 1857 banking law required the banks to publish quarterly financial data in major newspapers near each bank's principal business location. The parent branches of seven of the state's nine chartered banks were in St. Louis, and the newspapers there continued uninterrupted publication throughout the war. The best single source for these data was the *St. Louis Triweekly Missouri Republican*, but the *Daily Missouri Republican* and the *Daily Missouri Democrat* helped close gaps. The parent branch of the Farmers' Bank of Missouri was in Lexington, Missouri, and the nearest important newspaper was the *Liberty Tribune*. *Bankers' Magazine* and the *St. Joseph Morning Herald* were also helpful sources.

The banks' financial data needed much processing to yield useful information. The banks used nineteenth-century financial terminology, sometimes inconsistently. Also, individual branch banks published their own, unconsolidated data, making it possible to discover which banks accepted promissory notes. However, to get a picture of the banks' overall financial condition required consolidating branch-bank data for each of the nine banks, for each quarterly reporting period between January 1861 and December 1865. Next, each bank's balance sheet and income statement could be reconstructed from the consolidated data. Lastly, I used the financial statements to calculate financial ratios and to plot time series of key measures. The financial ratios are not precise, however. The banks' published data sometimes contained mathematical errors and the newspapers printing the data made misprints, which showed up when more than one newspaper published the same data. The banks' original books of record have not survived, so a few such errors remain unresolved.[22]

Legal sources included the published volumes of session laws and the journals of the

Missouri house and senate, as well as the much more fragmentary records of Missouri's Confederate government-in-exile. The house and senate journals provide a more summary account of the legislative sessions than such journals do today. St. Louis newspapers reported on the legislative proceedings, however, and filled in many gaps. The complete opinions of the Missouri Supreme Court were printed in the reports of that court and thoroughly indexed.

Contemporary newspapers also added useful information. After the outbreak of fighting in Missouri in June 1861 many of the country newspapers shut down, voluntarily or otherwise. Also, many issues of smaller newspapers have not survived. Arrow Rock, in Saline County, had two newspapers in 1861; not a single issue of either one survives today. A few papers in the interior of the state published uninterruptedly throughout the war, including the Columbia, Jefferson City, and Liberty newspapers. Such papers as a rule only reported local news from their home counties or nearby and major war items reprinted from the St. Louis papers. The St. Louis papers published throughout the war, but usually printed little news from the interior. Still, sometimes the St. Louis papers reprinted items from local newspapers that have not survived. Besides local, regional, and statewide newspapers, major eastern newspapers, such as the *New York Times*, the *New York Herald*, and the *Charleston Mercury* sometimes printed news from Missouri. Such coverage was haphazard but could give a valuable outside perspective on developments in the state.[23]

SAMPLING

To keep the study manageable, I selected a nonrandom judgment sample of three central and adjoining Boonslick counties: Cooper, Pettis, and Saline. There, the banks filed 310 debt suits against 369 defendants, about 11 percent of the total statewide, for promissory notes written between May 15, 1861, and June 30, 1862. I chose these counties because they are in the center of the main cluster of counties with the largest number of debt cases, and their records were intact. It was important to choose adjoining counties because defendants named in a case sometimes lived one county over. Also, a significant number of defendants signed notes in more than one county, which a sample of non-adjoining counties would have missed. To be certain the sample counties were typical of other counties with similar debt cases, I took a less detailed look at the court records of more distant counties.

Some of these samples were used to form benchmark comparisons for the different groups studied: bankers, defendants, planters, and guerrillas. Also, when considering such questions as population composition and demographic change, it was important to compare developments in Missouri to what was happening in other southern and western states. Slavery and slaveholding, in particular, differed in Missouri in several respects from the states that formed the Confederacy. Because almost all of this research is at the county, household, and individual level, there was little opportunity to use IPUMS data. The University of Virginia's Historical Census Browser extracted useful summaries of census data at the county and state level. Other summary statistics came from the decennial volumes published by the Bureau of the Census. Census data on specific individuals came from scanned images of the manuscript censuses available online at www.ancestry.com.

ANALYTICAL AND INTERPRETIVE ISSUES

Except for the records of the Missouri general assembly and the state supreme court, all the data sets studied were large enough to make data management and analysis a problem. Also, the court cases and the people who figured in them had complex interrelationships. Each defendant, for example, could appear in multiple cases, and each case could have multiple defendants. Individuals could also appear on multiple lists, as defendants, bankers, planters, and guerrillas. Finally, most of the people involved had kinship ties with one another, which played an important role in the events described. Relational-database software, Microsoft Access 2003, made data management easier. Analysis of the banks' financial measures was separate from everything else, requiring forensic accounting, financial-statement reconstruction, and eventually trend and ratio analysis.

A problem throughout this study is that key data sets are incomplete. Historians work with eroded sources all the time, and even the best historical data sets are seldom up to modern standards. However, this book attempts to provide answers to some questions of long-standing interest, and data quality is a serious issue. There are not enough data to answer any of the following questions:

1. The total amount of private money that Missouri's Confederates raised. The court records of many counties have not survived. Surviving court records do not show debts that borrowers paid off; such transactions would appear only in the banks' own books of record. Except for the account books of William H. Trigg & Company, a private banking firm in Boonville, none of the banks' original records from this period survive. An analysis of Trigg & Co.'s records, however, suggests borrowers paid off few defaulted loans. In the three sample counties, Trigg discounted eighty-six promissory notes the signers later defaulted. Trigg had to file suit on every single note.[24]

2. The total amount of private money that Missouri's Unionists raised. These data are so scattered they might as well be at the bottom of the ocean.

3. How likely young men from indebted families were to join guerrilla bands, compared to young men from nonindebted families. As explained in Chapter 6, the best answer the data will support is that young men from indebted families were more likely to join the guerrillas. There is, first of all, no good way to estimate the number of individuals, or families, that supported the rebellion in Missouri. Second, we not only do not have the names of all the guerrillas, but we do not know how many names are missing.

Answers to questions one and two are out of reach. For question three, some fragmentary data are available. In instances where some data were available but the data were insufficient, I used a construct-validity research strategy. That is, I tried to answer the same or related questions by designing multiple tests using different data sources. The idea is that a test has a greater likelihood of being correct if its results are consistent with those of other tests.

Another analytical problem was to identify and exclude ordinary defaulted loans from the data set. People bounce checks all the time, and the Civil War wreaked great havoc on

Missouri's economy. Debts incurred to arm rebel military units differed from simple bad debt cases as follows:

1. Southern military debt cases occurred in a pattern of small groups of individuals writing multiple promissory notes back and forth to one another. Simple bad debt cases did not show this pattern.

2. The defendants in southern military debt cases were uniformly southern sympathizers. Defendants in simple bad debt cases were of varying political sympathies. If data from other sources, such as militia rosters, showed that one or more of the signers was pro-Union, I excluded the case from the sample set.

3. Southern military debt cases occurred in counties that had a large slave population before the war.

4. There were no southern military debt cases anyplace where federal forces maintained uninterrupted control, such as St. Louis, Jefferson City, or Cape Girardeau.

5. German-American Missourians were almost all pro-Union, and southern military debt cases have almost no German-surnamed defendants.

These guidelines excluded most of the ordinary bad debt cases, but a few ambiguous cases remained. I did a final screening for ordinary bad debt cases using the R. G. Dun & Company credit reports, preserved in the Baker Library at the Harvard Business School. Defaulters on ordinary debts were often in financial difficulty before the war started, and Dun's correspondents noted such problems.

APPENDIX 2:
CALCULATIONS

SUMMARY

Calculations A–J are based on the three-county sample (Cooper, Pettis, and Saline). Calculations K–R are statewide measures.

A. Average number of endorsers per promissory note

    2.23 obligors/note

    1   payee/note

    3.23 total endorsers/note

B. Average judgment amount per promissory note, 1861 dollars

    $1,181.31

C. Average face amount per promissory note, 1861 dollars

    $1,017.54

D. Ratio of average judgment amount to average face amount

    1 : 0.8983

E. Three-county total face amount of promissory notes, 1861 dollars

    $315,437.40

F. Average debt obligation per signer, 1861 dollars

    $825.24

G. Average debt obligation as a percentage of signers' 1860 property

    8.8 percent of real property

    4.9 percent of all property

H. Promissory-note signers as a percentage of adult white male population

    4.6 percent

I. Promissory-note signers who were household heads as a percentage of all household heads

    6.2 percent

J. Promissory-note signers as a percentage of adult white male southern sympathizers

    10.6 percent

K. Total number of borrowers statewide

   3,487

L. Total face amount of promissory notes statewide, 1861 dollars

   $2,981,392.20

M. Total face amount of promissory notes statewide, 2008 dollars

   1. Calculated using the change in the consumer price index from 1860 to 2008

      $76,678,425.99

   2. Calculated in equivalent purchases of military sidearms

      $96,895,246.50

N. Total judgment amount statewide, 1861 dollars

   $3,461,238.30

O. Total acreage sold because of promissory note court judgments

   346,214 acres

P. Number of military encounters between hostile forces in indebted counties vs. in nonindebted counties, 1861–65

   Indebted counties: 11.7

   Nonindebted counties: 5.9

Q. Ratio of Missouri 1860 tax revenue to total promissory note borrowing

   1 : 1.76

R. Total number of eligible Missouri voters, 1860

   239,599

CALCULATION DETAILS

A. Average number of endorsers per promissory note[1]

There were a total of 310 promissory note cases in the three counties (Appendix 4). Each case corresponded to a single promissory note. The notes had a total of 1,001 endorsements. Nine hundred seventy-nine of these endorsements could be traced to 369 individual signers. The remaining 22 endorsements were illegible. The number of signers (endorsers) per promissory note therefore equals:

1001/310 notes = 3.23

The endorsements were by both obligors and by payees. Each promissory note had one or more obligors and a single payee. The average number of obligors per note thus equals:

3.23 − 1 = 2.23

B. Average judgment amount per promissory note, 1861 dollars[2]

The judgment amount equals the face amount of the original promissory note, plus accrued interest and court costs. Of the total 310 cases in the three counties, 279 were seen through to judgment. Thirty-one cases, or 10 percent, were apparently settled out of court. In the 279 cases, the cumulative dollar amount of judgments was $329,586.81. The average judgment for the 279 cases thus equals:

$329,586.81/279 = $1,181.31

C. Average face amount per promissory note, 1861 dollars[3]

In the three-county sample, there were 159 cases for which both the original amount of the note and the judgment amount are known. For these 159 cases, the face amount of the original notes totaled $161,788.48. The total judgment amount in these cases was $180,101.12. The average face amount for these 159 notes thus equals:

$161,788.48/159 = $1,017.54

The average judgment amount for these 159 notes equals:

$180,101.12/159 = $1,132.71

This figure is close to the average judgment figure for the 279 total cases that proceeded to judgment (Calculation B).

D. Ratio of average judgment amount to average face amount

Expressed as a proportion of the judgment amount, the face amount for these 159 notes (Calculation C) equals:

$180,101.12 : $161,788.48

or:

1 : 0.8983

E. Three-county total face amount of promissory notes, 1861 dollars

The total face amount of the notes written in Cooper, Pettis, and Saline Counties can be estimated by multiplying the average face amount (Calculation C) by the total number of notes:

$1,017.54 × 310 = $315,437.40

F. Average debt obligation per signer, 1861 dollars

The total face amount of the 310 promissory notes signed in the three counties was estimated at $315,437.40 (Calculation E). Under the law, all endorsers to a defaulted debt instrument are liable for repayment. A total of 1,001 endorsements appeared on these notes (Calculation A). Each endorsement therefore obligated the signer, on average, to pay:

$315,437.40/1,001 = $315.12

Twenty-two of the endorsements (2.2 percent), however, were illegible, and the signers could not be identified. Also, of the total 369 signers that could be identified, seven could not be located in the manuscript census. These seven individuals signed thirty-one separate promissory notes. Thus, of the total face amount of the promissory notes signed in the three counties, 53 endorsements' worth (22 + 31) represented debt assumed by an unknown number of persons, with unknown property holdings. The total amount of these obligations can be estimated at:

53 × $315.12 = $16,701.36

The total debt assumed by the 362 individual signers with known property holdings (369 − 7) can be estimated at:

$315,437.40 − $16,701.36 = $298,736.04

On average, therefore, each of the 362 individual signers with known property holdings obligated himself to pay:

$298,736.04/362 = $825.24

However, nineteen of these 362 signers owned no property of any kind. In the event of a default, no creditor would bother trying to recover from the men with no property. As a practical matter, then, the 343 (362 − 19) signers who owned property were the ones who would have to repay the debts. These signers had, therefore, in effect assumed an average debt obligation of:

$298,736.04/343 = $870.95

G. Average debt obligation as a percentage of signers' 1860 property[4]

The 362 signers with known property had obligated themselves to repay a face amount of $298,736.04 (Calculation F). According to their statements to the census takers, these signers owned real and personal property worth:

real property + personal property = total property
$3,402,465 + $2,702,496 = $6,104,961

As a percentage of the signers' real property, the signers' indebtedness was:

$298,736.04/$3,402,465 = .088 = 8.8 percent

As a percentage of the signers' total real and personal property, the signers' indebtedness was:

$298,736.04/$6,104,961 = .049 = 4.9 percent

H. Promissory note signers as a percentage of adult white male population[5]

Of 369 promissory note signers named in the debt cases in the three counties, 364 were men. In 1860 the counties had 7,931 white males aged twenty and over. The percentage of the counties' adult white males who signed promissory notes was therefore:

364/7,931 = .046 = 4.6 percent

I. Promissory note signers who were household heads as a percentage of all household heads[6]

In 1860 the three counties had 5,408 household heads. Of the 362 signers who could be identified in the manuscript census (Calculation F), 332, or 91.7 percent, were household heads. Of the seven that could not be identified in the manuscript census, the number of household heads can be estimated at:

$7 \times 0.917 = 6.4$

The total number of promissory note signers who were household heads was therefore about:

$332 + 6 = 338$

The percentage of household heads in the three counties who signed promissory notes thus equaled:

$338/5,409 = .062 = 6.2$ percent

J. Promissory note signers as a percentage of adult white male southern sympathizers[7]

Promissory note signers can in theory be compared to white male supporters of the rebellion, but there is no good way to determine how many persons there were in the latter group. A list of voters' names published in a Cooper County newspaper in 1866 gives a rough measure for that county. The list divided the county's voters into two categories, "accepted" (allowed to vote) and "rejected" (could not vote owing to their support for the rebellion). However, the list does not include voters who died or emigrated during the war, although it does include recent immigrants and men who came of age between 1861 and 1866. In this list, 464 voters (out of 1,995 total) were disqualified from voting owing to their support of the rebellion. The classification is itself suspect. The Radical Union party dominated Missouri politics in 1866, and the party took every excuse to disenfranchise Democrats and prevent them from voting. Even so, this admittedly imperfect source is the best we have. Based on this information, the percentage of the county's voters who supported the rebellion equaled:

$464/1,995 = .233 = 23.3$ percent

The list of voters, however, only contains 1,995 names, though in 1860 Cooper County had 4,298 white males aged 20 and over. Making some heroic assumptions, if the total number of adult white males in 1860 supported the rebellion in the same proportion as the 1866 voters, then the number of adult white male southern sympathizers in the county equaled:

$4,298 \times .233 = 1,001$

In the three-county sample of 310 promissory note cases, 106 signers lived in Cooper County in 1860. The percentage of Cooper County's adult white male southern sympathizers who signed promissory notes can thus be estimated at:

$106/1001 = .106 = 10.6$ percent

It would be a mistake to put much reliance in this number, but it seems safe to say that a small minority of southern sympathizers signed promissory notes.

K. Total number of borrowers statewide[8]

Each of the 310 promissory notes litigated in the three-county sample was signed by at least two persons. Altogether, a total of 369 separate individuals (ignoring illegible signatures) signed the notes. The number of unique signers per note in those counties thus equaled:

369/310 = 1.19

Statewide, surviving court records show forty counties with ten or more southern debt cases, for 2,930 cases in all. The total number of signers statewide can therefore be estimated at:

1.19 × 2,930 = 3,487

This is a conservative estimate. The total would be higher if the (unknown) number of signers who made the 22 illegible endorsements could be included.

L. Total face amount of promissory notes statewide, 1861 dollars

The total face amount of promissory notes statewide can be estimated by multiplying the average face amount per note (Calculation C) by the total number of promissory notes statewide. The total face amount of promissory notes statewide is therefore:

$1,017.54 × 2,930 = $2,981,392.20

M. Total face amount of promissory notes statewide, 2008 dollars[9]

1. *Calculated using the change in the consumer price index from 1860 to 2008*

From 1860 until 2003 (1860 = 100), the consumer price index for all items increased to 2,198, or by a factor of 2,198/100 = 21.98. According to the U.S. Bureau of Labor Statistics, from December 2003 to December 2008, the last full year available, the consumer price index increased from 184.0 to 215.303, or by a factor of 1.170. Therefore, from 1860 to the end of 2008, consumer prices increased by a factor of:

21.98 × 1.170 = 25.719

In 1861, Missouri's southern sympathizers raised about $2,981,392.20 using promissory notes (Calculation L). In December 2008 dollars, this sum would have equaled:

$2,981,392.20 × 25.719 = $76,678,425.99

2. *Calculated in purchases of military sidearms*

In 1861 the state-of-the-art military sidearm was the .44 caliber Colt's New Model Army revolver, which sold for twenty dollars (see Introduction). The money raised by the promissory note signers would have bought:

$2,981,392.20/$20 = 149,070 sidearms

Since 1985, the standard U.S. Army sidearm has been the Beretta M-9 pistol, sold to the public as the 92FS, for a manufacturer's suggested retail price of $650. To buy the same number of M-9s today, Missouri's southern sympathizers would have had to collect:

149,070 × $650 = $96,895,246.50

N. Total judgment amount statewide, 1861 dollars

The average judgment amount per promissory note in the three-county sample was $1,181.31 (Calculation B). There were a total of 2,930 promissory note cases statewide, so the total judgment amount statewide can be estimated at:

$1,181.31 × 2,930 = $3,461,238.30

O. Total acreage sold because of promissory note court judgments[10]

Not all promissory note cases resulted in property sales. Sometimes plaintiffs and defendants settled out of court. Some defendants were able to pay the judgments against them, while others might have no real property to sell. In Cooper County, 68 promissory note cases were litigated. These cases resulted in 34 known property sales, for a total of 8,035 acres and 10 town lots. (Cases settled out of court may have occasioned further property sales.) Ignoring the town lots, the average amount of acreage sold in Cooper County for each promissory note case equaled:

8,035/68 = 118.2 acres

For the 2,930 cases statewide, the total acreage sold as a result of the defaulted debts can be estimated at:

118.2 × 2,930 = 346,214 acres

P. Number of military encounters between hostile forces in indebted counties vs. in nonindebted counties, 1861–65[11]

Over the course of the war, there were approximately 945 clashes between hostile military forces in Missouri. In 904 instances, the county in which the fight took place can be identified. In the rest (for instance, "pursuit of Reeves," which occurred between December 23 and December 25, 1863), no county can be identified. Over the course of the war, the 40 counties with ten or more promissory note cases had a total of 468 military encounters between hostile forces. The remaining 74 nonindebted counties had a total of 436 military encounters. Thus, indebted counties had:

468/40 = 11.7 military encounters/county

Nonindebted counties had:

436/74 = 5.9 military encounters/county

Q. Ratio of Missouri 1860 tax revenue to total promissory note borrowing[12]

In 1860, the Missouri state government collected $1,691,934 in tax revenue. Missouri's southern sympathizers raised an estimated $2,981,392.20 using promissory notes (Calculation L). The ratio of promissory note borrowing to 1860 Missouri tax revenues is:

$1,691,934 : $2,981,392.20

or:

1 : 1.76

Put another way, Missouri's southern sympathizers raised more than one and one-half times the state's entire tax revenue in the last year of peacetime.

R. Total number of eligible Missouri voters, 1860[13]

Missourians cast 165,563 votes in the 1860 presidential election, estimated to be 69.1 percent of the state's total eligible voters. The total number of eligible voters in Missouri in 1860 was therefore about:

165,563/.691 = 239,599

APPENDIX 3:
PROMISSORY NOTE CASES—
THREE-COUNTY SAMPLE

The foundation of this study is an analysis of a three-county sample of the estimated 2,930 debt cases statewide that resulted from the banking conspiracy. The following is a list of the 310 circuit cases for defaulted debts arising out of the banking conspiracy for Cooper, Pettis, and Saline Counties. Each bibliographical reference—Book 8, for instance, in the first case, below—is to the entry in the circuit court minute book for when the case was adjudicated. To keep the cases straight, I assigned each one a unique alphanumeric code—CO633023, in the first case listed below. As of this writing, the circuit clerks in the different counties have custody of the original minute books. The Missouri State Archives in Jefferson City have microfilmed the minute books as part of the Archives' Local Records Preservation Program, but the microfilm is of uneven quality.

A. COOPER COUNTY—68 CASES

Cooper County Circuit Court records, Boonville, Missouri.

Bank of St. Louis v. Alfred Simmons, J. W. Bassett, Richard V. Simmons; adjudicated March 13, 1863. Book 8, p. 409 (CO633023).

Bank of St. Louis v. Charles M. McCormick, David Smith, Charles H. F. Greenlease; adjudicated September 9, 1863. Book 8, p. 410 (CO633026).

Bank of St. Louis v. Charles McCormick, Henry M. Meyers, Charles H. F. Greenlease; adjudicated September 11, 1863. Book 8, p. 581 (CO633025).

Bank of St. Louis v. David Smith, William Rankin, James Rankin; adjudicated March 13, 1863. Book 8, p. 411 (CO633031).

Bank of St. Louis v. Edward Chilton, Van Tromp Chilton, John J. Chilton; adjudicated February 17, 1863. Book 8, p. 325 (CO633036).

Bank of St. Louis v. Elisha W. Warfield, Administrator of John W. Young, deceased, Charles P. Alexander, John D. Stephens; adjudicated March 13, 1863. Book 8, p. 412 (CO633033).

Bank of St. Louis v. Elisha W. Warfield, Horace H. Brand; adjudicated March 13, 1863. Book 8, p. 409 (CO633021).

Bank of St. Louis v. George W. Miller, Gideon B. Miller, John Miller, L. W. Robinson; adjudicated February 28, 1868. Book 10, p. 98 (CO633193).

Bank of St. Louis v. James F. Conner, Henry Bousfield; March 23, 1863. Book 8, p. 474 (CO633204).

Bank of St. Louis v. James J. Harris, George W. Helm, John F. Drinkwater, James Y. Harris; adjudicated March 13, 1863. Book 8, p. 413 (CO633037).

Bank of St. Louis v. James Y. Harris, George W. Helm, Edward Hazell, James J. Harris; adjudicated March 3, 1863. Book 8, p. 472 (CO633030).

Bank of St. Louis v. James Y. Harris, James J. Harris, Frank Cole, George W. Helm; adjudicated September 9, 1863. Book 8, p. 561 (CO633141).

Bank of St. Louis v. Richard T. Ellis, Administrator for Richard P. Ellis, deceased, Thomas V. Ellis, H. W. Ferguson, Richard T. Ellis; adjudicated March 13, 1863. Book 8, p. 411 (CO633027).

Bank of St. Louis v. Thomas Monroe, J. F. Taylor, David Smith, W. W. Williams; adjudicated March 28, 1863. Book 8, p. 494 (CO633029).

Bank of St. Louis v. William B. Alexander, William Snyder, John P. Maddox, Marcus Williams; adjudicated March 28, 1863. Book 8, p. 494 (CO633024).

Bank of St. Louis v. William B. Short, Isaac Gearhart, William J. Smith, Daniel Berger; adjudicated February 18, 1863. Book 8, p. 325 (CO633034).

Bank of St. Louis v. William Rankin, James Rankin, S. S. Seat, J. H. Berry; adjudicated September 10, 1863. Book 8, p. 560 (CO633028).

William H. Trigg & Co. v. Alfred Simmons, J. T. Patton, Richard V. Simmons; adjudicated September 12, 1861. Book 8, p. 250 (CO619105).

William H. Trigg & Co. v. Andrew Meyers, William M. Taylor, Thomas J. Hughes, Samuel Hughes; adjudicated August 29, 1867. Book 9, p. 638 (CO61900G).

William H. Trigg & Co. v. Aquillus R. Priest, G. S. Priest, John W. Jamison, Nathaniel Sutherlin, William E. Jamison; adjudicated September 12, 1861. Book 8, p. 274 (CO619054).

William H. Trigg & Co. v. C. A. Phillips, Richard Van Simmons, T. C. Houx, Oliver Zeller, trustee of M. E. Phillips, deceased); adjudicated March 11, 1863. Book 8, p. 386 (CO633167).

William H. Trigg & Co. v. Edward Chilton, John J. Chilton, Van Tromp Chilton; adjudicated March 3, 1863. Book 8, p. 342 (CO633070).

William H. Trigg & Co. v. Edward Grey, Marcus Williams, William S. McCarty, Isaac McKee; adjudicated January 15, 1864. Book 9, p. 122 (CO633008).

William H. Trigg & Co. v. George W. Wallace, George Anderson, William A. Finley, Walker H. Finley; adjudicated September 11, 1863. Book 8, p. 587 (CO633086).

William H. Trigg & Co. v. George W. Wallace, Thomas S. Williams, Nathaniel Sutherlin; adjudicated March 11, 1863. Book 8, p. 384 (CO633083).

William H. Trigg & Co. v. George W. Wallace, William M. Rucker, Nathaniel Sutherlin; adjudicated September 9, 1863. Book 8, p. 536 (CO633001).

William H. Trigg & Co. v. Green S. Donthitt, Martin J. Warren, E. E. Rucker, Thomas A. Rucker; adjudicated March 13, 1863. Book 8, pg. 430 (CO61900C).

William H. Trigg & Co. v. H. A. B. Johnston, Samuel Wear, George L. Bell, E. C. Evans, Lawrence Woolery; adjudicated September 9, 1863. Book 8, p. 523 (CO633007).

William H. Trigg & Co. v. J. A. Hughes, Samuel Hughes, Thomas J. Hughes, George Lick-lider, Thomas Licklider; adjudicated March 11, 1863. Book 8, p. 377 (CO633011).

William H. Trigg & Co. v. J. J. Eubank, R. P. Eubank, Nancy Eubank, A. J. Eubank; adjudicated March 13, 1863. Book 8, p. 163 (CO61900D).

William H. Trigg & Co. v. J. W. Bassett, Richard Van Simmons; adjudicated March 11, 1863. Book 8, p. 378 (CO633006).

William H. Trigg & Co. v. James H. Hay, Walker H. Finley, S. P. Aldridge; adjudicated March 11, 1863. Book 8, p. 380 (CO633072).

William H. Trigg & Co. v. James J. Harris, George W. Helm, James Y. Harris; adjudicated March 11, 1863. Book 8, p. 379 (CO633045).

William H. Trigg & Co. v. James J. Harris, Samuel T. Melvin, Thomas M. Harris; adjudicated March 11, 1863. Book 8, p. 377 (CO633010).

William H. Trigg & Co. v. James Y. Harris, James J. Harris, James J. Harris, Jr.; adjudicated March 3, 1863. Book 8, p. 408 (CO633017).

William H. Trigg & Co. v. John P. Maddox, E. J. Bedwell, W. Weiland, Louis Weyland [sic]; adjudicated March 11, 1863. Book 8, p. 383 (CO633071).

William H. Trigg & Co. v. John T. Thornton, B. G. Tutt, Thomas McClanahan, Presley P. Thornton; adjudicated September 9, 1863. Book 8, p. 538 (CO633093).

William H. Trigg & Co. v. John W. Bryant, Vincent Marmaduke, Thomas Rodgers; adjudicated December 1, 1866. Book 9, p. 490 (CO619084).

William H. Trigg & Co. v. Nathaniel Sutherlin, George W. Wallace, Thomas S.[?]. Williams; adjudicated March 13, 1863. Book 8, p. 417 (CO633084).

William H. Trigg & Co. v. Nathaniel Sutherlin, Nathaniel T. Allison, James H. Hay; adjudicated March 13, 1863. Book 8, p. 407 (CO633016).

William H. Trigg & Co. v. Nathaniel Sutherlin, Walker H. Finley, William E. Jamison; adjudicated March 28, 1863. Book 8, p. 504 (CO633069).

William H. Trigg & Co. v. Nathaniel Sutherlin, William M. Rucker, Thomas S. Williams; adjudicated March 13, 1863. Book 8, p. 408 (CO633020).

William H. Trigg & Co. v. Nathaniel T. Allison, James H. Hay, Nathaniel Sutherlin; adjudicated March 11, 1863. Book 8, p. 380 (CO61900F).

William H. Trigg & Co. v. Nathaniel T. Allison, James H. Hay, Nathaniel Sutherlin; adjudicated March 11, 1863. Book 8, p. 379 (CO633054).

William H. Trigg & Co. v. Nathaniel T. Allison, James H. Hay, Walker H. Finley, Nathaniel Sutherlin; adjudicated March 11, 1863. Book 8, p. 382 (CO633066).

William H. Trigg & Co. v. Peter Pierce, William S. McCarty, Charles H. F. Greenlease; adjudicated March 13, 1863. Book 8, p. 412 (CO633035).

William H. Trigg & Co. v. Richard T. Ellis, Administrator of Richard P. Ellis, dec., H. W. Ferguson, James Y. Harris; adjudicated March 11, 1863. Book 8, p. 378 (CO633003).

William H. Trigg & Co. v. Samuel Cole, James W. Cole, Jacob Baughman; adjudicated March 13, 1863. Book 8, p. 408 (CO633004).

William H. Trigg & Co. v. Sinclair Morgan, Stokley S. Seat, James Rankin, William Rankin; adjudicated March 13, 1863. Book 8, p. 431 (CO633081).

William H. Trigg & Co. v. Thomas B. Smiley, T. S. Cole, Mark Cole; adjudicated September 9, 1863. Book 8, p. 537 (CO633018).

William H. Trigg & Co. v. Thomas J. Hughes, William M. Taylor, Samuel Hughes, James A. Hughes; adjudicated September 9, 1863. Book 8, p. 536 (CO61914B).

William H. Trigg & Co. v. Thomas J. Hughes, William M. Taylor, Samuel Hughes, James A. Hughes; adjudicated March 11, 1863. Book 8, p. 380 (CO61914A).

William H. Trigg & Co. v. Thomas J. Hughes, William M. Taylor, Samuel Hughes, James A. Hughes; adjudicated March 13, 1863. Book 8, p. 414 (CO633043).

William H. Trigg & Co. v. Thomas M. Harris, William M. McBride, James J. Harris; adjudicated March 11, 1863. Book 8, p. 380 (CO633076).

William H. Trigg & Co. v. Timothy Chandler, Henry W. Mills, John T. Thornton, Presley P. Thornton, William A. Thornton; adjudicated March 21, 1864. Book 9, p. 57 (CO633005).

William H. Trigg & Co. v. W. T. Allison, Nathaniel Sutherlin, William M. Rucker, James H. Hay; adjudicated March 11, 1863. Book 8, p. 385 (CO633078).

William H. Trigg & Co. v. Walker H. Finley, George W. Wallace, Nathaniel Sutherlin; adjudicated March 11, 1863. Book 8, p. 383 (CO633087).

William H. Trigg & Co. v. William Scott, R. W. Creel; adjudicated September 12, 1861. Book 8, p. 249 (CO619103).

William H. Trigg & Co. v. William B. Alexander, John P. Maddox, Peter G. Rea, William Snyder; adjudicated September 12, 1861. Book 8, p. 276 (CO61900E).

William H. Trigg & Co. v. William E. Jamison, John W. Jamison, Nathaniel Sutherlin, Thomas S. Williams; adjudicated March 13, 1863. Book 8, p. 386 (CO633091).

William H. Trigg & Co. v. William G. Tucker, Lewis E. Craig, Benjamin F. Craig; adjudicated March 11, 1863. Book 8, p. 381 (CO633068).

William H. Trigg & Co. v. William M. Rucker, George W. Wallace, Nathaniel Sutherlin; adjudicated March 13, 1863. Book 8, p. 418 (CO633088).

William H. Trigg & Co. v. William M. Rucker, Nathaniel Sutherlin, Nathaniel T. Allison, James H. Hay; adjudicated March 13, 1863. Book 8, p. 418 (CO633090).

William H. Trigg & Co. v. William M. Rucker, Nathaniel T. Allison, Nathaniel Sutherlin; adjudicated March 13, 1863. Book 8, p. 416 (CO633079).

William H. Trigg & Co. v. William M. Taylor, Samuel Briscoe, James B. Harris, Samuel Hughes, John Taylor, Thomas J. Hughes; adjudicated March 13, 1863. Book 8, p. 422 (CO633014).

William H. Trigg & Co. v. William S. McCarty, Richard McCarty, J. C. Ferguson; adjudicated March 13, 1863. Book 8, p. 432 (CO633092).

William H. Trigg & Co. v. William T. Cox, Thomas B. Smiley, John B. Dallas, Mark Cole; adjudicated March 13, 1863. Book 8, p. 537 (CO633015).

William H. Trigg & Co. v. William T. Cox, Thomas B. Smiley, Mark Cole; adjudicated September 9, 1863. Book 8, p. 538 (CO633002).

B. PETTIS COUNTY — 122 CASES

Pettis County Circuit Court records, Sedalia, Missouri.

Bank of St. Louis v. A. K. Sittington; adjudicated November 6, 1863. Book E, p. 221 (PE624062).

Bank of St. Louis v. Abram Darst, Benjamin F. Pollard, Seymour E. Pollard, Absalom Rearn; adjudicated November 6, 1863. Book E, p. 211 (PE624026).

Bank of St. Louis v. Absalom McVey; adjudicated November 6, 1863. Book E, p. 223 (PE624069).

Bank of St. Louis v. Absalom Rearn, Charles W. C. Walker, Samuel Durley; adjudicated November 6, 1863. Book E, p. 224 (PE624101).

Bank of St. Louis v. Albion Roberson, Andrew M. Forbes, Reece Hughes; adjudicated November 6, 1863. Book E, p. 215 (PE624028).

Bank of St. Louis v. Andrew M. Forbes, Albion Roberson, Oswald Kidd, Alfred P. Forbes; adjudicated November 6, 1863. Book E, p. 216 (PE624035).

Bank of St. Louis v. Benjamin E. Scrivener, William R. Trundle, Austin K. Walker; adjudicated April 30, 1862. Book E, p. 91 (PE624007).

Bank of St. Louis v. Benjamin F. Pollard, John Godfrey, George Spangenburger, Absalom Rearn; adjudicated November 6, 1863. Book E, p. 211 (PE624097).

Bank of St. Louis v. Benjamin H. Pollard, Absalom Rearn, John J. Monaghan; adjudicated November 6, 1863. Book E, p. 212 (PE624025).

Bank of St. Louis v. George Spangenburger, M. M. Harnsberger, Enrico Decatur Nelson; adjudicated November 6, 1863. Book E, p. 211 (PE624023).

Bank of St. Louis v. George W. Rothwell, Thomas F. Houston, E. P. Harris; adjudicated November 6, 1863. Book E, p. 215 (PE624031).

Bank of St. Louis v. H. C. Taylor; adjudicated November 6, 1863. Book E, p. 222 (PE624064).

Bank of St. Louis v. Hampton P. Gray; adjudicated November 6, 1863. Book E, p. 223 (PE624059).

Bank of St. Louis v. Jackson Quisenberry, Albion Roberson, Absalom Rearn; adjudicated November 6, 1863. Book E, p. 215 (PE624029).

Bank of St. Louis v. James A. Fisher, George D. Fisher, Wesley McClure, James S. Hopkins; adjudicated May 7, 1864. Book E, p. 311 (PE63B137).

Bank of St. Louis v. James Oldham; adjudicated November 6, 1863. Book E, p. 221 (PE624063).

Bank of St. Louis v. James S. Hopkins, Jr.; adjudicated November 6, 1863. Book E, p. 220 (PE624056).

Bank of St. Louis v. John B. Henderson; adjudicated November 6, 1863. Book E, p. 220 (PE624053).

Bank of St. Louis v. John C. Hughes, James M. Forbes, John M. Snead; adjudicated November 6, 1863. Book E, p. 225 (PE63B103).

Bank of St. Louis v. John C. Hughes; adjudicated November 6, 1863. Book E, p. 219 (PE624070).

Bank of St. Louis v. Joseph L. Cartwright; adjudicated November 6, 1863. Book E, p. 223 (PE624060).

Bank of St. Louis v. Nathaniel T. Allison, William H. Field, Absalom McVey; adjudicated November 6, 1863. Book E, p. 216 (PE624034).

Bank of St. Louis v. Samuel H. Brown; adjudicated November 6, 1863. Book E, p. 221 (PE624058).

Bank of St. Louis v. Thomas F. Houston, E. D. Williams, William Lowry; adjudicated November 6, 1863. Book E, p. 214 (PE624036).

Bank of St. Louis v. Thomas F. Houston, E. D. Williams, William Lowry; adjudicated November 6, 1863. Book E, p. 215 (PE624037).

Bank of St. Louis v. Thomas O. Sittington; adjudicated November 6, 1863. Book E, p. 222 (PE624065).

Bank of St. Louis v. Walker H. Finley, George Anderson, William A. Finley, Franklin Plummer; adjudicated May 7, 1864. Book E, p. 318 (PE645147).

Bank of St. Louis v. Walker H. Finley, George Anderson, William A. Finley, Franklin Plummer; adjudicated November 7, 1863. Book E, p. 236 (PE624057).

Bank of St. Louis v. Walker H. Finley, William A. Finley, George Anderson, William A. Powell, Aaron Jenkins; adjudicated November 6, 1863. Book E, p. 242 (PE63B138).

Bank of St. Louis v. Walker H. Finley, William A. Finley, George Anderson; adjudicated May 7, 1864. Book E, p. 318 (PE645146).

Bank of St. Louis v. William H. Field, George B. Newton; adjudicated November 6, 1863. Book E, p. 213 (PE624030).

Bank of St. Louis v. William H. Field, Henry Field; adjudicated November 6, 1863. Book E, p. 214 (PE624032).

Bank of St. Louis v. William R. Scott, George Anderson, Ebenezer Magoffin, Gideon B. Miller, William L. Powell; adjudicated April 6, 1864. Book E, p. 277 (PE624024).

Bank of St. Louis v. Willis G. Craig, James R. Hughes, John R. Ford; adjudicated November 6, 1863. Book E, p. 278 (PE624033).

Bank of the State of Missouri v. Aaron Jenkins, James Jenkins, Josiah Joplin; adjudicated November 4, 1863. Book E, p. 180 (PE63B110).

Bank of the State of Missouri v. Aaron Jenkins, William O. Powell; adjudicated May 6, 1864. Book E, p. 279 (PE645145).

Bank of the State of Missouri v. Aquillus R. Priest, George S. Priest, William E. Jamison; adjudicated November 4, 1863. Book E, p. 169 (PE624079).

Bank of the State of Missouri v. Benjamin Greer, Charles Q. Shouse, John Greer, Frank Woodson; adjudicated November 4, 1863. Book E, p. 170 (PE624089).

Bank of the State of Missouri v. Charles Q. Shouse, W. C. Wilson, W. H. Sellers; adjudicated November 4, 1865. Book E, p. 446 (PE63B105).

Bank of the State of Missouri v. Charles W. C. Walker, George S. Brown, Samuel Durley; adjudicated November 4, 1863. Book E, p. 171 (PE624090).

Bank of the State of Missouri v. Charles Younger, Harvey C. Howe, Nathaniel Sutherlin, William M. Rucker; adjudicated November 4, 1863. Book E, p. 168 (PE624081).

Bank of the State of Missouri v. David M. Williams, John H. Williams; adjudicated November 5, 1863. Book E, p. 181 (PE63B114).

Bank of the State of Missouri v. David W. Bouldin, Ferris E. Cravens, William R. Scott; adjudicated November 4, 1863. Book E, p. 170 (PE624078).

Bank of the State of Missouri v. George S. Priest, Aquillus R. Priest, William E. Jamison; adjudicated November 4, 1863. Book E, p. 170 (PE624080).

Bank of the State of Missouri v. George W. Miller, William R. Scott, Nimrod B. Miller,

Nathaniel T. Allison, Walker H. Finley, John Miller; adjudicated May 6, 1864. Book E, p. 278 (PE645141).

Bank of the State of Missouri v. George W. Rothwell, William L. Powell, David M. Williams; adjudicated November 4, 1863. Book E, p. 170 (PE624077).

Bank of the State of Missouri v. Gideon B. Miller, George S. Priest, M. R. Priest, Aquillus R. Priest, William Grinstead, William L. Powell; adjudicated November 4, 1863. Book E, p. 180 (PE63B109).

Bank of the State of Missouri v. Gideon B. Miller, John Miller, George W. Miller, Andrew M. Forbes; adjudicated November 4, 1863. Book E, p. 181 (PE63B111).

Bank of the State of Missouri v. James A. Fisher, George D. Fisher, William R. Scott, V. Volney Thomson; adjudicated November 4, 1863. Book E, p. 169 (PE624082).

Bank of the State of Missouri v. James S. Hopkins, John R. Ford, Joshua Hopkins; adjudicated November 4, 1863. Book E, p. 181 (PE63B112).

Bank of the State of Missouri v. John H. Williams, Thomas F. Houston; adjudicated November 4, 1863. Book E, p. 181 (PE63B106).

Bank of the State of Missouri v. John H. Williams, Thomas F. Houston; adjudicated November 5, 1863. Book E, p. 181 (PE63B115).

Bank of the State of Missouri v. John R. Ford, James S. Hopkins, James R. Hughes; adjudicated November 4, 1863. Book E, p. 172 (PE624093).

Bank of the State of Missouri v. Joseph Cartwright, Charles Q. Shouse, William L. Powell; adjudicated November 4, 1863. Book E, p. 169 (PE624088).

Bank of the State of Missouri v. Joseph L. Cartwright, George Anderson, Joseph C. Donahoo, Albion Roberson, Charles O. Jones, Peter H. Stone, Albert Casson; adjudicated May 6, 1864. Book E, p. 278 (PE645142).

Bank of the State of Missouri v. Madison G. Purdom, Thomas O. Sittington, Andrew M. Forbes, James S. Hopkins, James R. Hughes; adjudicated November 3, 1863. Book E, p. 171 (PE624076).

Bank of the State of Missouri v. Madison G. Purdom; adjudicated April 30, 1862. Book E, p. 93 (PE624015).

Bank of the State of Missouri v. Nathaniel T. Allison, Andrew M. Forbes, James M. Jones, J. R. Davis; adjudicated November 5, 1863. Book E, p. 182 (PE63B116).

Bank of the State of Missouri v. Nathaniel T. Allison, William L. Powell, Reece Hughes, Ellis W. Jones; adjudicated November 5, 1863. Book E, p. 181 (PE63B113).

Bank of the State of Missouri v. Reece Hughes, Alden A. Glasscock, William L. Powell; adjudicated November 4, 1863. Book E, p. 169 (PE624087).

Bank of the State of Missouri v. Samuel H. Brown, Reece Hughes, Samuel Durley; adjudicated November 4, 1863. Book E, p. 180 (PE63B107).

Bank of the State of Missouri v. Solomon Cunningham, Walker H. Finley, Aaron Jenkins; adjudicated November 4, 1863. Book E, p. 180 (PE63B108).

Bank of the State of Missouri v. Thomas F. Houston, E. D. Williams, William Lowry; adjudicated November 4, 1863. Book E, p. 168 (PE624085).

Bank of the State of Missouri v. Thomas F. Houston, John W. Jamison, William E. Jamison; adjudicated November 4, 1863. Book E, p. 167 (PE624084).

Bank of the State of Missouri v. Thomas O. Sittington, Madison G. Purdom, James R. Hughes, James S. Hopkins; adjudicated November 4, 1863. Book E, p. 171 (PE624075).

Bank of the State of Missouri v. William H. Field, Henry Field, Thomas F. Houston; adjudicated November 4, 1863. Book E, p. 172 (PE624091).

Bank of the State of Missouri v. William H. Field, Henry Field; adjudicated November 4, 1863. Book E, p. 172 (PE624092).

Bank of the State of Missouri v. William R. Scott, Charles Q. Shouse, Abner Clopton; adjudicated November 4, 1863. Book E, p. 168 (PE624086).

Exchange Bank of St. Louis v. Gideon B. Miller, George W. Miller, John Miller; adjudicated May 7, 1864. Book E, p. 316 (PE63B134).

Exchange Bank of St. Louis v. John W. Jamison, William E. Jamison, Thomas F. Houston; adjudicated May 7, 1864. Book E, p. 315 (PE63B136).

Exchange Bank of St. Louis v. Nathaniel T. Allison, William A. Finley; adjudicated May 7, 1864. Book E, p. 315 (PE63B135).

Farmers' Bank of Missouri v. Absalom Rearn, Oswald Kidd, Albion Roberson; adjudicated November 4, 1863. Book E, p. 173 (PE63B124).

Farmers' Bank of Missouri v. Alfred Graves, Baxter E. Morrow, Benjamin F. Dobyns, Jonathan Graves; adjudicated November 3, 1865. Book E, p. 425 (PE645140).

Farmers' Bank of Missouri v. Andrew M. Forbes, Alfred P. Forbes, Albion Roberson; adjudicated November 4, 1863. Book E, p. 174 (PE63B125).

Farmers' Bank of Missouri v. Gideon B. Miller, William L. Powell, Nimrod B. Miller, George W. Miller, John Miller; adjudicated May 7, 1864. Book E, p. 315 (PE63B131).

Farmers' Bank of Missouri v. Isaac McGirk, John R. Ford, James A. Quarles, administrator of William H. Field, deceased, George S. Priest, Thomas H. Allen; adjudicated November 4, 1863. Book E, p. 173 (PE63B126).

Farmers' Bank of Missouri v. Jackson Quisenberry, George W. McClure, Albion Roberson; adjudicated May 7, 1864. Book E, p. 286 (PE644127).

Farmers' Bank of Missouri v. M. B. Steele, J. N. Steele, Andrew M. Forbes; adjudicated May 7, 1864. Book E, p. 315 (PE63B132).

Farmers' Bank of Missouri v. Oswald Kidd, Andrew M. Forbes, Albion Roberson; adjudicated November 4, 1863. Book E, p. 173 (PE63B122).

Farmers' Bank of Missouri v. Oswald Kidd, Andrew M. Forbes, Albion Roberson; adjudicated November 4, 1863. Book E, p. 173 (PE63B123).

Farmers' Bank of Missouri v. Samuel H. Brown, George S. Brown; adjudicated May 7, 1864. Book E, p. 314 (PE63B130).

Farmers' Bank of Missouri v. William L. Cahill, Ferris E. Cravens, Andrew M. Forbes; adjudicated May 7, 1864. Book E, p. 314 (PE63B129).

Mechanics' Bank of St. Louis v. Jackson Quisenberry, Absalom Rearn, Reece Hughes; adjudicated November 6, 1863. Book E, p. 226 (PE624098).

Mechanics' Bank of St. Louis v. John J. Monaghan, George Spangenburger; adjudicated November 7, 1863. Book E, p. 238 (PE628100).

Union Bank of Missouri v. Absalom McVey, William F. Marshall, Albion Roberson; adjudicated November 6, 1863. Book E, p. 230 (PE63B118).

Union Bank of Missouri v. Benjamin S. Hawkins, Daniel M. Douglass, Henry L. Douglas; adjudicated August 29, 1866. Book F, p. 26 (PE645148).

Union Bank of Missouri v. Reece Hughes, H. C. Taylor, John Henderson, John Taylor; adjudicated November 6, 1863. Book E, p. 230 (PE63B117).

Union Bank of Missouri v. Thomas F. Houston, William Lowry, John Motz; adjudicated November 6, 1863. Book E, p. 230 (PE63B119).

William H. Trigg & Co. v. Absalom Rearn, Albion Roberson, Erbin Warren; adjudicated November 6, 1863. Book E, p. 212 (PE624019).

William H. Trigg & Co. v. Austin K. Walker, Thomas A. Fowler, Abram Darst; adjudicated November 6, 1863. Book E, p. 213 (PE624020).

William H. Trigg & Co. v. B. H. Barrett; adjudicated November 6, 1863. Book E, p. 225 (PE624099).

William H. Trigg & Co. v. Benjamin E. Scrivener, F. A. Yost, William B. Trundle, Thomas B. Evans, George L. Bell; adjudicated April 30, 1862. Book E, p. 91 (PE624004).

William H. Trigg & Co. v. Benjamin E. Scrivener, John G. Fowler, Andrew M. Forbes, F. A. Yost; adjudicated April 30, 1862. Book E, p. 90 (PE624002).

William H. Trigg & Co. v. Charles Younger, Nathaniel Sutherlin, James Faulconer, Harvey C. Howe; adjudicated November 6, 1863. Book E, p. 217 (PE624049).

William H. Trigg & Co. v. George Anderson, Charles Younger, Harvey C. Howe; adjudicated April 30, 1862. Book E, p. 93 (PE624014).

William H. Trigg & Co. v. George Spangenburger, Absalom Rearn, M. M. Harnsberger; adjudicated November 6, 1863. Book E, p. 211 (PE624017).

William H. Trigg & Co. v. Gideon B. Miller, Aaron Jenkins, S. H. Jenkins, Nimrod B. Miller; adjudicated November 6, 1863. Book E, p. 217 (PE624044).

William H. Trigg & Co. v. Gideon B. Miller, S. H. Jenkins, William R. Scott; adjudicated April 30, 1862. Book E, p. 92 (PE624012).

William H. Trigg & Co. v. Harvey C. Howe, George Anderson, Charles Younger; adjudicated April 30, 1862. Book E, p. 93 (PE624013).

William H. Trigg & Co. v. Henry Field, William H. Field; adjudicated November 6, 1863. Book E, p. 216 (PE624040).

William H. Trigg & Co. v. James Faulconer, Harvey C. Howe, George Anderson, Samuel B. Scott; adjudicated April 30, 1862. Book E, p. 91 (PE624006).

William H. Trigg & Co. v. John C. Shy, Buriah M. Shy, C. L. Shy, David J. Shy, Albion Roberson; adjudicated November 6, 1863. Book E, p. 212 (PE624022).

William H. Trigg & Co. v. John G. Fowler, Charles W. C. Walker, Austin K. Walker; adjudicated November 6, 1863. Book E, p. 219 (PE624047).

William H. Trigg & Co. v. John Henderson, George R. Smith, Absalom McVey, William H. Lightfoot; adjudicated April 30, 1862. Book E, p. 92 (PE624008).

William H. Trigg & Co. v. John Henderson, William H. Lightfoot, Ebenezer Magoffin, John B. Henderson; adjudicated April 30, 1862. Book E, p. 92 (PE624009).

William H. Trigg & Co. v. John J. Monaghan, Abram Darst, Benjamin F. Pollard, Seymour E. Pollard; adjudicated November 6, 1863. Book E, p. 212 (PE624039).

William H. Trigg & Co. v. John J. Monaghan, Benjamin F. Pollard, Martha Phillips, E. M. Phillips; adjudicated November 6, 1863. Book E, p. 216 (PE624027).

William H. Trigg & Co. v. John J. Monaghan, George Spangenburger, Absalom Rearn; adjudicated November 6, 1863. Book E, p. 212 (PE624016).

William H. Trigg & Co. v. John Miller, George W. Miller, Gideon B. Miller; adjudicated November 6, 1863. Book E, p. 218 (PE624045).

William H. Trigg & Co. v. John Motz, James M. Jones, Thomas F. Houston; adjudicated November 6, 1863. Book E, p. 225 (PE63B102).

William H. Trigg & Co. v. N. N. Parberry, Absalom Rearn, John Ryan; adjudicated November 6, 1863. Book E, p. 212 (PE624021).

William H. Trigg & Co. v. Nathaniel Sutherlin, Harvey C. Howe, R. B. Howe, James Faulconer, Charles Younger; adjudicated November 6, 1863. Book E, p. 217 (PE624048).

William H. Trigg & Co. v. Nelson Oldfield, John J. Monaghan, Robert Boggs, John Godfrey, Thomas B. Stephens, Abram Darst, Thomas Owen, Seymour E. Pollard, William Owen, R. J. Burcham; adjudicated April 30, 1862. Book E, p. 92 (PE624010).

William H. Trigg & Co. v. R. G. Wallace, John G. Fowler, William R. Trundle, Benjamin E. Scrivener, F. A. Yost, George A. Whitney; adjudicated April 30, 1862. Book E, p. 91 (PE624005).

William H. Trigg & Co. v. Thomas F. Houston, John W. Jamison, William E. Jamison; adjudicated November 6, 1863. Book E, p. 218 (PE624046).

William H. Trigg & Co. v. Van Tromp Chilton, George W. Embree, William E. Combs; adjudicated April 30, 1862. Book E, p. 89 (PE624001).

William H. Trigg & Co. v. Walker H. Finley, George Anderson, Gideon B. Miller, George W. Miller, John Miller; adjudicated November 6, 1863. Book E, p. 216 (PE624050).

William H. Trigg & Co. v. Walker H. Finley, George Anderson, Nathaniel Sutherlin, William E. Jamison; adjudicated November 6, 1863. Book E, p. 216 (PE624041).

William H. Trigg & Co. v. Walker H. Finley, Nathaniel Sutherlin, Gideon B. Miller, George W. Miller, Nathaniel T. Allison; adjudicated November 6, 1863. Book E, p. 218 (PE624043).

William H. Trigg & Co. v. Walker H. Finley, Nathaniel T. Allison, Gideon B. Miller, John Miller, George W. Miller; adjudicated November 6, 1863. Book E, p. 217 (PE624042).

William H. Trigg & Co. v. William E. Combs, Joseph Brown, J. R. Vandyke; adjudicated April 30, 1862. Book E, p. 90 (PE624003).

William H. Trigg & Co. v. William R. Trundle, Milton Huffman, James R. Major, Thomas E. Fristoe; adjudicated November 6, 1863. Book E, p. 213 (PE624018).

C. SALINE COUNTY — 120 CASES

Saline County Circuit Court records, Marshall, Missouri.

Bank of St. Louis v. William T. Harrison, Sabrina Shroyer, administratrix and Charles W. Hall and Jesse Davis, administrators for the estate of Presley Shroyer, deceased; adjudicated November 13, 1863. Book F, p. 141 (SA63B014).

Bank of the State of Missouri v. Asa P. Thomson, William E. Thomson; adjudicated November 13, 1863. Book F, p. 144 (SA63B020).

Bank of the State of Missouri v. David Vaughan, Isaac S. Parsons, W. S. Bates; adjudicated November 13, 1863. Book F, p. 142 (SA63B017).

Bank of the State of Missouri v. Hugh H. McDowell, John Spears, William O. Maupin; adjudicated November 13, 1863. Book F, p. 155 (SA63B031).

Bank of the State of Missouri v. James H. Huey, J. Ingram, Jacob H. Smith, Henry B. Winslow, Robert Huey; adjudicated November 13, 1863. Book F, p. 145 (SA63B023).

Bank of the State of Missouri v. Jeremiah Leggett, Thomas Jackson, John Thornton, James B. Brown; adjudicated November 10, 1863. Book F, p. 64 (SA63B038).

Bank of the State of Missouri v. John B. Davis, James R. Davis, Joseph Marshall; adjudicated November 13, 1863. Book F, p. 143 (SA63B019).

Bank of the State of Missouri v. Joseph G. Francisco, Andrew J. Francisco, Joshua C. Hays; adjudicated November 13, 1863. Book F, p. 142 (SA63B016).

Bank of the State of Missouri v. Strother T. Hamm, Alfred L. Towles, Charles P. Bondurant, Archibald Paxton, Joseph Audsley; adjudicated November 13, 1863. Book F, p. 145 (SA63B024).

Bank of the State of Missouri v. Vincent Marmaduke, Thomas J. Rogers; adjudicated November 13, 1863. Book F, p. 144 (SA63B021).

Bank of the State of Missouri v. Walker H. Finley, H. M. Ramsey, Richard Marshall Jr., David M. Williams, J. B. Wallace; adjudicated November 13, 1863. Book F, p. 178 (SA63B033).

Bank of the State of Missouri v. Walker H. Finley, Solomon Cunningham, John Mann, Mandeville B. Hancock; adjudicated November 13, 1863. Book F, p. 154 (SA63B029).

Bank of the State of Missouri v. William E. Thomson, Asa P. Thomson; adjudicated November 13, 1863. Book F, p. 146 (SA63B025).

Bank of the State of Missouri v. William T. Harrison, Jacob H. Smith; adjudicated November 13, 1863. Book F, p. 153 (SA63B027).

Bank of the State of Missouri v. Alfred L. Towles, Thomas J. Rogers, Richard E. Snelling; adjudicated November 13, 1863. Book F, p. 141 (SA63B015).

Bank of the State of Missouri v. James W. Craig, Robert E. Kirtley; adjudicated May 13, 1865. Book F, p. 338 (SA63B035).

Exchange Bank of St. Louis v. Alfred L. Towles, Stephen Wheeler, Thomas J. Rogers; adjudicated November 13, 1863. Book F, p. 168 (SA63B046).

Exchange Bank of St. Louis v. Archibald Paxton, Timothy Harris; adjudicated November 13, 1863. Book F, p. 170 (SA63B051).

Exchange Bank of St. Louis v. Henry Garnett, William W. Graves; adjudicated May 14, 1864. Book G, p. 15 (SA645170).

Exchange Bank of St. Louis v. John N. Garnett, Henry Garnett, William W. Graves, Thomas Garnett, Edward G. Garnett; adjudicated November 13, 1863. Book F, p. 167 (SA63B044).

Exchange Bank of St. Louis v. Joseph Audsley, Archibald Paxton; adjudicated November 13, 1863. Book F, p. 165 (SA63B041).

Exchange Bank of St. Louis v. Thomas H. Booker, William S. Booker; adjudicated November 13, 1863. Book F, p. 170 (SA63B050).

Exchange Bank of St. Louis v. Walker H. Finley, Nathaniel Allison, George Anderson; adjudicated May 14, 1864. Book F, p. 360 (SA63B056).

Exchange Bank of St. Louis v. Walker H. Finley, Nathaniel Allison, George Anderson; adjudicated May 4, 1864. Book F, p. 360 (SA63B055).

Exchange Bank of St. Louis v. Charles P. Bondurant, Strother T. Hamm, Archibald Paxton; adjudicated November 13, 1863. Book F, p. 170 (SA63B052).

Exchange Bank of St. Louis v. Flora Thomson, administratrix of Quincy A. Thomson, deceased, Asa P. Thomson, William E. Thomson; adjudicated November 13, 1863. Book F, p. 169 (SA63B048).

Exchange Bank of St. Louis v. John N. Garnett, Thomas Garnett, Edward G. Garnett; adjudicated November 13, 1863. Book F, p. 166 (SA63B042).

Exchange Bank of St. Louis v. John N. Garnett, Thomas Garnett; adjudicated November 13, 1863. Book F, p. 166 (SA63B043).

Exchange Bank of St. Louis v. Philander Y. Irvine, administrator of John R. Brown, William Brown, William S. Brown; adjudicated November 13, 1863. Book F, p. 172 (SA63B057).

Exchange Bank of St. Louis v. Reuben Seay, John A. Walden; adjudicated November 13, 1863. Book F, p. 173 (SA63B058).

Exchange Bank of St. Louis v. Thornton P. Bell, Alfred L. Towles, James S. Jones; adjudicated November 13, 1863. Book F, p. 164 (SA63B039).

Farmers' Bank of Missouri v. Addison Huston, Mary B. Craig, John H. Lewis with William B. S. Lewis as administrators of John M. Lewis, deceased; adjudicated November 13, 1863. Book F, p. 231 (SA63B060).

Farmers' Bank of Missouri v. Alfred L. Towles, Thomas J. Rogers, Charles P. Bondurant; adjudicated November 13, 1863. Book F, p. 118 (SA63B069).

Farmers' Bank of Missouri v. Charles P. Bondurant, James M. Stonesiffer, Threesivellus M. Minor, Jr.; adjudicated November 12, 1863. Book F, p. 119 (SA63B071).

Farmers' Bank of Missouri v. George J. Fackler, John J. Major, Alexander M. Creel; adjudicated November 13, 1863. Book F, p. 229 (SA63B074).

Farmers' Bank of Missouri v. Hugh H. Chrisman, Osbert Miller, William M. Chrisman; adjudicated November 10, 1863. Book F, p. 64 (SA63B059).

Farmers' Bank of Missouri v. James W. Craig, Robert E. Kirtley, administrator of George R. Kirtley, Robert E. Nunnelly, Richard P. Samuel; adjudicated December 12, 1863. Book F, p. 116 (SA63B064).

Farmers' Bank of Missouri v. John B. Ervin, John H. Lewis and William B. S. Lewis, administrators of John M. Lewis, deceased, Cave J. Kirtley, William Prewitt; adjudicated November 13, 1863. Book F, p. 231 (SA63B062).

Farmers' Bank of Missouri v. John H. Lewis, William B. S. Lewis, administrators of John M. Lewis, deceased, William O. Maupin, John B. Ervin; adjudicated November 13, 1863. Book F, p. 232 (SA63B061).

Farmers' Bank of Missouri v. Robert E. Kirtley, administrator of George R. Kirtley, deceased, George J. Fackler; adjudicated November 12, 1863. Book F, p. 118 (SA63B068).

Farmers' Bank of Missouri v. Strother T. Hamm, James M. Stonesiffer, Charles P. Bondurant; adjudicated November 12, 1863. Book F, p. 119 (SA63B070).

Farmers' Bank of Missouri v. Thornton P. Bell, Daniel T. Guthrey, John H. Lewis and William B. S. Lewis, administrators of John M. Lewis, deceased; adjudicated May 12, 1865. Book G, p. 71 (SA63B077).

Farmers' Bank of Missouri v. William O. Maupin, John Spears, Hugh H. McDowell, George L. Chrisman; adjudicated November 12, 1863. Book F, p. 117 (SA63B066).

Farmers' Bank of Missouri v. William Price, Henry Cooper, A. Fletcher Brown, William J. Brown; adjudicated May 14, 1864. Book F, p. 384 (SA645173).

Merchants' Bank of St. Louis v. Abram Jordan, John J. Latimer, Nathaniel G. Cruzen; adjudicated November 13, 1863. Book F, p. 325 (SA63B126).

Merchants' Bank of St. Louis v. Archibald Paxton, Joseph Audsley, John Harris; adjudicated November 13, 1863. Book F, p. 195 (SA625011).

Merchants' Bank of St. Louis v. Archibald Paxton, Joseph Audsley, John Harris; adjudicated November 13, 1863. Book F, p. 210 (SA63B112).

Merchants' Bank of St. Louis v. Charles P. Bondurant, James M. Stonesiffer, Curtis W. Pendleton; adjudicated May 13, 1864. Book F, p. 324 (SA63B105).

Merchants' Bank of St. Louis v. Charles P. Bondurant, James S. Jones, Edward A. Carter; adjudicated November 13, 1863. Book F, p. 208 (SA63B106).

Merchants' Bank of St. Louis v. Charles P. Bondurant, Thomas J. Rogers, George W. Outcalt; adjudicated November 13, 1863. Book F, p. 207 (SA63B103).

Merchants' Bank of St. Louis v. Charles P. Bondurant, Thomas J. Rogers, John Rogers; adjudicated November 13, 1863. Book F, p. 207 (SA63B104).

Merchants' Bank of St. Louis v. Daniel T. Guthrey, James S. Jones; adjudicated November 13, 1863. Book F, p. 203 (SA63B096).

Merchants' Bank of St. Louis v. Daniel T. Guthrey, John Brown and William S. Brown; adjudicated November 13, 1863. Book F, p. 204 (SA63B224).

Merchants' Bank of St. Louis v. David Herndon Lindsey; adjudicated May 12, 1866. Book G, p. 300 (SA65C219).

Merchants' Bank of St. Louis v. David Herndon Lindsey, Alfred L. Towles, William C. Hill; adjudicated November 13, 1863. Book F, p. 210 (SA63B111).

Merchants' Bank of St. Louis v. David Herndon Lindsey, Jesse J. Ferrel; adjudicated February 29, 1864. Book F, p. 248 (SA642164).

Merchants' Bank of St. Louis v. David Vaughan, Isaac S. Parsons, Alfred L. Towles; adjudicated November 13, 1863. Book F, p. 197 (SA63B087).

Merchants' Bank of St. Louis v. Edward A. Carter, Charles P. Bondurant, James S. Jones; adjudicated November 13, 1863. Book F, p. 206 (SA63B102).

Merchants' Bank of St. Louis v. Edward A. Carter, Reuben Seay, James S. Jones, Charles P. Bondurant; adjudicated November 13, 1863. Book F, p. 194 (SA63B082).

Merchants' Bank of St. Louis v. Edward G. Garnett, John N. Garnett, Thomas Garnett; adjudicated November 13, 1863. Book F, p. 220 (SA63B131).

Merchants' Bank of St. Louis v. Edward S. Carpenter, Edmund Brown, William O. Smith; adjudicated November 13, 1863. Book F, p. 195 (SA63B085).

Merchants' Bank of St. Louis v. J. H. Youley [Yonley?], *Isaac S. Parsons, David Vaughan*; adjudicated November 13, 1863. Book F, p. 197 (SA63B086).

Merchants' Bank of St. Louis v. James S. Jones, Daniel T. Guthrey; adjudicated November 13, 1863. Book F, p. 204 (SA63B098).

Merchants' Bank of St. Louis v. James S. Jones, John B. Jones, Edward A. Carter, Charles P. Bondurant; adjudicated November 13, 1863. Book F, p. 204 (SA63B097).

Merchants' Bank of St. Louis v. James S. Jones, Reuben Seay, John A. Walden; adjudicated November 13, 1863. Book F, p. 206 (SA63B101).

Merchants' Bank of St. Louis v. James S. Jones, Thornton P. Bell, Alfred L. Towles; adjudicated November 13, 1863. Book F, p. 205 (SA63B100).

Merchants' Bank of St. Louis v. John D. Patrick, Wilson Calhoun, William S. Brown; adjudicated May 12, 1864. Book F, p. 299 (SA63B093).

Merchants' Bank of St. Louis v. John N. Garnett, Edward G. Garnett, Thomas Garnett; adjudicated November 13, 1863. Book F, p. 215 (SA63B121).

Merchants' Bank of St. Louis v. John N. Garnett, Thomas Garnett, Edward G. Garnett; adjudicated November 13, 1863. Book F, p. 216 (SA63B124).

Merchants' Bank of St. Louis v. John S. Deaderick, Alfred L. Towles, and Benjamin F. Reynolds comprising the firm of Deaderick, Reynolds & Co., and Philip S. Reynolds; adjudicated May 13, 1864. Book F, p. 326 (SA645177).

Merchants' Bank of St. Louis v. Joseph Audsley, Archibald Paxton, Isaac N. Graves; adjudicated November 13, 1863. Book F, p. 213 (SA63B118).

Merchants' Bank of St. Louis v. Joseph Audsley, Strother T. Hamm, Charles P. Bondurant; adjudicated November 13, 1863. Book F, p. 214 (SA63B120).

Merchants' Bank of St. Louis v. Joseph N. Laurie, Edward A. Carter; adjudicated November 13, 1863. Book F, p. 220 (SA63B130).

Merchants' Bank of St. Louis v. Joseph T. Jones, David Vaughan; adjudicated May 13, 1864. Book F, p. 326 (SA645175).

Merchants' Bank of St. Louis v. Osbert Miller, Hugh H. Chrisman; adjudicated May 13, 1864. Book F, p. 328 (SA645179).

Merchants' Bank of St. Louis v. Reuben Seay, John A. Walden, Edward A. Carter; adjudicated November 13, 1863. Book F, p. 199 (SA63B089).

Merchants' Bank of St. Louis v. Reuben Seay, John A. Walden; adjudicated May 13, 1864. Book F, p. 326 (SA645176).

Merchants' Bank of St. Louis v. Robert C. Wilson, Alfred L. Towles; adjudicated May 13, 1864. Book F, p. 327 (SA645178).

Merchants' Bank of St. Louis v. Robert C. Wilson, Stephen Wheeler, Richard E. Snelling; adjudicated November 13, 1863. Book F, p. 198 (SA63B080).

Merchants' Bank of St. Louis v. Thomas Garnett, John N. Garnett, Edward G. Garnett; adjudicated November 13, 1863. Book F, p. 216 (SA63B123).

Merchants' Bank of St. Louis v. Thomas Garnett, John N. Garnett; adjudicated November 13, 1863. Book F, p. 215 (SA63B122).

Merchants' Bank of St. Louis v. Thornton P. Bell, Alfred L. Towles, Threesivellus M. Minor, Jr., James S. Jones, Edward A. Carter; adjudicated November 13, 1863. Book F, p. 211 (SA63B114).

Merchants' Bank of St. Louis v. Thornton P. Bell, Edward A. Carter, Alfred L. Towles, James S. Jones, William C. Hill; adjudicated November 13, 1863. Book G, p. 68 (SA63B116).

Merchants' Bank of St. Louis v. Thornton P. Bell, John A. Walden, James S. Jones; adjudicated November 13, 1863. Book F, p. 212 (SA63B115).

Merchants' Bank of St. Louis v. William H. Shaughnessy, William S. Booker, Curtis W. Pendleton; adjudicated November 13, 1863. Book F, p. 201 (SA63B092).

Merchants' Bank of St. Louis v. William L. Walden, William T. Williams, John A. Walden, Alfred L. Towles; adjudicated November 13, 1863. Book F, p. 198 (SA63B088).

Merchants' Bank of St. Louis v. William O. Burgis, Angus A. Rucker, William S. Brown; adjudicated May 13, 1864. Book F, p. 325 (SA63B110).

Western Bank of Missouri v. William L. Walden, John D. Patrick; adjudicated May 14, 1864. Book F, p. 368 (SA645213).

Western Bank of Missouri v. Addison Carthrae, Abram H. Lewis; adjudicated October 30, 1866. Book G, p. 347 (SA63B147).

Western Bank of Missouri v. Alfred L. Towles, Thornton P. Bell, James S. Jones; adjudicated November 13, 1863. Book F, p. 241 (SA63B163).

Western Bank of Missouri v. Andrew J. Sydenstriker, Thomas S. Sydenstriker; adjudicated February 27, 1864. Book F, p. 248 (SA642190).

Western Bank of Missouri v. Archibald Paxton, Joseph Audsley; adjudicated November 13, 1863. Book F, p. 186 (SA63B160).

Western Bank of Missouri v. Benjamin F. Willis; adjudicated November 13, 1863. Book F, p. 186 (SA63B162).

Western Bank of Missouri v. Dudley H. Cooper; adjudicated May 14, 1864. Book F, p. 368 (SA645211).

Western Bank of Missouri v. Edmund Brown; adjudicated November 13, 1863. Book F, p. 182 (SA63B149).

Western Bank of Missouri v. James C. Kitchen; May 14, 1864. Book F, p. 355 (SA63B146).

Western Bank of Missouri v. James S. Jones, Charles P. Bondurant, Thomas J. Rogers; adjudicated November 13, 1863. Book F, p. 184 (SA63B158).

Western Bank of Missouri v. James S. Jones, Charles P. Bondurant, Thomas J. Rogers; adjudicated November 13, 1863. Book F, p. 184 (SA63B137).

Western Bank of Missouri v. James S. Jones, John A. Walden; adjudicated November 13, 1863. Book F, p. 182 (SA63B151).

Western Bank of Missouri v. John A. Walden; adjudicated November 13, 1863. Book G, p. 180 (SA63B155).

Western Bank of Missouri v. John C. Barkley; adjudicated May 14, 1864. Book F, p. 361 (SA63B161).

Western Bank of Missouri v. John N. Garnett, Thomas Garnett, Edward G. Garnett; adjudicated November 13, 1863. Book F, p. 184 (SA63B157).

Western Bank of Missouri v. Joseph Audsley; adjudicated April 13, 1863. Book F, p. 182 (SA63B150).

Western Bank of Missouri v. Joseph H. Marshall, William T. Williams; adjudicated May 14, 1864. Book F, p. 367 (SA645209).

Western Bank of Missouri v. Samuel W. Williams; adjudicated May 14, 1864. Book F, p. 355 (SA63B145).

Western Bank of Missouri v. Thomas J. Edwards; adjudicated May 14, 1864. Book F, p. 355 (SA63B142).

Western Bank of Missouri v. Thomas J. Rogers; adjudicated May 11, 1864. Book F, p. 284 (SA645196).

Western Bank of Missouri v. Thornton P. Bell, James S. Jones, William C. Hill; adjudicated May 14, 1864. Book F, p. 351 (SA63B136).

Western Bank of Missouri v. Thornton P. Bell; adjudicated November 13, 1863. Book F, p. 181 (SA63B143).

Western Bank of Missouri v. Walker H. Finley, William A. Finley, George Anderson; adjudicated May 14, 1864. Book F, p. 351 (SA63B156).

Western Bank of Missouri v. William Brown; adjudicated May 11, 1864. Book F, p. 284 (SA645198).

Western Bank of Missouri v. William Clark, Jacob Boatright; adjudicated May 12, 1864. Book F, p. 356 (SA63B154).

Western Bank of Missouri v. William Clark, William M. Hall; adjudicated November 13, 1863. Book F, p. 183 (SA63B153).

Western Bank of Missouri v. William E. Roller, Edward S. Carpenter, William O. Burgess; adjudicated May 14, 1864. Book F, p. 364 (SA645204).

Western Bank of Missouri v. William J. Brown; adjudicated May 14, 1864. Book F, p. 363 (SA645205).

Western Bank of Missouri v. William O. Smith; adjudicated November 13, 1863. Book F, p. 180 (SA63B140).

Western Bank of Missouri v. William P. Hicklin, Curtis W. Pendleton; adjudicated May 14, 1864. Book F, p. 369 (SA645216).

Western Bank of Missouri v. William S. Brown; adjudicated May 11, 1864. Book F, p. 285 (SA641995).

Western Bank of Missouri v. William S. Brown; adjudicated May 11, 1864. Book F, p. 285 (SA645200).

William H. Trigg & Co. v. Vincent Marmaduke, Thomas J. Rogers, John W. Bryant; adjudicated May 14, 1864. Book F, p. 381 (SA63B133).

APPENDIX 4:
DATA TABLES

The following tables list the six most important types of data used in researching this study: banks, bankers, defendants, cases, guerrillas, and planters. Each individual banker, defendant, guerrilla, and planter is listed by name, but the accompanying information is a small extract of the biographical data collected. The backbone of this study is research on the court cases, defendants, banks, bankers, and planters of a sample of three Boonslick counties, Cooper, Pettis, and Saline. Sections B, C, E, and F summarize the data for these three counties. Section B lists the names and locations of all branches of the nine chartered banking corporations in the state in 1861. The list includes an additional, private banking firm, William H. Trigg & Company, not associated with the other banking corporations. Trigg & Company was located in Boonville, and was plaintiff in nearly a hundred promissory note cases in the three counties. Banks that were plaintiffs in the three sample counties are indicated, as well as the number of promissory note cases for each. Section C lists officers and directors only for those banks that were plaintiffs in promissory-note cases heard in the three counties, and not for every bank listed in Section B. Section G contains the names of the ninety-eight guerrillas identified for the two samples: fifty-three guerrillas from Cooper, Pettis, Saline, Chariton, and Lafayette Counties, making up the central-west sample; and forty-five guerrillas from Jasper and Newton Counties, in the southwest sample.

A. St. Louis Bank Promoters, 1857–58

Name (2 or more incorporations)	Post–1857 Bank	Total Incorporations, 14th–20th general assemblies
Anderson, David	Union	2
Anderson, John J.	Bank of St. Louis	7
Barnet, George J.	Mechanics'	4
Bissell, Lewis	Union	2
Blow, Henry Taylor	Merchants'	12
Bogy, Louis V.	Exchange	7
Brotherton, John	Union	2
Brownlee, John A.	Merchants'	2
Campbell, Robert H.	Merchants'	7
Charless, Joseph	Merchants'	7
Christy, Andrew	Exchange	2
Christy, William T.	Merchants'	5
Clark, William G.	Merchants'	3
Davis, Samuel C.	Union	2
Dorsheimer, Lewis	Exchange	3
Evans, John C.	Mechanics'	2
Evil, John	Mechanics'	2
Grimsley, Thornton	Merchants'	2
Harrison, James	Bank of St. Louis	5
Hart, Oliver A.	Mechanics'	3
Haskell, Stephen	Bank of St. Louis	2
January, Derrick A.	Merchants'	9
Knapp, George	Bank of St. Louis	7
Ladew, A. P.	Bank of St. Louis	2
McCune, John S.	Merchants'	3
McElhanny, William J.	Southern	4
Miller Madison	Bank of St. Louis	10
Morrison, William M.	Merchants'	8
Overstoltz, Henry	Union	2
Parks, Robert M.	Merchants'/Mechanics'	6
Peck, Charles H.	Mechanics'	3
Priest, John G.	Bank of St. Louis	3
Rice, Bartholomew	Exchange	3
Runyan, Benjamin M.	Merchants'	5
Sturgeon, Isaac H.	Union	3
Thornburgh, John W.	Mechanics'	2

Name (2 or more incorporations)	Post–1857 Bank	Total Incorporations, 14th–20th general assemblies
Watson, James S.	Southern	3
Wiggins, Samuel B.	Exchange	2
Wimer, John M.	Mechanics'	6
Wood, William T.	Southern	2
Yeatman, James E.	Merchants'	9

B. Parent and Branch Banks, 1861

Bank Name	Location	Max age as of 12/1860 (months)	Founded after	Founded before	County	Parent/branch	Plaintiff	Total cases
Bank of Missouri	Arrow Rock	18	6/1859	12/1859	Saline	B	Y	47
Bank of Missouri	Canton	18	6/1859	12/1859	Lewis	B		
Bank of Missouri	St. Joseph	18	6/1859	12/1859	Buchanan	B		
Bank of Missouri	St. Louis			1/1859	St. Louis	P	Y	2
Bank of Missouri	Cape Girardeau			1/1859	Cape Girardeau	B		
Bank of Missouri	Chillicothe			1/1859	Livingston	B		
Bank of Missouri	Fayette			1/1859	Howard	B		
Bank of Missouri	Louisiana			1/1859	Pike	B		
Bank of Missouri	Palmyra			1/1859	Marion	B		
Bank of Missouri	Springfield			1/1859	Greene	B		
Bank of St. Louis	Kirksville	18	6/1859	12/1859	Adair	B	Y	1
Bank of St. Louis	St. Louis			1/1859	St. Louis	P	Y	51
Bank of St. Louis	Boonville			1/1859	Cooper	B		
Exchange Bank	Columbia	24	1/1859	6/1859	Boone	B		
Exchange Bank	St. Louis			1/1859	St. Louis	P	Y	7
Exchange Bank	Glasgow			1/1859	Howard	B	Y	11
Farmers' Bank	Lexington			1/1859	Lafayette	P	Y	24
Farmers' Bank	Liberty			1/1859	Clay	B		
Farmers' Bank	Paris			1/1859	Monroe	B		
Mechanics' Bank	Kansas City	18	6/1859	12/1859	Jackson	B		
Mechanics' Bank	St. Louis			1/1859	St. Louis	P		

Bank Name	Location	Max age as of 12/1860 (months)	Founded after	Founded before	County	Parent/ branch	Plaintiff	Total cases
Mechanics' Bank	Warsaw			1/1859	Benton	B	Y	2
Mechanics' Bank	Weston			1/1859	Platte	B		
Merchants' Bank	Ste. Genevieve	24	1/1859	6/1859	Ste. Genevieve	B		
Merchants' Bank	St. Louis			1/1859	St. Louis	P		
Merchants' Bank	Brunswick			1/1859	Chariton	B	Y	43
Merchants' Bank	Osceola			1/1859	St. Clair	B		
Southern Bank	St. Charles	24	1/1859	6/1859	St. Charles	B		
Southern Bank	Savannah	18	6/1859	12/1859	Andrew	B		
Southern Bank	St. Louis			1/1859	St. Louis	P		
Southern Bank	Independence			1/1859	Jackson	B		
Union Bank	St. Louis	24	1/1859	6/1859	St. Louis	P		
Union Bank	Kansas City	18	6/1859	12/1859	Jackson	B		
Union Bank	La Grange	18	6/1859	12/1859	Lewis	B		
Union Bank	Richmond	18	6/1859	12/1859	Ray	B		
Union Bank	Warrensburg	18	6/1859	12/1859	Johnson	B	Y	4
Union Bank	Charleston	12	12/1859	3/1860	Mississippi	B		
Union Bank	Milan	9	3/1860	6/1860	Sullivan	B		
Western Bank	St. Joseph	24	1/1859	6/1859	Buchanan	P		
Western Bank	Glasgow	24	1/1859	6/1859	Howard	B	Y	32
Western Bank	Bloomington	6	6/1860	12/1860	Macon	B		
Western Bank	Fulton	6	6/1860	12/1860	Callaway	B		
William H. Trigg	Boonville			1/1859	Cooper	N/A	Y	86
Total								310

C. Bankers—Three-County Sample

Name	Bank	Title	Age 1860	Nativity	Home county 1860	Other occupation(s)
Adams, Andrew	Bank of St. Louis–Boonville	Dir	46	KY	Cooper	retired trader
Adderton, Joseph A. J.	Bank of Missouri–Arrow Rock	Dir	42	MD	Saline	merchant
Anderson, George	Bank of Missouri–Arrow Rock	Dir	38	AR	Pettis	farmer, stockman, cattle trader
Anderson, William Harrison	Union Bank of St. Louis–Warrensburg	Cshr	47	TN	Johnson	
Atkisson, James	Mechanics' Bank of St. Louis–Warsaw	Pres	40	KY	Benton	merchant
Aull, Robert	Farmers' Bank of Missouri–Lexington	Pres	53	DE	Lafayette	merchant
Bacon, Robert Bell	Bank of St. Louis–Boonville	Pres	50	KY	Cooper	merchant
Bartholow, Thomas Jeremiah	Exchange Bank of St. Louis–Glasgow	Dir	34	MD	Howard	tobacco dealer
Birch, Thomas Erskine	Western Bank of Missouri–Glasgow	Dir	44	VA	Howard	farmer
Birch, Weston Favel	Western Bank of Missouri–Glasgow	Cshr	55	VA	Howard	private banker
Boon, William Crawford	Exchange Bank of St. Louis–Glasgow	Cshr	38	MO	Howard	merchant
Borland, William P.	Mechanics' Bank of St. Louis–Warsaw	Cshr	34	MD	unknown	merchant

Name	Bank	Title	Age 1860	Nativity	Home county 1860	Other occupation(s)
Boyer, Dr. William L.	Bank of Missouri–Arrow Rock	Cshr	38	TN	Saline	merchant
Bradford, Dr. Charles Manfield	Bank of Missouri–Arrow Rock	Dir	42	NY	Saline	physician
Brewster, Chester Hilliard	Bank of St. Louis–Boonville	Dir	33	CT	Cooper	steamboat captain, tobacco merchant
Brown, Elisha Warfield	Bank of St. Louis–Boonville	Dir	42	KY	Cooper	farmer, commission merchant, miller, private banker
Burr, William Edward	Bank of St. Louis–Boonville	Cshr	31	KY	Cooper	private banker
Collins, Major May Burton	Western Bank of Missouri–Glasgow	Dir	43	VA	Howard	farmer
Conner, James F.	Bank of St. Louis–Boonville	Dir	49	MO	Cooper	farmer, steam miller
Cunningham, Dr. John Frederick	Merchants' Bank of St. Louis–Brunswick	Dir	41	NY	Chariton	druggist, physician
Davis, John Mason	Merchants' Bank of St. Louis–Brunswick	Dir	43	KY	Chariton	farmer
Dunn, James Jr.	Mechanics' Bank of St. Louis–Warsaw	Cshr	41	KY	Benton	
Earickson, John K.	Exchange Bank of St. Louis–Glasgow	Dir	26	MO	Howard	tobacconist
Elliott, Thomas T.	Merchants' Bank of St. Louis–Brunswick	Dir	41	VA	Chariton	circuit clerk, real estate broker
Fisher, Jacob Harness	Bank of Missouri–Arrow Rock	Dir	50	VA	Saline	farmer

Name	Bank	Position	Age	State	County	Occupation
Forbis, James Brown	Western Bank of Missouri–Glasgow	Dir	41	KY	Howard	merchant
Garth, Dabney Crenshaw	Exchange Bank of St. Louis–Glasgow	Pres	56	VA	Howard	planter
Hayden, Luke Fyler	Exchange Bank of St. Louis–Glasgow	Dir	42	CT	Howard	farmer, brick yard owner
Henderson, Robert Morrison	Farmers' Bank of Missouri–Lexington	Dir	42	KY	Lafayette	grocer
Hendrix, Colonel Adam	Bank of Missouri–Fayette	Cshr	47	PA	Howard	
Hoffmann, Robert H.	Farmers' Bank of Missouri–Lexington	Cshr	42	VA	Lafayette	clerk
Hudgins, James Foster	Farmers' Bank of Missouri–Lexington	Dir	74	VA	Livingston	farmer
Hutchison, Solomon C.	Western Bank of Missouri–Glasgow	Dir	42	KY	Howard	hemp manufacturer
Johnson, Adamantine	Merchants' Bank of St. Louis–Brunswick	Cshr	36	KY	Chariton	merchant, farmer
Lewis, Colonel John Murray	Farmers' Bank of Missouri–Lexington	Dir	52	VA	Saline	planter
Lightner, James Shields	Farmers' Bank of Missouri–Lexington	Dir	40	VA	Lafayette	farmer
Locke, John D.	Exchange Bank of St. Louis–Glasgow	Dir	57	VA	Chariton	farmer
Mauzey, Stark	Merchants' Bank of St. Louis–Brunswick	Dir	39	IN	Chariton	tin and stove dealer
McMahan, Jesse Nelson	Bank of Missouri–Arrow Rock	Dir	47	MO	Saline	merchant

Name	Bank	Title	Age 1860	Nativity	Home county 1860	Other occupation(s)
Mills, Henry Samuel	Bank of Missouri–Arrow Rock	Dir	39	NY	Saline	merchant
Mitchell, William C.	Union Bank of St. Louis–Warrensburg	Pres	40	VA	Johnson	farmer
Morehead, Charles Robert	Farmers' Bank of Missouri–Lexington	Cshr	60	VA	Lafayette	
Morehead, Garrett W.	Exchange Bank of St. Louis–Glasgow	Dir	41	MD	Howard	farmer
Morrison, William	Farmers' Bank of Missouri–Lexington	Dir	42	PA	Lafayette	tinner and coppersmith, merchant, financier
Nelson, James M.	Bank of St. Louis–Boonville	Pres	44	VA	Cooper	planter
Offutt, Alfred H.	Farmers' Bank of Missouri–Lexington	Dir	42	KY	Lafayette	
Payne, William	Bank of Missouri–Fayette	Pres	44	KY	Howard	farmer
Plunkett, Willis Hawkins	Merchants' Bank of St. Louis–Brunswick	Pres	44	VA	Chariton	grocer, newspaper publisher
Price, Thomas Henry	Merchants' Bank of St. Louis–Brunswick	Dir	31	VA	Chariton	attorney
Roper, Alfred William	Western Bank of Missouri–Glasgow	Dir	41	KY	Howard	farmer
Sappington, William Breathitt	Bank of Missouri–Arrow Rock	Pres	39	TN	Saline	planter, manufacturer
Sawyer, Samuel Locke	Farmers' Bank of Missouri–Lexington	Dir	46	NH	Lafayette	attorney, farmer

Name	Bank	Position	Age	State	County	Occupation
Shackelford, Judge Thomas	Exchange Bank of St. Louis–Glasgow	Dir	38	MO	Howard	attorney
Shortridge, Alfred Lewis	Bank of St. Louis–Boonville	Dir	47	KY	Moniteau	physician
Slaughter, Martin	Farmers' Bank of Missouri–Lexington	Dir	47	VA	Lafayette	farmer
Southworth, Dr. James Walsh	Exchange Bank of St. Louis–Glasgow	Dir	50	NY	Howard	physician
Speed, William Pope	Bank of St. Louis–Boonville	Dir	44	KY	Cooper	druggist
Spratt, William A. Hall	Farmers' Bank of Missouri–Lexington	Dir	56	VA	Lafayette	farmer
Stephens, Captain Joseph Lafayette	Bank of St. Louis–Boonville	Cshr	34	MO	Cooper	attorney
Strancke, Samuel B.	Farmers' Bank of Missouri–Lexington	Dir	47	NY	Lafayette	farmer
Swinney, Captain William Daniel	Western Bank of Missouri–Glasgow	Pres	61	VA	Howard	planter
Townsend, Sanders Alexander Hamilton	Bank of Missouri–Arrow Rock	Dir	28	MO	Saline	farmer
Tracy, Benjamin N.	Western Bank of Missouri–Glasgow	Dir	51	VA	Randolph	merchant
Trigg, Dr. William Hodge	William H. Trigg & Co.–Boonville	Pres	52	TN	Cooper	
Turner, Henry Atchison	Exchange Bank of St. Louis–Glasgow	Dir	36	MO	Howard	farmer
Waddell, John William	Farmers' Bank of Missouri–Lexington	Dir	28	KY	Lafayette	merchant, farmer, stockman
Walker, Austin Kendrick	Bank of St. Louis–Boonville	Dir	40	KY	Pettis	farmer
Ward, George W.	Western Bank of Missouri–Glasgow	Dir	49	KY	Howard	farmer

Name	Bank	Title	Age 1860	Nativity	Home county 1860	Other occupation(s)
Warden, William E.	Merchants' Bank	Dir	35	MO	Chariton	farmer
Wentworth, Stephen Girard	Farmers' Bank of Missouri–Lexington	Dir	48	MA	Lafayette	public administrator
Wilcoxson, Hiram	Merchants' Bank of St. Louis–Brunswick	Dir	54	KY	Carroll	farmer
Williams, John Peter	Merchants' Bank of St. Louis–Brunswick	Dir	50	VA	Chariton	farmer
Wilson, Samuel	Farmers' Bank of Missouri–Lexington	Pres	62	Ireland	Lafayette	merchant
Withers, Marquis W.	Farmers' Bank of Missouri–Lexington	Dir	45	KY	Lafayette	farmer
Wood, William Henry	Bank of Missouri–Arrow Rock	Dir	29	MO	Saline	commission merchant
Woods, John Creigler	Western Bank of Missouri–Glasgow	Dir	42	MO	Howard	farmer

D. Promissory Note Cases per County — Summary

County	Total cases	County total real property (1860)	County total personal property (1860)	County total all property (1860)	Est. total face amt of notes	% of county real property	Est. total judgment amt of notes	% of county real property
Adair	10	$2,024,334	$1,029,102	$3,053,436	$10,612	1%	$11,813	1%
Andrew	23	$4,090,160	$2,344,302	$6,434,462	$24,407	1%	$27,170	1%
Audrain	15	$4,600,203	$2,600,290	$7,200,493	$15,918	0%	$17,720	0%
Benton	61	$1,595,101	$1,553,761	$3,148,862	$64,732	4%	$72,060	5%
Boone	20	$6,382,562	$6,296,091	$12,678,653	$21,224	0%	$23,626	0%
Buchanan	59	$11,501,897	$4,714,642	$16,216,539	$62,610	1%	$69,697	1%
Caldwell	16	$1,536,190	$582,065	$2,118,255	$16,979	1%	$18,901	1%
Callaway	11	$5,752,294	$5,863,579	$11,615,873	$11,673	0%	$12,994	0%
Carroll	51	$3,375,671	$2,616,750	$5,992,421	$54,120	2%	$60,247	2%
Cass	30	$3,948,650	$2,458,391	$6,407,041	$31,835	1%	$35,439	1%
Chariton	85	$3,158,149	$4,170,393	$7,328,542	$90,200	3%	$100,411	3%
Clark	12	$3,998,124	$2,198,076	$6,196,200	$12,734	0%	$14,176	0%
Clay	200	$6,228,620	$4,730,580	$10,959,200	$212,236	3%	$236,262	4%
Clinton	34	$3,482,895	$1,966,205	$5,449,100	$36,080	1%	$40,165	1%
Cooper	68	$7,684,256	$7,020,517	$14,704,773	$72,160	1%	$80,329	1%
Dade	17	$1,534,370	$1,377,331	$2,911,701	$18,040	1%	$20,082	1%
Greene	132	$4,426,995	$4,366,622	$8,793,617	$140,076	3%	$155,933	4%
Henry	138	$3,642,190	$2,981,470	$6,623,660	$146,443	4%	$163,021	4%
Hickory	62	$868,509	$594,128	$1,402,637	$65,793	8%	$73,241	9%

County	Total cases	County total real property (1860)	County total personal property (1860)	County total all property (1860)	Est. total face amt of notes	% of county real property	Est. total judgment amt of notes	% of county real property
Howard	13	$7,022,371	$9,588,023	$16,610,394	$13,795	0%	$15,357	0%
Jackson	123	$11,698,943	$8,672,756	$20,371,699	$130,525	1%	$145,301	1%
Johnson	365	$5,321,125	$4,002,354	$9,323,479	$387,331	7%	$431,178	8%
Lafayette	284	$11,210,267	$8,494,462	$19,704,729	$306,681	3%	$341,399	3%
Lawrence	18	$1,720,492	$1,595,637	$3,316,129	$19,101	1%	$21,264	1%
Lewis	31	$4,814,378	$2,908,122	$7,722,500	$32,897	1%	$36,621	1%
Linn	50	$2,656,303	$1,636,795	$4,293,098	$53,059	2%	$59,066	2%
Livingston	73	$2,402,531	$1,310,701	$3,713,232	$77,466	3%	$86,236	4%
Macon	29	$3,258,285	$2,163,963	$5,422,248	$30,774	1%	$34,258	1%
Mississippi	57	$1,649,645	$1,518,197	$3,167,842	$60,487	4%	$67,335	4%
Monroe	22	$3,013,767	$3,770,748	$6,784,515	$23,346	1%	$25,989	1%
Pettis	122	$5,605,464	$3,246,514	$8,851,978	$129,464	2%	$144,120	3%
Platte	23	$7,448,361	$5,278,213	$12,726,574	$24,407	0%	$27,170	0%
Polk	25	$2,295,432	$1,943,463	$4,238,895	$26,530	1%	$29,533	1%
Randolph	35	$3,171,840	$3,736,956	$6,908,796	$37,141	1%	$41,346	1%
Ray	254	$4,208,815	$4,905,265	$9,114,080	$269,540	6%	$300,053	7%
Saline	120	$6,837,227	$6,534,729	$13,371,956	$127,342	2%	$141,757	2%
Schuyler	37	$1,286,025	$689,825	$1,975,850	$39,264	3%	$43,708	3%
Scott	18	$984,226	$740,205	$1,724,431	$19,101	2%	$21,264	2%
St. Charles	18	$6,687,683	$3,605,397	$10,293,080	$19,101	0%	$21,264	0%
St. Clair	169	$1,566,155	$1,491,327	$3,057,482	$179,339	11%	$199,641	13%
Totals	2,930	$174,630,505	$137,297,947	$311,928,452	$3,114,563	2%	$3,467,145	2%

Real and personal property figures are from *Statistics of the United States*, 307.

E. Defendants—Three-County Sample

Name	Age 1860	Nativity	Home county 1860	Occupation(s)	Number of cases
Aldridge, Sanford P.	42	VA	Pettis	farmer	1
Alexander, Charles B.	30	KY	Cooper	farmer	1
Alexander, William B.	64	KY	Cooper	farmer	2
Allin, Thomas Hoos	42	KY	Chariton	gentleman	1
Allison, Nathaniel Thompson	62	KY	Cooper	farmer	16
Anderson, George	38	AR	Pettis	farmer, stockman, cattle trader	15
Barkley, John C.	26	KY	Saline	farmer	2
Bassett, John W.	43	NY	Cooper	farmer	2
Bates, William S.	41	MO	Saline	farmer	1
Baughman, Jacob	57	KY	Cooper	farmer	1
Bedwell, Elisha J.	41	VA	Cooper	stonecutter	1
Bell, George Lafayette	48	NC	Cooper	merchant	2
Bell, Thornton Pagett	42	VA	Saline	merchant	9
Berger, Daniel	58	VA	Cooper	boarding house keeper	1
Berry, Major Joshua H.	62	NC	Cooper	farmer	1
Boatright, Jacob	61	SC	Saline	farmer	1
Boggs, Robert	23	MO	Pettis	farmer	1
Bondurant, Captain Charles Palmore	57	VA	Saline	merchant, farmer	15
Booker, Thomas Henry	25	VA	Saline	farmer	1
Booker, William S.	30	VA	Saline	farmer	2
Bouldin, David William	32	VA	Pettis	farmer	1
Bousfield, Henry	78	UK	Cooper	farmer	1

Name	Age 1860	Nativity	Home county 1860	Occupation(s)	Number of cases
Brand, Horace Holley	27	KY	Cooper	farmer	1
Briscoe, Samuel Logan	43	KY	Cooper	farmer	1
Brown, Asbury Fletcher	31	VA	Saline	farmer	1
Brown, Edmund	68	VA	Saline	farmer	2
Brown, George Isbell	28	KY	Pettis	farmer	1
Brown, James Burton	42	VA	Saline	farmer	1
Brown, John Royal	28	VA	Saline	farmer	2
Brown, Joseph	65	KY	Pettis	none (infirm)	1
Brown, Samuel H.	28	KY	Pettis	farmer	2
Brown, Reverend William J.	45	VA	Saline	clergyman	3
Brown, William Spencer	40	VA	Saline	banker	36
Bryant, John W.	39	VA	Saline	circuit attorney	2
Burcham, Reuben James	39	NC	Pettis	farmer	1
Burgess, William Oscar	30	VA	Saline	miller	2
Cahill, William L.	24	KY	Pettis	saddler	2
Calhoun, Wilson	34	VA	Saline	clerk	1
Carpenter, Edward S.	25	VA	Saline	none	2
Carter, Edward A.	58	VA	Saline	farmer	8
Carthrae, Addison Fletcher	49	VA	Saline	farmer	1
Cartwright, Dr. Joseph Lafayette	35	KY	Pettis	planter, government freighter, physician	3
Chandler, Timothy	33	VA	Cooper	farmer	1
Chilton, Dr. Edward	45	VA	Cooper	physician	2
Chilton, John James	50	VA	Cooper	farmer	2
Chilton, Van Tromp	42	VA	Pettis	farmer	3

Name	Age	Birthplace	County	Occupation	
Chrisman, George L.	66	KY	Saline	no information	1
Chrisman, Hugh H.	31	KY	Saline	farmer	2
Chrisman, William M.	28	KY	Saline	farmer	1
Clark, William	37	TN	Saline	farmer	2
Clopton, Abner	52	VA	Pettis	farmer	1
Cole, James W.	58	KY	Cooper	farmer, stock raiser	1
Cole, Mark	54	KY	Cooper	farmer	3
Cole, Samuel	60	VA	Cooper	farmer	1
Cole, Samuel Franklin	27	MO	Cooper	farmer	1
Cole, Thomas Smiley	34	MO	Cooper	farmer	1
Combs, William Lorenzo	42	KY	Pettis	hotel keeper	2
Conner, James F.	49	MO	Cooper	farmer, steam miller	1
Cooper, Dudley Hancock	40	MO	Saline	farmer	1
Cooper, Henry	22	PA	Saline	miller	1
Cox, William T.	55	KY	Cooper	no information	2
Craig, Benjamin F.	38	KY	Cooper	farmer	1
Craig, James William	26	KY	Saline	farmer	2
Craig, Lewis Easterday	49	KY	Cooper	farmer	1
Craig, May Burton	33	VA	Saline	farmer	1
Craig, William Gasper Lafayette	27	MO	Nebraska Territory	laborer	1
Cravens, Ferris Ewing	42	MO	Pettis	farmer	3
Creel, Alexander M.	39	VA	Saline	farmer	1
Creel, Reuben Wagenner	44	KY	Pettis	farmer	1
Cruzen, Nathaniel Greene North	33	VA	Saline	farmer	1
Cunningham, Solomon	39	VA	Saline	farmer	2
Dallas, John Brinton	21	MO	Cooper	farmer	1
Darst, Abraham	32	OH	Pettis	farmer	4

Name	Age 1860	Nativity	Home county 1860	Occupation(s)	Number of cases
Davis, James Robinson	44	VA	Saline	farmer	1
Davis, John Boyden	26	VA	Pettis	merchant	1
Deaderick, John S.	42	GA	Saline	planter	1
Dobyns, Dr. Benjamin Franklin	43	KY	Johnson	physician	1
Donahoo, Joseph C.	44	KY	Pettis	farmer	1
Douglas, Daniel M.	38	MO	Johnson	farmer	1
Douglass, Henry L.	50	MO	Boone	none	1
Douthitt, Green Lee	45	KY	Cooper	farmer	1
Drinkwater, John Thurston	39	MO	Cooper	blacksmith	1
Durley, Samuel	55	KY	Pettis	farmer	3
Edwards, Thomas J.	36	VA	Saline	farmer	1
Ellis, Richard Petrop	50	VA	Cooper	farmer, miller, stock raiser	2
Ellis, Richard T.	23	MO	Cooper	farm laborer	1
Ellis, Thomas V.	30	VA	Cooper	farmer	1
Embree, George E.	35	KY	Cooper	boarding house keeper	1
Ervin, John B.	52	VA	Saline	farmer	2
Eubank, Achilles Jackson	29	MO	Cooper	farmer	1
Eubank, Joseph James	22	MO	Cooper	trader	1
Eubank, Nancy	47	KY	Cooper	none	1
Eubank, Richard Presley	22	MO	Cooper	trader	1
Evans, Dr. Edwin Chalmers	32	DC	Pettis	physician	1
Evans, Dr. Thomas	55	DC	Pettis	physician, farmer	1
Fackler, George Jacob	45	VA	Saline	farmer	2
Faulconer, James Harvey	30	KY	Pettis	farmer	3

Name	Age	State	County	Occupation	No.
Ferguson, James Sharp	61	VA	Howard	planter, stock raiser	1
Ferguson, Horace Willis	33	KY	Cooper	farmer	2
Ferrel, Jesse J.	38	MO	Saline	cabinetmaker	1
Field, Henry	24	KY	Pettis	farmer	4
Field, Colonel William Hill	51	VA	Pettis	planter	7
Finley, Judge Walker Hodnet	41	KY	Saline	farmer, stock dealer	20
Finley, William Adam	54	VA	Saline	farmer	7
Fisher, George Dunlap	23	KY	Pettis	none	2
Fisher, Colonel James Adam	48	KY	Pettis	farmer	2
Forbes, Alfred P.	24	MO	Pettis	trader	2
Forbes, Andrew Miller	53	KY	Pettis	farmer, stock dealer	12
Forbes, James M.	22	MO	Pettis	student	1
Ford, Colonel John Richardson Sr.	59	KY	Pettis	farmer	4
Fowler, John Goodon	37	KY	Pettis	farmer	3
Fowler, Thomas Armstrong	26	MO	Pettis	farmer	1
Francisco, Andrew J.	51	KY	Saline	farmer	1
Francisco, George	47	KY	Saline	farmer	1
Fristoe, Thomas Edward	28	MO	Pettis	farmer	1
Garnett, Edward Graves	41	VA	Saline	county judge	8
Garnett, Henry	50	VA	Saline	farmer	1
Garnett, Dr. John Newton	38	VA	Saline	physician	10
Garnett, Thomas T.	50	VA	Saline	planter	9
Garnett, William J.	22	KY	St. Louis	none	2
Gearhart, Isaac	67	VA	Howard	farmer, steamboat owner	1
Glasscock, Aldea Amazon	63	VA	Pettis	attorney, farmer, merchant, county school commissioner	1
Godfrey, John	44	KY	Pettis	farmer	2

Name	Age 1860	Nativity	Home county 1860	Occupation(s)	Number of cases
Graves, Alfred	23	VA	Johnson	merchant	1
Graves, Isaac Newton	30	KY	Saline	farmer	1
Graves, Jonathan	49	VA	Johnson	farmer	1
Graves, William Willis	50	KY	Illinois	farmer	2
Greenlease, Charles H. F.	47	VA	Cooper	farmer	3
Greer, Benjamin	75	VA	Pettis	farmer	1
Greer, John Wesley	30	MO	Pettis	blacksmith	1
Grey, Edward	54	UK	Cooper	bootmaker	1
Grinstead, William Wallace	30	KY	Pettis	farmer	1
Guthrey, Daniel Travis	43	VA	Saline	farmer, stock raiser	4
Hall, William M.		unknown	unknown	no information	1
Hamm, Dr. Strother Thrift	50	VA	Saline	physician	4
Hancock, Mandeville B.	30	KY	Saline	farmer	1
Hansberger, Mitchell	44	VA	Pettis	farmer	2
Harris, Edward Hazelwood	30	KY	Cooper	farmer	1
Harris, James Berry	49	MO	Cooper	farmer	1
Harris, James J.	62	VA	Cooper	farmer	7
Harris, James J. Jr.	21	VA	Cooper	farmer	1
Harris, James Y.	49	VA	Cooper	farmer	6
Harris, John	59	VA	Saline	farmer	3
Harris, Thomas Marcellius	64	VA	Cooper	farmer	2
Harris, Timothy	59	KY	Saline	renter	1
Harrison, William T.	47	KY	Saline	planter	2
Hawkins, Benjamin S.	42	KY	Pettis	farmer	1

Name	Age	Birthplace	County	Occupation	
Hay, James H.	43	KY	Cooper	farmer	7
Hays, Joshua Craig	42	KY	Saline	farmer	1
Hazell, Edward	47	KY	Cooper	blacksmith	1
Helm, George W.	57	VA	Cooper	farmer	4
Henderson, John B.	32	KY	Pettis	overseer	2
Henderson, John Moore	60	KY	Pettis	farmer	3
Hicklin, William P.	48	KY	Saline	ferryman	1
Hill, William Cackley	48	VA	Saline	farmer, trader	4
Hopkins, Major James Speed Sr.	61	KY	Pettis	planter	5
Hopkins, Joshua Barbee	28	KY	Pettis	farmer	1
Houston, Thomas Franklin	41	NC	Pettis	planter, stock raiser	12
Houx, Thomas C.	25	MO	Cooper	farm laborer	1
How, Robert William	33	MO	Pettis	farmer	1
Howe, Harvey C.	38	MO	Pettis	farmer	6
Huffman, Milton	37	OH	Pettis	farmer	1
Hughes, James A.	27	MO	Cooper	none	4
Hughes, James R.	39	KY	Pettis	planter, physician	4
Hughes, John C.	43	KY	Pettis	no information	2
Hughes, Colonel Reece Jr.	41	TN	Pettis	farmer, attorney, steam sawmill owner	6
Hughes, Samuel	54	TN	Cooper	farmer	6
Hughes, Thomas J.	31	MO	Cooper	merchant	6
Huston, Addison	33	VA	Saline	farmer	1
Ingram, James Samuel	58	VA	Saline	farmer	1
Jackson, Thomas	59	KY	Saline	farmer	1
Jamison, John Wesley	35	MO	Cooper	farmer	5
Jamison, William Ephraim	39	MO	Cooper	farmer	9
Jenkins, Aaron	57	TN	Pettis	farmer	5

Name	Age 1860	Nativity	Home county 1860	Occupation(s)	Number of cases
Jenkins, James	26	MO	Pettis	farmer	1
Jenkins, Samuel H.	48	TN	Cooper	farmer	2
Jones, Charles O.	46	KY	Pettis	farmer	1
Jones, Ellis W.		VA	Lafayette	farmer	1
Jones, James M.	42	KY	Pettis	farmer	2
Jones, James S.	51	VA	Saline	none	17
Jones, John Bright	49	KY	Saline	farmer	2
Jones, Joseph T.	38	KY	Saline	blacksmith	1
Jopling, Josiah	42	VA	Pettis	farmer	1
Jordan, Abram	48	VA	Saline	farmer	1
Kidd, Oswald	60	VA	Pettis	hotel keeper	4
Kirtley, Cave Johnson	34	KY	Lafayette	merchant	1
Kirtley, George Robertson	36	KY	Saline	county surveyor	3
Kirtley, Robert Edwards	40	KY	Saline	farmer	1
Kitchen, James C.	24	VA	Saline	farmer	2
Latimer, John T.	32	KY	Saline	farmer	1
Laurie, Judge Joseph Nourse	48	DC	Saline	probate judge	1
Lewis, Abraham Henry	34	VA	Saline	farmer	2
Lewis, Colonel John Murray	52	VA	Saline	planter	4
Licklider, George W.	23	OH	Cooper	tenant farmer	1
Licklider, Thomas	49	VA	Cooper	farmer	1
Liggett, Jeremiah	32	MO	Saline	merchant	1
Lightfoot, William H.	40	KY	Pettis	merchant clerk	2
Lindsey, David Herndon	32	KY	Saline	teacher	3

Name	Age	Birthplace	County	Occupation	#
Long, Gabriel B.	68	SC	Lafayette	farmer	1
Lowry, William	48	VA	Pettis	planter	4
Maddox, John P.	56	VA	Cooper	shoemaker	3
Magoffin, Ebenezer	43	KY	Pettis	farmer	2
Major, James R.	52	KY	Pettis	farmer	1
Major, John James	65	KY	Saline	farmer	1
Mann, John W.	32	KY	Cooper	farmer	1
Marmaduke, Vincent	29	MO	Saline	planter, stock dealer	4
Marshall, Joseph Hurst	31	KY	Saline	miller, distiller	3
Marshall, Richard Sr.	69	VA	Saline	farmer, coal dealer	1
Marshall, William F.	38	MO	Pettis	farmer	1
Maupin, William Overton	51	VA	Saline	planter	3
McBride, William Henry	42	KY	Cooper	farmer	1
McCarty, Richard	32	KY	Cooper	stock trader	1
McCarty, William S.	38	VA	Cooper	livery stable owner, jailor	3
McClanahan, Thomas	51	TN	Cooper	farmer	1
McClure, George W.	40	KY	Pettis	grocer	1
McClure, Wesley	33	KY	Pettis	sheriff	1
McCormick, Charles M.	50	VA	Cooper	trader	2
McDowell, Hugh H.	34	VA	Saline	farmer	2
McGirk, Isaac Carlock		MO	Johnson	physician	1
McKee, Isaac	38	KY	Cooper	steamboat captain, livery stable owner	1
McVey, Absalom	57	MD	Pettis	farmer	4
Melvin, Samuel T.	22	VA	Cooper	clerk	1
Meyers, Andrew	24	KY	Cooper	farmer	1
Meyers, Henry Marke	46	VA	Cooper	farmer	1
Miller, George Wear Jr.	27	MO	Kansas	territorial legislator	9

Name	Age 1860	Nativity	Home county 1860	Occupation(s)	Number of cases
Miller, Gideon Blackburn	52	VA	Pettis	farmer	12
Miller, John	79	SC	Cooper	farmer	8
Miller, Nimrod B.	23	MO	Pettis	none	3
Miller, Osbert	55	VA	Saline	farmer	2
Mills, Henry Winslow	45	VA	Cooper	farmer	1
Minor, Threesivellus M. Jr.	44	VA	Saline	farmer	2
Monaghan, John J.	47	PA	Pettis	farmer	6
Monroe, Thomas B.	41	TN	Cooper	farmer, state senator	1
Morgan, St. Clair	45	TN	Cooper	farmer	1
Morrow, Baxter E.	36	MO	Johnson	merchant	1
Motz, John	50	NC	Pettis	farmer	2
Nelson, Enrico Decatur	28	VA	Pettis	farmer	1
Newton, George Brigham	44	MA	Pettis	teacher	1
Nunnelly, Robert C.	40	KY	Saline	farmer	1
Oldfield, Nelson	26	OH	Pettis	plasterer	1
Outcalt, George Washington	43	NJ	Chariton	banker, manufacturer	1
Owen, Thomas	67	GA	Pettis	farmer	1
Owen, William	31	MO	Pettis	farmer	1
Parberry, Nathaniel Newbill	39	VA	Pettis	farmer	1
Parsons, Isaac	63	VA	Saline	farmer	3
Patrick, John D.	50	MO	Saline	planter	3
Patton, John Dysart	34	TN	Howard	farmer	2
Paxton, Archibald	50	VA	Saline	farmer	8
Pendleton, Curtis W.	34	KY	Saline	saddler	3

Name	Age	State	County	Occupation	No.
Phillips, Charles A.	18	MO	Cooper	farm laborer	1
Phillips, Elijah M.	19	PA	Pettis	farmer	1
Phillips, Martha	53	PA	Pettis	farmer	1
Phillips, Mary E.	40	MD	Cooper	none	1
Pierce, Colonel Peter	66	VA	Cooper	hotel keeper	1
Plummer, Franklin	41	PA	Saline	farmer	2
Pollard, Benjamin F.	32	NY	Pettis	merchant	5
Pollard, Seymour E.	29	NY	Pettis	merchant clerk	2
Powell, William H.	45	VA	Pettis	farmer	1
Powell, William L.	35	TN	Pettis	farmer	8
Price, William	29	PA	Saline	miller	1
Priest, Aquillus Rhodham	34	KY	Pettis	farmer	4
Priest, George Stubblefield	57	KY	Pettis	farmer	5
Priest, Martin Rush	32	KY	Pettis	farmer	1
Pruitt, William Henry	38	KY	Lafayette	merchant	1
Purdom, Madison G.	46	KY	Pettis	farmer	3
Quisenberry, Jackson	60	KY	Pettis	farmer	3
Ramsey, Higginbottom M.	43	VA	Saline	farmer	1
Rankin, James	55	VA	Cooper	farmer	3
Rankin, William	53	VA	Cooper	miller	3
Rea, Reverend Peter Goodman	40	VA	Cooper	clergyman	1
Ream, Absalom	36	MO	Pettis	farmer	11
Reynolds, Benjamin F.	35	VA	Saline	farmer	2
Reynolds, Philip Swan	54	VA	Saline	no information	1
Roberson, Albion	47	VA	Pettis	farmer	12
Robinson, Lewis Wilton	44	KY	Boone	lawyer	1
Rogers, John	28	TN	Saline	farmer	1

Name	Age 1860	Nativity	Home county 1860	Occupation(s)	Number of cases
Rogers, Thomas J.	48	TN	Saline	farmer	11
Rollen, William E.		unknown	unknown	no information	1
Rothwell, Dr. George W.	48	VA	Pettis	farmer, physician	2
Rucker, Dr. Angus Alexander	38	VA	Saline	physician	1
Rucker, Elizabeth Elrod	55	KY	Pettis	wife	1
Rucker, Thomas Allen	16	KY	Lafayette	none	1
Rucker, William Michael	36	MO	Cooper	farmer	7
Ruffner, Catherine P.	33	VA	Cooper	keeping house	1
Ryan, John Q.	49	VA	Pettis	farmer	1
Samuel, Richard Presley	24	KY	Saline	farmer	1
Scott, Samuel B.	42	KY	Pettis	farmer	1
Scott, William R.	53	KY	Pettis	farmer	6
Scott, William Wilson	40	KY	Cooper	farmer	1
Scrivener, Benjamin E.	56	KY	Pettis	hotel keeper	4
Seat, Stokely S.	50	TN	Cooper	farmer	2
Seay, Reuben Jr.	58	VA	Saline	farmer	5
Sellers, William H.	46	PA	Saline	farmer	1
Shaughnessy, William H.	27	IL	Saline	saddler	1
Short, William B.	34	KY	Cooper	saddler	1
Shouse, Reverend Charles Q.	23	KY	Pettis	farmer, clergyman	4
Shroyer, Presley	59	KY	Saline	farmer	3
Shy, Buriah M.	39	KY	Pettis	farmer	1
Shy, Christopher Lillard	39	KY	Pettis	farmer	1
Shy, David Jones	46	KY	Pettis	farmer	1

Name	Age	Birthplace	County	Occupation	No.
Shy, John C.	30	KY	Pettis	farmer	1
Simmons, Alfred	57	KY	Cooper	farmer	2
Simmons, Richard Van	23	KY	Cooper	farmer	4
Sitlington, Thomas Oliver	42	VA	Pettis	farmer	3
Smiley, Thomas B. Jr.	28	MO	Cooper	farmer	3
Smith, David	54	KY	Cooper	farmer	3
Smith, Sheriff Jacob H.	44	KY	Saline	sheriff	2
Smith, William J.	55	KY	Cooper	farmer	1
Smith, William Orlando	42	VA	Saline	farmer	2
Sneed, John M.	34	KY	Pettis	farmer	1
Snelling, Richard Elam	55	VA	Saline	farmer	2
Snyder, William J.	40	PA	Cooper	farmer	2
Spangenburger, George	45	PA	Pettis	farmer	5
Spears, John	28	VA	Saline	farmer	2
Steel, James Harvey	26	MO	Cooper	farmer	1
Steel, Morgan B.	30	KY	Pettis	renter	1
Stephens, Captain John H.	32	MO	Cooper	farmer	1
Stephens, Thomas Hart Benton	28	MO	Pettis	farmer	1
Stone, Peter H.	43	KY	Pettis	farmer	1
Stoneseffer, James M.	30	VA	Saline	farm laborer	3
Sutherlin, Nathaniel	59	VA	Cooper	farmer	21
Sydenstriker, Andrew J.	32	VA	Saline	farmer	1
Sydenstriker, Thomas Lewis	27	VA	Saline	farmer	1
Taylor, Henry Clay	29	MO	Pettis	farmer	2
Taylor, James Archer	23	MO	Pettis	farmer	1
Taylor, John	49	KY	Cooper	farmer, stock dealer	2
Taylor, William M.	62	GA	Cooper	farmer	8

Name	Age 1860	Nativity	Home county 1860	Occupation(s)	Number of cases
Thomson, Asa Peyton	29	MO	Saline	farmer	3
Thomson, Quincy Adams	31	MO	Saline	farmer	2
Thomson, Volney V.	35	KY	Pettis	farmer	1
Thomson, William Ellis	39	KY	Saline	farmer	3
Thornton, John	46	TN	Saline	none	1
Thornton, John Taylor	61	VA	Cooper	farmer	2
Thornton, Presley P.	23	MO	Cooper	farmer	2
Thornton, William A.	30	VA	Cooper	farmer	1
Towles, Dr. Alfred Lewis	42	VA	Saline	physician	15
Trundle, William R.	29	KY	Pettis	farmer	4
Tucker, William G.	41	KY	Cooper	farmer	1
Tutt, Reverend Benjamin George	21	MO	Cooper	clergyman	1
Vandyke, John R.	33	TN	Pettis	farmer	1
Vaughan, David	38	PA	Saline	farmer	4
Walden, John A.	40	VA	Saline	overseer	8
Walden, William L.	41	VA	Saline	teamster	3
Walker, Austin Kendrick	40	KY	Pettis	farmer	3
Walker, Charles W. C.	39	KY	Pettis	farmer, trader	3
Wallace, George Washington	41	MO	Cooper	farmer	6
Wallace, Joseph B.	34	MO	Cooper	farmer	1
Wallace, Robert Green Jr.	39	MO	Texas (state)	farmer	1
Warfield, Elisha Nicholas	36	KY	Cooper	farmer, county public administrator	1
Warren, Erbin	45	KY	Pettis	farmer	1
Warren, Martin V.	23	MO	Lafayette	farmer	1

Wear, Samuel	41	MO	Cooper	farmer	1
Weyland, Louis	35	Germany	Cooper	upholsterer	1
Wheeler, Stephen	48	KY	Saline	farmer	2
Whitney, George A.	23	KY	Pettis	grocer	1
Williams, David M.	25	KY	Pettis	farmer	3
Williams, John H.	23	KY	Pettis	farmer	3
Williams, Marcus	44	VA	Cooper	miller	2
Williams, Samuel W.	31	KY	Saline	miller	1
Williams, Thomas L.	48	VA	Cooper	farmer	5
Williams, Wallace W.	47	KY	Moniteau	teacher	1
Williams, William T.	33	KY	Saline	farmer	2
Willis, Benjamin F.	34	VA	Saline	farmer	2
Wilson, Robert Cresap	34	MD	Saline	farmer	2
Wilson, William H.	35	KY	Pettis	merchant	1
Winslow, Henry	49	VA	Saline	farmer	1
Woodson, Frank	32	KY	Pettis	hotel keeper	1
Woolery, Lawrence Gabriel	24	MO	Cass	none	1
Young, John Wesley	30	KY	Cooper	farmer	1
Younger, Charles	33	MO	Pettis	farmer	5

Total 979

F. Planters—Three-County Sample

Name	Age 1860	Nativity	Home county 1860	Real prop 1860	Slaves 1860	Acres 1860	Notes
Booker, Pinkethman Davis (Pink)*	60	VA	Saline	$20,000	28	1,200	2, 4
Bruce, Aaron Franklin	52	KY	Saline	$90,000	22	2,000	1, 4
Cartwright, Dr. Joseph Lafayette*	35	KY	Pettis	$23,600	25	650	4
Cheatham, Edward O.	52	KY	Pettis	$24,000	25	600	4
Cockrill, George S.	38	VA	Cooper	$24,000	27	1,300	1, 3
Deaderick, John S.*	42	GA	Saline	$100,000	30	2,550	2
Demoss, John	78	NC	Saline	$30,000	35	1,360	2
Field, Colonel William Hill*	51	VA	Pettis	$123,000	40	1,985	
Fields, Joseph	44	VA	Saline	$20,000	24	800	1, 4
Fisher, Jacob Harness*	50	VA	Saline	$20,000	38	1,670	1, 3
Gentry, Richard	52	KY	Pettis	$114,000	41	7,600	1, 4
Gibson, William	66	SC	Cooper	$60,000	25	1,200	2, 4
Gilliam, William Taylor	52	VA	Saline	$134,750	50	2,190	2, 4
Goodwin, John Chapman Garland	48	VA	Cooper	$49,700	24	1,580	2, 3
Hardeman, Dr. Glenn Owen	34	MO	Saline	$20,000	28	1,129	
Harrison, Willam T.*	50	KY	Saline	$20,000	20	1,200	1, 3
Hereford, George W.	49	VA	Saline	$20,000	20	880	1, 4
Hopkins, Major James Speed Sr.*	61	KY	Pettis	$83,000	35	2,400	3
Houston, Thomas Franklin*	41	NC	Pettis	$100,000	24	10,000	3
Hughes, Dr. James R.*	39	KY	Pettis	$29,000	21	1,440	
Jackson, Hon. Claiborne Fox*	54	KY	Saline	$21,000	48	1,240	1, 3
Jones, John Stycks	49	KY	Pettis	$54,000	31	1,800	1

Name	Age	State	County	Wealth	No.	Acres	Notes
Lewis, Colonel John Murray*	52	VA	Saline	$25,000	28	1,000	1, 4
Lowry, William*	47	VA	Pettis	$21,000	21	985	4
Marmaduke, Hon. Meredith Miles*	68	VA	Saline	$37,800	54	2,200	2, 3
Marmaduke, Vincent*	29	MO	Saline	$25,000	23	1,400	2, 3
Maupin, William Overton*	51	VA	Saline	$20,000	22	1,400	1, 3
Mayo, William H.	45	VA	Cooper	$36,000	32	1,000	
McDaniel, Reuben Ellis	61	VA	Saline	$24,000	48	1,250	2, 4
Moore, John R.	59	KY	Pettis	$20,000	22	1,160	
Napton, Judge William Barclay	51	NJ	Saline	$25,000	30	1,500	1, 3
Neff, Isaac	63	TN	Saline	$16,000	27	1,012	2, 4
Nelson, James M.*	43	VA	Cooper	$13,200	35	1,320	1, 3
O'Banion, Minor W.	48	VA	Saline	$20,000	29	1,600	1
Patrick, John Dennis*	50	MO	Saline	$40,000	22	2,000	
Piper, Willis	50	VA	Saline	$25,800	23	904	1
Ragland, John Kelly	42	VA	Cooper	$36,710	81	2,000	2, 4
Sappington, Mrs. Penelope Caroline	27	KY	Saline	$20,750	66	830	2, 4
Sappington, William Breathitt*	48	TN	Saline	$41,000	65	2,300	2, 4
Smith, Crawford Early	35	MO	Saline	$40,000	106	2,500	1
Smith, N. J.	25	KY	Saline	$20,000	21	1,060	4
Thomson, Mentor	49	KY	Pettis	$41,320	20	800	1, 4
Thomson, Robert Yancey*	60	KY	Saline	$22,700	30	1,600	2, 3
Walker, Anthony Smith	55	KY	Cooper	$54,000	29	13,000	1, 4
Walker, Henry R.	57	KY	Cooper	$25,080	20	1,254	1, 4

Notes

* Individual was a banker, was a promissory note signer, or had a son who was a promissory note signer.

1. Individual or nuclear family present in 1850 — non-planter

2. Individual or nuclear family member present in 1850 — planter

3. Individual or nuclear family member present in 1870 — non-elite landowner

4. Individual or nuclear family member present in 1870 — elite landowner

G. Guerrillas—Seven-County Sample (ordered by county)

Name	Age 1860	Nativity	Home county 1860	Occupation
Gilliam, James Anthony*	18	MO	Chariton	none
Gooch, Joseph	17	MO	Chariton	none
Hines, Claiborne*	13	MO	Chariton	none
Hines, William*	14	MO	Chariton	none
Rucker, Dr. Minor Jackson*	30	VA	Chariton	physician
Swearengen, John	9	MO	Chariton	none
Watson, Andrew J.	23	MO	Chariton	none
Wisdom, Green*	15	NC	Chariton	none
Bell, James S.*	23	VA	Cooper	none
Baker, Captain Moses Jefferson	44	KY	Jasper	farmer
Bedford, Littleberry	46	KY	Jasper	farmer
Bishop, John	45	KY	Jasper	farmer
Brison (Bryson), John W.	28	MO	Jasper	farmer
Buskirk, James	56	KY	Jasper	farmer
Buskirk, Taylor	16	IL	Jasper	none
Hall, Richard	14	KY	Jasper	none
Hawkins, Thomas H.	24	MO	Jasper	farmer
Hines, Simeon	15	MO	Jasper	none
Humbard, Absalom	23	TN	Jasper	farmer
Hydon, Whitton	15	VA	Jasper	none
Ireland, Austin (John)	25	IN	Jasper	farmer
Jackson, Chancey	24	IN	Jasper	farm laborer
Johnson, Callaway	26	TN	Jasper	grocer
Johnson, Peter	37	NC	Jasper	farmer
McKey, John (Jack)	29	TN	Jasper	blacksmith
Meador, Moses Greer	46	VA	Jasper	farmer
Nichols, James	40	KY	Jasper	farmer
Norris, Milton	21	KY	Jasper	medical student
Ozment, Ferd	24	NC	Jasper	farmer
Parkinson, William	29	MO	Jasper	merchant
Petty, James	30	KY	Jasper	farmer
Petty, Washington	30	MO	Jasper	farmer
Rader, William	16	MO	Jasper	none
Rusk, David	22	IN	Jasper	farmer
Scott, Robert A.	19	KY	Jasper	farm laborer
Shirley, John Allison M. (Bud)	18	MO	Jasper	none
Sunday, David	38	PA	Jasper	farmer

Name	Age 1860	Nativity	Home county 1860	Occupation
Tingle, William	49	DE	Jasper	merchant
Walker, George B.	16	MO	Jasper	none
Webb, Austin	15	MO	Jasper	none
Webb, Thomas	36	TN	Jasper	farmer
Bledsoe, James Lauderdale*	16	TN	Lafayette	none
Bledsoe, Josiah Lauderdale*	19	MO	Lafayette	farmhand
Burton, Peter*	21	MO	Lafayette	none
Gann, Isaac Luther*	17	MO	Lafayette	none
Gann, Wesley Benton*	19	MO	Lafayette	none
Gann, William Butler*	12	MO	Lafayette	none
Graves, John Robinson*	29	KY	Lafayette	farmer
Hammond, Charles W.*	14	MO	Lafayette	none
Kincheloe, James Thomas*	16	MO	Lafayette	none
Marshall, Julius*	28	MO	Lafayette	druggist
Mitchell, Nathaniel Baxter*	20	MO	Lafayette	none
Poisal, James Hamilton	25	VA	Lafayette	no information
Poisal, McKendrie R. (Mack)	22	VA	Lafayette	no information
Pool, Francis Marion (Dave)*	22	MO	Lafayette	no information
Pool, John Adams*	21	MO	Lafayette	none
Poole, William*	17	MO	Lafayette	none
Prewitt, John Allen*	13	MO	Lafayette	none
Reinhardt, Jack*	39	KY	Lafayette	merchant
Sanders, Theodore*	18	KY	Lafayette	none
Sutherland, Zacharius (Zack)*	18	MO	Lafayette	none
Thompson, James*	32	TN	Lafayette	farmer
Waller, James*	30	KY	Lafayette	farmer
Warren, James*	20	MO	Lafayette	none
Warren, John*	19	MO	Lafayette	none
Warren, Thomas B.*	20	MO	Lafayette	none
Goode, John R.	26	MO	Newton	farmer
Harmon, John	17	MO	Newton	none
Henson, William	23	TN	Newton	farmer
Johnson, Rector	36	MO	Newton	grocer
Martin, Elijah M.	30	TN	Newton	farmer
Matthews, Allen	44	KY	Newton	merchant
Matthews, John	18	MO	Newton	saddler's apprentice
Mayfield, Hiram	37	NC	Newton	farmer
McCullough, Edward	27	VA	Newton	merchant
Price, Lafayette (Fay)	17	MO	Newton	none

Name	Age 1860	Nativity	Home county 1860	Occupation
Ramsey, James	26	TN	Newton	blacksmith
Ray, William F.	27	MO	Newton	farm laborer
Waggoner, George	17	TN	Newton	none
Jones, Edmond A.*	13	MO	Pettis	none
Nichols, John*	18	KY	Pettis	farmer
Woodson, Thomas Jefferson*	24	MO	Pettis	miller
Allen, Richard*	20	MO	Saline	none
Allen, Thomas*	42	KY	Saline	gentleman
Benson, Dr. John W.*	24	MO	Saline	physician
Cruzen, George Richardson*	15	VA	Saline	none
Cruzen, Isaac Champlain*	19	VA	Saline	none
Davis, Simon (Simeon) G.	14	MO	Saline	none
Durrett, Richard*	24	MO	Saline	none
Durrett, William Silas*	25	MO	Saline	farmer
Ervin, John Chalmers*	21	MO	Saline	none
Ferrell, David*	27	MO	Saline	farmer
Jackson, William Sappington*	26	MO	Saline	farmer
Noten, John W.	24	ME	Saline	renter
O'Donnell, Thompson	17	PA	Saline	none
Pulliam, John Drury	15	MO	Saline	none
Shaull, Joseph Lewis*	14	VA	Saline	no information
Stephens, William M.*	31	MO	Saline	farmer
Surbaugh, Henry Clay	15	MO	Saline	none

* Guerrilla or family member signed one or more promissory notes (guerrillas from Chariton, Cooper, Lafayette, Pettis, and Saline Counties only)

NOTES

INTRODUCTION

1. Colt wholesale price list for 1860, reproduced in Haven and Belden, *History of the Colt Revolver*, 380. In June 1861 the U.S. War Department purchased Colt revolvers "of the latest pattern" (probably Colt New Model Army revolvers) for $25 each. Report from Lt. Col. James W. Ripley to Hon. Simon Cameron, Secretary of War, dated June 8, 1861, in *The War of the Rebellion: A Compilation of the Official Records of the Union and Confederate Armies* (hereafter cited as *Official Records*), ser. 3, vol. 1, 260. A few months previously the Texas Secession Convention appointed Major (later Brigadier General, C.S.A.) Ben McCulloch to purchase one thousand Colt revolvers, among other arms, for the defense of the state. McCulloch also paid twenty-five dollars apiece for the revolvers. *Official Records*, ser. 4, vol. 1, 721. Over the course of the war Colt dropped its price to the U.S. War Department, since the government was purchasing the revolver in such large volumes. From 1861 to 1866 the U.S. War Department purchased 129,730 Colt's New Model Army revolvers, at an average price of $17.69 apiece. Haven and Belden, *History of the Colt Revolver*, 100.
2. Marler, "Rural Merchants and Consumers," 176–79.

CHAPTER 1. FINANCIAL CONSPIRACY

1. McPherson, *Battle Cry of Freedom*, 232, 276–77. Long, *Civil War Day by Day*, 4, 12, 76.
2. McPherson, *Battle Cry of Freedom*, 284, 290. Parrish, *History of Missouri*, 3. *Historical Census Browser. Compendium of the Enumeration of the Inhabitants and Statistics of the United States*, 90. "State of Missouri, Table Number 3, Population of Cities, Towns, &c," in Kennedy, *Population of the United States in 1860*, 1:297. Hurt, *Agriculture and Slavery in Missouri's Little Dixie*, 125–54.
3. Phillips, *Missouri's Confederate*, 19, 77. *Jefferson City Inquirer*, June 30, 1860, 2. *Liberty*

Tribune, May 16, 1856, 2. Parrish, *History of Missouri*, 3. U.S. Census (manuscript), population schedule, 8th census (1860).

4. Parrish, *History of Missouri*, 1, 3. McCandless, *History of Missouri*, 247–53. Phillips, *Missouri's Confederate*, 201, 230, 235. Jackson had won a plurality of the popular vote with 47 percent of the total, compared to 42 percent for his nearest rival, Sample Orr. 158,579 popular votes were cast, and Jackson won by 7,863 votes.

5. The Breckinridge Democrats had sixty-two members in the house and senate as compared with forty-six Douglas Democrats, forty-four Constitutional Unionists, and thirteen Republicans. This alignment included fourteen holdover Breckinridge senators. Parrish, *History of Missouri*, 1, 4–6. Snead, *Fight For Missouri*, 66–67.

6. McPherson, *Battle Cry of Freedom*, 234–35. Long, *Civil War Day By Day*, 31. "Progress of the Revolution—What is to Be Done?" *New York Herald*, January 11, 1861. It is not clear how the writer thought the "full measure of justice" might be conceded, other than for Lincoln to voluntarily resign. "The Crisis in Kansas," *Charleston Mercury*, March 16, 1861. Jones, "Civil War Letters," April 22, 1861, and May 4, 1861. George Graham Vest was a Boonville lawyer, an ardent secessionist, and later representative and senator from Missouri to the Confederate Congress. Dyer, *Boonville*, 103. U.S. Senate, *Biographical Directory of the U.S. Congress.*

7. "Border Ruffians Invading Nebraska," *New York Times*, August 11, 1856, reprinted from the *Council Bluffs Chronotype*, July 30, 1856. "From Kansas to St. Louis Overland," *New York Daily Times*, February 14, 1857, 10. Missouri's bonds sold at a discount when this article appeared, but the state had no problem borrowing money. "Commercial Affairs," *New York Times*, March 4, 1857.

8. "The Kansas Swindle," *Frederick Douglass' Paper*, August 3, 1855. "Southern Dragooning," *Frederick Douglass' Paper*, July 20, 1855; "The Spirit of Despotism," *Frederick Douglass' Paper*, May 18, 1855; "Shooting Fugitives in Illinois on the Fourth," *Chatham Provincial Freeman*, August 22, 1857, reprinted from the Chicago *Congregational Herald*; "Kansas," Washington, D.C. *National Era*, July 10, 1856; *Frederick Douglass' Paper*, August 12, 1853; "Southern Justice," Boston, Mass. *Liberator*, June 28, 1834; "Gov. Reeder, and the Missourians; What will the President Do?" *Frederick Douglass' Paper*, May 18, 1855. "Important from Kansas," *New York Daily Times*, February 25, 1856, 3. Also "The Ex-Border Ruffianism of the West—Experience of it in California," *New York Times*, June 11, 1856, 2.

9. "The Escape of Missouri," *New York Times*, July 8, 1861, 4.

10. Connolly, *Quantrill and the Border Wars*, 35.

11. McGrath, *State Almanac and Official Directory of Missouri* (1879), 11–116. U.S. Senate, *Biographical Directory of the U.S. Congress.* McPherson, *Battle Cry of Freedom*, 122. "'The Cause of Kansas, the Cause of the South,'" *Frederick Douglass' Paper*, November 23, 1855, from the *Charleston Mercury*. Ibid., April 30, 1861. "The Crisis in Kansas," ibid., March 16, 1861. Also "Our Cincinnati Correspondence," Ibid., June 19, 1861. "Shall the Slaveholders Give up Kansas," *Provincial Freeman*, May 10, 1856, reprinted from the *Richmond Enquirer*. "Organized Movement to Make Kansas a Slave State," *Frederick Douglass' Paper*, April 13, 1855, reprinting from the *Jackson Missis-*

sippian, March 20, 1855. "The Situation of Affairs," *New York Herald*, May 18, 1861. Entries on Senators Waldo Johnson and Trusten Polk, Representatives John Bullock Clark Sr. and John W. Reid, in U.S. Senate, *Biographical Directory of the U.S. Congress*. Davis, speech to Mississippi State Legislature, Jackson, Mississippi, November 4, 1857, in *The Papers of Jefferson Davis, 1856–1860*, 6:160. Davis, speech to Cumberland County (Maine) Democratic Convention, Portland, Maine, August 26, 1858, ibid., 221. McPherson, *Battle Cry of Freedom*, 284. Davis, *Papers of Jefferson Davis*, 4:7, 50–51n2.

12. Long, *Civil War Day by Day*, 38. Parrish, *Turbulent Partnership*, 7–8. McPherson, *Battle Cry of Freedom*, 258–59.

13. Parrish, *Turbulent Partnership*, 6–14, 23. Snead, *Fight for Missouri*, 66–67.

14. Myers, *Financial History of the United States*, 149. *St. Louis Missouri Republican*, January 1, 1861, 2.

15. *St. Louis Missouri Republican*, January 1, 1861, 2. Cable, *Bank of the State of Missouri*, 274.

16. Cable, *Bank of the State of Missouri*, 274. "An Act to Regulate Banks and Banking Institutions and to Create the Offices of Bank Commissioners" (March 2, 1857), Article 1, Section 9, in *Laws of the State of Missouri, Nineteenth General Assembly*, 5, 14. Phillips, *Missouri's Confederate*, 85–86. In addition to these family members, the governor's brothers-in-law Charles M. Bradford and Darwin W. Marmaduke and his first cousin once removed Captain William E. Warden were all bank officers or directors at the time of Jackson's election as governor. Each of these allied families had other family members who were involved in banking. The Jackson extended clan particularly dominated the board of directors of the Bank of Missouri at Arrow Rock. *Marshall Democrat*, March 7, 1860, 2. Phillips, *Missouri's Confederate*, 220–21.

17. "An Act for the Relief of the Bank of the State of Missouri, the Merchants' Bank, the Mechanics' Bank, the Exchange Bank, the Southern Bank, the Bank of St. Louis, the Farmers' Bank of Missouri, and the Western Bank of Missouri" (March 18, 1861), *Laws of the State of Missouri, Twenty-First General Assembly*, 9. Hubbard and Davids, *Banking in Mid-America*, 93.

18. The letter from Robert A. Barnes to Jackson, dated May 10, 1861, made it clear that the banks had not yet paid the money. *St. Louis Daily Missouri Democrat*, June 22, 1861, 2. My thanks to Jack Kennedy of Columbia, Missouri, who drew my attention to these letters, after noticing them while conducting his own research on the plot to seize the United States arsenal in St. Louis in 1861. Primm, *Lion of the Valley*, 233.

19. Long, *Civil War Day by Day*, 56–57, 59, 60. Parrish, *History of Missouri*, 10. Parrish, *Turbulent Partnership*, 17.

20. Jackson to Walker, April 19, 1961, folder 3, Claiborne Fox Jackson, General Correspondence, 1861, in the Governors' Papers Collection, Missouri State Archives; quoted in Phillips, "Calculated Confederate," 405. Phillips, *Missouri's Confederate*, 246. Bartels, *Civil War in Missouri Day by Day*, 6. *St. Louis Daily Missouri Democrat*, June 25, 1861. Parrish, *Turbulent Partnership*, 17.

21. Parrish, *History of Missouri*, 11. Phillips, *Damned Yankee*, 165, 202–3.

22. Parrish, *History of Missouri*, 5–6. McPherson, *Battle Cry of Freedom*, 282.

23. *New York Times*, December 8, 1861, 3, reprinted from the *St. Louis Missouri Republican*, December 3, 1861. *St. Louis Daily Missouri Democrat*, June 22, 1861, 2.

24. *St. Louis Daily Missouri Democrat*, June 22, 1861, 2. The Brunswick branch of the Merchants' Bank of St. Louis, the Glasgow branches of the Exchange Bank of St. Louis and the Western Bank of Missouri, the Arrow Rock and Fayette branches of the Bank of Missouri, and the Boonville branch of the Bank of St. Louis. *Liberty Tribune*, April 20, 1860, 2. Castel, *General Sterling Price*, 7.

25. Castel, *General Sterling Price*, 13. Parrish, *History of Missouri*, 14.

26. "An Act to Provide for the Organization, Government, and Support of the Military Forces in the State of Missouri" (May 14, 1861), *Laws of the State of Missouri, Twenty-First General Assembly, Called Session*, 3. "An Act to Authorize Counties to Loan Money to the State" (May 15, 1861), ibid., 51. Castel, *General Sterling Price*, 34. "An Act to Raise Money to Arm the State, Repel Invasion, and Protect the Lives and Property of the People of Missouri" (May 11, 1861), Section 2, *Laws of the State of Missouri, Twenty-First General Assembly, Called Session*, 52–53. Parrish, *History of Missouri*, 24–25.

27. Castel, *General Sterling Price*, 14–15. Eakin and Hale, *Confederate Records*, 5:283.

28. *New York Times*, May 26, 1861, 3; ibid., May 30, 1861, 3; ibid., June 17, 1861, 3.

29. Phillips, *Damned Yankee*, 209, 224–25.

30. Steward, *Duels and the Roots of Violence*, 131. Parrish, *Turbulent Partnership*, 31.

31. Castel, *General Sterling Price*, 25–26; Parrish, *Turbulent Partnership*, 32.

32. The first sea battle was Fort Sumter, on April 12; First Manassas was on July 21. McPherson, *Battle Cry of Freedom*, 273, 340. Parrish, *Turbulent Partnership*, 14. *New York Times*, June 18, 1861, 4. Also Hale, *Branded as Rebels*, 2:226. Kirkpatrick, "Missouri's Secessionist Government," 124–37.

33. Castel, *General Sterling Price*, 11. Nancy Chapman Jones to May Jones McCarthy (Gibson), 22 April 1861, 4 May 1861, and 11 May 1861, in Jones, "Civil War Letters." "The Escape of Missouri," *New York Times*, July 8, 1861, 4. Public Resolution No. 1, approved December 24, 1861, in Rives, *Congressional Globe, Thirty-Seventh Congress, Second Session*, appendix, 419.

34. *Journal of the Missouri State Convention, July, 1861*, 25–32.

35. *New York Times*, June 18, 1861, 1; June 21, 1861, 1; June 30, 1861, 1. *Harper's Weekly*, July 13, 1861, 1; July 27, 1861, 1. "The War in Missouri," *New York Times*, July 28, 1861, 2. *Chicago Tribune*, June 25, 1861, 2. *St. Louis Daily Missouri Democrat*, June 22, 1861, 2. *New York Times*, May 25, 1861, 4; May 30, 1861, 3; June 18, 1861, 4.

36. "An Act to Give Aid to the People of the State of Missouri," August 6, 1861, *Official Records*, ser. 1, vol. 53, 721. "An Act Declaring the Political Ties Heretofore Existing Between the State of Missouri and the United States of America Dissolved" (October 28, 1861), *Journal of the Senate, Extra Session of the Rebel Legislature (Missouri)*, 39. "An Act to Provide for the Defense of the State of Missouri" (November 1, 1861), ibid., 34–35. Parrish, *Turbulent Partnership*, 268–69. Long, *Civil War Day by Day*, 144. Act of November 28, 1861, *Official Records*, Series 1, vol. 53, 754–55.

37. The individual bond certificates were printed "Receivable in Payment of all Dues to the

State." While the act stopped short of declaring the bonds legal tender for debts, Section 11 did empower the bond commissioners to negotiate or hypothecate any amount of the bonds for the purpose of raising funds to defray expenses incurred in the defense of the state. "An Act to Provide for the Defense of the State of Missouri" (November 1, 1861), *Journal of the Senate, Extra Session of the Rebel Legislature (Missouri)*, 34–35. Bond from personal collection, John Karel. Kirkpatrick, "Missouri's Secessionist Government," 127–29. *Columbia Missouri Statesman*, May 16, 1862, 2. Act of January 27, 1862, *Official Records*, ser. 4, vol. 1, 882. Act of February 15, 1862, *Official Records*, ser. 4, vol. 1, 939. Kirkpatrick, "Missouri's Secessionist Government," 128, 130. Phillips, *Missouri's Confederate*, 273. Parrish, *Turbulent Partnership*, 31–32. Parrish, *History of Missouri*, 48.

38. Smith, *History and Debates*, 37–40, 175–83.

39. The act assigned a specific amount of bonds that each bank was obliged to buy. The Bank of Mobile was to purchase $319,150; the Southern Bank of Alabama $212,800; and the Northern Bank of Alabama $106,400. "An Act to legalize the suspension of specie payments by certain banks of Alabama" (February 2, 1861), *Acts of the Called Session of the General Assembly of Alabama (1861)*, 9–11. "An Act to raise money and to provide for the Military Defence of the State of Alabama" (January 29, 1861), ibid., 41–43.

40. Mississippi also sent a commissioner to Missouri, Daniel L. Russell, who gave a speech to the Missouri General Assembly on January 18, 1861. *Journal of the House of Representatives of the State of Missouri, Twenty-First General Assembly, Regular Session*, 113–14. *St. Louis Missouri Republican*, December 30, 1860. Quoted in the *New York Times*, "Missouri Legislature and Secession," January 1, 1860, 8. Report of William Cooper, Commissioner to Missouri, presented to Governor Moore, January 7, 1861. Smith, *History and Debates*, 405–12.

41. *New York Times*, July 28, 1861.

CHAPTER 2. NEW BANKS

1. Article 8, "Of Banks," *Constitution of the State of Missouri*, 22. Cable, *Bank of the State of Missouri*, 247. *Laws of the State of Missouri, Ninth General Assembly, First Session*, 11. For a complete list of parent and branch banks, see Appendix 4. "Semi-Annual Statement of the Condition of the Banks of Missouri, on the First day of January, 1859," etc., *Bankers' Magazine and Statistical Register* (hereafter *Bankers' Magazine*) 8, no. 11 (May 1859), 886–87. "Condition of the Banks of the State of Missouri on the First Day of July, 1859," etc., *Bankers' Magazine* 9, no. 3 (September 1859), 202–3. "Semi-Annual Statement of the Condition of the Banks of the State of Missouri on the first day of January, 1860," etc., in *Journal of the House of Representatives of Missouri, Twentieth General Assembly, Called Session*, 14–15 (Appendix E, Bank Commissioner's Report). *St. Louis Daily Missouri Republican*, April 8, 1860, 3; July 7, 1860, 2.

2. As of October 16, 1854, the State Bank and its branches had $1,737,250 in outstanding circulation. There are no precise figures for Missouri's population at that time, but the 1850 census gave a total state population of 682,044. In 1860, the state's population

stood at 1,182,012. The average of these two numbers, used here for the circulation per head, is 932,028. Using this figure, the banknote circulation per person in Missouri computes to $1.86. *Historical Census Browser*. Cable, *Bank of the State of Missouri*, 244. McCandless, *History of Missouri*, 95, 103. As of October 16, 1854, stockholders' equity in the Bank of Missouri stood at $1,215,405.22, of which the state had provided $954,205.22. Report of the Committee Appointed by the Governor to Examine the Condition of the Bank of the State of Missouri and its Branches to the Eighteenth General Assembly, *Journal of the House of Representatives of the State of Missouri, First Session, Eighteenth General Assembly*, 15, 92 (appendix). The bank's charter limited circulation to a two-to-one ratio to paid-in capital. With $1.2 million in paid-in capital, the bank could have circulated up to $2.4 million in paper currency. Section 46, "An Act to Charter the Bank of the State of Missouri," *Laws of the State of Missouri, First Session, Ninth General Assembly*, 22.

3. Miller and VanHoose, *Essentials of Money, Banking and Financial Markets*, 301 (citing Timberlake, *Monetary Policy in the United States*). Myers, *Financial History of the United States*, 130, 134. Hepburn, *History of Currency in the United States*, 66–67. Cable, *Bank of the State of Missouri*, 207–8, 244.

4. *St. Louis Missouri Democrat*, February 26, 1857, 2. Dillistin, *Bank Note Reporters*, 1. Cable, *Bank of the State of Missouri*, 246, quoting from *Report of the Committee Appointed by the Chamber of Commerce of St. Louis on "Trade, Commerce and Manufacturing."* In the late 1850s the St. Louis newspapers quoted current prices for "Eastern exchange" and "Eastern sight." Eastern exchange referred to bills of exchange payable at an eastern city, usually New York. Eastern sight referred to bills with so little time remaining that they would be due by the time they were physically transferred to the place of payment. "Sight" equals payable on demand. Dewey, *State Banking Before the Civil War*, 111.

5. *Bankers' Magazine* 9, no. 12 (June 1860), 60–61. Willcox, *History of the Philadelphia Savings Fund Society*, 5, 12. "An Act to Incorporate the Boatman's Savings Institution," in *Laws of the State of Missouri, First Session, Fourteenth General Assembly*, 224–26. "An Act to Incorporate the Boatmen's Savings Institution," in *Local and Private Acts of the State of Missouri, Adjourned Session, Eighteenth General Assembly*, 148–51. *St. Louis Missouri Democrat*, January 13, 1857. The first such institution was founded in Dumfriesshire, Scotland, by the Reverend Henry Duncan in 1810. McCandless, *History of Missouri*, 2:161. Cable, *Bank of the State of Missouri*, 237.

6. Cable, *Bank of the State of Missouri*, 237. For example, "The payment of the stock subscribed shall be made and completed by the subscribers, respectively, at such time and in such manner as such Directors may prescribe." "An Act to Incorporate the Independence Savings Institution," article 4, in *Local and Private Acts of the State of Missouri, Adjourned Session, Eighteenth General Assembly*, 163. "Report of the Committee Appointed by the Governor to Examine the Condition of the Bank of the State of Missouri and its Branches to the Eighteenth General Assembly," *Journal of the House of Representatives of the State of Missouri, First Session, Eighteenth General Assembly*, 92 (Appendix). Section 1, "An Act to Charter the Bank of the State of Missouri," *Laws of the State of Missouri, First Session, Ninth General Assembly*, 13. "An Act Concerning

Corporations," chapter 34, *Revised Statutes of the State of Missouri* (1856), 1:369–79. "An Act to Create Loan and Fund Associations, and to Extend the Benefits Thereof," chapter 36, ibid., 1:381–83.

7. Governor's Message, *Journal of the House of Representatives of the State of Missouri, First Session, Eighteenth General Assembly*, 22–24.

8. U.S. Senate, *Biographical Directory of the U.S. Congress*. There are no census figures for 1837 and 1854, so an exact comparison is impossible. The closest years available for comparison are 1840 and 1860. From 1840 to 1860 Missouri's population more than tripled, from 383,702 to 1,182,012. *Historical Census Browser*. In his message to the Eighteenth General Assembly, Governor Price reported that state revenues for the two years ending October 1, 1856, totaled $1,007,113.53. During the same period the state had spent $871,818.72, leaving a balance in the treasury of $271,899.94. This latter amount included $200,000 set aside to redeem state bonds maturing the following July. Meanwhile, the state was stretching its credit to extend financing to railroad companies for construction, and it was not in a position to sell yet more bonds to expand the banking system. *Journal of the House of Representatives of the State of Missouri, First Session, Eighteenth General Assembly*, 15–17. Missouri's Eighth Senatorial District at the time was composed of Platte and Clinton Counties. *Liberty Tribune*, August 18, 1854, 2. *Journal of the Senate of the State of Missouri, First Session, Eighteenth General Assembly*, 40–41, 248. *Laws of the State of Missouri, First Session, Nineteenth General Assembly*, 6. Governor's Message, *Journal of the House of Representatives of the State of Missouri, First Session, Nineteenth General Assembly*, 17.

9. Rolnick and Weber, "Free Banking, Wildcat Banking, and Shinplasters," 12. Bodenhorn, *State Banking in Early America*, 262. Rolnick and Weber, "New Evidence on the Free Banking Era," 1082–83.

10. *Bankers' Magazine* 9, no. 12 (June 1860), 974–1000. In 1837, the state enacted a law prohibiting foreign banking companies from doing business in Missouri and from circulating out-of-state banknotes. "An Act to Prevent Foreign Banking Companies from setting up Agencies or transacting Banking business within the limits of the State," in *Laws of the State of Missouri, First Session, Ninth General Assembly*, 24. In 1840, a law was passed restricting the right to circulate banknotes to the Bank of Missouri. *Laws of the State of Missouri, First Session, Eleventh General Assembly*, 30. In 1843, the legislature enacted "An Act to Prevent Illegal Banking, and to Suppress the Circulation of Small Bank Notes, and Other Depreciated Paper Currency Within the Limits of this State (February 28, 1843)." In *Laws of the State of Missouri, First Session, Twelfth General Assembly*, 20. Other laws date from 1845 and 1855. Chapter 16, "An Act to Prevent Illegal Banking, and the Circulation of Depreciated Paper Currency Within the Limits of this State (March 26, 1845)," in *Revised Statutes of the State of Missouri* (1845), 166–70. Article 4 of the state's corporation law barred any corporation not created for banking purposes from issuing banknotes ("An Act Concerning Corporations," chapter 34, in *Revised Statutes of the State of Missouri* (1856), 371. An 1855 law encouraged brokers to buy up out-of-state banknotes, and thus remove them from circulation. "An Act to Prevent Illegal Banking, and the Circulation of Depreciated Paper Currency, within this State," chapter 16, ibid., 285. The general banking law of 1857 contained several

clauses restricting Missouri's banks of issue from circulating out-of-state banknotes. Article 42 made it illegal for the new banks to circulate any note payable outside the state, or at any other place than at the bank or its branches. Article 43 barred the banks from taking in payment any funds but gold and silver, and the notes of specie-paying banks of the state. *St. Louis Daily Missouri Republican*, December 16, 1856, 2.

11. Rockoff, for instance, found that by 1860 there were several states with sound free banking systems. Rockoff further argued that in the states where the free banking system failed, the failure could be traced to defects in the bond security system for circulating notes. Rockoff, "Varieties of Banking and Regional Economic Development," 167, 169. Rolnick and Weber also found that the free banking period was not as chaotic as once thought; nor were free banking systems as costly to depositors and note holders as has been assumed. Rolnick and Weber, "New Evidence on the Free Banking Era," 1084–85. Nor, when free banks did fail, were their problems contagious. Rolnick and Weber, "Banking Instability and Regulation." *Laws of the State of Missouri, First Session, Nineteenth General Assembly*, 6. *Journal of the Senate of the State of Missouri, First Session, Nineteenth General Assembly*, 94. For example, on January 17, one day after the Senate passed the bank bill, citizens of Liberty, Missouri, met to form a delegation to the assembly to urge that a bank be placed their city. *Liberty Tribune*, January 23, 1857, 2. *St. Louis Missouri Republican* January 17, 1857, 2. *Liberty Tribune*, February 7, 1857, 2, reprinted from the *St. Louis Herald*.

12. *Journal of the House of Representatives of the State of Missouri, First Session, Nineteenth General Assembly*, 389, 401–2, 409. *Journal of the Senate of the State of Missouri, First Session, Nineteenth General Assembly*, 313, 339. Appendix, "Report of the Joint Committee on Banks," ibid., 343. "An Act to Regulate Banks and Banking Institutions, and to Create the Offices of Bank Commissioners," in *Laws of the State of Missouri, First Session, Nineteenth General Assembly*, 14–40.

13. *St. Louis Missouri Republican*, February 26, 1857, 2. *Journal of the House of Representatives of the State of Missouri, First Session, Nineteenth General Assembly*, 331; *Journal of the Senate of the State of Missouri, First Session, Nineteenth General Assembly*, 339. For instance, an editorial in December 1856 in the *St. Louis Missouri Republican* included a long list of provisions that the writer argued should be incorporated into any new law. *St. Louis Missouri Republican*, December 16, 1856, 2. Senator James L. Minor of Cole County in the senate session of February 25, 1857, reported in the *St. Louis Daily Missouri Democrat*, February 27, 1857, 2.

14. "An Act Establishing General Regulations for the Incorporation of Banks, passed March 22, 1837," in *Acts of the General Assembly of Virginia* (1837), 59–68. "An Act to Regulate Banks and Banking Institutions, and to Create the Offices of Bank Commissioners," in *Laws of the State of Missouri, First Session, Nineteenth General Assembly*, 14–40. *Bankers' Magazine* 9, no. 12 (June 1860), 974–1000. Ibid. 6, no. 10 (April 1857), 328.

15. Cable, *The Bank of the State of Missouri*, 256. *Bankers' Magazine* 6, no. 10 (April 1857), 828. *St. Louis Missouri Democrat*, February 26, 1857, 2. Price's successor, Trusten Polk, was inaugurated January 5, 1857, while the Nineteenth General Assembly was in session. Leopard and Shoemaker, *Messages and Proclamations*, 3:10. Governor's Message,

Journal of the House of Representatives of the State of Missouri, First Session, Nineteenth General Assembly, 20–21.

16. Governor's Message, *Journal of the House of Representatives of the State of Missouri, First Session, Nineteenth General Assembly*, 20–21.

17. With a group of other investors, Frank P. Blair, Jr., publisher of the *St. Louis Missouri Democrat*, and future U.S. congressman and Union general, applied to the legislature to charter the Laclede Bank, with paid-in capital of two million dollars. So did the Boatmen's Savings Institution, the chief competitor of the State Bank as a depository and lending institution, under the leadership of its president, Sullivan Blood. Cable, *Bank of the State of Missouri*, 232. Blood, too, was strongly pro-Union. A group of German investors also sought to form a bank; they too were denied. *Jefferson City Inquirer*, February 7, 1857, 2. *Journal of the House of Representatives of the State of Missouri, First Session, Nineteenth General Assembly*, 411. "An Act to Regulate Banks and Banking Institutions, and to Create the Offices of Bank Commissioners," article 37, in *Laws of the State of Missouri, First Session, Nineteenth General Assembly*, 22.

18. "An Act to Regulate Banks and Banking Institutions, and to Create the Offices of Bank Commissioners," in *Laws of the State of Missouri, First Session, Nineteenth General Assembly*, 21, 24.

19. *Journal of the Senate of the State of Missouri, First Session, Eighteenth General Assembly*, 27. *Journal of the House of Representatives of the State of Missouri, First Session, Eighteenth General Assembly*, 39. *Journal of the House of Representatives of the State of Missouri, First Session, Nineteenth General Assembly*, 36. *Journal of the Senate of the State of Missouri, First Session, Nineteenth General Assembly*, 62. In the Nineteenth General Assembly's Joint Committee on Banks, the house members represented the counties of Adair, Benton, Cooper, Howard, Jackson, Livingston, New Madrid, Macon, Marion, Pike, and St. Louis. The senate members represented the counties of Jefferson, Ste. Genevieve, and St. Francois (Fifteenth District); Adair, Knox, Scotland, Schuyler, Putnam and Sullivan (Fourth District); Benton, Pettis, Henry, Hickory, and St. Clair (Twenty-Third District); and Buchanan, DeKalb, and Gentry (Seventh District). *Revised Statutes of the State of Missouri* (1856), 2:1320–22. "An Act to Regulate Banks and Banking Institutions, and to Create the Offices of Bank Commissioners," in *Laws of the State of Missouri, First Session, Nineteenth General Assembly*, 31–40.

20. In Howard County there were five banks within a few miles of each other (Bank of Missouri at Arrow Rock, Western Bank of Missouri at Glasgow, Bank of Missouri at Fayette, Exchange Bank of St. Louis at Brunswick, and the Bank of St. Louis branch at Boonville. In the Kansas City–Independence area, there were four banks within a few miles of each other. Clayton, *Landings on all the Western Rivers and Bayous*, 41–43. *Liberty Tribune*, April 3, 1857, 4. *Liberty Tribune*, March 13, 1857, 2; June 5, 1857, 1. *Columbia Missouri Statesman*, March 13, 1857, 3.

21. The banks that were able to close their subscription books early were the Bank of St. Louis, the Exchange Bank of St. Louis, the Farmers' Bank of Missouri, and the Western Bank of Missouri. Cable, *Bank of the State of Missouri*, 259, referencing the *St. Louis Missouri Democrat*, March 18, 1857. *St. Louis Triweekly Missouri Republican*, February 1, 1861, 1. The branch with the lowest percentage of its capital provided by the

parent bank was the Southern Bank of St. Louis branch at Independence, at 15 percent. The branch bank with the highest percentage of its capital provided by the parent bank was the Mechanics' Bank of St. Louis branch at Kansas City, with 49 percent. *St. Louis Missouri Republican*, January 7, 1860, 2; October 5, 1860; October 6, 1860; October 8, 1860.

22. Hurt, *Agriculture and Slavery*, 69–74. McCandless, *History of Missouri*, 143–44. Primm, *Lion of the Valley*, 128–36. Hammond, *Sovereignty and an Empty Purse*, 27.

23. Cable, *Bank of the State of Missouri*, 259. Hurt, *Agriculture and Slavery*, 13–14, 219–23. Writing about the future Confederate states, Eugene Genovese found that banking served as an auxiliary to the plantation economy there as well. Genovese, *Political Economy of Slavery*, 21–22. Dewey, *State Banking Before the Civil War*, 154, 182–84. Hammond, *Sovereignty and an Empty Purse*, 76.

24. Contact with outside sources of information and connections with banks in distant commercial locations have been important banking functions since earliest times. In antebellum Missouri, besides contact by letter and word of mouth with their counterparts at corresponding banks, the banks' chief source of information about financial markets was the newspapers. St. Louis was the funnel through which financial information passed, and the leading newspapers of the city would regularly report financial news. Mostly this took the form of quoting portions of articles from other newspapers, usually two to three per issue. For example, "In the exchange market the rate was firmly fixed at 5 per cent. premium for Eastern sight, and 6 for New Orleans. . . . Gold is at 4 1/2 premium, and silver 2." *St. Louis Missouri Republican*, January 25, 1861, 3. Translated, this means that $100 in notes issued by reputable, secure, first-rate New York banks may be purchased with $105 in Missouri money issued by banks of the same character. Similarly, $106 in Missouri money buys $100 in New Orleans money, $104.50 in Missouri money buys $100 in gold, and $102 in Missouri money buys $100 in silver.

25. McCandless, *History of Missouri*, 150. Before the telegraph, obtaining current information about business conditions, interest rates, and banknotes' value in distant cities was a real problem for bankers, something they were usually only able to accomplish by having correspondents in these places. Refer for example to Brown, *A Hundred Years of Merchant Banking*, 19 ff. Weston F. Birch & Son account books, vol. 2, Exchange Book, 1859–1871. Lloyd, *Lloyd's Railroad, Telegraph and Express Map*.

26. Most scholarship on innovation focuses on technological innovation, though there are other kinds. Joseph Alois Schumpeter defined entrepreneurship as the carrying out of "new combinations" in one of five different areas: introducing a new product, production method, or source of supply; opening a new market; or creating a new organizational form. Schumpeter, *Theory of Economic Development*, 66, 78. Paul H. Wilken has a similar breakdown, classifying innovations as either technological, organizational, material, product, market, financial, or labor. Wilken, *Entrepreneurship*, 86. The state with the highest per capita circulation was Rhode Island, with $20.86 in circulation. Comparable figures for New York, Massachusetts, and Pennsylvania were $7.59, $18.77, and $4.47, respectively. The state with the highest specie reserves for each dollar of circulation was Louisiana, with $1.20 in gold or silver for every paper dollar. Illinois

currency had the lowest specie backing in the country. For New York, Massachusetts, and Pennsylvania, specie reserves per dollar of circulation were $.84, $.33, and $.58, respectively. *Bankers' Magazine* 9, no. 12 (June 1860), 974–1000.

27. *St. Louis Triweekly Missouri Republican*, February 1, 1861, 1. *Historical Census Browser.* The six additional banks near Fayette were the Arrow Rock branch of the Bank of Missouri, the Glasgow and Columbia branches of the Exchange Bank of St. Louis, the Glasgow branch of the Western Bank of Missouri, the Brunswick branch of the Merchants' Bank of St. Louis, and the Boonville branch of the Bank of St. Louis. *St. Louis Triweekly Missouri Republican*, February 1, 1861, 1.

28. The three banks in the southeast quarter of the state were the Bank of Missouri branch at Cape Girardeau, the Merchants' Bank of Missouri branch at Ste. Genevieve, and the Union Bank of Missouri branch at Charleston. The rest of Missouri's southeast (the modern counties of Butler, Camden, Carter, Christian, Cole, Crawford, Dallas, Dent, Douglas, Dunklin, Franklin, Gasconade, Howell, Iron, Laclede, Madison, Maries, Miller, Morgan, New Madrid, Oregon, Osage, Ozark, Pemiscot, Phelps, Pulaski, Reynolds, Ripley, Shannon, St. Francois, Stoddard, Stone, Taney, Texas, Washington, Wayne, and Wright) had no banks at all. This area is greater than the 1860 states of Rhode Island, Delaware, Connecticut, New Jersey, New Hampshire, Vermont, Massachusetts, and Maryland, as well as the later states of Hawaii and West Virginia. Total land area of Missouri counties available at Digital-Topo-Maps.com. Origins of Missouri counties available at "Missouri History," Missouri Secretary of State web page. *Historical Census Browser.*

29. Excluding St. Louis, the population of the counties without banks grew by 92 percent between 1850 and 1860. Over the same period, the population of the counties with banks grew by 53 percent. *Historical Census Browser.* The Granby lead mines, near Joplin, opened in 1857 and by 1860 had produced fifteen million pounds of lead. Holibaugh, *Lead and Zinc Mining Industry*, 154–56. Pinney, *History of Wine in America*, 177–79. Walker, *Compendium of the Ninth Census*, 704 (see Table XCI). Since the Volstead Act took effect in January 1920, the 1920 U.S. agricultural census does not contain statistics for wine production in that year. The census does, however, report production in 1909. In that year California produced 16,005,519 gallons of wine, eclipsing the production of every other state. After California, the major wine producing states were New York (346,973 gallons), Ohio (264,218 gallons), Missouri (245,656 gallons), and North Carolina (205,152 gallons). *Fourteenth Census of the United States*, 871. Henry Overstoltz, an incorporator of the Union Bank of Missouri, was born in Germany. "An Act to Incorporate the Union Bank of Missouri," approved March 2, 1859, in *Laws of the State of Missouri, First Session, Twentieth General Assembly*, 21. U.S. Census (manuscript), population schedule, 8th census (1860), St. Louis County [Missouri]. "An Act to Regulate Banks and Banking Institutions and to Create the Offices of Bank Commissioners," article 4, "Establishing Banks and Branches," in *Laws of the State of Missouri, First Session, Nineteenth General Assembly*, 31–36. Charles Everts, cashier of the Mechanics' Bank of St. Louis parent branch in 1860, was born in Germany. U.S. Census (manuscript), population schedule, 8th census (1860), St. Louis County [Missouri]. *Bankers' Magazine* 9, no. 12 (June 1860), 996.

30. *Historical Census Browser.*
31. *Jefferson City Inquirer,* April 23, 1859, 3, reprinting from the *St. Louis Herald. Jefferson City Inquirer,* May 21, 1859, 2. The bank's March 3, 1857, published financial data showed a total capital of $1,215,405, of which the state owned $954,205. Cable, *Bank of the State of Missouri,* 246. The proportion of state ownership was shrinking, however, as the bank opened new branches and sold additional stock after the passage of the 1857 law. As of January 1859, the state owned one million dollars' worth of stock in the state bank, and individuals owned $1,383,750. *Bankers' Magazine* 8, no. 11 (May 1859), 886. On January 1, 1861, the state owned $1,086,300 in capital stock, and individuals owned $2,305,676.51 in stock. *St. Louis Missouri Republican,* February 1, 1861. *Liberty Tribune,* January 30, 1857, 2, 4. *Chicago Daily Tribune,* January 27, 1857, 2.
32. *Jefferson City Inquirer,* April 23, 1859, 3, reprinting from the *St. Louis Herald. Jefferson City Inquirer,* May 21, 1859, 2. *Liberty Tribune,* June 17, 1859, 2.
33. *Chicago Press and Tribune,* May 12, 1859, 2. *Jefferson City Inquirer,* April 23, 1859, 3, reprinting from the *St. Louis Herald. Jefferson City Inquirer,* May 21, 1859, 2. *Liberty Tribune,* June 17, 1859, 2. *Chicago Press and Tribune,* June 25, 1859, 4; June 29, 1859, 2.
34. "An Act to Regulate Banks and Banking Institutions and to Create the Offices of Bank Commissioners," section 26, in *Laws of the State of Missouri, First Session, Nineteenth General Assembly,* 21. In this period Massachusetts, Pennsylvania, and New York banks were likewise limited in the amount of capital they could invest in real estate. Dewey, *State Banking Before the Civil War,* 45–46. In contrast some banks, particularly in the South, had been formed with aid to agricultural improvements in mind, such as the Union Bank of Louisiana and the Planters' Bank of Mississippi. Ibid., 47. *Boatmen's Savings Institution v. Bank of the State of Missouri,* in *Reports of Cases Argued and Determined in the Supreme Court of the State of Missouri* (1863), 33:497, 522. "An Act Respecting Savings Institutions and other Corporations doing a Banking Business," in *Laws of the State of Missouri, First Session, Twentieth General Assembly,* 13. "Official Corruption," *New York Times,* February 21, 1859. *Jackson v. Boatmen's Saving Institution,* Missouri Supreme Court Historical Database.
35. "Report of the Joint Committee on Banks," in *Journal of the Senate of the State of Missouri, First Session, Nineteenth General Assembly,* 343. *Columbia Statesman,* reprinted in the *Liberty Tribune,* April 3, 1857, 4. *Liberty Tribune,* March 13, 1857, 2.
36. Trusten Polk, after serving as Missouri governor for less than two months, resigned at the end of February 1857 after the Assembly chose him to be U.S. Senator from Missouri. U.S. Senate, *Biographical Directory of the U.S. Congress.* Lieutenant Governor Hancock Jackson assumed office as acting governor until a special election was held in August 1857; Robert M. Stewart was elected and assumed office in October. Leopard and Shoemaker, *Messages and Proclamations,* 3:24–25. Hubbard and Davids, *Banking in Mid-America,* 87–88. Cable, *Bank of the State of Missouri,* 256. Castel, *General Sterling Price,* 7.
37. For a detailed history of upper-class Kentuckians who relocated to Pettis County, Missouri, see Claycomb, *History of Northeast Pettis County,* 39–40. The total population of Missouri in 1850 was 682,044. In 1860 the total population of Missouri was 1,182,012: a 73 percent increase over the decade. In 1850, there were 87,422 slaves in Missouri. By

1860, there were 114,931: a 31 percent increase. In the seven counties with most slaves (Boone, Callaway, Clay, Cooper, Howard, Lafayette, and Saline), the total number of slaves went from 21,015 in 1850 to 27,574 in 1860: also a 31 percent increase. In these same seven counties, the overall population increased from 74,900 to 97,959: again a 31 percent increase. However, the number of slave owners overall in these counties did not keep pace, increasing from 4,690 in 1850 to 5,340 in 1860: a 15.7 percent increase. Also, during the decade, slave ownership became proportionately more concentrated in the hands of the large operators. In these seven counties with most slaves, the total number of slave owners with twenty or more slaves went from 147 to 213: a 45 percent increase. *Historical Census Browser.* Hurt, *Agriculture and Slavery*, 309–10.

CHAPTER 3. NEW BANKERS

1. *New York Times*, May 25, 1861, 4.
2. Schumpeter, *Theory of Economic Development*, 137.
3. "An Act to Regulate Banks and Banking Institutions, and to Create the Offices of Bank Commissioners," in *Laws of the State of Missouri, First Session, Nineteenth General Assembly*, 31–36. "An Act to Incorporate the Union Bank of Missouri," in *Laws of the State of Missouri, First Session, Twentieth General Assembly*, 21. *Laws of the State of Missouri, First Session, Fourteenth General Assembly*, 180, 214, 221. *Laws of the State of Missouri, Fifteenth General Assembly*, 219, 368. *Laws of the State of Missouri, Sixteenth General Assembly*, 77, 362, 379, 467, 480, 484. *Laws of the State of Missouri, Second Session, Seventeenth General Assembly*, 30, 37, 46, 56, 311, 318. *Laws of the State of Missouri, Second Session, Eighteenth General Assembly*, 36, 61, 64, 66, 69, 77, 103, 126, 127, 210, 215, 231, 243, 250, 253, 257, 260, 265, 311, 324, 372, 379, 383, 423, 428. *Local and Private Acts of the State of Missouri, Adjourned Session, Eighteenth General Assembly*, 149, 198, 147, 158, 207, 221, 230, 288, 311. *Laws of the State of Missouri, First Session, Nineteenth General Assembly*, 588, 615, 633, 648, 588, 606, 615, 617, 624, 633, 648. *Laws of the State of Missouri, First Session, Twentieth General Assembly*, 294, 359, 419. The group of forty-one incorporated 6 currency-issuing banks, 22 insurance companies, 16 savings banks, 8 manufacturing firms, 4 railroads, 7 other transportation firms, 6 hotels, 5 mines, and 3 utilities, and 4 other organizations. The core group of fourteen incorporated more financial firms than any other sort. Of the 68 companies this group incorporated, 19 were insurance companies, 9 were savings banks, and 6 were currency-issuing banks.
4. *Dartmouth College v. Woodward*, 17 U. S. 518 (1819). "An Act to Establish an Academy in the Town of Jackson, in the county of Cape Girardeau," in *Acts of the First General Assembly of the State of Missouri, First Session*, 10. "An Act to Incorporate the Cape Girardeau Mill Company," in *Laws of the State of Missouri, Second Session, Third General Assembly*, 8. Before it passed its first general incorporation law, the state passed an earlier law affecting the legal standing of corporations in 1835: "An Act to Regulate the Proceedings Against Corporations," dated February 6, 1835. *Revised Statutes of the State of Missouri*, 1840, 125–27. "An Act Concerning Corporations," chapter 35, in *Revised Statutes of the State of Missouri*, 1845, 230. The most important feature of the 1855

corporation law was to reduce shareholder liability to its modern level. "An Act Concerning Corporations," chapter 34, articles 13 and 15, in *Revised Statutes of the State of Missouri*, 1856, 372–73.

5. U.S. Census (manuscript), slave schedule, 8th census (1860), St. Louis County [Missouri]. For more detailed biographical information see Supporting Data available on the Yale University Press website (hereafter referred to as Supporting Data). John J. Anderson, president of the Bank of St. Louis, was the only one of the core group of fourteen promoters involved in bank management. Anderson, too, was strongly pro-Confederate, and Union military authorities arrested him after fighting broke out in St. Louis in May 1861. Geiger, "Missouri's Hidden Civil War," 117.

6. *Bankers' Magazine* 10, no. 12 (June 1861), 996. John J. Anderson, one of the founders of the Bank of St. Louis, had previously headed the private banking firm of John J. Anderson & Co. *The St. Louis Directory*, 1854, 215. Chell, Haworth, and Brearley, *The Entrepreneurial Personality*, 245–67. Miner, *Psychological Typology of Successful Entrepreneurs*, 21–31. Robert A. Barnes, president of the State Bank, gave his occupation as merchant to the census taker. John J. Anderson gave his occupation as banker, inasmuch as he continued to head his own private banking firm, John J. Anderson & Co., while at the same time being president of the Bank of St. Louis. Junius Brutus Alexander gave his occupation to the census taker as merchant wholesaler; John A. Brownlee as wholesale dry goods merchant; George E. Harding as commission merchant. Ezekiel B. Kimball reported no occupation. Of the seven, John W. Wills was the only one who reported his occupation as bank president. *Bankers' Magazine* 10, no. 12 (June 1861), 996. U.S. Census (manuscript), population schedule, 8th census (1860), St. Louis County [Missouri]. However, at this time Wills was also treasurer of an insurance company. *Liberty Tribune*, May 7, 1858, 3. John C. Cawelti traces the evolution of the ideology of the self-made man that swept the country in the second quarter of the nineteenth century, eclipsing the Jeffersonian idea of a natural aristocracy. At this time, Cawelti writes, the self-made man was identified with commercial pursuits and business enterprise. Cawelti, *Apostles of the Self-Made Man*, 4–5, 46. In St. Louis in the election of 1860 Lincoln received a majority of all the votes cast for him in *all* the southern states and carried the city. Primm, *Lion of the Valley*, 244. See Supporting Data for more biographical information.

7. Edwards and Hopewell, *Edwards' Great West*, 193. Darby, *Personal Recollections*, 416–17. Gould, *Fifty Years on the Mississippi*, 567. "Biographical Sketch," Robert Augustus Barnes papers. Scharf, *History of Saint Louis City and County*, 2:1101–2. Conard, *Encyclopedia of the History of Missouri*, 1:150.

8. Stevens, *St. Louis*, 321–25. *Official Records*, ser. 2, vol. 1, 554. Conard, *Encyclopedia of the History of Missouri*, 1:43. Stevens, *Missouri the Center State*, 2:410 (opposite), 528–30. Letter dated September 12, 1861, naming John Anderson of St. Louis and Ephraim Converse and William C. Kennett of New Orleans and St. Louis, Missouri Secretary of State, Missouri Union Provost Marshal Papers, Reel F1581. The letter concerns circuit court proceedings involving the Crescent City Bank, Mechanics' and Traders Bank, and Louisiana State Bank, all of New Orleans, and John Anderson and Company.

9. *Compendium of the Enumeration of the Inhabitants and Statistics of the United States,*

from the Returns of the Sixth Census, 90. State of Missouri, Table Number 3, "Population of Cities, Towns, &c," in Kennedy, *Population of the United States in 1860*, 1:297. In 1860, St. Louis County had 96,086 foreign-born inhabitants, or 51.6 percent, out of a total population of 186,178. The nativity of slaves was not recorded in the 1860 census, and the figures for St. Louis County are only for the free population. State of Missouri, Table 4, "Free Population, Native and Foreign, by Counties," ibid., 1:300. New York County, New York, had 386,345 foreign-born inhabitants, or 47.4 percent, out of a total population of 813,669. State of New York, Table 4, "Free Population, Native and Foreign, by Counties," ibid., 1:345. Junius B. Alexander, president of the Exchange Bank, had moved from Kentucky about 1858; the census shows that his youngest child (Lucy Fitzhugh Alexander) was born in Kentucky in 1857. John J. Anderson came to St. Louis sometime before 1838, when his eldest child, Cora, was born in Missouri. U.S. Census (manuscript), population schedule, 8th census (1860), St. Louis County [Missouri]. Robert A. Barnes moved to St. Louis in 1830. Shoemaker, *Missouri Day by Day*, 2:388–89. John A. Brownlee, president of the Merchants' Bank, moved to St. Louis in 1839. Edwards, *Edwards' Great West*, 219–20. Ezekiel B. Kimball first came to St. Louis some time prior to 1838 but soon left again. Kimball did not settle in St. Louis permanently until sometime after 1853. John Wills, president of the Mechanics' Bank, came to St. Louis between 1852 (Wills's son John was born in Kentucky, 1852) and 1858 (when Wills was named as an officer in an insurance company). *Liberty Tribune*, April 30, 1858, 3–1. George E. Harding, president of the Union Bank, came to St. Louis in 1856. Stevens, *St. Louis*, 2:322–23. The birthplaces of Kimball's children, recorded in the 1860 census, show that the family had lived in Missouri, Mexico, Illinois, Missouri again, and Louisiana, before settling in Missouri permanently. U.S. Census (manuscript), population schedule, 8th census (1860), St. Louis County [Missouri]. In 1875–76, James H. Britton, in 1861 cashier of the Southern Bank and later its president, served one term as mayor of St. Louis on a Democratic ticket. Hyde and Conard, *Encyclopedia of the History of St. Louis*, 1:238. See Supporting Data for more detailed biographical information.

10. The smallest town with a branch bank was Fayette, in Howard County, with a population in 1860 of 647. State of Missouri, Table Number 3, "Population of Cities, Towns, &c," in Kennedy, *Population of the United States in 1860*, 1:288–98.

11. Atherton, "Pioneer Merchant in Mid-America," 107. Besides settlement of monetary debts, the new year was the time for renewal of contractual agreements of all sorts, including farm tenancies and the hiring out of slaves. Hurt, *Agriculture and Slavery*, 242. Hammond, *Sovereignty and an Empty Purse*, 93.

12. See Supporting Data for more detailed information.

13. *Bankers' Magazine* 10, no. 12 (June 1861), 996. *The Daily News' History of Buchanan County*, 883–84. *Liberty Tribune*, June 24, 1859, 2.

14. *Bankers' Magazine* 10, no. 12 (June 1861), 996. *Illustrated Atlas Map of Howard County*, 14, 27. *United States Biographical Dictionary*, 720–21. Bloch, *Paintings of George Caleb Bingham*, A108, 52, 158.

15. Lynne Doti and Larry Schweikart describe the same evolution elsewhere in the American West. Many banks grew out of other businesses: Wells Fargo Bank and American

Express were both originally freighting companies. Doti and Schweikart, *Banking in the American West*, 21, 26–28. Lewis Atherton found that 14 percent of the pioneer merchants he studied shifted to banking in later life, the second-largest occupational shift for this group after politics. Atherton, "Pioneer Merchant in Mid-America," 30, 105. Schweikart, *Banking in the American South*, 7, 191–92.

16. Anderson played an important role in founding the Ohio & Mississippi Railroad, the Pacific Railroad, the Iron Mountain Railroad, and the North Missouri Railroad. Conard, *Encyclopedia of the History of Missouri*, 1:43. Stevens, *Missouri the Center State*, 2:410 (opposite), 528–30. U.S. Census (manuscript), slave schedule, 8th census (1860), Green, Saline, Randolph, Cape Girardeau Counties [Missouri]. On Berry, see Hubble, *Personal Reminiscences*, 54–55. On Garth, see White, *General History of Macon County*, 786.

17. Jones, "Civil War Letters." U.S. Census (manuscript), population schedule, 8th census (1860), Cooper County [Missouri]. Johnson, *History of Cooper County*, 915–16. Ancestry.com.

18. Stevens, *Missouri the Center State*, 3:356–57. U.S. Census (manuscript), population schedule, 8th census (1860), Pettis County [Missouri]. Claycomb, "John S. Jones," 434–50. *Missouri State Gazetteer and Business Directory*, 10. U.S. Census (manuscript), slave schedule, 8th census (1860), Saline County [Missouri].

19. *Boonville Weekly Advertiser*, December 20, 1889, quoted in Dyer, *Boonville*, 115–16. Eakin and Hale, *Branded as Rebels*, 1:50. Jones, "Civil War Letters."

20. *Bankers' Magazine* 10, no. 12 (June 1861), 996. Davis and Durrie, *Illustrated History of Missouri*, 546; McCarty portrait opposite p. 372. *Liberty Tribune*, August 23, 1856, 1–5. Stevens, *Missouri the Center State*, 4:89. Douglass on Reverend Johnson in "The Kansas Swindle," *Frederick Douglass' Paper*, August 3, 1855.

21. See Supporting Data for more detailed information on individual bankers. The banks named in Jackson's letter were the Brunswick branch of the Merchants' Bank of St. Louis, the Glasgow branches of the Exchange Bank of St. Louis and the Western Bank of Missouri, the Arrow Rock and Fayette branches of the Bank of Missouri, and the Boonville branch of the Bank of St. Louis. (See Chapter 1.) Jackson and Price had family members who were either officers or directors of the Merchants' Bank at Brunswick, the Exchange Bank at Glasgow, the Arrow Rock and Fayette branches of the Bank of Missouri, and the Exchange Bank of Missouri branch at Columbia. Jackson himself had once been the cashier of the Fayette branch of the Bank of Missouri, a position he got because his brother Wade was one of the bank's directors. Phillips, *Missouri's Confederate*, 85.

22. Lamoreaux, *Insider Lending*, 1–4, 25–26, 49.

23. Lamoreaux, "Banks, Kinship, and Economic Development," 653–54. The capital structure of Missouri's banks was similar in this respect to that of the New England banks in Lamoreaux's study. As of December 31, 1859, Missouri's banks had $9.1 million of paid-in capital, compared to $3.3 million in deposits. "Semi-Annual Statement of the Condition of the Banks of the State of Missouri on the first day of January, 1860," etc., in *Journal of the House of Representatives of Missouri, Twentieth General Assembly,*

Called Session, 14–15 (Appendix E, Bank Commissioner's Report). An overview of traditional Islamic banking can be found in Aggarwal and Yousef, "Islamic Banks and Investment Financing." Woodman, *King Cotton and his Retainers*, 37–49. Cable, *Bank of the State of Missouri*, 219.

24. Maurer, *The Power and the Money*, 1–10.

25. Maurer, *The Power and the Money*, 8–10; Lamoreaux, "Banks, Kinship, and Economic Development," 662, 664.

26. Lamoreaux, "Banks, Kinship, and Economic Development," 647. Maurer, *The Power and the Money*, 1–10, 95.

27. The average age of branch presidents was 46, and of cashiers 42. U.S. Census (manuscript), population schedule, 8th census (1860) [Missouri]. By 1860 branch bank presidents had lived in Missouri an average of 27 years and cashiers 29 years. See Supporting Data for bankers' biographies. Of Missouri's total population of 1,182,012 in 1860, 273,500 were born in slaveholding states (other than Missouri), almost all of them from the Upper South states of Kentucky, Tennessee, Virginia, and North Carolina. Fellman, *Inside War*, 6–7. Twenty-four of thirty-three branch presidents were merchants, as were seventeen out of thirty-three branch cashiers. U.S. Census (manuscript), population schedule, 8th census (1860) [Missouri]. The bank officers with prior banking experience were Hendrix, Birch, Northrup, and Price. See Supporting Data for more information on individual bankers.

28. To cite just a few examples, Judge Irvine O. Hockaday, later president of the Fulton branch of the Western Bank of Missouri, had been one of the original founders of Callaway County and at one point had held most of the county offices himself. Shoemaker, *Missouri and Missourians*, 3:18. John Calvin McCoy, president of the Southern Bank of St. Louis branch at Independence, was a co-founder of Westport and Kansas City. *Here Lies Kansas City*, 94–95. Captain William David Swinney and William F. Dunnica, respectively the president of the Western Bank branch and cashier of the Exchange Bank branch at Glasgow, were co-founders of that town. Bloch, *Paintings of George Caleb Bingham*, A108, 52, 158. *Illustrated Atlas Map of Howard County*, 14, 15, 27. See Supporting Data for more information on individual bankers. Eugene Genovese argues that this pattern of social relations—planters dominating bankers—was typical throughout the cotton South. Genovese, *Political Economy of Slavery*, 22, 187.

29. Though the Boonslick was home to many German immigrants, they virtually never appear in surviving banking records, or as defendants in bad-debt suits brought by banks in the civil courts. William H. Trigg Papers; also Weston F. Birch & Son account books. Fellman, *Inside War*, 7.

30. The term "factor" was rarely used in antebellum Missouri, whereas the term "commission merchant" was common. According to Bouvier's law dictionary, the terms are synonymous. Bouvier, *Law Dictionary*. Morrison-Fuller, "Plantation Life in Missouri." U.S. Census (manuscript), agricultural schedule, 8th census (1860), Howard County [Missouri].

31. See Supporting Data for more information on individual bankers.

CHAPTER 4. INSIDER LENDING

1. U.S. Census (manuscript), population schedule, 8th census (1860), Buchanan County [Missouri]. In September 1861, when Confederate troops occupied St. Joseph, Donnell was president of the St. Joseph branch of the Bank of Missouri. *Bankers' Magazine* 11, no. 12 (June, 1860), 996. *St. Louis Triweekly Missouri Republican*, March 11, 1861, 2. *Daily News' History of Buchanan County*, 516. Testimony of David Pinger in the case of R. W. Donnell (February 28, 1862), microfilm reel F1303, Missouri Union Provost Marshal Papers.

2. *Daily News' History of Buchanan County*, 516. Fuenfhausen, *Guide to Historic Clay County*, 81–82. In this letter, Loan named Israel Landis and William K. Richardson, as well as Donnell, as being the three rebels most "potent for evil" in St. Joseph. Brigadier General Benjamin F. Loan, Missouri State Militia, to General J. M. Schofield, St. Louis, dated March 18, 1862, in St. Joseph. *Official Records*, ser. 2, vol. 1, 272.

3. *St. Louis Triweekly Missouri Republican*, September 3, 1861, 3. Sampson, "The Honorable John Brooks Henderson," 237–41. See Supporting Data for more information on Henderson.

4. The nonparticipating banks were the seven banks in St. Louis; the Bank of Missouri branches in Louisiana, Cape Girardeau, and Fayette; the Merchants' Bank at Ste. Genevieve; and the Union Bank at Milan. Louisiana, Cape Girardeau, and Ste. Genevieve are on the Mississippi River, and U.S. troops acted swiftly and decisively to take control of the river traffic and towns. Also, the bank president in Louisiana was the staunchly pro-Union John Brooks Henderson (see Chapter 3). (The town of Charleston, Missouri, is also on the Mississippi River, but in the far southeastern corner of the state where Missouri, Arkansas, Kentucky, and Tennessee meet. U.S. forces were able to police this area only intermittently for much of the war.) The town of Milan is in Sullivan County, in north-central Missouri, and settled mainly by Midwesterners from nonslave states. The town of Fayette is in Howard County, the heart of Missouri's slave-holding district. Nevertheless, the bank's officers and directors refused to have anything to do with the promissory notes (see Chapter 5).

5. Courthouses in the following Missouri counties burned during the war: Adair, Barton, Bates, Cedar, Chariton, Christian, Dade, Dallas, Dent, Dunklin, Greene, Howell, Jasper, McDonald, Monroe, Montgomery, Newton, Oregon, Ozark, Pike, Platte, Reynolds, Ripley, St. Clair, Saline, Shannon, Stoddard, Texas, Vernon, and Wright. See "Local History." Geiger, "Missouri Banks and the Civil War," 101. See Appendix 4 for the names and locations of banks, and for the number of promissory notes written in each county.

6. *Statistics of the United States, (Including Mortality, Property, &c.,) in 1860*, 511. Cable, *Bank of the State of Missouri*, 273. On the first of July, 1861, the thirty participating banks held $2,952,970.18 in gold coin, close to the estimated amount that the banks paid out on the promissory notes. Six months later, on January 1, 1862, these banks held $1,419,941.71 in coin, but the shrinkage in the banks' lending portfolio would have contributed at least this much money. On July 1, 1860, the thirty banks had a total lending portfolio of $7,839,228.65, after deducting suspended debt. By the following

January the banks' aggregate portfolio had shrunk to $6,497,186.14, a net decrease of $1,342,042.51. *St. Louis Missouri Triweekly Republican,* August 1, 1861, 2. *St. Louis Triweekly Missouri Republican,* April 16, 1862, 2.

7. See Appendix 2 for calculations. The exact amount of the largest note was $8,177.10. *Exchange Bank of St. Louis v. John N. Garnett, Henry Garnett, William W. Graves, Thomas Garnett, Edward G. Garnett* [Case SA63B044], Saline County Circuit Court records, October 1863 session. The smallest note was for $60.90. *Western Bank of Missouri at Glasgow versus John B. Jones, William S. Brown* [Case SA63B145], Saline County Circuit Court records, October 1863 session. Six of the twelve banks accounted for 283 cases of the cases filed, or 91.3 percent of the three-county total. These banks were the Bank of St. Louis at Boonville; the Farmers' Bank of Missouri at Lexington; the Bank of Missouri at Arrow Rock; the Merchants' Bank of St. Louis at Brunswick; William H. Trigg (a private banking firm in Boonville); and the Western Bank of Missouri at Glasgow. See Appendix 3 for a complete list of cases in the three counties.

8. William H. Trigg Papers.

9. Castel, *General Sterling Price,* 56. U.S. Census (manuscript), population schedule, 8th census (1860), Cooper, Pettis, and Saline Counties [Missouri].

10. Speech by Missouri Senator John Doniphan to the Twenty-Second General Assembly, Avord Papers, Folder 102. McPherson, *Battle Cry of Freedom,* 313.

11. Bartels, *Civil War in Missouri Day by Day,* 33. Dyer, *Boonville,* 114–16, 122–27. *Liberty Tribune,* November 14, 1862, 1.

12. Cooper County Circuit Court minute books 8–9, Boonville, Missouri.

13. U.S. Census (manuscript), population, slave, and agricultural schedules, 8th census (1860), Saline County [Missouri]. Napton, *Past and Present of Saline County,* 363. On Finley's arrest see Lieutenant James Crissy's report, October 2, 1862, in the Missouri Union Provost Marshal Papers, reel F1317. For the suits against Finley and his cosigners, see Appendix 3. The following cases were heard in the Pettis County Circuit Court, Sedalia, Missouri: PE624041, PE624042, PE624043, PE624050, PE624057, PE63B108, PE63B138, PE645141, PE645146, PE645147. The following cases were heard in the Cooper County Circuit Court, Boonville, Missouri: CO633069, CO633087, CO633086, CO633066, CO633072. The following cases were heard in the Saline County Circuit Court, Marshall, Missouri: SA63B029, SA63B033, SA63B055, SA63B056, SA63B156. U.S. Census (manuscript), population schedule, 9th census (1870), Saline County [Missouri].

14. U. S. Census (manuscript), population schedule, 8th census (1860), Cooper, Pettis, and Saline Counties [Missouri]. *History of Howard and Cooper Counties,* 751. Newspaper article listing accepted and rejected voters in Cooper County, entitled "To the Conservative Men of Cooper County," *Boonville Central Missouri Advertiser,* October 1866, in William H. Trigg Papers, vol. 5.

15. Confederate generals with close family connections to bankers and defendants in the three-county sample include General John Cabell Breckenridge of Fayette County, Kentucky, with the Thomsons of Saline County (Warner, *Generals in Gray,* 34); Brigadier Generals John Bullock Clark, Jr. and Sr., of Howard County, Missouri, to the Clarks of Chariton County and the Turners of Howard County (*Biographical Direc-*

tory of the United States Congress; Allardice, *More Generals in Gray*, 59–61); Brigadier General John Hall Chilton of Loudon County, Virginia, to the Chiltons of Cooper County (Warner, *Generals in Gray*, 49); Brigadier Generals Richard Brooke Garnett and Robert Selden Garnett of Essex County, Virginia, to the Garnetts of Saline County (ibid., 99–100); General James Patrick Major of Howard County, Missouri, to the Majors of Pettis and Saline counties (ibid., 209–10); General John Sappington Marmaduke to the Marmaduke, Harwood, Sappington, and Jackson families (including Governor Claiborne Fox Jackson) of Howard and Saline counties (see below, this chapter); General James H. McBride to the McBrides of Cooper County (Allardice, *More Generals in Gray*, 155–56); General Mosby Monroe Parsons of Cole County to the Parsons of Saline County, Missouri (Warner, *Generals in Gray*, 228); and Generals Sterling Price and Edwin Price to the Price and Garth families of Chariton and Howard Counties, Missouri. Forty-four of 362 defendants whose 1860 census records could be found listed a real estate value of zero; thirty-six defendants had real and personal property valued at a total of one thousand dollars or less. U.S. Census (manuscript), population schedule, 8th census (1860), Cooper, Pettis, and Saline Counties [Missouri]. See Supporting Data for more information on individual defendants.

16. See Appendix 3 for details of individual cases. One family group among the defendants was the Harris family: Thomas M., James Y., James J., and James J. Jr. The second family group was the Hughes family: James A., Samuel, and Thomas J. The third family group was the Sutherlin-Jamison-Hay group. In a war where many military units were known as "Gordon's Cavalry," "Elliott's command," and so forth, many of the commanders so named officered units of Shelby's Iron Brigade: George P. Gordon, Benjamin Elliott, Upton Hays, David Shanks. O'Flaherty, *General Jo Shelby*, 124, 141. The nine colonels who signed notes were Hugh Chrisman, George J. Fackler, and Vincent Marmaduke in Saline County; Ebenezer Magoffin, Thomas F. Houston, and Henry Clay Taylor in Pettis County; and Charles B. Alexander, Horace Holley Brand, and Thomas B. Monroe in Cooper County. These persons were first identified as defendants in the promissory-note cases; then their service records were traced to Confederate muster rosters, county histories, and personal reminiscences at the Missouri State Historical Society, the Missouri State Archives, and the United Daughters of the Confederacy.

17. Very few of the individual borrowers and bankers were prominent individuals. Consequently, biographical data were fragmented and scattered, requiring many separate lookups for each individual. The number of sources consulted was too large to list in a single footnote. Types of sources examined included the U.S. Census for the years 1850 through 1900; county and local histories; family histories; local government records, including civil court, probate, and marriage records; military records; tombstone inscriptions, genealogical databases, local newspapers; archival material; and R. G. Dun & Company credit reports. All sources used are listed in the bibliography.

18. Cashin, "Structure of Antebellum Planter Families," 55–70; Mann, "Mountains, Land and Kin Networks," 411–34. Kenzer, *Kinship and Neighborhood*, 2, 7, 37–38, 40–46.

19. Peck, *Forty Years of Pioneer Life*, 146; quoted in Hurt, *Agriculture and Slavery*, 24. For example, Kentuckians who in 1860 lived in Cooper, Pettis, and Saline Counties came

largely from the Bluegrass counties near Lexington. U.S. Census (manuscript), population schedule, 8th census (1860), Cooper, Pettis, and Saline Counties [Missouri]. Of 369 defendants and 74 bankers in the sample, a total of 382, or 86 percent, had a kinship connection to other members of the sample. See Supporting Data for more information on kinship connections.

20. In the Miller family, John, Gideon B., George W. Jr., and Nimrod B. In the Shy family, Christopher L., John C., David J., and Buriah M. Other families just as large or nearly so among the defendants were the Fergusons, Wallaces, Ellises, and Lewises. Ancestry .com; Phillips, *Missouri's Confederate*, 6. For family connections in the families of large planters, see Scarborough, *Masters of the Big House*, 22–26.

21. See Supporting Data. The eleven intermarriages between the families were:

> 1. John Sappington to Jane Breathitt, 22 November 1804, in Russellville, Logan County, Kentucky. Dodd, "Kentucky Marriages 1802–1850."
>
> 2. Cardwell Breathitt to Rebecca Harwood, 26 March 1810, in Montgomery County, Maryland. Dodd, Maryland Marriages, 1655–1850.
>
> 3. Levin Harwood to Elizabeth Breathitt, 9 December 1818, in Russellville, Logan County, Kentucky. Dodd, "Kentucky Marriages 1802–1850."
>
> 4. Meredith Miles Marmaduke to Lavinia Sappington, 1 January 1826, in Saline County, Missouri. Dodd, Missouri Marriages to 1850.
>
> 5. Claiborne Fox Jackson to Mary Jane Breathitt Sappington, 17 February 1831, in Saline County, Missouri. Phillips, *Missouri's Confederate*, 67–68.
>
> 6. Claiborne Fox Jackson to Louisa Catherine Sappington, 12 September 1833, in Saline County, Missouri. Phillips, *Missouri's Confederate*, 69–70.
>
> 7. Erasmus Darwin Sappington to Penelope Breathitt, 16 November 1838. Bloch, *Paintings of George Caleb Bingham*, 169.
>
> 8. Claiborne Fox Jackson to Eliza W. (Sappington) Pearson, 27 November 1838, in Saline County, Missouri. Phillips, *Missouri's Confederate*, 91.
>
> 9. William Breathitt Sappington to Mary Mildred Breathitt, 3 September 1844, in Saline County, Missouri. Dodd, "Missouri Marriages to 1850."
>
> 10. Levin Breathitt Harwood to Jane Breathitt Marmaduke, 1 September 1846, in Saline County, Missouri. Ibid.
>
> 11. Darwin William Marmaduke to Jane C. Sappington 15, September 1860, in Saline County, Missouri. Ibid. Phillips, *Missouri's Confederate*, 71. Morrow, *John Sappington*, 18.

22. Soldiers were approximately 245 of 369 total defendants in the sample, including Colonels Alexander, Brand, Chrisman, Fackler, Houston, Magoffin (brother of Kentucky's pro-Confederate governor, Beriah Magoffin), Marmaduke, Monroe, and Taylor. Soldiers Database: War of 1812–World War I, Missouri State Archives. See Appendix 4 for individual names.

23. Merchants were approximately 85 of 369 total defendants in the sample. See Appendix 4 for individuals' names.

24. Cosigners were approximately 39 of 369 total defendants in the sample. See Appen-

dix 4 for individual names. The bonds the Jackson government had issued were declared receivable in payment of all dues to the state. Also, the Jackson government's legislation authorizing the bond issue stated that the bonds should be paid out "as the exigencies of the state should require." Another act levied a property tax on Missouri counties for the defense of the state. The monies so received were to be paid into an escrow account held by the county court of each county, which court could draw warrants on the account in payment for military supplies. "An Act to Provide for the Defense of the State of Missouri" (November 1, 1861), *Journal of the Senate, Extra Session of the Rebel Legislature*, 34–35.

25. Phillips, *Missouri's Confederate*, 7n12. U.S. Census (manuscript), population schedule, 7th census (1850), Saline County [Missouri]. U.S. Census (manuscript), population and slave schedules, 8th census (1860), Saline County [Missouri]. See Appendix 3 for cases. See Supporting Data for kinship connections.

26. Morrow, *John Sappington*, 18. Phillips, *Missouri's Confederate*, 65–71. Collins, *Historical Sketches of Kentucky*, 211–12.

27. Morrow, *John Sappington*, 18. *Marshall Democrat*, March 7, 1860, 2. U.S. Census (manuscript), population schedule, 7th census (1850), Saline County [Missouri]. U.S. Census (manuscript), population and slave schedules, 8th census (1860), Saline County [Missouri].

28. Brigadier General Benjamin F. Loan to Major General Samuel Curtis, November 19, 1862, *Official Records*, ser. 1, vol. 13, 806–87. U.S. Census (manuscript), population, slave, and agricultural schedules, 8th census (1860), Saline County [Missouri]. Napton, *Past and Present of Saline County*, 847. Russell Trust Association, 1913 catalog. Sturm, "Great Chicago Conspiracy," 55–61. *Columbia Missouri Statesman*, July 10, 1863, 2. *Sedalia Daily Democrat*, February 20, 1872; September 24, 1876. *Boonville Weekly Advertiser*, October 6, 1876. *Atlanta Constitution*, November 27, 1897, 1. Provost Marshal's File on Confederate Civilians, Missouri State Archives.

29. By railroad from St. Joseph to Hannibal (194 miles), by steamboat from Hannibal to St. Louis (130 miles), and then by a different steamboat from St. Louis to New Madrid (about 242 miles)—a total distance of 566 miles. The alternative would be by steamboat from St. Joseph to St. Louis (448 miles), and then from St. Louis to the mouth of the Ohio (180 miles), and from there to New Madrid (about 62 miles)—a total distance of about 690 miles. The distance from St. Louis to New Orleans is 1,039 miles. National Oceanic and Atmospheric Administration and the National Ocean Service, *Distances Between United States Ports*, T-19 through T-21. Missouri Highway and Transportation Department, *Official Highway Map*.

30. Sageman, *Understanding Terrorist Networks*, 137–58. Gould, "Why Do Networks Matter?" 233–57. Marsden and Friedkin, "Network Studies of Social Influence," 2–26.

31. Shortfield, *Western Merchant*, preface; quoted in Atherton, "Pioneer Merchant in Mid-America," 7.

32. McCandless, *History of Missouri*, 2:272–73. No written records of the Blue Lodge have ever been found. Given that it was a conspiratorial organization, this is not surprising. However, there are several personal accounts of individuals who came in contact with the group or its members. See for example the story of General George Rappen Smith,

in *History of Pettis County*, 424. O'Flaherty writes that during Shelby's Missouri campaign of 1864 the Knights of the Golden Circle "had come into [Shelby's] camp with mysterious books, innumerable signs, grips, signals, passwords and incantations, to aid the cause; General Sterling Price, riding about in a buggy because of his great bulk had placed great reliance on them, though they had never enabled a Confederate soldier to take or hold a foot of ground." O'Flaherty, *General Jo Shelby*, 241–42.

33. Sageman identifies the al-Qaeda terrorist network as a small-world network and argues that the network would survive even if Osama bin Laden were captured or killed. Sageman, *Understanding Terrorist Networks*, 137–58.

34. The picture is incomplete owing to a number of courthouse fires, during the Civil War and after, which destroyed the pertinent records. Precise determination of regional hubs would depend on more detailed analysis of the case and defendants in these counties, similar to what I did with the three-county sample. But based on the information at hand, there are probably six regional hubs in the central region: Pettis-Saline, Clay-Jackson, Schuyler, Lafayette-Carroll, Henry-St. Clair, and Greene.

35. Geiger, "Missouri Banks and the Civil War," Appendix 2, "Sources and Uses of Funds," 185–215.

36. Marcellus Harris was a prosperous thirty-five-year-old farmer in St. Clair County. Harris himself was killed from ambush on January 26, 1862, less than a quarter mile from Osceola. No one ever took credit for Harris's murder, but it was presumed to be revenge for Vaughan's killing. U.S. Census (manuscript), population schedule, 8th census (1860), St. Clair County [Missouri]. Miles, *Bitter Ground*, 261. *History of Henry and St. Clair Counties, Missouri*, 834, 937. Missouri, vol. 33, 293 and 298, R. G. Dun & Co. Collection, Baker Library, Harvard Business School, Cambridge, Massachusetts.

CHAPTER 5. THE UNIONISTS REGAIN CONTROL

1. Parrish, *History of Missouri*, 2–3, 6. Primm, *Lion of the Valley*, 260.
2. *St. Louis Triweekly Missouri Republican*, August 1, 1861, 2. Stevens, *St. Louis*, 312.
3. Garth was a brother-in-law of Sterling Price (*Jefferson City People's Tribune*, June 17, 1874, 2), owner of twenty-two slaves (U.S. Census [manuscript], slave schedule, 8th census [1860], Howard County [Missouri]), and an anti-Benton representative from Randolph County in the state Democratic convention in August 1854 (*Liberty Tribune*, August 18, 1854, 2). Boon was imprisoned at the beginning of the war and confined to the Alton prison because he refused to take the oath of allegiance. W. C. Boon biography, United Daughters of the Confederacy Missouri Records. Hubbard and Davids, *Banking in Mid-America*, 93; Stevens, *St. Louis*, 315. *Journal of the Missouri State Convention* (June 1862), 6. See Supporting Data for more biographical information.
4. *Journal of the Missouri State Convention* (July 1861), 16–17. *Proceedings of the Missouri State Convention* (July 1861), 49, 56–61. *Harper's Weekly*, October 19, 1861, 657–58.
5. Parrish, *Turbulent Partnership*, 47, 55–56. *Missouri Troops in Service during the Civil War*, 18, 21–23.
6. Inaugural Address of Abraham Lincoln, March 4, 1861, in *Inaugural Addresses of the Presidents of the United States. New York Times*, June 21, 1861, 1. Parrish, *History of Mis-*

souri, 27–29. Lincoln ordered Missouri to be added to the Department of the Ohio, commanded by General George McClellan, on June 6. Lyon's command was reduced at the same time. Phillips, *Damned Yankee*, 223–24.

7. McPherson, *Battle Cry of Freedom*, 352–53. Most Missouri historians are highly critical of Fremont's performance in Missouri and blame his decisions for contributing to the Union defeats at the Battles of Wilson's Creek and Lexington. Parrish, *History of Missouri*, 28, 34–35; also Parrish, *Turbulent Partnership*, 73–76. St. Louis *Missouri Republican*, August 31, 1861, 2.

8. Cable, *Bank of the State of Missouri*, 273. Grant, *Personal Memoirs of U. S. Grant*, 1:18. *Official Records*, ser. 1, vol. 3, 54. *St. Louis Missouri Republican*, August 19, 1861, 2. Bartels, *Civil War in Missouri Day by Day*, 25–56. Nancy Chapman Jones to May Jones McCarthy (Gibson), August 27, 1861, in Jones, "Civil War Letters."

9. Bartels, *Civil War in Missouri Day by Day*, 31–36. Parrish, *Turbulent Partnership*, 66–68. Parrish, *History of Missouri*, 37–38.

10. *New York Times*, September 25, 1861, 4. Davis, *Rise and Fall*, 431. National Park Service, *Civil War Sites Advisory Commission Report*, Table 2. *St. Louis Missouri Republican*, September 28, 1861, 3. *Liberty Tribune*, October 4, 1861, 2; October 11, 1861, 2; October 18, 1861, 1.

11. Colonel Dewitt Clinton Hunter, Seventh Cavalry Regiment, Eighth Division (Raines), Missouri State Guard, was originally from Vernon County, Missouri, and later became a partisan leader in northwest Arkansas. Hale, *Branded as Rebels*, 2:152. Brigadier General James S. Rains, originally of Jasper County, Missouri, was a state senator and commanding officer of the Eighth Military District of the Missouri State Guards. Eakin and Hale, *Branded as Rebels*, 1:223, 363.

12. The bank was the successor to a private banking partnership of William L. Vaughan, Waldo P. Johnson, and John F. Weidemeyer. Johnson was Missouri's treasonous senator, expelled from the Senate January 10, 1862, who later served as a Confederate officer and in the Confederate Congress. Weidemeyer was a wealthy fifty-year-old Osceola merchant and the father of Captain John M. Weidemeyer, who had led the defense of the town against General Jim Lane's troops. *Biographical Directory of the American Congress* (1950), 1384. U.S. Census (manuscript), population schedule, 8th census (1860), St. Clair County [Missouri]. Miles, *Bitter Ground*, 132, 135, 145–46, 261. *History of Henry and St. Clair Counties, Missouri*, 834, 937. Brigadier General James H. Lane in a dispatch to Major General Fremont, dated September 24, 1861. *Official Records*, ser. 1, vol. 3, 196.

13. Several accounts of the Osceola raid, including three by eyewitnesses, are recounted in Miles, *Bitter Ground*, 133–51. Brigadier General James H. Lane in a dispatch to Major General Fremont, dated September 24, 1861, *Official Records*, ser. 1, vol. 3, 196, 506. *New York Times*, October 5, 1861, 1, reprinting from the *Leavenworth (KS) Conservative*, September 28, 1861. Miles, *Bitter Ground*, 132, 135, 145–46. *St. Louis Missouri Republican*, October 1, 1861, 3.

14. "An Act for the Relief of the Merchants Bank of St. Louis" (March 23, 1863), in *Laws of the State of Missouri, Regular Session, Twenty-Second General Assembly*, 5–7.

15. Nancy Chapman Jones to May Jones McCarthy (Gibson), October 3, 1861, in Jones,

"Civil War Letters." Goodrich, *Black Flag*, 16–18. Richard Reed and Rev. Lawrence Lewis, in interviews with the author, December 10, 2004; Castel, "Kansas Jayhawking Raids," 1–11. *New York Times*, October 1, 1861, 1. Miles, *Bitter Ground*, 148. *St. Louis Missouri Republican*, October 1, 1861, 3.

16. Cable, *Bank of the State of Missouri*, 273. Stevens, *Centennial History of Missouri*, 3:730–31. Goodrich, "In the Earnest Pursuit of Wealth," 155–84. Brownlee, *Gray Ghosts of the Confederacy*, 95.

17. U.S. Senate, *Biographical Directory of the U.S. Congress*. Phillips, *Missouri's Confederate*, 85. *St. Louis Missouri Republican*, September 3, 1861, 3. *Liberty Tribune*, September 13, 1861, 3, reprinting from the *St. Louis Missouri Republican*. *Columbia Missouri Statesman*, August 30, 1861, 2. Stevens, *Centennial History of Missouri*, 3:730–31.

18. In the three-county sample of Cooper, Pettis, and Saline, the Glasgow branch of the Exchange Bank of Missouri had twenty cases (see Appendix 3). Besides this, the Howard County Circuit Court records show the Exchange Bank as plaintiff in an additional five cases, or twenty-five cases in all. The other bank, the Western Bank of Missouri at Glasgow, was plaintiff in thirty-one cases in the three-county sample. In the Howard County Circuit Court, the Western Bank was plaintiff to one case, for thirty-two cases in all. The Exchange Bank's twenty-five cases and the Western Bank's thirty-two total fifty-seven. Howard County Circuit Court records, minute books 12–13, December, 1862 session. Microfilm Roll 2826, County and Municipal Records Series, Missouri State Archives. Stevens, *St. Louis*, 1:312–315.

19. At the beginning of May, U.S. forces were commanded by General William S. Harney. He was relieved on May 30 and replaced by Brigadier General Nathaniel Lyon. Less than two weeks earlier Lyon had been a captain, but he had been elected general by the volunteer troops he had mustered into U.S. service on May 17. President Lincoln confirmed Lyon's rank on May 20, retroactive to May 18, which placed Lyon in command of all U.S. forces in the West. Lyon held this post for little more than a month. Missouri's Governor Hamilton Gamble, appointed Jackson's successor by the provisional government, considered Lyon too rash. On Gamble's urging Lyon was relieved and Missouri placed under General George McClellan's Department of the Ohio. McClellan found the command too unwieldy even for his formidable administrative abilities. Lincoln ordered the command reorganized and on July 1 appointed General John C. Fremont as commander of the United States Department of the West, which included Missouri. Lyon was given command of U.S. forces in southwest Missouri. Fremont was relieved on November 2 and replaced by General David Hunter, who held this post exactly one week before being transferred to the newly created Department of Kansas. Hunter was replaced on November 9, 1861, by General Henry Halleck. Parrish, *History of Missouri*, 20–21, 26–28, 34–35, 40–41. Parrish, *Turbulent Partnership*, 73–76. Phillips, *Damned Yankee*, 208. Primm, *Lion of the Valley*, 239–40. Castel, *General Sterling Price*, 232–77. Fellman, *Inside War*, 231–42.

20. *St. Louis Missouri Democrat*, August 6, 1861, quoted in Stanley, Wilson, and Wilson, *Death Records from Missouri Newspapers*, vol. 2. *Official Records*, ser. 2, vol. 1, 554. James M. Carpenter to Mrs. Octavia Boyle, New York, November 27, 1862, Mullanphy Family Collection. William M. McPheeters papers. United Daughters of the Con-

federacy, Missouri Division, *Reminiscences*, 238–40. *Jefferson City Daily Tribune*, November 28, 1893, 4. *Staunton Spectator*, September 3, 1861, available at "Valley of the Shadow: Two Communities in the American Civil War," Virginia Center for Digital History. U.S. Census (manuscript), population schedule, 9th census (1870), Shelby County [Tennessee]. Keating, *History of the Yellow Fever*, 391.

21. Trigg: List of disloyal citizens, Boonville, Missouri, dated December, 1864, Provost Marshal's File on Groups of Two or More Confederate Civilians. Barnes: James M. Carpenter to Mrs. Octavia Boyle, New York, November 27, 1862, Mullanphy Family Collection. Wills: William M. McPheeters papers. The first loyalty oath was prescribed by the Convention on October 16, 1861. *Journal of the Missouri State Convention* (October 1861), 74–78. Parrish, *History of Missouri*, 42. Smith, "Experiment in Counterinsurgency," 362–64. Primm, *Lion of the Valley*, 233, 242. *Official Records*, ser. 2, vol. 2, 250. Major J. McKinstry, U.S. Assistant Provost Marshal, Office of Provost-Marshal, St. Louis, to Lt. Col. S. Burbank, U.S. Army, Commanding Arsenal, dated August 21, 1861, *Official Records*, ser. 2, vol. 1, 128. *St. Louis Missouri Republican*, October 11, 1861, 2; October 14, 1861, 2. Bay, *Reminiscences of the Bench and Bar*, 514. United Daughters of the Confederacy, Missouri Division, *Reminiscences*, 238–40. *Liberty Tribune*, May 29, 1863, 2. *New York Times*, January 5, 1892, 5.

22. *Columbia Missouri Statesman*, November 21, 1862, 4; reprinted from the *Lexington Union*. *Liberty Tribune*, November 14, 1862, 1. Brigadier General Benjamin F. Loan to Major General Samuel Curtis, November 19, 1862, *Official Records*, ser. 1, vol. 13, 806–7. Geiger, "Missouri Banks and the Civil War," Appendix 2, "Sources and Uses of Funds," 185–223.

23. Geiger, "Missouri Banks and the Civil War," Appendix 2, "Sources and Uses of Funds," 209–15. *St. Louis Missouri Republican*, August 29, 1861, 3.

24. *St. Louis Daily Missouri Democrat*, October 15, 1861, 3; October 16, 1861, 3.

25. *St. Louis Missouri Republican*, October 16, 1861, 3. *St. Louis Daily Missouri Democrat*, October 15, 1861, 3. Geiger, "Missouri Banks and the Civil War," 194, 199. Federal Deposit Insurance Corporation, "Statistics at a Glance."

26. Hammond, *Sovereignty and an Empty Purse*, 224 ff. Geiger, "Missouri Banks and the Civil War," Appendix 3, "Liquidity, Leverage, and Profitability," 219–24.

27. Sandage, *Born Losers*, 30, 215. "An Act for the Relief of Insolvent Persons Confined on Criminal Process" (November 23, 1855), *Revised Statutes of the State of Missouri* (1856), 1:255. "An Act to Provide for Suits of Attachment," ibid., section 54, 236. Mann, *Republic of Debtors*, 48. For calculation of acreage, see Appendix 2, calculation O. For percentages of the counties' total real estate in 1860, see Appendix 4.

28. Wyatt-Brown, *Southern Honor*, 345–46. Mann, *Republic of Debtors*, 16–17.

29. Some provision was made for Missourian troops fighting for the Union to vote; nevertheless, the distances involved and the difficulties of communication prevented many from doing so. Laughlin, "Missouri Politics During the Civil War," 99–102. *Ordinances in Relation to Elections, Voters, and Civil Officers*, 4–7. Kirkpatrick, "Missouri's Secessionist Government," 130.

30. No returns were received for Bollinger, Butler, Douglas, Dallas, Dunklin, Howell, Jasper, McDonald, Oregon, Ozark, Pemiscot, Reynolds, Ripley, Shannon, Stoddard,

Taney, Texas, and Vernon Counties. *Journal of the House of Representatives of Missouri, First Session, Twenty-Second General Assembly,* 88–92, appendix. See Appendix 2 for approximation of eligible voters in Missouri in 1860.

31. Laughlin, "Missouri Politics During the Civil War," 99–102.

32. Each political faction had pejorative names for the others: The Emancipationists called the Radicals "Charcoals," after the prewar "Black Republicans"; the Radicals returned the favor by calling their opponents "Claybanks," meaning colorless. Democrats were variously called by that name, or else Conservatives, Anti-Emancipationists, or Snowflakes (meaning white man's party). Parrish, *History of Missouri,* 93, 95, 101–2.

33. The Twenty-Second General Assembly house considered about 975 bills, and the senate about 743. The succeeding General Assembly, the Twenty-Third, considered altogether slightly over a thousand bills, or just less than 60 percent as many as the Twenty-Second. *Journal of the Senate of Missouri, First Session, Twenty-Second General Assembly,* index. *Journal of the House of Representatives of Missouri, First Session, Twenty-Second General Assembly,* index. *Journal of the House of Representatives of Missouri, Adjourned Session, Twenty-Second General Assembly,* index; *Journal of the Senate of the State of Missouri, Adjourned Session, Twenty-Second General Assembly,* index; *Journal of the House of Representatives of the State of Missouri, Regular Session, Twenty-Third General Assembly,* index; *Journal of the Senate of the State of Missouri, Regular Session, Twenty-Third General Assembly,* index.

34. Examples of debt-relief legislation are Senate Bill 7, entitled "An Act Protecting the Real Estate of Married Women," *Journal of the Senate of Missouri, First Session, Twenty-Second General Assembly,* 35; and Senate Bill 309, entitled "An Act Authorizing the Redemption of Real Estate," ibid., 85. Section 2 of the bill gave the debtor the right of redemption within twelve months of the sale of the property. House Bill 31, "An act to amend an act entitled an act to regulate executions, approved December 1, 1855," would have barred the sale of a debtor's property for less than two-thirds of its value, as appraised by three householders. *Journal of the House of Representatives of Missouri, First Session, Twenty-Second General Assembly,* 80, 626.

35. Missouri's Seventh Senatorial District was at that time composed of the north central counties of Schuyler, Adair, Knox, Macon, and Shelby; the Thirteenth Senatorial District was composed of the northwest counties of Buchanan and Platte. "An Act to Apportion Representation, and to Divide the State into Senatorial Districts" (November 17, 1857), *Laws of the State of Missouri, Adjourned Session, Nineteenth General Assembly,* 8. Avord Papers, Folder 102. U.S. Census (manuscript), population schedule, 8th census (1860), Buchanan County [Missouri]. *Journal of the Senate of Missouri, First Session, Twenty-Second General Assembly,* 22–23 (index). Conard, *Encyclopedia of the History of Missouri,* 2:297. Fuenfhausen, *Guide to Historic Clay County,* 67. *Daily News' History of Buchanan County,* 344–46.

36. Parrish, *Turbulent Partnership,* 148, 170. *Journal of the House of Representatives of the State of Missouri, Regular Session, Twenty-Third General Assembly,* index; *Journal of the Senate of the State of Missouri, Regular Session, Twenty-Third General Assembly,* index.

37. "An Act to Prevent Illegal Banking and the Circulation of Depreciated Paper Currency

Within This State," section 9, *Revised Statutes of the State of Missouri* (1856), 371. *Bank of the State of Missouri v. Snelling*, et al., *Reports of Cases, Supreme Court, Missouri* (1865), 35:190. "An Act to Regulate Banks and Banking Institutions, and to Create the Offices of Bank Commissioners" (March 2, 1857), *Laws of the State of Missouri, Regular Session, Nineteenth General Assembly; Merchants' Bank of St. Louis v. Farmer*, 43 *Reports of Cases, Supreme Court, Missouri* (1869), 214.

38. "An Act for the Relief of the Bank of the State of Missouri, the Merchants' Bank, the Mechanics' Bank, the Exchange Bank, the Southern Bank, the Union Bank, the Bank of St. Louis, the Farmers' Bank of Missouri, and the Western Bank of Missouri" (March 18, 1861), 9–17. *Merchants' Bank of St. Louis v. Sassee et al. Reports of Cases, Supreme Court, Missouri* (1863), 33:350; *Coots and Ferrier v. Mechanics' Bank of Missouri* (1863), Missouri Supreme Court Historical Database; *Fox and Coots v. Mechanics' Bank of Missouri* (1863), ibid.; *Moore, Wallace, Hays, and Cochran v. Mechanics' Bank of Missouri* (1863), ibid.; *Cochran, Hays, Waller, Frost v. Mechanics' Bank of Missouri* (1863), ibid.

CHAPTER 6. GUERRILLAS

1. On November 16, 1861, the Confederate Congress passed a law for easy transfer of Missouri State Guard troops into the Confederate army. On April 8, 1862, accompanied by about five thousand men, General Sterling Price resigned as Commander of the Missouri State Guard and entered Confederate service in the Army of the West. After Price's resignation and the expiration of the terms of enlistment of most of the volunteers, the remaining Missouri State Guard troops served as auxiliaries to General Hindman's command in Arkansas. Bartels, *Civil War in Missouri Day by Day*, 53; Parrish, *History of Missouri*, 47–48.

2. Fellman, *Inside War*, xvi; Sutherland, "Guerrilla Warfare," 263; McPherson, *Battle Cry of Freedom*, 292; Phillips, *Missouri's Confederate*, 278; Parrish, *History of Missouri*, 199.

3. In 1860 Kentucky's white population was 919,484 compared with Missouri's 1,063,489. The total populations of the two states in 1860 were 1,155,684 and 1,182,012, respectively. Kennedy, *Population of the United States in 1860*, 179, 285. Frederick H. Dyer counted a total of 10,455 military movements of all sorts listed in the *Official Records*. Counted in this way, Virginia ranked first (2,154), Tennessee second (1,462), Missouri third (1,162), and Kentucky ninth (453). Dyer's count, however, is too expansive, including such events as South Carolina's secession ordinance and thirteen actions of various kinds in Minnesota that in fact were fights with Indians. Dyer, *Compendium*, 2:765, 830. Looking only at entries on Dyer's list that appear to have been violent clashes between opposing military forces (excluding "expeditions," "reconaissances," "scouts," and "occupations"), the rank order of the states remains the same. Based on Dyer's list, Virginia had 1,875 violent clashes on its soil, more than any other state. Tennessee came second with 1,245, Missouri third with 945, and Kentucky ninth with 409. Dyer, *Compendium*, 2:582. As to the size of these various battles, the *Civil War Sites Advisory Commission Report* of the National Park Service (NPS) classifies battles from A to D,

in order of importance. Under the NPS classification, Missouri had 29 total battles, A through D, making it the third-ranked state in this respect as well, again after Virginia and Tennessee. Kentucky again ranks ninth with eleven battles, A through D. National Park Service, *Civil War Sites Advisory Commission Report.*

4. Neely, *Civil War and the Limits of Destruction,* 42–45.

5. "Trouble in Missouri," *New York Times,* September 22, 1863, 4.

6. Reports vary on exactly how many were killed at Lawrence. Fellman gives a figure of one hundred and fifty in *Inside War,* 25–26. Other sources make a case for a minimum death count of two hundred. Summarized in Stiles, *Jesse James,* 412n11. Neely, "Was the Civil War a Total War?" 454.

7. Watts, *Babe of the Company,* 6–7. Watts's obituary states that he joined the guerrillas in 1862: *Higbee News,* December 16, 1921. However, in his memoir, he writes that he joined Bill Anderson in the spring of 1864 (p. 6). According to Watts's death certificate, he was born January 14, 1848, so he joined Bill Anderson's band not long after his sixteenth birthday. Hampton B. Watts, Certificate of Death, Bureau of Vital Statistics, Missouri State Board of Health. In "Missouri Death Certificates, 1910–1958," database, Missouri State Archives. Younger, *Story of Cole Younger,* 6–7, 13–15, 53; Barton, *Three Years with Quantrill,* 49–52.

8. *New York Times,* July 28, 1861, 2. Robinson, *Mountain Max.* In addition to Watts, Younger, and McCorkle, in the decades that followed the war many former guerrillas recounted their stories—or parts of them—to their hometown newspapers. These accounts, which also almost exclusively describe gunfights, have been anthologized by Hale in *We Rode with Quantrill.* Edwards also mentions "robbery of all [their] personal possessions" as one of the reasons that young men joined the guerrillas. Edwards, *Noted Guerrillas,* 21. Mackey, *Uncivil War,* 8. Sutherland, "Guerrilla Warfare," 285–86.

9. Francis Lieber, *Guerrilla Parties Considered with Reference to the Laws and Usages of War,* in *Official Records,* ser. 2, vol. 5, 671–82. For a useful discussion of Lieber's ideas see Mackey, *Uncivil War,* 5–11.

10. "Partisans are soldiers armed and wearing the uniform of their army but belonging to a corps which acts detached from the main body for the purpose of making inroads into the territory occupied by the enemy. If captured they are entitled to all the privileges of the prisoner of war." General Orders, No. 100, in *Official Records,* ser. 2, vol. 5, 676, paragraphs 81, 82. Lieber defined guerrillas, as they are commonly understood today, in paragraphs 82 and 85. Ibid., 677. Lieber, *Guerrilla Parties,* 18–19.

11. "An Act to Organize Bands of Partizan Rangers" (April 21, 1862), in *Military Laws of the Confederate States,* 65. Sutherland, "Guerrilla Warfare," 283–85; Russell, *Memoirs of John Singelton Mosby,* 192.

12. Mackey, *Uncivil War,* 37–39, 203–6; Sutherland, "Guerrilla Warfare," 283–85, 291. Connolly interview with Strieby, William E. Connolly Collection, quoted in Castel and Goodrich, *Bloody Bill Anderson,* 15. The Confederate Congress passed "An Act to Repeal an Act to Organize Bands of Partisan Rangers, Approved April 21, 1862, and for Other Purposes" on February 17, 1864. See *Journal of the Congress of the Confederate States of America* 6:628, 802, 828–29, 849, 863. Published in Senate Document No. 234, vol. 6, 58th U.S. Congress, 2nd session.

13. Edwards, *Shelby and His Men*, 39–53, 93–104, 193–226. Barton, *Three Years with Quantrill*, 48, 63. In a public letter addressed to the two newspapers of Lexington, Missouri, Bill Anderson wrote, "I have never belonged to the Confederate Army, nor do my men." Anderson's letter is quoted in Brownlee, *Gray Ghosts of the Confederacy*, 201. Nevertheless, when Bill Anderson was killed, a written order from Confederate general Sterling Price was found on Anderson's body, instructing him to proceed north of the Missouri River and destroy the North Missouri Railroad. Brownlee, *Gray Ghosts of the Confederacy*, 223–24. Also see General Orders, No. 100, in *Official Records*, ser. 2, vol. 5, 677; General Orders, No. 32, Department of the Missouri, dated December 22, 1861, by order of Major General Halleck, *Official Records*, ser. 1, vol. 8, 463–64; General Orders, No. 1, Department of the Missouri, dated January 1, 1862, by order of Major General Halleck, *Official Records*, ser. 1, vol. 8, 476–78; and General Orders, No. 2, Department of the Mississippi, March 3, 1862, by order of Major General Halleck, *Official Records*, ser. 1, vol. 22, pt. 1, 865.

14. The most notable study of guerrillas outside of Missouri that has principally relied on identification of individuals is Noe, "Who Were the Bushwhackers?" Missouri historians have generally not used this approach, with the notable exception of Don R. Bowen.

15. The names of voters denied the right to vote in the 1866 state elections because of support for the rebellion is one possible source of names, but such a list survives for only one of the five counties, Cooper. Newspaper clipping, *Boonville Central Missouri Advertiser*, October, 1866, in William H. Trigg Papers, vol. 5. Even a complete list of rejected voters in 1866 would exclude persons who died or emigrated during the war, but such a list would include persons who immigrated to the area and who came of age between 1861 and 1866. Persons who initially supported the rebellion but later changed their minds might not appear on the list. Finally, some voters were disenfranchised for spurious reasons. The Radical Union Party—the state's version of the Radical Republicans—dominated Missouri politics in 1866 and used every excuse it could to disenfranchise Democrats. Parrish, *History of Missouri*, 136, 140–42.

16. The starting point for identifying guerrillas by name from the sampled counties is the compilation by Eakin and Hale, *Branded as Rebels*, vol. 1; and Hale, *Branded as Rebels*, vol. 2. Both books are compilations of names and biographical information on Missouri rebels, culled from many sources, including the provost marshals' records, the *Official Records*, Missouri newspapers, John Newman Edwards's books, muster rosters, and everything else the authors could find. *Branded as Rebels* thus contains many references to murders, house-burnings, and robberies committed by the guerrillas against civilians, which are not included in Dyer's count. Starting with Eakin and Hale, the original sources that they referenced could be traced. In instances where there was enough information to know where to look, the 1860 manuscript census showed the guerrillas' counties of residence and details of their families and households.

17. See Appendix 2, calculation P.

18. Geiger, "Missouri's Hidden Civil War," 218. The earliest such debt cases were heard in the fall court sessions, 1861. By spring 1865, all the cases had been adjudicated and closed, with the exception of a few garnishments. In the sampled counties, the circuit

court minute books, which contain summary entries for the cases, are as follows: Chariton County (85 cases): Volume E; Cooper County (68 cases): Volumes 8–9; Lafayette County (284 cases): Books 17–19, 19 1/2; Pettis County (122 cases): Books E–F; and Saline County (120 cases): Books E–F. Dyer, *Compendium*, 2:582.

19. Eakin and Hale, *Branded as Rebels*, vol. 1, and Hale, *Branded as Rebels*, vol. 2. The number of guerrillas from each county was as follows: Chariton — 8; Cooper — 1; Lafayette — 25; Pettis — 3; Saline — 16. See Appendix 4 for a list of guerrillas' names. Geiger, "Missouri's Hidden Civil War," 246–49.

20. The six guerrillas who signed promissory notes were Thomas H. Allen, Julius Marshall, Jack Reinhardt, James Waller, James Warren, and John Warren. Eakin and Hale, *Branded as Rebels*, 1:283, 367, 449, 454; and Hale, *Branded as Rebels*, 2:338. For James Waller, the cases were *Farmers' Bank of Missouri v. Richard Bledsoe, James T. Waller*; Lafayette County Circuit Court Minute Book 19 1/2, 339 [LF639060]; *Farmers' Bank of Missouri v. Richard H. Bledsoe, Lewis N. Sanders, James T. Waller*; Lafayette County Circuit Court Minute Book 19 1/2, 338 [LF639061]. For Julius Marshall: *Farmers' Bank of Missouri v. Benjamin Eliot, Julius S. Marshall, William Corse*; May–June 1864 session, Lafayette County Circuit Court Minute Book 19, 303 [LF639045]. For Jack Reinhardt: *Farmers' Bank of Missouri v. Daniel Trigg, William K. Trigg, Paul Reinhard, Jacob Reinhardt, Thomas M. Shields*; May 1862 session, Lafayette County Circuit Court Minute Book 17, 370, 378 [LF625008]. For James Warren: *Farmers' Bank of Missouri v. Anderson Warren, Martin V. Warren, James Warren*; May–June 1864 session, Lafayette County Circuit Court Minute Book 19, 363 [LF646162]. For John Warren: *Farmers' Bank of Missouri v. Martin V. Warren, Anderson Warren, John M. Warren*; May–June 1864 session, Lafayette County Circuit Court Minute Book 19, 321 [LF646143]. For Allen, *Farmers' Bank of Missouri v. Isaac McGirk, et al.*; November 1863 session, Pettis County Circuit Court Minute Book E, p. 173 [PE63B126]. For the guerrillas named in the text whose relatives were being sued, the relatives' names were as follows: For Woodson, his brother Frank Woodson, and his uncle David Hearndon Lindsey. For the Cruzens, their brother Nathaniel Green North Cruzen and his father-in-law, Abram Jordan. For Ferrell, his brother Jesse J. Ferrell, brother-in-law William Cackley Hill, and uncle Phares Ferrell (Lafayette County). For Benson, cousins Daniel T. Guthrie, John R. Brown, and William S. Brown.

21. See Appendix 4 for list of individual guerrillas. See Supporting Data for detailed individual data. In the group of thirty-six recruits who were being sued or had a close family member being sued, the four who became guerrillas were J. L. Bledsoe, Dr. John W. Benson, Isaac Cruzen, and William S. Jackson. In the second group of thirty-eight recruits who had no connection to the debts, the recruit who became a guerrilla was Drury Pulliam (or Pullum). U.S. Census (manuscript), population schedule, 8th census (1860), Lafayette and Saline Counties [Missouri]. Also *Official Records*, ser. 1, vol. 41, pt. 1, 678. Geiger, "Missouri's Hidden Civil War," 151–68; Circuit Court records, Saline and Lafayette Counties, Missouri. Soldiers Database: War of 1812–World War I, Missouri State Archives; *History of Lafayette County, Missouri*, 368–70, 380–82.

22. Three Confederate generals came from the five counties sampled, including the senior leadership of all Missourians serving in the southern armies: Major Generals Sterling

Price and John Sappington Marmaduke, and Brigadier General Joseph Orville Shelby. Many more generals came from Missouri's Boonslick region as a whole.

23. See Appendix 4 for list of individual guerrillas and details.

24. Overall, the southwestern guerrillas differ from their central-west counterparts in one significant respect. On average the southwesterners were several years older, and therefore more often heads of households. The reason for this age difference is unclear.

25. Brownlee, *Gray Ghosts of the Confederacy*, 142–56. Brigadier General Benjamin F. Loan to Major General Samuel R. Curtis, January 27, 1863, *Official Records*, ser. 1, vol. 22, pt. 2, 80; Geiger, "Missouri's Hidden Civil War," 218. "Memorial of Citizens of Jackson County to Change County Seat" (November 25, 1863), in *Journal of the House of Representatives of Missouri, Adjourned Session, Twenty-Second General Assembly*, appendix, 60. See Chapter 4, note 5, on courthouse fires.

26. "An Act Concerning the Records of the County of Chariton," approved February 9, 1864, in *Laws of the State of Missouri, Adjourned Session, Twenty-Second General Assembly*, 411. *History of Howard and Chariton Counties*, 537; Conard, *Encyclopedia of the History of Missouri*, 1:567; U.S. Census (manuscript), population schedule, 8th census (1860), Chariton County [Missouri]. Chariton County Circuit Court records (microform), Missouri State Archives.

27. U.S. Census (manuscript), population, slave, and agricultural schedules, 8th census (1860), Lafayette County [Missouri]. For the promissory note cases in which Waller was a defendant, see Chapter 6, note 20. Report of Capt. James B. Moore, First Missouri State Militia Cavalry, to Col. James McFerran, April 1, 1864, *Official Records*, ser. 1, vol. 34, pt. 1, 861–62. *Columbia Missouri Statesman*, April 15, 1864, 4. Lafayette County marriage records show that Waller's widow, Fanny, married George W. Ferrell in 1868. Missouri census and marriage records show through 1880 no other record of the Ferrells or any of James and Fanny Waller's children, except one: Maggie Waller married Isaac Wisler in Clay County, Missouri, in 1870. Neither the 1870 nor the 1880 census shows any record of the Wislers.

28. According to the family history the slaves said, "We don't want to be set free. We want to stay with Mr. Waller." This quote and the rest of the family version of Waller's story in the text were written in a copy of the Bible presented to Riley Rosalie Callahan, December 25, 1934, and cited in entry on James T. Waller in the Speare, Haseltine, Armstrong, Waddell, Schulz family tree, Ancestry.com.

29. Family members include Martin D. Warren, Anderson Warren, Martin V. Warren, John Warren, G. B. Warren, Samuel W. Warren, W. W. Warren, J. S. Warren. U.S. Census (manuscript), population, slave, and agricultural schedules, 8th census (1860), Lafayette County [Missouri]. Dodd, "Kentucky Marriages 1802–1850"; "Missouri Marriages to 1850"; and "Missouri Marriages, 1851–1900," Ancestry.com (accessed October 27, 2009). See the following note for references on the promissory notes. See Appendix 4 for list of individual guerrillas. See Supporting Data for more biographical information.

30. Benjamin Loan to Samuel R. Curtis, November 19, 1862, in *Official Records*, ser. 1, vol. 13, 806–7; *Liberty Tribune*, November 14, 1862, 1. Cases heard in the Lafayette County Circuit Court were: *Farmers' Bank of Missouri v. John P. Bowman, William J. Seeber,*

Anderson Warren, May 1862 session, Circuit Court Minute Book 17, 423 [LF625024]; *Farmers' Bank of Missouri v. James Rucker, Elizabeth Rucker, Martin D. Warren, Martin V. Warren,* May–June 1864 session, Circuit Court Minute Book 18, 336 [LF63B065]; *Farmers' Bank of Missouri v. John R. Warren, Martin D. Warren administrator of George W. Warren (deceased), James A. Fishback,* May–June 1864 session, Circuit Court Minute Book 19, 311 [LF646139]; *Farmers' Bank of Missouri v. Martin V. Warren, Anderson Warren, John M. Warren,* May–June 1864 session, Circuit Court Minute Book 19, 321 [LF646143]; *Farmers' Bank of Missouri v. Anderson Warren, Martin V. Warren, James Warren,* May–June 1864 session, Circuit Court Minute Book 19, 363 [LF646162]; *Farmers' Bank of Missouri v. Martin D. Warren, John Warren and John R. Warren,* Circuit Court Minute Book 19, 364; *Farmers' Bank of Missouri v. Martin D. Warren, See A. Neill* [?], May–June 1864 session, Circuit Court Minute Book 19, 371 [LF646176]; *Farmers' Bank of Missouri v. James W. Rucker, Martin V. Warren, Anderson Warren,* May–June 1864 session, Circuit Court Minute Book 19 1/2, 39 [LF646232]; *Farmers' Bank of Missouri v. Martin D. Warren,* May–June 1864 session, Circuit Court Minute Book 19 1/2, 190 [LF646262]. The case heard in the Cooper County Circuit Court was *William H. Trigg v. Green S. Donthitt, Martin J. [sic] Warren, E. E. Rucker, Thomas A. Rucker,* March 1863 session, Circuit Court Minute Book 8, 430 [CO61900C]. The case heard in the Pettis County Circuit Court was *Merchants' Bank v. G. B. Warren, John Harbert, D. Vandyke,* June 1865 session, Circuit Court Minute Book E, 364 [PE656152]. St. Joseph *Daily Journal of Commerce,* July 22, 1863, quoted in Eakin and Hale, *Branded as Rebels,* 1:451, and Hale, *Branded as Rebels,* 2:338. Another report of the Warrens' bushwhacking can be found in the statement by Andrew A. Belt to Capt. D. A. Calvert on the robbery of the steamboat "Marcella" in October 1863. Microfilm reel F1607, Missouri Union Provost Marshal Papers. In 1870, the only remaining Warren household of the four was that of Martin D. Warren. U.S. Census (manuscript), population schedule, 9th census (1870), Lafayette County [Missouri]. Martin V. Warren had moved with his family to Kansas. U.S. Census (manuscript), population schedule, 9th census (1870), Cherokee County [Kansas]. The whereabouts of the families of John and Anderson Warren in 1870 are unknown.

31. Fellman, *Inside War,* 38, 57, 235. Dennis, *Eugene Field's Creative Years,* 14–15, 28–30. St. Louis *Republican,* September 24, 1874. "Good Citizens Indignant," *New York Times,* September 8, 1883, 1; "The Amenities of Travel," *New York Times,* August 29, 1873, 4.

CHAPTER 7. THE TRANSFORMATION
OF REGIONAL IDENTITY

1. Woodward, *Origins of the New South,* 179. To employ Gavin Wright's terminology in *Old South New South,* the planters were able to transform themselves from "labor-lords" before the Civil War to landlords after the war. Wright, *Old South New South,* 47–51. Eric Foner also views the lack of any significant land redistribution after the war to be the critical factor in planter persistence there. Foner, *Short History of Reconstruction,* 172–78.

2. Oakes, *Ruling Race*, 52. Fogel and Engerman, *Time on the Cross*, 200. Wiener, "Planter Persistence and Social Change," 235–36. Formwalt, "Antebellum Planter Persistence," 412. Campbell, "Population Persistence and Social Change," 190–96. Moneyhon, "Impact of the Civil War in Arkansas," 105–18.

3. In the 1860 census for Missouri, 4 persons identified themselves as planters, against 124,989 farmers. Also in 1860, there were 561 farms greater than five hundred acres, and 540 owners of twenty or more slaves. The comparable figures for Mississippi were 3,098 planters, 46,308 farmers, 2,349 farms greater than five hundred acres, and 5,895 owners of twenty or more slaves. In Mississippi there were 1,675 owners of fifty slaves or more. Table 6, "Occupations," in Kennedy, *Population of the United States in 1860*, 1:273, 302–3. *Historical Census Browser*. See Appendix 4 for planters in the three sampled counties.

4. In 1850 for the three counties, the top 3 percent of property owners by valuation or acreage would include all farms equal to or greater than 890 acres, or six thousand dollars in valuation. In 1860 in Cooper County, a farm in the top 3 percent by valuation or acreage would be a farm valued at $16,000, or of 800 acres. In Pettis County, a farm in the top 3 percent by valuation or acreage would be a farm valued at $22,320, or of 1,000 acres. In Saline County, a farm in the top 3 percent by valuation or acreage would be a farm valued at $20,000, or of 1,200 acres. In 1870 in Cooper County, the top 3 percent of farms by valuation or acreage correspond to a valuation of $13,200, or just short of 500 acres. In 1870 in Pettis County, a farm in the top 3 percent by valuation or acreage would be a farm valued at $17,000, or 510 acres. In 1870 in Saline County, a farm in the top 3 percent by valuation or acreage would be a farm valued at $12,500, or 500 acres. DeBow, *Seventh Census of the United States*, Table I: Statistics on Missouri, 644–46, cxxv. *Historical Census Browser. Ninth Census of the United States: Statistics of Population. Tables I to VIII Inclusive*, Table 2: Missouri, 43.

5. Wiener, "Planter Persistence and Social Change," 238, 248; Formwalt, "Antebellum Planter Persistence," 414–16; Campbell, "Population Persistence and Social Change," 198.

6. Moneyhon, "Impact of the Civil War in Arkansas," 114. Townes, "Effect of Emancipation," 407–10. In the three Missouri counties, out of three hundred and ninety-six landowners with five hundred or more acres in 1860, seventy-five were still present in 1870. Using the top 3 percent of valuation, out of one hundred and seven landowners in the three Missouri counties in 1860, twenty-three were still in the top 3 percent of landowners by 1870.

7. Wiener, "Planter Persistence and Social Change," 239–40, 250, 252, 256; Formwalt, "Antebellum Planter Persistence;" 414, 416, 424–25; Campbell, "Population Persistence and Social Change;" 197, 199, 201–2.

8. U. S. Census (manuscript), population schedule, 9th census (1870), Saline County, Missouri [for Harrison], Cole County [for Deaderick], and Pettis County [for Hopkins]. Goodrich and Oster, eds. "Few Men But Many Widows," 273–304.

9. *Historical Census Browser*. Population in the three counties went from 41,447 in 1860 to 61,070 in 1870.

10. Missouri had 88,553 farms in 1860 and 148,418 in 1870. The average-size farm went

from 226 acres in 1860 to 146 acres in 1870, a 35 percent decrease. The three counties had 3,093 farms in 1860 and 5,976 in 1870, a 93 percent increase. *Historical Census Browser.* "First Annual Report of the Missouri State Board of Agriculture, for the Year 1865," in *Appendix to the Journal of the Senate, Adjourned Session, Twenty-Third General Assembly of Missouri,* 156–58.

11. Missouri's white population was 906,540 in 1860 and 1,380,972 in 1870. African Americans were omitted from this calculation because the 1860 census did not record the slaves' nativity, making a comparison to 1870 figures impossible. The number of native-born Missourians grew from 475,246 in 1860 to 788,491 in 1870, an increase of 66 percent, in spite of the war. Foreign-born Missourians increased from 160,541 in 1860 to 222,267 in 1870, a 38 percent increase. Missourians born in free states increased from 185,990 in 1860 to 355,262 in 1870, an increase of 91 percent. In 1860, 274,146 Missourians had been born in southern states; in 1870, the number was 265,187. *Historical Census Browser.* Clevenger, "Missouri Becomes a Doubtful State," 551–53.

12. Little Dixie comprised Callaway, Boone, Howard, Cooper, Saline, Lafayette, and Clay counties. Frizzell, "Southern Identity," 271. O'Flaherty, *General Jo Shelby,* 51.

13. Frizzell, "Southern Identity," 239–40, 254–58.

14. Population figures for Boone, Callaway, Clay, Cooper, Howard, Lafayette, and Saline counties from *Historical Census Browser.* Frizzell, "Southern Identity," 258n50, 259.

15. There were a total of 365 defendants in the three-county sample whose later history is known. Of these, 34 (9 percent) did not survive the war. Of the remaining 331, 92 left the state, though 9 later returned. Defendants and bankers were traced mainly through the 1870 and 1880 censuses. Family histories and genealogical databases provided some supplemental information. See Supporting Data for detailed individual data.

16. Harter, *Lost Colony of the Confederacy,* 19, 33, 64–65; Knapp, "New Source on the Confederate Exodus," 369. O'Flaherty, *General Jo Shelby,* 235–52. U.S. Senate, *Biographical Directory of the U.S. Congress.* Castel, *General Sterling Price,* 273–77.

17. Cooper County Circuit Court records. *Boonville Weekly Advertiser,* February 22, 1878, 7; June 26, 1885. *St. Louis Missouri Republican,* October 11, 1861, 2; October 14, 1861, 2. *Nathaniel T. Allison, Plaintiff in Error, v. Nathaniel Sutherlin, et al, Defendants in Error,* 50 *Reports of Cases, Supreme Court, Missouri* (1873), 274. *St. Louis Missouri Republican,* July 4, 1868, quoted in Stanley, Wilson, and Wilson, *Death Records from Missouri Newspapers: January 1, 1866–December 31, 1870.*

18. For instance, the *St. Louis Missouri Republican* noted in May 1862 that there was no lack of money for investment, but there was little employment for it save in government securities. *St. Louis Missouri Republican,* May 4, 1862. Primm, *Lion of the Valley,* 270–71. Cronon, *Nature's Metropolis,* 301–3.

19. "An Act to Enable the Banks and Branch Banks in this State to Wind up their Business and Organize under the Law of Congress to Furnish a National Currency" (February 12, 1864), *Laws of the State of Missouri, Adjourned Session, Twenty-Second General Assembly,* 9. Hubbard and Davids, *Banking in Mid-America,* 95, 102.

20. Hammond, *Sovereignty and an Empty Purse,* 224–26, 342, 355–59. *St. Louis Missouri Republican,* May 24, 1862, 3. Myers, *Financial History,* 163. Eaton, "Development and Later Decline of the Hemp Industry," 344–59. O'Flaherty, *General Jo Shelby,* 51.

21. *Journal of the House of Representatives of Missouri, First Session, Twenty-Second General Assembly,* 1–21 (index). *Journal of the Senate of Missouri, First Session, Twenty-Second General Assembly,* 21–28 (index). *Journal of the Senate of the State of Missouri, Regular Session, Twenty-Third General Assembly,* 2–3. *Journal of the House of Representatives of the State of Missouri, Regular Session, Twenty-Third General Assembly,* 33–35.

22. Hunter, "Missouri's Confederate Leaders," 371–96.

23. Frizzell, "Southern Identity," 260. Between 1872 and 1905, Missouri had seven governors who had taken part in the Civil War in the state: Silas Woodson, Charles H. Hardin, John S. Phelps, Thomas T. Crittenden, John S. Marmaduke, Albert P. Morehouse, and Alexander M. Dockery. Of this group, Marmaduke was the only former Confederate. Missouri's Legislative Leaders, Missouri State Archives.

24. Clevenger, "Missouri Becomes a Doubtful State," 541. Missouri's Legislative Leaders, Missouri State Archives. Elazar, *American Federalism,* quoted in Hardy, Dohm, and Leuthold, *Missouri Government and Politics,* 26. In Elazar's analysis, Missouri's political culture resembles that of no other state save Hawaii. Elazar makes no comment on this resemblance, which he may view as a chance occurrence.

25. Hunter, "Missouri's Confederate Leaders," 379. Parrish, *History of Missouri,* 128, 254–55. Kremer and Christiansen, *History of Missouri,* 17. N. D. Allen Papers, journals and diaries, entry dated March 2, 1863. *Columbia Missouri Statesman,* June 8, 1883, 4. Cutler, *History of the State of Kansas,* Part 10. Stevens, *Missouri the Center State,* 89. Goodrich, "'In the Earnest Pursuit of Wealth,'" 155–84. Waldo was already unstable, to judge by his past history.

26. Geiger, "Missouri Banks and the Civil War," 145; Stevens, *St. Louis,* vol. 2, 560–64. Stevens, *Centennial History of Missouri,* 3:669. See Supporting Data for more biographical information.

27. Williams and Shoemaker, *Missouri, Mother of the West,* 3:142. Conard, *Encyclopedia of the History of Missouri,* 1:495–6. *History of Buchanan County* (1881), 241–43. Hyde and Conard, *Encyclopedia of the History of St. Louis,* 1:238, 3:1384. Sampson, "The Honorable John Brooks Henderson," 237–41. U.S. Senate, *Biographical Directory of the U.S. Congress.* "Domestic Intelligence," *Harpers Weekly,* January 23, 1864, 51; February 27, 1864, 130.

28. To name only two bankers who left Missouri, Robert Hoffman, cashier of the Farmers' Bank of Missouri in Lexington, by 1880 was a planter in Mississippi (U.S. Census [manuscript], population schedule, 10th census [1880], Madison County [Mississippi]); Waldo Johnson, former United States senator and one of the principal investors in the Merchants' Bank of Missouri branch at Osceola, was in Canada. U.S. Senate, *Biographical Directory of the U.S. Congress. Columbia Missouri Statesman,* March 9, 1883, 2–2. Hyde and Conard, *Encyclopedia of the History of St. Louis,* 1:26. *Liberty Tribune,* December 13, 1867, 2. *Columbia Missouri Statesman,* March 9, 1883, 2; May 27, 1863, 1–7; June 8, 1883, 4. "Alexander Family," 184. *Columbia Missouri Statesman, Daily News' History of Buchanan County,* 516. Robert W. Donnell, life sketch, *Boonville Weekly Eagle,* August 9, 1872, 3. *New York Times,* January 13, 1893, 5.

29. Fuenfhausen, *Clay County*. Ancestry.com. Robert W. Donnell, life sketch, *Boonville Weekly Eagle*, August 9, 1872, 3. *New York Times*, August 8, 1878. U.S. Census (manuscript), population schedule, 7th census (1850),Cooper and Buchanan counties [Missouri]. *Butte Daily Miner*, January 23, 1883, 3; March 13, 1877, 3; March 20, 1877, 3. PBS documentary, *Las Vegas: An Unconventional History*.

30. U.S. Census (manuscript), population schedule, 10th census (1880). *Daily News' History of Buchanan County*, 516. *New York Times*, January 5, 1892, 5. Robert W. Donnell, life sketch, *Boonville Weekly Eagle*, August 9, 1872, 3. *New York Times*, January 5, 1892, 5.

31. Levens and Drake, *History of Cooper County*, 96–118. Hubbard and Davids, *Banking in Mid-America*, 116. Jackson, *Missouri Democracy*, 3:165. Gentry, *Bench and Bar*, 18–19, portrait of Edward A. Lewis opposite p. 16.

32. Morrison-Fuller, "Plantation Life in Missouri." *Glasgow Missourian*, June 2, 1938; June 9, 1938; June 23, 1938; June 30, 1938; July 7, 1938. *United States Biographical Dictionary and Portrait Gallery of Eminent and Self-Made Men: Missouri Volume*, 720–721. *Illustrated Atlas Map of Howard County*, 14, 27.

33. As of October 2005, the United Daughters of the Confederacy had 305 members in Missouri, 165 in Kentucky, and 86 in Maryland. Telephone conversation with reference librarian, Goodlett Memorial Library, United Daughters of the Confederacy, Richmond, Virginia, February 24, 2006. *Frederick Douglass' Paper*, January 26, 1855.

34. The film *Bad Men of Missouri* was released by Warner Brothers in 1941. Robinson, *Mountain Max*. Olpin, "Missouri and the Civil War Novel," 1. Lowman, *Narrative of the Lawrence Massacre*. The first films about Jesse James and William Clarke Quantrill were, respectively, *The James Boys in Missouri*, Essanay Film Manufacturing Company, 1908; and *Quantrell's Son*, Vitagraph Film Company of America, 1914. Video games featuring Jesse James include "Gunfighter: The Legend of Jesse James," and "Gunfighter 2: The Return of Jesse James," both for the Sony Playstation.

35. Nichols, "Thoroughly Bad Guy," 1. *The Unforgiven* won the 1992 Academy Awards for Best Picture, Best Supporting Actor (Gene Hackman), Best Directing (Clint Eastwood), and Best Film Editing. James Stewart starred in *Bend of the River* (Universal International Pictures, 1952); Clint Eastwood in *The Unforgiven* (Malpaso Productions, 1992); the Carradine, Keach, Quaid, and Guest brothers in *The Long Riders* (United Artists, 1980); and Brad Pitt in *The Assassination of Jesse James by the Coward Robert Ford* (Warner Brothers, 2007).

CHAPTER 8. WAR AND THE
ADMINISTRATIVE STATE

1. Bensel, *Yankee Leviathan*, 94. More than two million men were in the Union army at one time or another during the Civil War. Kreidberg and Henry, *History of Military Mobilization*, 97. Estimates of Confederate enlistments throughout the war vary from 1,227,890 to 1,406,180. Eicher and Eicher, *Civil War High Commands*, 71. In 1860 the population of the United States and territories was 31,443,321. Kennedy, *Population of*

the United States in 1860, 599. Message of the President of the United States, to the 37th Congress 1st Session. In Rives, *Congressional Globe, First Session, Thirty-Seventh Congress* (hereafter *Cong. Globe* 1 [1861]), 2 (appendix).

2. Hesseltine, *Lincoln and the War Governors*, 146. Shannon, *Organization and Administration*, 1:29–30.

3. Meneely, *War Department*, 23–24. The army's strength was further reduced by the defection of the last four seceding states. Shannon, *Organization and Administration*, 1:27. In January 1861, the total U.S. officer corps numbered 1,098. Of these, 313 (29 percent) resigned their commissions and joined the Confederate forces. Kreidberg and Henry, *History of Military Mobilization in the United States Army*, 89–91.

4. *Official Records*, ser. 3, vol. 1, 145–46. Hesseltine, *Lincoln and the War Governors*, 165, 178–79. Secretary of War Simon Cameron to the President of the United States, dated July 1, 1861, in *Official Records*, ser. 3, vol. 1, 303–4. Message of the President of the United States, in *Congressional Globe* 1 (1861), 2 (appendix). "An Act to authorize the Employment of Volunteers to aid in the Enforcing of Laws and Protecting Public Property" (July 22, 1861), *U.S. Statutes at Large*, 12:268. Shannon, *Organization and Administration*, 1:46–47. *Official Records*, ser. 3, vol. 1, 383–84. Huston, *Sinews of War*, 175.

5. *Register of Officers and Agents*, 102, 104–7. Shannon, *Organization and Administration*, 1:53–54. *Official Records*, ser. 3, vol. 1, 132, 177. Meneely, *War Department*, 25–26, 115. "An Act to indemnify the States for Expenses incurred by them in Defence of the United States" (July 27, 1861), 37th Congress, 1st Session, *U.S. Statutes at Large*, 12:276. Huston, *Sinews of War*, 86, 103, 216. Kreidberg and Henry, *History of Military Mobilization*, 87. Rives, *Congressional Globe, Second Session, Thirty-Sixth Congress*, 46.

6. Hesseltine, *Lincoln and the War Governors*, 116, 128–30. "An Act to Establish a Board of Ordnance and an Ordnance Bureau, and for Other Purposes" (November 13, 1860), *Acts of the General Assembly of the State of South Carolina*, 856. On December 17, 1860, three days before South Carolina voted to secede, the legislature authorized the governor to call out the militia for the defense of the state against external enemies. "An Act to Provide an Armed Military Force" (December 17, 1860), ibid., 848. Long, *Civil War Day by Day*, 5–6. Stamp, *And the War Came*, 89–90. Terrell, *Indiana in the War of the Rebellion*, 1:3, 563 (appendix).

7. Shannon, *Organization and Administration*, 262. One such charter was "An Act to Authorize the Formation of a New Volunteer Company of Infantry within the Limits of the Fifteenth Regiment of South Carolina Militia, to be Called the 'Lexington Volunteer Rifle Company,' and to Incorporate the Same, and to Authorize the Formation of Certain Other New Volunteer Companies, and for Other Purposes" (January 28, 1861), in *Acts of the General Assembly of the State of South Carolina*, 867–69. "An Ordinance to Provide a Board, to Whom Shall be Referred all Claims for Expenditures Arising from the Organization, Equipment and Support of the Land and Naval Forces Called or to be Called out for the Defence of the Commonwealth under the Present Emergency" (April 27, 1861), in "Ordinances Adopted by the Convention of Virginia, in Secret Session, in April and May 1861 [First session]," *Acts of the General Assembly*

of the State of Virginia (1862), 18–19; "An Act Creating a War Fund and to Provide for Auditing all Accounts and Disbursements Arising Under the Call for Volunteers" (May 2, 1861), in *Laws of the State of Illinois, Passed by the Twenty-Second General Assembly, at its Extraordinary Session* 22, sections 1 and 4. The Illinois act provided for the auditing and payment for "all accounts for supplies and munitions of war, camp equipage and provisions, equipments, clothing and supplies, furnished for any portion of the Illinois troops on special service, under the orders of the governor, and all accounts in any way or manner originating under the call of the president for volunteers, or the proclamation of the governor for such volunteers, or which should properly be charged to the state war fund." "An Act Providing for Auditing all Accounts and Disbursements Arising Under the Call for Volunteers from Iowa, and also for all Men Organized as the State Militia of Iowa" (May 28, 1861), in *Acts and Resolutions, Iowa,* 9; "An Act to Make Valid Certain Irregular Proceedings of the County Courts of this State, and for Other Purposes" (May 11, 1861), in *Public Laws of the State of North-Carolina,* 102, sections 1 and 2; "An Act to Authorize the Governor to Furnish Arms to Organized Volunteer Companies not Uniformed" (December 18, 1860 [1861]), in *Acts of the General Assembly of the State of Georgia,* 52. Hesseltine, *Lincoln and the War Governors,* 183, 185–86. Also Secretary of War Simon Cameron to Gen. Robert Patterson, April 28, 1861, in *Official Records,* ser. 3, vol. 1, 124–25. J. Leslie, Jr., Chief Clerk War Department, to Col. John A. Wright, August 6, 1861, in *Official Records,* ser. 3, vol. 1, 390. Ibid., ser. 3, vol. 1, 443. "An Act to Raise Money to Arm the State, Repel Invasion, and Protect the Lives and Property of the People of Missouri" (May 13, 1861), *Laws of the State of Missouri, Called Session, Twenty-First General Assembly,* 53, section 2; "An Act for the Organization, Government, and Support of the Military Forces of Missouri" (May 10, 1861), ibid., 18–20, sections 96, 100–107.

8. Alexander Hamilton, "Federalist No. 26." "An Act Declaring the Rights and Liberties of the Subject and Settling the Succession of the Crown," Avalon Project, Yale Law School. Huston, *Sinews of War,* 4. "Assize of Arms," in Adams and Stephens, *Select Documents,* 23–24. In the English Bill of Rights, the right to bear arms was limited: "Subjects which are Protestants may have arms for their defence suitable to their conditions and as allowed by law." "The English Bill of Rights, 1689," Avalon Project, Yale Law School. Cowen, Nichols, and Bennet, *United States Court of Claims,* 2:1, 4.

9. Cowen, Nichols, and Bennet, *United States Court of Claims,* 2:9–10.

10. "Proposed Adjustment of the Account of the State of South Carolina."

11. Shannon, *Organization and Administration,* 1:58. *New York Tribune,* July 8, 1861; July 15, 1861; September 5, 1861. War Department, Adjutant General's Office, General Orders, No. 71, dated September 5, 1861, in *Official Records,* ser. 3, vol. 1, 483–84 [New York]. War Department, Adjutant General's Office, Special Orders, No. 241, dated September 7, 1861, in *Official Records,* ser. 3, vol. 1, 489 [Pennsylvania]. War Department, Adjutant General's Office, Special Orders, No. 243, dated September 10, 1861, in *Official Records,* ser. 3, vol. 1, 495–96 [Ohio]. Shannon, *Organization and Administration,* 1:261. Adjutant General's Office, General Orders, No. 78, dated September 16, 1861, in *Official Records,* ser. 3, vol. 1, 518. Adjutant General's Office, General Orders,

No. 18, dated February 21, 1862, in *Official Records*, ser. 3, vol. 1, 898. Major General John E. Wool to Major General Henry E. Halleck, dated September 20, 1862, in *Official Records*, ser. 3, vol. 2, 422.

12. Adjutant General's Office, General Orders, No. 18, dated February 21, 1862, in *Official Records*, ser. 3, vol. 1, 898. Huston, *Sinews of War*, 216. Military expenditures for fiscal 1860–61 were $22,981,000 for the army and $12,421,000 for the navy; for fiscal 1861–62, $394,368,000 for the army and $42,668,000 for the navy; for fiscal 1864–65, $1,031,323,000 for the army and $122,613,000 for the navy. Series Y457–465, "Outlays of the Federal Government, 1789 to 1970," in U.S. Department of Commerce, *Historical Statistics of the United States, Bicentennial Edition*, 2:1114.

13. McPherson, *Battle Cry of Freedom*, 447. Foner, *Short History of Reconstruction*, 115.

14. Chapter 53, "An Act to audit the accounts of the respective States against the Confederacy" (August 30, 1861), in Matthews, *Statutes at Large of the Provisional Government of the Confederate States of America*, 197. Also chapter 58, "An Act to provide a mode of authenticating claims for money against the Confederate States, not otherwise provided for" (August 30, 1861), ibid., 199. Parrish, *Turbulent Partnership*, 31–32; Parrish, *History of Missouri*, 48; Kirkpatrick, "Missouri, the Twelfth Confederate State," 270–81.

15. "An Act to indemnify the States for Expenses incurred by them in Defence of the United States" (July 27, 1861), 37th Congress, 1st Session, *U.S. Statutes at Large*, 12:276. "An Act Making Appropriations for the Support of the Army for the Year ending June thirty, Eighteen Seventy-Two, and for Other Purposes" (March 3, 1871), 41st Congress, 3rd Session, *U.S. Statutes at Large* 16:524–25. The commission considered claims filed between March 3, 1871, and March 3, 1873. The commission received 22,298 claims for a total sum of $60,258,144.44, of which the commission allowed $4,636,920.69. Klingberg, *Southern Claims Commission*, 157. "An Act to Legalize and Confirm Certain Acts of the County Court" (September 20, 1861), chapter 19, *Public Laws of the State of North-Carolina, Second Extra Session, 1861*, 48. Cowen, Nichols, and Bennet, *United States Court of Claims*, 2:87. Wilson, *Business of Civil War*, appendix A, 228.

16. Goldin and Lewis, "Economic Cost of the American Civil War." "An Act to indemnify the States for Expenses incurred by them in Defence of the United States" (July 27, 1861), 37th Congress, 1st Session, *U.S. Statutes at Large*, 12:276. Blaine, "War Debts of the Loyal States," 2.

17. Meneely, *War Department*, 121. Byers, *Iowa in War Times*, 47–48. This source lists other prominent Iowans and several of the state's banks that did the same. Todd, *Confederate Finance*, 173. Shannon, *Organization and Administration*, 45, citing the *New York Tribune*, June 1, 1861. Shannon cites other examples of major private contributions by banks, businesses, and individuals. Ibid., 24.

18. Dyer, *Compendium*, 2:583–94. Eicher, *Longest Night*, 99. At First Manassas, U.S. forces numbered 28,450 and the Confederate forces 32,230. At Wilson's Creek, Union forces numbered about 5,400 troops, the Confederates about 11,000. National Park Service, American Battlefield Protection Program. Dyer, *Compendium*, 2:587.

19. At Shiloh, U.S. forces totaled 65,085, Confederate forces 44,968. Casualties at Shiloh

were 13,047 U.S., and 10,699 Confederate. Union casualties at Antietam were 12,401, Confederate 10,316. U.S. National Park Service, American Battlefield Protection Program. Goldin, "War," 3:938. According to Dyer, Union battlefield deaths totaled 1,226 for the last six months of 1861. During 1862, Union forces had 18,084 battlefield deaths, so 9,042 for six months. 9,042 – 1,226 = 7,818. At Antietam, Union battlefield deaths totaled 2,108. Dyer, *Compendium*, 2:583–94.

20. Skowronek, *Building a New American State*, 3–18. Following Skowronek's work, two notable books about the postwar expansion of the U.S. government are Skocpol, *Protecting Soldiers and Mothers*, and Dunlavy, *Politics and Industrialization*. However, Richard Bensel's book *Yankee Leviathan* describes lasting changes in the centralization of state power that grew out of the American Civil War.

21. Besides military units drawn from the same counties, villages, or neighborhoods, other units formed along racial, occupational, sentimental, and sometimes eccentric lines. Many Western organizations were German, and, in the East, there were regiments of French. Volunteer fire companies in New York City formed a regiment of Fire Zouaves. Shannon, *Organization and Administration*, 1:37, 42. Testimony of Edward Padelford, in Williams, *Civil War Suits*, 140. Shackelford, "Shackelford Amendment," 121–28. Mitchell, *Vacant Chair*, 32–33.

22. Mitchell, *Vacant Chair*, 19–37.

APPENDIX 1. RESEARCH DESIGN AND METHODOLOGY

1. *Official Records*, ser. 2, vol. 5, 681, paragraph 149.

2. Ash, *When the Yankees Came*, 48–49, 41–47. Ash also presents evidence that the ranks of the guerrillas were swelled by returning Confederate troops whose enlistments had expired and by deserters. Ibid., 47–49, 125, 168, 181. Corroborating Ash's findings, Kenneth W. Noe also found that the guerrillas in western Virginia came from every social class. Noe, "Who Were the Bushwhackers?" 1–25.

3. Fisher, *War at Every Door*, 163–64, 173–75.

4. Brownlee, *Gray Ghosts of the Confederacy*, 31; *Report to the Committee of the House of Representatives of the Twenty-Second General Assembly of the State of Missouri*, 98, 180–81, 192–94, 296–305, 316–41, 349–50, 373–76, 391–93, 409, 415, 425, 437–38, 442.

5. Fellman, *Inside War*, 21–22, 35–37, 90–91, 239–40.

6. Major General H. W. Halleck to Brigadier General Lorenzo Thomas, St. Louis, January 18, 1862, in *Official Records*, ser. 1, vol. 8, 507; General J. M. Schofield to Hon. E. M. Stanton, St. Louis, May 16, 1862, in *Official Records*, ser. 1, vol. 13, 386; Fellman, *Inside War*, 35–37, 213–14.

7. See note 2, above.

8. Bowen, "Guerilla War in Western Missouri," 38. Bowen found that four of the eight families who owned more than fifty slaves in Jackson County in 1860 included family members who were guerrillas. Many more guerrillas came from families not quite as wealthy but still very well off. Ibid., 45, 47.

9. Woodward, *Origins of the New South, 1877–1913*, 1–23.

10. Wiener, *Social Origins of the New South*, 35. Billings, *Planters and the Making of the "New South,"* 70–74, 197, 213, 223–27.

11. Phillips, *Missouri's Confederate*, 235, 291. Thelen, *Paths of Resistance*, 70–71. Phillips, "Judge Napton's Private War," 214. Woodward, *Burden of Southern History*, 27, 7 (page citations are to the reprint edition).

12. Kremer and Christensen, *History of Missouri*, 1–27. Thelen, *Paths of Resistance*, 13–17, 29–35, 59–65, 70–77. Cassity, *Defending a Way of Life*, 206–12.

13. Abraham Lincoln to Attorney General Edward Bates, November 29, 1862, in *Official Records*, ser. 3, vol. 2, 882–83.

14. Fellman, *Inside War*, 247–64. Stiles, *Jesse James*, 20–21, 53–54, 289, 38.

15. Ball, *Financial Failure and Confederate Defeat*, 1–2, 14–17, 22–23. Schweikart, *Banking in the American South*, 2–5. Roark, *Masters Without Slaves*, 136–37, 173–77, 178.

16. Goldin and Lewis, "Economic Cost of the American Civil War," 304, 308.

17. Blaine, "War Debts of the Loyal States," 2. Goldin takes her figures for state and local military outlays from Bolles, *Financial History of the United States*. Goldin, Supplementary Tables for "The Economic Cost of the American Civil War: Estimates and Implications," table 7 (unpublished data, courtesy of the author). Except for state enlistment bounties, which Goldin adds to Bolles's figures, Bolles's own data come from Blaine. Bolles, *Financial History of the United States*, 245. Sinisi, *Sacred Debts*, 23.

18. "An Act to indemnify the States for Expenses incurred by them in Defence of the United States" (July 27, 1861), 37th Congress, 1st Session, *U.S. Statutes at Large*, 12:276. Blaine, "War Debts of the Loyal States," 2.

19. Goldin, Supplementary Tables for "The Economic Cost of the American Civil War: Estimates and Implications," table 13 (unpublished data, courtesy of the author). Todd, *Confederate Finance*, 135, 171–74.

20. Blaine, "War Debts of the Loyal States," 2. Missouri received about $6.5 million from the state's first claim against the U.S. government, in December 1866. *Liberty Tribune*, December 21, 1866, 2. In 1882, the state received $234,594.10 for its second claim. *Jefferson City People's Tribune*, August 16, 1882, 3. In 1904, Missouri received its final claims payment of $475,198.13 from the U.S. government, for interest the state had paid on war bonds. *Jefferson City State Tribune*, January 7, 1904, 1. The U.S. Court of Claims dismissed Missouri's final suit for compensation, amounting to about two million dollars, in 1908. *Jefferson City Daily Tribune*, April 7, 1908, 1. *Missouri Troops in Service During the Civil War*, 21–23, 48, 59, 61, 67. *Letter from the Secretary of the Treasury.*

21. *Bank of St. Louis v. Walker H. Finley, et al*, Pettis County, Missouri, Circuit Court Minute Book E, 472, June 15, 1865 [PE645147].

22. Geiger, "Missouri Banks and the Civil War," Appendix 2, "Sources and Uses of Funds," and Appendix 3, "Liquidity, Leverage, and Profitability," 185–239.

23. In one involuntary newspaper closure, Union troops chased off the editor of the Boonville *Observer*, then crated up the printing press and sent it to Jefferson City. Johnson, *History of Cooper County*, 189.

24. William H. Trigg Papers.

APPENDIX 2. CALCULATIONS

1. See Appendix 4 for cases per county and signers' names. See Supporting Data for details of individual cases and additional biographical detail on signers.
2. See Appendix 3 for list of cases. See Supporting Data for details of individual cases.
3. See Appendix 3 for list of cases. See Supporting Data for details of individual cases.
4. See Appendix 3 for list of cases, Appendix 4 for signers' names. See Supporting Data for additional biographical detail on signers.
5. *Historical Census Browser.*
6. *Historical Census Browser.*
7. Newspaper clipping, *Boonville Central Missouri Advertiser,* October 1866, in William H. Trigg Papers, vol. 5. *Historical Census Browser.* See Appendix 4 for signers' names and counties of residence.
8. See Appendix 4 for signers' names in the three-county sample, and for cases per county.
9. "Consumer Price Indexes, for all items," Table series Cc1–65, in Carter, et al., *Historical Statistics of the United States,* "Table Containing History of CPI-U: U.S. All Items Indexes and Annual Percent Changes from 1913 to Present," U.S. Bureau of Labor Statistics. "M-9 Pistol Factfile for the U.S. Army." Beretta USA website.
10. For cases per county, see Appendix 4. Cooper County Deed records, Boonville, Missouri. Books C-2, p. 618; Book D-2, pp. 210, 615, 626; Book E-2, 26, 59–60, 63, 73, 85, 87, 119, 135, 148, 152, 171, 212, 221, 225, 251, 319, 334–335, 380, 382, 385–386, 532, 535, 614, 738; Book H-2, pp. 128, 197, 343.
11. For cases per county, see Appendix 4. Dates and locations of military encounters between hostile forces are drawn from Dyer, *Compendium,* 2:790–815.
12. *Statistics of the United States, (Including Mortality, Property, &c.,) in 1860,* 511.
13. Leip, *Atlas of U.S. Presidential Elections.* U.S. Department of Commerce, Bureau of the Census, *Historical Statistics of the United States, Bicentennial Edition* 2:1072.

Bibliography

ARCHIVAL SOURCES

Baker Library, Harvard University, Cambridge, Mass.
    R. G. Dun & Company Collection.
Boone County Circuit Court records. Columbia, Missouri.
Chariton County Circuit Court records. Keytesville, Missouri.
Clay County Circuit Court records. Liberty, Missouri.
Cooper County Circuit Court records. Boonville, Missouri.
Cooper County deed records. Boonville, Missouri.
Howard County Circuit Court records. Fayette, Missouri.
Jackson County Circuit Court records. Independence, Missouri.
Kansas State Archives, Kansas State Historical Society, Topeka, Kansas.
    Election returns 1854–61, Executive Department, Territorial Records Series.
    William E. Connolly Collection, box 13.
Kentucky Department for Libraries and Archives, Frankfort, Kentucky.
Lafayette County Circuit Court records. Lexington, Missouri.
Missouri Historical Society, St. Louis, Missouri.
    N. D. Allen Papers.
    Robert Augustus Barnes papers, Collection A0085 (accessed October 27, 2009). http://archon.mohistory.org/controlcard.php?id=864. (This collection is divided into five sections. One of these sections, the Robert A. Barnes Personal Papers Series, contains a subsection, Correspondence, which contains correspondence relating to Barnes's southern sympathies during the War.)
    Civil War Collection.
    William M. McPheeters papers.
    Morrison Family Papers.
    Mullanphy Family Collection.
    Sappington Family Papers.

Missouri Secretary of State. Missouri State Archives. Jefferson City, Missouri.

  Digital collections, http://www.sos.mo.gov/archives/resources/resources.asp#onlinedb
      (accessed October 27, 2009):
  Missouri Death Certificates 1910–1958.
  Missouri History.
  Missouri Supreme Court Historical Database.
  Missouri Union Provost Marshal Papers: 1861–1866. (The Provost Marshal Papers for
      the state of Missouri are part of the War Department Collection of Confederate
      Records, Record Group 109, National Archives, Washington, DC. The National
      Archives refers to this collection as the Union Provost Marshals' File of Papers Re-
      lating to Individual Civilians; it is made up of three hundred rolls of microfilmed
      documents [NAMS M-345] for the period from 1861 to 1866. The records at the
      Missouri State Archives are copied from the Missouri portion of the National Ar-
      chives collection.)
  Missouri's Legislative Leaders.
  Soldiers Database: War of 1812–World War I.
  Non-digital collections:
  Governors' Papers collection, 1840–1875.
  Missouri County Circuit Court Records. Missouri Local Records Preservation Pro-
      gram.
  Provost Marshal's File on Confederate Civilians, Provost Marshal Papers for the State
      of Missouri. National Archives and Records Administration, Record Group 109,
      War Department Collection of Confederate Records.
National Archives, Washington, DC.
  "List of Leading and Influential Men in the 2nd Subdistrict-Central District of Missouri-
      Cooper County." Records Group 393, Part 1, c. 2637, "Two or More Citizens File."
      Box 3, National Archives, Washington, DC.
  Provost Marshal's File on Confederate Civilians: Arrests of Two or More Civilians,
      Microfilm Roll 13719 (original in National Archives, Washington, DC). Also available
      at Special Collections, Ellis Library, University of Missouri, Columbia, Missouri.
Pettis County Circuit Court records. Sedalia, Missouri.
Saline County Circuit Court records. Marshall, Missouri.
Transylvania University, Lexington, Kentucky. Student records.
University of Missouri, Columbia, Missouri—Special Collections, Ellis Library.
  Provost Marshal's File on Groups of Two or More Confederate Civilians, Microfilm Roll
      13719 (original in National Archives, Washington, DC).
Western Historical Manuscript Collection, State Historical Society of Missouri, Columbia,
      Missouri.
  Lisbon Applegate Collection, Collection 996.
  Avord Papers, Collection 970.
  Bingham Family Papers, Collection 998.
  Weston F. Birch & Son account books, Collection 2310.
  William C. Breckenridge Papers, Collection 1036.
  Claiborne Fox Jackson File, Collection 2447.

Claiborne Fox Jackson Letters, Collection 1789.

Lilian Kingsbury Collection, Collection 3724.

Meredith Miles Marmaduke Papers, Collection 1021.

Bryan Obear Collection, Collection 1387.

William M. Paxton Papers, Collection 2903.

John Sappington Collection, Collection 1036.

John Sappington Family Papers, Collection 2889.

John S. Sappington Papers, Collection 1027.

William B. Sappington Papers, Collection 1421.

Meriwether Jeff Thompson Papers, Collection 1030.

William H. Trigg Papers. Collection 281.

United Daughters of the Confederacy Missouri Records, Collection 3188.

Washburne Family Papers, Collection 2971.

Marie Oliver Watkins Papers, Collection 2689.

Roy D. Williams Papers, Collection 3769.

PERIODICALS

Banker's Magazine and Statistical Register, various issues, 1857–65.

Bicknell's Counterfeit Detector, Banknote Reporter, and General Price Current, various issues, 1857–58.

Boonville (MO) Weekly Advertiser, various issues, 1880–1930.

Boonville (MO) Weekly Eagle, various issues, 1866–77.

Boonville (MO) Weekly Observer, various issues, 1855–61.

Boston *Liberator,* various issues, 1831–35. Accessible Archives. http://www.accessible.com/accessible/ (accessed October 27, 2009).

Brunswick (MO) Brunswicker, various issues, 1852.

Brunswick (MO) Central City and Brunswicker, various issues, 1863.

Butler (MO) Bates County Democrat, January 28, 1915.

Butte (MT) Miner, various issues, 1876–85.

Charleston (SC) Mercury, various issues, 1860–1865. Accessible Archives, http://www.accessible.com/accessible/ (accessed October 27, 2009).

Chicago Press and Tribune, various issues, 1855–59.

Chicago Tribune, various issues, 1860–65. http://www.proquest.com/en-US/catalogs/databases/detail/pq-hist-news.shtml (accessed October 27, 2009).

Columbia (MO) Missouri Statesman, various issues, 1855–65.

Covington (KY) Kentucky Post, August 18, 2003.

Frederick Douglass' Paper (formerly *The North Star*), various issues, 1851–55. Accessible Archives. http://www.accessible.com/accessible/ (accessed October 27, 2009).

Glasgow (MO) Missourian, various issues, 1938.

Glasgow (MO) Weekly Times, various issues, 1858.

Harper's Weekly, various issues, 1853–65.

Jefferson City (MO) Daily Tribune, various issues, 1885–1908.

Jefferson City (MO) State Tribune, January 7, 1904.

Jefferson City (MO) Inquirer, various issues, 1856–70.

Jefferson City (MO) Missouri Republican, February 13, 1841.

Jefferson City (MO) Missouri State Tribune, October 4, 1901.

Jefferson City (MO) People's Tribune, various issues, 1874.

Jefferson City (MO) Weekly Examiner, 1861.

Journal of Money, Credit and Banking 32, no. 1 (February 2000).

Kansas City Genealogist, various issues, 1992.

Kansas City Western Journal of Commerce, various issues, 1860–65.

Lexington (MO) Advertiser News, May 9, 1940.

Lexington (MO) Intelligencer, February 23, 1889.

Lexington (MO) Register, February 21, 1889.

Lexington (MO) Weekly Union, September 17, 1864.

Liberty (MO) Tribune, various issues, 1855–80.

Marion County (MO) Magazine 1, no. 6 (1904).

Marshall (MO) Democrat, various issues, 1860.

Marshall (MO) Saline County Weekly Progress, various issues, 1915.

Memphis (MO) Reveille, various issues, 1885.

Missouri Alumnus, various issues, 1920–36.

Missouri Historical Review, various issues, 1908–2004.

New York Colored American, various issues, 1837–41. Accessible Archives. http://www
.accessible.com/accessible/ (accessed October 27, 2009).

New York Freedom's Journal, various issues, 1827–29. Accessible Archives. http://www
.accessible.com/accessible/ (accessed October 27, 2009).

New York Herald, various issues, 1861–65. Accessible Archives. http://www.accessible.com/
accessible/ (accessed October 27, 2009).

New York Times, various issues, 1853–83. http://www.nytimes.com/ (accessed October 27,
2009).

New York Tribune, June 1, 1861.

North Star (later *Frederick Douglass' Paper*), various issues, 1847–51. Accessible Archives.
http://www.accessible.com/accessible/ (accessed October 27, 2009).

Plattsburg (MO) Leader, 3 October 1902.

Staunton (VA) Spectator, September 3, 1861. Virginia Center for Digital History, University of Virginia. http://valley.lib.virginia.edu/VoS/choosepart.html (accessed October 27,
2009).

St. Joseph (MO) Daily Journal of Commerce, various issues, 1863–65.

St. Joseph (MO) Journal, various issues, 1861.

St. Louis Invincible Magazine 1 (April 1913–April 1914).

St. Louis Missouri Argus, various issues, 1835–36.

St. Louis Missouri Democrat, various issues, 1855–65.

St. Louis Missouri Intelligencer, various issues, 1823–35.

St. Louis Missouri Republican, various issues, 1855–65.

Sedalia (MO) Capital, March 13, 1915.

Sedalia (MO) Central Missouri News, June 12, 1991.

Sedalia (MO) Weekly Democrat, various issues, 1870.

Southern Bivouac 5 (1886–87).

Toronto Provincial Freeman, various issues, 1854–57. Accessible Archives, http://www .accessible.com/accessible/ (accessed October 27, 2009).

Warrensburg (MO) Star Journal, various issues, 1993.

Washington, DC, National Era, various issues, 1847–60. Accessible Archives, http://www .accessible.com/accessible/ (accessed October 27, 2009).

PRINTED SOURCES

Acts and Resolutions Passed at the Extra Session of the Eighth General Assembly of the State of Iowa, which Convened at the Capitol in Des Moines on Wednesday, the 15th Day of May, 1861. Des Moines, IA: F. W. Palmer, State Printer, 1861.

Acts of the Called Session of the General Assembly of Alabama, Held in the City of Montgomery, Commencing on the Second Monday in January, 1861. Montgomery, AL: Shorter & Reid, State Printers, 1861.

Acts of the First General Assembly of the State of Missouri; Passed at the First Session, which was begun and held at the town of Saint Louis, on Monday, the 18th of September, 1820. St. Louis: Isaac M. Henry & Company, 1820.

Acts of the General Assembly of the State of Georgia, Passed in Milledgeville, at an Annual Session in November and December, 1861. Milledgeville, GA: Boughton, Nisbet and Barnes, State Printers, 1862.

Acts of the General Assembly of the State of South Carolina, Passed in November and December, 1860, and January, 1861. Columbia, SC: R. W. Gibbes, Printer to the State, 1861.

Acts of the General Assembly of the State of Virginia, Passed in 1861–2, in the Eighty-Sixth Year of the Commonwealth. Richmond, VA: William F. Ritchie, Public Printer, 1862.

Acts of the General Assembly of Virginia, Passed at the Session of 1836–1837, Commencing 5th December, 1836, and Ending 31st March, 1837, in the Sixty-First Year of the Commonwealth. Richmond: Thomas Ritchie, Printer to the Commonwealth, 1837.

Adams, George Burton, and H. Morse Stephens, *Select Documents of English Constitutional History*. New York: MacMillan and Company, 1939 (reprint of 1901 ed.).

Adler, Jeffrey S. "Yankee Colonizers and the Making of Antebellum St. Louis." *Gateway Heritage* 12, no. 3 (Winter 1992): 4–19.

Aggarwal, Rajesh K., and Tarik Yousef. "Islamic Banks and Investment Financing." *Journal of Money, Credit and Banking* 32, no. 1 (February 2000): 93–120.

"Alexander Family." *William and Mary College Quarterly Historical Magazine* 10, no. 3 (January 1902), 178–85.

Allardice, Bruce S. *More Generals in Gray*. Baton Rouge: Louisiana State University Press, 1995.

Anders, Leslie. "The Blackwater Incident." *Missouri Historical Review* 88 (July 1994): 416–29.

Appendix to the Journal of the House of Representatives of the Adjourned Session of the Twenty-Second General Assembly of Missouri. Jefferson City, MO: J. P. Ament, 1863.

Appendix to the Journal of the Senate of the Adjourned Session of the Twenty-Third General Assembly of Missouri. Jefferson City, MO: Emory S. Foster, 1865–66.

Ash, Stephen V. *When the Yankees Came: Conflict and Chaos in the Occupied South, 1861–1865*. Chapel Hill: University of North Carolina Press, 1995.

Atherton, Lewis. "James and Robert Aull: Pioneer Merchants in Western Missouri." *Missouri Historical Review* 30, no. 3 (October 1935): 3–27.

———. "The Pioneer Merchant in Mid-America." *University of Missouri Studies* 14, no. 1 (January 1, 1939): 1–127.

Atkeson, William Oscar. *History of Bates County, Missouri*. Topeka, KS: Historical Publishing Company, 1918.

Atlas Map of Lafayette County, Missouri. St. Louis: Missouri Publishing Company, 1877.

The Avalon Project: Documents in Law, History, and Diplomacy, Lillian Goldman Law Library. http://avalon.law.yale.edu/default.asp (accessed October 27, 2009).

Baker, H. F. "Outline History of Banking in the United States." *Bankers' Magazine and Statistical Register* 6, no. 4 (October 1856): 241–56; 6, no. 5 (November 1856): 321–41; 6, no. 6 (December 1856): 416–30.

Ball, Douglas B. *Financial Failure and Confederate Defeat*. Urbana: University of Illinois Press, 1991.

Balleisen, Edward J. *Navigating Failure: Bankruptcy and Commercial Society in Antebellum America*. Chapel Hill: University of North Carolina Press, 2001.

Bancroft, Hubert Howe. *Works*. Vol. 31. *History of Washington, Idaho, and Montana, 1845–1889*. San Francisco: The History Company, 1890.

Barnhill, Frank Clinton. *History of Freemasonry in Saline County*. N.p.: Missouri Lodge of Research, 1956.

Barns, C. R., ed. *The Commonwealth of Missouri, a Centennial Record*. St. Louis: Bryan, Brand & Company, 1877.

Bartels, Caroline. *Marriage Records of Cooper County*. Shawnee Mission, KS: by the author, n.d.

Bartels, Caroline. *The Civil War in Missouri Day by Day: 1861–1865*. Shawnee Mission, KS: Two Trails, 1992.

Barton, O. S. *Three Years With Quantrill: A True Story Told by his Scout*. Norman, OK: University of Oklahoma Press, 1992.

Bay, William Van Ness. *Reminiscences of the Bench and Bar of Missouri . . .* St. Louis: F. H. Thomas and Company, 1878.

Belser, Thomas A., Jr. "Military Operations in Missouri and Arkansas, 1861–1865." Ph.D. diss., Vanderbilt University, 1958.

The Bench and Bar of St. Louis, Kansas City, Jefferson City, and other Missouri Cities. St. Louis: American Biographical Publishing, 1884.

Bensel, Richard Franklin. *Yankee Leviathan: The Origins of Central Authority in America, 1861–1877*. Cambridge: Cambridge University Press, 1994.

Beretta U.S.A. https://www.berettausa.com/Default.aspx (accessed October 27, 2009).

Billings, Dwight. *Planters and the Making of the "New South": Class, Politics and Development in North Carolina, 1865–1900*. Chapel Hill: University of North Carolina Press, 1979.

Biographical Directory of the American Congress, 1774–1949, the Continental Congress, September 5, 1774, to October 21, 1788, and the Congress of the United States from the

First to the Eightieth Congress, March 4, 1789, to January 3, 1949, Inclusive. Washington, DC: United States Government Printing Office, 1950.

Biographical Directory of the American Congress, 1771–1971. Washington, DC: United States Printing Office, 1971.

Biographical history of Nodaway and Atchison counties, Missouri: Compendium of National Biography. Chicago: Lewis Publishing, 1901.

Blaine, James G. "War Debts of the Loyal States, to Accompany H. R. Bill 282," dated February 16, 1866. U.S. Congress, House Report, 39th Congress, 1st sess., 1866, H. Doc. 16, serial 1272. LexisNexis Congressional. http://web.lexis-nexis.com (accessed October 27, 2009).

Bloch, E. Maurice. *The Paintings of George Caleb Bingham: A Catalog Raisonné.* Columbia: University of Missouri Press, 1986.

Bodenhorn, Howard. *State Banking in Early America: A New Economic History.* New York: Oxford University Press, 2003.

Boggs, Karen Carmichael, and Louise Muir Coutts. *Howard County Cemetery Records.* N.p.: by the authors, n.d.

Bolles, Albert D. *A Financial History of the United States from 1861 to 1885.* New York: D. Appleton and Company, 1886.

Bouvier, John. *A Law Dictionary Adapted to the Constitution and Laws of the United States of America and of the Several States of the American Union.* Philadelphia: Childs & Peterson, 1856. http://www.constitution.org/bouv/bouvier.htm (accessed October 27, 2009).

Bowen, Don R. "Guerilla War in Western Missouri, 1862–1865: Historical Extensions of the Relative Deprivation Hypothesis." *Comparative Studies in Society and History* 19 (January 1977): 30–51.

Brown, John Crosby. *A Hundred Years of Merchant Banking.* New York: private printing, 1909.

Browning, James A. *Violence Was No Stranger: A Guide to the Gravesites of Famous Westerners.* Stillwater, OK: Barbed Wire Press, 1993.

Brownlee, Richard S. *Gray Ghosts of the Confederacy: Guerrilla Warfare in the West, 1861–1865.* Baton Rouge: Louisiana State University Press, 1984.

Brunetti, Marty Helm, comp. *Lafayette County, Missouri Cemetery Inscriptions.* Odessa, MO: by the author, 1977.

Bryan, William S., and Robert Rose. *A History of the Pioneer Families of Missouri.* St. Louis: Bryan, Brand, 1876.

Byers, S. H. M. *Iowa in War Times.* Des Moines, IA: W. D. Condit & Company, 1888.

Cable, John R. *The Bank of the State of Missouri,* in *Columbia University Studies in History, Economics and Public Law* 102. New York: Columbia University Press, 1923.

Campbell, Randolph B. "Population Persistence and Social Change in Nineteenth-Century Texas: Harrison County, 1850–1880." *Journal of Southern History* 48, no. 2 (May 1982): 185–204.

Carter, Genevieve L., comp. *Pioneers of Pettis County, Missouri.* N.p.: by the author, 1976.

———. *Pioneers of Pettis and Adjoining Missouri Counties.* N.p.: by the author, 1966.

Carter, Susan, Scott Gartner, Michael Haines, Alan Olmstead, Richard Sutch, and Gavin Wright, eds. *Historical Statistics of the United States: Millennial Edition Online.* New

York: Cambridge University Press, 2002. http://www.cambridge.org (accessed October 27, 2009).

Cashin, Joan E. "The Structure of Antebellum Planter Families: 'The Ties that Bound us was Strong.'" *Journal of Southern History* 56, no. 1 (February 1990): 55–70.

Cassity, Michael. *Defending a Way of Life: An American Community in the Nineteenth Century.* Albany: State University of New York Press, 1989.

Castel, Albert. *General Sterling Price and the Civil War in the West.* Baton Rouge: Louisiana State University Press, 1968.

———. "Kansas Jayhawking Raids into Western Missouri in 1861." *Missouri Historical Review* 54, no. 1 (October 1959): 1–11.

Castel, Albert, and Thomas Goodrich. *Bloody Bill Anderson: The Short, Savage Life of a Civil War Guerrilla.* Mechanicsburg, PA: Stackpole Books, 1998.

Catalog of the Officers and Students of the University of Missouri for the Year Ending June, 1866, Together With a List of Former Officers and Graduates of the Institution. Columbia: William F. Switzler, 1866.

Cawelti, John C. *Apostles of the Self-Made Man.* Chicago: University of Chicago Press, 1965.

Chell, Elizabeth, Jean Haworth, and Sally Brearley. *The Entrepreneurial Personality: Concepts, Cases and Categories.* London: Routledge, 1991.

Chitty, Joseph, and John Walter Hulme. *A Practical Treatise on Bills of Exchange, Checks on Bankers, Promissory Notes, Bankers' Cash Notes, and Bank Notes, with Reference to the Law of Scotland, France, and America.* 12th American edition from the 9th London edition. Springfield, MA: Merriam, 1854.

Circuit Court of Jackson County, Missouri: A History of the Sixteenth Judicial Circuit, 1826–1989. N.p.: The Court, 1989.

Claycomb, William B. *History of Northeast Pettis County, Missouri.* Sedalia, MO: Morningside Press, 1996.

———. "James Brown: Forgotten Trail Freighter." *Wagon Tracks: Santa Fe Trail Association Quarterly* 8, no. 2 (February 1994): 4–6.

———. "John S. Jones: Farmer, Freighter, Frontier Promoter." *Missouri Historical Review* 73, no. 4 (July 1979): 434–50.

Clayton, Frank M., comp. *Landings on all the Western Rivers and Bayous, Showing the Location, Post-Offices, Distances, &c.* St. Louis: Woodward, Tiernan, and Hale, 1884.

Clevenger, Homer. "Missouri Becomes a Doubtful State." *Mississippi Valley Historical Review* 29, no. 4 (March 1943): 541–56.

Cochran, Mr. and Mrs. John, comp. *Cemetery Records of Saline County, Missouri.* Columbia: Church of Jesus Christ and Latter Day Saints, 1964.

Collins, Lewis. *Historical Sketches of Kentucky . . .* Maysville, KY: 1847. Reprint, Lexington, KY: Henry Clay Press, 1968.

Compendium of the Enumeration of the Inhabitants and Statistics of the United States, as obtained at the Department of State, from the Returns of the Sixth Census, etc. Washington, DC: Thomas Allen, Printer, 1841.

Conard, Howard L. *Encyclopedia of the History of Missouri: a Compendium of History and Biography for Ready Reference.* New York: Southern History, 1901.

Congressional Globe. Hein Online, William S. Hein & Company, Inc. http://www .heinonline.org (accessed October 27, 2009).

Connolly, William Else. *Quantrill and the Border Wars.* Cedar Rapids, IA: The Torch Press, 1910.

Constitution of the State of Missouri. St. Louis: I. N. Henry & Company, 1820.

Couch, Robert, and May Couch, comps. *Chariton County Cemetery Inscriptions.* Marcelline, MO: by the authors, 1985.

Cowen, Wilson, Philip Nichols, Jr., and Marion T. Bennet. *The United States Court of Claims: A History,* Part 2, *Origin-Development-Jurisdiction, 1855–1978.* Washington, DC: Committee on the Bicentennial of Independence and the Constitution of the Judicial Conference of the United States, 1978.

Cox, James. *Old and New St. Louis.* St. Louis: Central Biographical Publishing, 1894.

Crisler, Robert M. "Missouri's 'Little Dixie.'" *Missouri Historical Review* 42, no. 2 (January 1948): 130–39.

Cronon, William. *Nature's Metropolis: Chicago and the Great West.* New York: W. W. Norton, 1991.

Cutler, William G. *History of the State of Kansas.* Chicago: A.T. Andreas, 1883. The Kansas Collection, http://www.kancoll.org/books/cutler/terrhist/terrhist-p50.html (accessed October 27, 2009).

Daily News' History of Buchanan County and St. Joseph, Missouri, From the Platte Purchase to the End of the Year 1898. St. Joseph, MO: St. Joseph Publishing Company, 1898.

Darby, John F. *Personal Recollections of Many Prominent People Whom I Have Known: and of Events, Especially of Those Relating to the History of St. Louis, During the First Half of the Present Century.* St. Louis: G.I. Jones, 1880.

Davis, Jefferson. *The Papers of Jefferson Davis.* Edited by Haskell Monroe. Vol. 6, *1856–60.* Baton Rouge: Louisiana State University Press, 1989.

———. *The Papers of Jefferson Davis.* Edited by Haskell Monroe. Vol. 7, *1861.* Baton Rouge: Louisiana State University Press, 1992.

———. *The Rise and Fall of the Confederate Government.* New York: D. Appleton, 1881.

Davis, Walter Bickford, and Daniel S. Durrie. *Illustrated History of Missouri.* St. Louis: A. S. Hall, 1876.

DeBow, J. D. B., Superintendent of the United States Census. *Seventh Census of the United States: 1850.* Washington, DC: Robert Armstrong, 1853.

Demaree, L. Steven. "Post–Civil War Immigration to Southwest Missouri, 1865–1873." *Missouri Historical Review* 69, no. 2 (January 1975): 169–90.

Dennis, Charles H. *Eugene Field's Creative Years.* Garden City, NY: Doubleday, Page, 1924.

Denslow, Ray V. *A Missouri Frontier Lodge: The Story of "Franklin Union Lodge No. 7" at Old Franklin, Missouri, 1822–1832.* N.p.: Masonic Service Association of Missouri, 1929.

Dewey, Davis R. *State Banking Before the Civil War.* Washington, DC: Government Printing Office, 1910.

Dickey, Michael. *Arrow Rock: Crossroads of the Missouri Frontier.* Arrow Rock, MO: Friends of Arrow Rock, 2004.

Dillistin, William H. *Bank Note Reporters and Counterfeit Detectors, 1826–1866; with a*

Discourse on Wildcat Banks and Wildcat Bank Notes. New York: American Numismatic Society, 1949.

Dodd, Jordan R. "Missouri Marriages to 1850." Provo, UT: The Generations Network, Inc., 1997. Ancestry.com. http://www.ancestry.com/search/db.aspx?dbid=2094 (accessed October 27, 2009).

Dodd, Jordan R. "Tennessee Marriages, 1851–1900." Provo, UT: The Generations Network, Inc., 2000. Ancestry.com. http://www.ancestry.com/search/db.aspx?dbid=4125 (accessed October 27, 2009).

Dodd, Jordan R. "Tennessee Marriages to 1825." Provo, UT: The Generations Network, Inc., 1997. Ancestry.com. http://www.ancestry.com/search/db.aspx?dbid=2099 (accessed October 27, 2009).

Dodd, Jordan R., comp. "Kentucky Marriages, 1851–1900." Provo, UT: The Generations Network, Inc., 2001. Ancestry.com. http://www.ancestry.com/search/db.aspx?dbid=4428 (accessed October 27, 2009).

Dodd, Jordan R, et al., comps. "Kentucky Marriages 1802–50." Ancestry.com. http://www.ancestry.com/search/db.aspx?dbid=2089 (accessed October 27, 2009).

Dodd, Jordan R., Liahona Research, comp. "Maryland Marriages, 1655–1850." Provo, UT: The Generations Network, Inc., 2004. Ancestry.com. http://www.ancestry.com/search/db.aspx?dbid=7846 (accessed October 27, 2009).

Dodd, Jordan R., Liahona Research, comp. "Missouri Marriages, 1851–1900." Provo, UT: The Generations Network, Inc., 2000. Ancestry.com. http://www.ancestry.com/search/db.aspx?dbid=4474 (accessed October 27, 2009).

Dodd, Jordan, Liahona Research, comp. "Virginia Marriages, 1851–1929." Provo, UT: The Generations Network, Inc., 2000. Ancestry.com. http://www.ancestry.com/search/db.aspx?dbid=3976 (accessed October 27, 2009).

Doti, Lynne Pierson, and Larry Schweikart. *Banking in the American West: From the Gold Rush to Deregulation.* Norman: University of Oklahoma Press, 1991.

Douglass, Robert S. *History of Southeast Missouri: A Narrative Account of its Historical Progress, its People and its Principal Interests.* Chicago: Goodspeed Publishing Company, 1888.

Drake, Charles Daniel. *An Examination of the "Bankable Funds" System of the Missouri Banks, in Connection with the Depreciation of Missouri Bank Paper.* St. Louis: George Knapp, 1860.

Dunlavy, Colleen A. *Politics and Industrialization: Early Railroads in the United States and Prussia.* Princeton: Princeton University Press, 1994.

Dyer, Frederick H. *A Compendium of the War of the Rebellion.* New York: T. Yoseloff, 1959.

Dyer, Robert L. *Boonville: An Illustrated History.* Boonville, MO: Pekitanoui Publications, 1987.

Dyson, Verne, ed. *Picturesque Fayette and its People.* Fayette, MO: Press of the Advertiser, 1905.

Eakin, Joanne C., and Donald R. Hale. *Branded as Rebels.* Vol. 1. Independence, MO: Wee Print, 1993.

Eakin, Joanne C., and Donald R. Hale, comps. *Confederate Records from the United Daughters of the Confederacy Files.* Vol. 5. Independence, MO: Two Trails, 1999.

Eakin, Joanne C., and Donald R. Hale, comps. *Missouri Prisoners of War from Gratiot Street Prison and Myrtle Street Prison, St. Louis, Missouri, and Alton Prison, Alton, Illinois; Including Citizens, Confederates, Bushwhackers and Guerrillas.* Independence, MO: by the authors, 1995.

Eaton, Miles W. "The Development and Later Decline of the Hemp Industry in Missouri." *Missouri Historical Review* 43, no. 4 (July 1949): 344–59.

Edwards, John Newman. *Noted Guerillas, or the Warfare on the Border.* St. Louis: Bryan, Brand, 1877.

Edwards, John Newman. *Shelby and His Men; or, The War in the West.* Cincinnati: Miami Printing and Publishing Company, 1867.

Edwards, John Newman. *Shelby's Expedition to Mexico: An Unwritten Leaf of the War.* Fayetteville: University of Arkansas Press, 2002.

Edwards, Richard, and M. Hopewell, M.D. *Edwards' Great West and her Commercial Metropolis. Embracing a General View of the West and a Complete History of St. Louis.* St. Louis: Edwards' Monthly, 1860. Northern Illinois University Library Digitization Projects, http://lincoln.lib.niu.edu/cgi-bin/philologic/getobject.pl?c.2536:1.lincoln (accessed October 27, 2009).

Eicher, David J. *The Longest Night: A Military History of the Civil War.* New York: Simon & Schuster, 2001.

Eicher, John H., and David J. Eicher. *Civil War High Commands.* Stanford: Stanford University Press, 2001.

Elazar, Daniel J. *American Federalism: A View from the States.* New York: Harper and Row, 1984.

Ellsberry, Elizabeth Prather, comp. *Cooper County, Missouri, Cemetery Records.* Chillicothe, MO: by the author, n.d.

———. *Marriage Records 1819–1850 and Will Records 1820–1870 of Cooper County, Missouri.* Chillicothe, MO: by the author, 1959.

———. *Saline County, Missouri, Cemetery Records.* Chillicothe, MO: by the author, n.d.

———. *Saline County Marriage Records 1820–1850.* Chillicothe, MO: by the author, n.d.

———. *Wills and Administrations of Howard County, Missouri.* Vol. 2, 1837–1847. Chillicothe, MO: by the author, n.d.

———, comp. *Wills and Administrations of Saline County, Missouri, 1821–1863.* Chillicothe, MO: by the author, n.d.

Evans, Gen. Clement A. *Confederate Military History: A Library of Confederate States History.* Secaucus, NJ: Blue & Grey Press, 1975.

FamilySearch International Genealogical Index v5.0. http://www.familysearch.org/Eng/Search/frameset_search.asp.

Farmer, Phillip S. *United States Marshals of the Western District of Missouri.* N.p.: privately published, 1987.

Federal Deposit Insurance Corporation, "Statistics at a Glance," as of December 31, 2007. http://www.fdic.gov/bank/statistical/stats/2007dec/industry.html (accessed October 27, 2009).

FedStats. http://www.fedstats.gov/qf/states/29000.html (accessed October 27, 2009).

Fellman, Michael. *Inside War: The Guerrilla Conflict in Missouri During the American Civil War*. New York: Oxford University Press, 1989.

Fisher, Noel C. *War at Every Door: Partisan Politics and Guerrilla Violence in East Tennessee, 1860–1865*. Chapel Hill: University of North Carolina Press, 1997.

Fogel, Robert William, and Stanley L. Engerman. *Time on the Cross: The Economics of American Negro Slavery*. Boston: Little, Brown, 1974.

Foner, Eric. *A Short History of Reconstruction*. New York: Harper & Row, 1990.

Ford, James E. *History of Jefferson City, Missouri's State Capital and of Cole County, Illustrated*. Jefferson City, MO: New Day Press, 1938.

Formwalt, Lee W. "Antebellum Planter Persistence: Southwest Georgia—A Case Study." *Plantation Society in the Americas* 1, no. 3 (October 1981): 410–29.

Fourteenth Census of the United States Taken in the Year 1920. Vol. 5, *Agriculture*. Washington, DC: Government Printing Office, 1922.

Fox-Genovese, Elizabeth, and Eugene D. Genovese. *Fruits of Merchant Capital: Slavery and Bourgeois Property in the Rise and Expansion of Capitalism*. New York: Oxford University Press, 1983.

Frizzell, Robert W. "Southern Identity in Nineteenth-Century Missouri: Little Dixie's Slave-Majority Areas and the Transition to Midwestern Farming." *Missouri Historical Review* 99, no. 3 (April 2005): 238–60.

Fuenfhausen, Gary G. *A Guide to Historic Clay County, Missouri*. Kansas City: Little Dixie Publications, 1996.

Geiger, Mark W. "Missouri Banks and the Civil War." M.A. thesis, University of Missouri, 2000.

Geiger, Mark W. "Missouri's Hidden Civil War: Financial Conspiracy and the Decline of the Planter Elite." Ph.D. diss., University of Missouri, 2006.

Genovese, Eugene D. *The Political Economy of Slavery: Studies in the Economy and Society of the Slave South*. Middletown, CT: Wesleyan University Press, 1989.

Gentry, North Todd. *Bench and Bar of Boone County*. Columbia: privately published, 1916.

Goldin, Claudia D. "War." In Glenn Porter, ed., *The Encyclopedia of American Economic History: Studies of the Principal Movements and Ideas*, 3:935–57. New York: Charles Scribner and Sons, 1980.

Goldin, Claudia D., and Frank D. Lewis. "The Economic Cost of the American Civil War: Estimates and Implications." *Journal of Economic History* 35, no. 2 (June 1975): 299–326.

Goldstein, Max Aaron. *One Hundred Years of Medicine and Surgery in Missouri: Historical and Biographical Review of the Careers of the Physicians and Surgeons of the State of Missouri and Sketches of Some of its Notable Medical Institutions*. St. Louis: St. Louis Star, 1900.

Goodrich, James W. "'In the Earnest Pursuit of Wealth': David Waldo in Missouri and the Southwest, 1820–1878." *Missouri Historical Review* 66 (January 1972): 155–84.

Goodrich, James W., and Donald B. Oster, eds. "'Few Men But Many Widows': The

Daniel B. Fogle Letters, August 8–September 4, 1867." *Missouri Historical Review* 80 (April 1986): 273–304.

Goodrich, Thomas. *Black Flag: Guerrilla Warfare on the Western Border, 1861–1865.* Bloomington, IN: Indiana University Press, 1999.

Gould, Emerson W. *Fifty Years on the Mississippi, or Gould's History of River Navigation.* St. Louis: Nixon-Jones Printing Company, 1889.

Gould, Roger V. "Why Do Networks Matter? Rationalist and Structuralist Interpretations." in Mario Diani and Doug McAdam, *Social Movements and Networks: Rational Approaches to Collective Action*, 233–57. New York: Oxford University Press, 2003.

Grant, Ulysses S. *Personal Memoirs of U.S. Grant.* Vol. 1. New York: Charles L. Webster & Company, 1885–86. Project Gutenberg. http://www.gutenberg.org/etext/4367 (accessed October 27, 2009).

Gray, Marcus L., and Ward M. Baker. *1806–1906: The Centennial Volume of Missouri Methodism, Methodist Episcopal Church, South.* Kansas City: Burd & Fletcher, 1907.

Gray, Wood. *The Hidden Civil War: The Story of the Copperheads.* New York: Viking Press, 1942.

Greenfield, Sidney M., Arnold Strickon, and Robert T. Aubey, eds. *Entrepreneurs in Cultural Context.* Albuquerque: University of New Mexico Press, 1979.

Hale, Donald R. *Branded as Rebels.* Vol. 2. Independence, MO: Blue & Gray Book Shoppe, 2003.

———. *We Rode with Quantrill: Quantrill and the Guerrilla War as Described by the Men and Women Who Were with Him, with a True Sketch of Quantrill's Life.* Clinton, MO: The Printery, 1974.

Haley, T. P., *Dawn of the Reformation: History and Biography of the Early Churches and Pioneer Preachers of the Christian Church of Missouri*, St. Louis: Christian Publishing, 1888.

Hall, Thomas B. "John Sappington." *Missouri Historical Review* 24, no. 2 (January 1930): 177–99.

Hall, Thomas B. II, and Thomas B. Hall III. *Dr. John Sappington of Saline County, Missouri, 1776–1856.* Arrow Rock, MO: Friends of Arrow Rock, 1975.

Hamilton, Jean Tyree. *Missouri's Historic National Landmarks: Village of Arrow Rock; George Caleb Bingham Home.* Columbia: Friends of Arrow Rock, 1963.

———. *Arrow Rock: Where Wheels Started West.* Centralia, MO: Guard Printing and Publishing, 1972.

Hamilton, Alexander. "Federalist No. 26, The Idea of Restraining the Legislative Authority in Regard to the Common Defense Considered." First published in *The Independent Journal*, December 22, 1787. Library of Congress, http://thomas.loc.gov/home/histdox/fedpapers.html (accessed October 27, 2009).

Hammond, Bray. *Sovereignty and an Empty Purse: Banks and Politics in the Civil War.* Princeton: Princeton University Press, 1970.

Hanna, Alfred J., and Kathryn A. Hanna. *Confederate Exiles in Venezuela.* Tuscaloosa, AL: Confederate Publishing, 1960.

Harter, Eugene C. *The Lost Colony of the Confederacy.* College Station, TX: Texas A & M University Press, 2000.

Hardy, Richard J., Richard R. Dohm, and David A. Leuthold, eds. *Missouri Government and Politics.* Columbia: University of Missouri Press, 1995.

Haven, Charles T., and Frank A. Belden. *A History of the Colt Revolver and the Other Arms Made by Colt's Patent Fire Arms Manufacturing Company from 1836 to 1940.* New York: Bonanza Books, 1940.

Hepburn, Alonzo Barton. *A History of Currency in the United States.* New York: Macmillan Company, 1924.

Heritage Auctions, Inc. http://currency.ha.com/?ic=Tab-Home-041408 (accessed October 27, 2009).

Hesseltine, William B. *Lincoln and the War Governors.* New York: Alfred A. Knopf, 1955.

Hickman, W. Z. *History of Jackson County.* Cleveland: Historical Publishing, 1920.

Hill, Lawrence F. "The Confederate Exodus to South America." *Southwestern Historical Quarterly* 39 (October 1935): 100–34; 39 (January 1936): 161–99; 39 (April 1936): 309–26.

Hines, Thomas H. "The Northwestern Conspiracy." *Southern Bivouac* 5 (1886–87): 441.

Historical and Descriptive Review of Missouri. Kansas City: John Lethem, 1891.

Historical Census Browser. University of Virginia, Geospatial and Statistical Data Center. http://fisher.lib.virginia.edu/collections/stats/histcensus/index.html (accessed October 27, 2009).

History of Andrew and Dekalb Counties, Missouri. . . . St. Louis: Goodspeed Publishing Company, 1888.

History of Boone County, Missouri. . . . St. Louis: Western Historical Company, 1882.

History of Buchanan County, Missouri. . . . St. Joseph, MO: Union Historical Company, 1881.

History of Buchanan County and St. Joseph, Missouri. . . . St. Joseph, MO: Midland Printing Company, 1915.

History of Caldwell and Livingston Counties, Missouri. . . . St. Louis: National Historical Company, 1886.

History of Callaway County, Missouri. . . . St. Louis: National Historical Company, 1884.

History of Carroll County, Missouri. . . . St. Louis: Missouri Historical Company, 1881.

History of the City of St. Louis and Vicinity. St. Louis: John Devoy, 1898.

History of Clay and Platte Counties, Missouri. . . . St. Louis: National Historical Company, 1885.

History of Clinton County, Missouri. St. Joseph, MO: National Historical Company, 1881.

History of Cole, Moniteau, Morgan, Benton, Miller, Maries and Osage Counties, Missouri. . . . Chicago: Goodspeed Publishing Company, 1889.

History of Colorado. Vol. 5. Denver: Linderman Company, 1927.

History of Daviess County, Missouri. . . . Kansas City: Birdsall & Dean, 1882.

History of Greene County, Missouri. . . . St. Louis: Western Historical Company, 1883.

History of Henry and St. Clair Counties, Missouri. . . . St. Joseph: National Historical Company, 1883.

History of Hickory, Polk, Cedar, Dade, and Barton Counties, Missouri. . . . Chicago: Goodspeed Publishing Company, 1889.

History of Holt and Atchison Counties, Missouri. . . . St. Joseph: National Historical Company, 1882.

History of Howard and Chariton Counties, Missouri. . . . St. Louis: National Historical Company, 1883.

History of Howard and Cooper Counties, Missouri. . . . St. Louis: National Historical Company, 1883.

History of Jackson County, Missouri. . . . Kansas City: Union Historical Company, 1881.

History of Johnson County, Missouri. . . . Kansas City: Kansas City Historical Society, 1881.

History of Lafayette County, Missouri. . . . St. Louis: Missouri Historical Company, 1881.

History of Lewis, Clark, Knox, and Scotland Counties, Missouri. . . . St. Louis: Goodspeed Publishing Company, 1887.

History of Lincoln County, Missouri. . . . Chicago: Goodspeed Publishing Company, 1888.

History of Linn County, Missouri. . . . Kansas City: Birdsall & Dean, 1882.

History of Monroe and Shelby Counties, Missouri. . . . St. Louis: National Historical Company, 1884.

History of Pettis County, Missouri. . . . N.p.: F. A. North, 1882. Reprint, Clinton, MO: The Printery.

History of Pike County, Missouri. . . . Des Moines, IA: Mills and Company, 1883.

History of Saline County, Missouri. St. Louis: Missouri Historical Company, 1881.

History of St. Charles, Montgomery, and Warren Counties, Missouri. . . . St. Louis: National Historical Company, 1885.

History of St. Louis Medical College. St. Louis: T. G. Waterman, Publisher, 1898.

History of Southeast Missouri. Chicago: Lewis Publishing, 1912.

History of Vernon County, Missouri. St. Louis: Brown & Company, 1887.

Holibaugh, John R. *The Lead and Zinc Mining Industry of Southwest Missouri and Southeast Kansas*. New York: Scientific Publishing Company, 1895.

Hubbard, Timothy W., and Lewis E. Davids. *Banking in Mid-America: A History of Missouri Banks*. Washington, DC: Public Affairs Press, 1969.

Hubble, Martin Jones. *Personal Reminiscences and Fragments of the Early History of Springfield and Greene County, Missouri*. Springfield, MO: Inland Printing, 1914.

Hunter, Lloyd A. "Missouri's Confederate Leaders after the War." *Missouri Historical Review* 67, no. 2 (April 1973): 371–96.

Hunting For Bears, comp. Mississippi Marriages, 1776–1935. Provo, UT: The Generations Network, Inc., 2004. Ancestry.com. http://www.ancestry.com/search/db.aspx?dbid=7842 (accessed October 27, 2009).

Hunting For Bears, comp. Missouri Marriages, 1766–1983. Provo, UT: The Generations Network, Inc., 2004. Ancestry.com. http://www.ancestry.com/search/db.aspx?dbid=7843 (accessed October 27, 2009).

Hurt, R. Douglas. *Agriculture and Slavery in Missouri's Little Dixie*. Columbia: University of Missouri Press, 1992.

Huston, James A. *Sinews of War: Army Logistics, 1775–1953*. Army Historical Series. Washington, DC: Office of the Chief of Military History, United States Army, 1966.

Hyde, William, and Howard L. Conard. *Encyclopedia of the History of St. Louis.* St. Louis: Southern History, 1899.

Illustrated Atlas Map of Cooper County, Missouri. St. Louis: St. Louis Atlas Publishing, 1877.

Illustrated Atlas Map of Howard County, Missouri. St. Louis: Missouri Publishing, 1876.

Illustrated Atlas Map of Lewis County, Missouri. Philadelphia: Edward Brothers of Missouri, 1878.

Illustrated Atlas Map of Pike County, Missouri. N.p. [IL]: W. R. Brink, 1875.

Illustrated Historical Atlas Map of Buchanan County, Missouri. N.p.: Brink, McDonough, 1877.

Illustrated Historical Atlas of Marion County, Missouri. Quincy, IL: T. M. Rogers, 1875.

Illustrated Historical Atlas of Monroe County, Missouri. Philadelphia: Edwards Brothers of Missouri, 1876.

Inaugural Addresses of the Presidents of the United States. Washington, DC: U.S. Government Printing Office, 1989.

Jackson, William Rufus. *Missouri Democracy: A History of the Party and its Representative Members, Past and Present.* St. Louis: S. J. Clarke, 1935.

Janda, Lance. "Shutting the Gates of Mercy: The American Origins of Total War, 1860–1880." *Journal of Military History* 59, no. 1 (January 1995): 7–26.

Johnson, William Foreman. *History of Cooper County, Missouri.* Topeka, KS: Historical Publishing, 1919.

Jones, Nancy Chapman. "The Civil War Letters of Nancy née Chapman Jones." Edited by Nan O'Meara Strang. http://cooper.mogenweb.org/Military/Jones_Letters.pdf (accessed October 27, 2009).

Journal of the Congress of the Confederate States of America. Vol. 6. Published in Senate Document No. 234, 58th U.S. Congress, 2nd session. LexisNexis Congressional. http://web.lexis-nexis.com (accessed October 27, 2009).

Journal of the Missouri Constitutional Convention of 1875. Jefferson City, MO: Hugh Stephens, 1920.

Journal of the House of Representatives of the State of Missouri at the First Session of the Eighteenth General Assembly. Jefferson City, MO: James Lusk, Public Printer, 1855.

Journal of the House of Representatives of the State of Missouri at the First Session of the Nineteenth General Assembly, Begun and Held at the City of Jefferson, on Monday, the 29th Day of December, 1856. Jefferson City, MO: James Lusk, Public Printer, 1857.

Journal of the House of Representatives of the State of Missouri, at the Called Session of the Twentieth General Assembly. Jefferson City, MO: W. G. Cheeney, 1860.

Journal of the House of Representatives of the State of Missouri at the Regular Session of the Twenty-First General Assembly. Jefferson City, MO: W. G. Cheeney, 1861.

Journal of the House of Representatives of the State of Missouri at the First Session of the Twenty-Second General Assembly, Begun and Held at the City of Jefferson, on Monday, December Twenty-Ninth, 1862. Jefferson City, MO: W. A. Curry, 1863.

Journal of the House of Representatives of the State of Missouri at the Adjourned Session of the Twenty-Second General Assembly, Begun and Held at the City of Jefferson, on Tuesday, November Tenth, 1863. Jefferson City, MO: W. A. Curry, 1863.

Journal of the House of Representatives of the State of Missouri at the Regular Session of the Twenty-Third General Assembly. Jefferson City, MO: W. A. Curry, 1865.

Journal of the Missouri State Convention, Held at Jefferson City, July, 1861. St. Louis: George Knapp & Company, 1861.

Journal of the Missouri State Convention, Held at the City of St. Louis, October, 1861. St. Louis: George Knapp & Company, 1861.

Journal of the Missouri State Convention Held in Jefferson City, June 1862. St. Louis: George Knapp & Company, 1862.

Journal of the Senate of the State of Missouri, at the First Session, Being the Regular Session, of the Eighteenth General Assembly. Jefferson City, MO: James Lusk, Public Printer, 1855.

Journal of the Senate of the State of Missouri, at the Adjourned Session of the Eighteenth General Assembly. Jefferson City, MO: James Lusk, Public Printer, 1856.

Journal of the Senate of the State of Missouri, at the First Session, being the Regular Session, of the Nineteenth General Assembly. . . . Jefferson City, MO: James Lusk, Public Printer, 1857.

Journal of the Senate, Extra Session of the Rebel Legislature: Called Together by a Proclamation of C. F. Jackson Begun and Held at Neosho, Newton County, Missouri, on the Twenty-First of October, 1861. Jefferson City, MO: Emory S. Foster, 1865.

Journal of the Senate of Missouri at the First Session of the Twenty-Second General Assembly, Begun and Held at the City of Jefferson, on Monday, December Twenty-Ninth, 1862. Jefferson City, MO: W. A. Curry, 1863.

Journal of the Senate of the State of Missouri at the Adjourned Session of the Twenty-Second General Assembly, Begun and Held at the City of Jefferson, on Tuesday, November Tenth, 1863. Jefferson City, MO: W. A. Curry, 1863.

Journal of the Senate of the State of Missouri at the Regular Session of the Twenty-Third General Assembly. Jefferson City, MO: W. A. Curry, 1865.

Keating, John McLeod. A *History of the Yellow Fever: The Yellow Fever Epidemic of 1878, in Memphis. . . .* Memphis, TN: The Howard Association, 1878.

Kennedy, C. G. *Agriculture of the United States in 1860, Compiled from the Original Returns of the Eighth Census Under the Direction of the Secretary of the Interior.* Washington, DC: Government Printing Office, 1864.

Kennedy, Robert V., ed. *St. Louis City Directory for the Year 1857.* St. Louis: R. V. Kennedy, 1857.

Kenzer, Robert C. *Kinship and Neighborhood in a Southern Community: Orange County, North Carolina, 1849–1881.* Knoxville: University of Tennessee Press, 1987.

Kirkpatrick, Arthur Roy. "The Admission of Missouri to the Confederacy." *Missouri Historical Review* 55, no. 4 (July 1961): 366–86.

———. "Missouri, the Twelfth Confederate State." Ph.D. diss., University of Missouri, 1954.

———. "Missouri on the Eve of the Civil War." *Missouri Historical Review* 55, no. 2 (January 1961): 99–108.

———. "Missouri's Secessionist Government, 1861–1865." *Missouri Historical Review* 45, no. 2 (January 1951): 124–37.

Klingberg, Frank W. *The Southern Claims Commission.* Berkeley: University of California Press, 1955.

Knapp, Frank A. Jr. "A New Source on the Confederate Exodus to Mexico: The Two Republics." *Journal of Southern History* 19, no. 3 (August 1953): 364–73.

Krauthoff, Louis Charles. "The Supreme Court of Missouri." *Green Bag* 3 (April 1891): 157–90.

Kreidberg, Lt. Col. Marvin A., and 1st Lieutenant Merton G. Henry, *History of Military Mobilization in the United States Army, 1775–1945.* Department of the Army Pamphlet 20–212. Washington, DC: U.S. Government Printing Office, 1955.

Kremer, Gary R., and Lawrence O. Christensen. *History of Missouri.* Vol. 4, *1875 to 1919.* Columbia: University of Missouri Press, 2004.

Lafferty, Rev. John J. *Sketches and Portraits of the General Conference of the Methodist Episcopal Church, South. Held in Richmond, Virginia May, 1886.* Richmond, VA: Christian Advocate Office, 1886.

Lamoreaux, Naomi R. "Banks, Kinship, and Economic Development: The New England Case." *Journal of Economic History* 46, no. 3 (September, 1986): 647–67.

———. *Insider Lending: Banks, Personal Connections, and Economic Development in Industrial New England.* New York: Cambridge University Press, 1994.

Las Vegas: An Unconventional History. WGBH Educational Foundation and Goodhue Pictures, 2005. PBS documentary. http://www.pbs.org/wgbh/amex/lasvegas/peopleevents/p_clark.html (accessed October 27, 2009).

Laughlin, Sceva Bright. "Missouri Politics During the Civil War." *Missouri Historical Review* 24 (October 1929): 87–113.

"The Law of Bills of Exchange: An Appendix to 'The Manual for Notaries Public.'" *Bankers' Magazine and Statistical Register* 6, no. 9 (March 1857): 708–20; 6, no. 10 (April 1857): 765–84.

Laws of the State of Illinois, Passed by the Twenty-Second General Assembly, at its Extraordinary Session, Convened April 23, 1861. Springfield, IL: Bailhache & Baker, Printers, 1861.

Laws of the State of Missouri Passed at the Second Session of the Third General Assembly, and the First Session of the Fourth General Assembly, Begun and Held at the City of Jefferson, November 20, 1826. N.p.: C. Keemle, Printer, 1827.

Laws of the State of Missouri Passed at the First Session of the Ninth General Assembly, Begun and Held at the City of Jefferson, on Monday, the Twenty-First Day of November, in the Year of Our Lord One Thousand Eight Hundred and Thirty-Six. City of Jefferson, MO: Calvin Gunn, Jeffersonian Office, 1837.

Laws of the State of Missouri Passed at the First Session of the Twelfth General Assembly, Begun and Held at the City of Jefferson, on Monday, the Twenty-First Day of November, Eighteen Forty-Two, and Ended Tuesday, the Twenty-Eighth Day of February, Eighteen Hundred and Forty-Three. Jefferson City, MO: Alan Hammond, 1843.

Laws of the State of Missouri, Passed at the First Session of the Fourteenth General Assembly, Begun and Held at the City of Jefferson, on Monday, the Sixteenth Day of November, Eighteen Hundred and Forty-Six, and Ended on Tuesday, the Sixteenth Day of February,

Eighteen Hundred and Forty-Seven. City of Jefferson, MO: James Lusk, Public Printer, 1847.

Laws of the State of Missouri, Passed at the Session of the Fifteenth General Assembly, Begun and Held at the City of Jefferson, on Monday, the Twenty-Fifth Day of December, Eighteen Hundred and Forty-Eight, and Ended on Monday the Twelfth Day of March, Eighteen Hundred and Forty-Nine. City of Jefferson, MO: Hampton L. Boon, Public Printer, 1849.

Laws of the State of Missouri Passed at the Session of the Sixteenth General Assembly. Begun and Held at the City of Jefferson on Monday the Thirtieth Day of December, A. D. 1850. City of Jefferson, MO: James Lusk — Public Printer, 1851.

Laws of the State of Missouri, Passed at the First Session of the Seventeenth General Assembly, Begun and Held at the City of Jefferson on Monday the Thirtieth Day of August, A. D. 1852. City of Jefferson, MO: James Lusk, Public Printer, 1853.

Laws of the State of Missouri, Passed at the Second Session of the Seventeenth General Assembly, Begun and Held at the City of Jefferson on Monday the Twenty-Seventh Day of December, A. D. 1852. City of Jefferson, MO: James Lusk, Public Printer, 1853.

Laws of the State of Missouri Passed at the First Session of the Eighteenth General Assembly, begun and held at the City of Jefferson, on Monday, the 25th Day of December, 1854. Jefferson City, MO: James Lusk, Public Printer, 1855.

Laws of the State of Missouri Passed at the Nineteenth General Assembly, begun and held at the City of Jefferson, on Monday, the 29th Day of December, 1856. City of Jefferson, MO: James Lusk, Public Printer, 1857.

Laws of the State of Missouri Passed at the Adjourned Session of the Nineteenth General Assembly, Begun and Held at the City of Jefferson, on Monday, the 19th Day of October, 1857. Jefferson City, MO: C. G. Corwin, 1858.

Laws of the State of Missouri Passed at the First Session of the Twentieth General Assembly, begun and held at the City of Jefferson, on Monday, the 27th Day of December, 1858. Jefferson City, MO: J. Corwin, Public Printer, 1859.

Laws of the State of Missouri, Passed at the Adjourned Session of the Twentieth General Assembly, Begun and Held at the City of Jefferson on Monday, the Twenty-Eighth Day of November, 1859. Jefferson City, MO: W. G. Cheeney, Public Printer, 1860.

Laws of the State of Missouri Passed at the Regular Session of the Twenty-First General Assembly, Begun and Held at the City of Jefferson, on Monday, December Thirty-First, 1860. Jefferson City, MO: W. G. Cheeney, 1861.

Laws of the State of Missouri Passed at the Called Session of the Twenty-First General Assembly, Begun and Held at the City of Jefferson, on Thursday, May Second, 1861. Jefferson City, MO: W. G. Cheeney, 1861.

Laws of the State of Missouri Passed at the Regular Session of the Twenty-Second General Assembly, Begun and Held at the City of Jefferson, on Monday, December Twenty-Ninth, 1862. Jefferson City, MO: J. P. Ament, 1863.

Laws of the State of Missouri Passed at the Adjourned Session of the Twenty-Second General Assembly, Begun and Held at the City of Jefferson, on Tuesday, November Tenth, 1863. Jefferson City, MO: W. A. Curry, 1864.

Laws of the State of Missouri Passed at the Regular Session of the Twenty-Third General Assembly Begun and Held at the City of Jefferson On Monday, December Twenty-Sixth, 1864. Jefferson City, MO: W. A. Curry, 1865.

Laws of the State of Missouri Passed at the Adjourned Session of the Twenty-Third General Assembly, Begun and Held at the City of Jefferson, on Wednesday, November First, 1865. Jefferson City, MO: Emory S. Foster, 1866.

Leavy, William A. *A Memoir of Lexington and Its Vicinity.* N.p.: privately published, n.d.

Leip, David. *Atlas of U.S. Presidential Elections.* http://uselectionatlas.org/ (accessed October 27, 2009).

Leopard, Buel, and Floyd C. Shoemaker, comps. *Messages and Proclamations of the Governors of the State of Missouri.* Vol. 3. Columbia: State Historical Society of Missouri, 1922.

Letter from the Secretary of the Treasury, Transmitting, in response to Senate Resolution of March 8, 1880, a statement showing the expenditures of the government on account of the war of the rebellion from July 1, 1861, to June 30, 1879, inclusive, &c. Senate Executive Document No. 206, dated June 10, 1880. 46th Congress, 2nd Session.

Levens, Henry C., and Nathanial M. Drake. *A History of Cooper County, Missouri, From the First Visit by White Men, in February, 1804, to the 5th Day of July, 1876.* St. Louis: Perrin & Smith, 1876.

Lieber, Francis. *Guerrilla Parties Considered with Reference to the Laws and Usages of War. Written at the request of Major-Gen. Henry W. Halleck.* New York: D. Van Nostrand, 1862.

Lloyd, James T. *Lloyd's Railroad, Telegraph and Express Map of the United States and Canadas from Official Information.* New York: James T. Lloyd, 1867.

Local and Private Acts of the State of Missouri, Passed at the Adjourned Session of the Eighteenth General Assembly, Begun and Held in the City of Jefferson, on Monday, the Fifth of November, Eighteen Hundred and Fifty-Five. City of Jefferson, MO: James Lusk, Public Printer, 1856.

"Local History." University Extension, University of Missouri–Columbia. http://extension.missouri.edu/main/DisplayCategory.aspx?C=226 (accessed October 27, 2009).

Long, Everette B., with Barbara Long. *The Civil War Day by Day: An Almanac, 1861–1865.* Garden City, NY: Doubleday, 1971.

Lowman, H. E. *Narrative of the Lawrence Massacre.* Lawrence, KS: Journal Press, 1864.

"M-9 Pistol Factfile for the U.S. Army." http://www.army.mil/factfiles/equipment/individual/m9.html (accessed October 27, 2009).

Mackey, Robert R. *Uncivil War: Irregular Warfare in the Upper South, 1861–1865.* Norman: University of Oklahoma Press, 2004.

Mallory, Rudena Kramer, ed. *Claims by Missourians for Compensation of Enlisted Slaves.* N.p.: by the author, 1992.

Mann, Bruce H. *Republic of Debtors: Bankruptcy in the Age of American Independence.* Cambridge, MA: Harvard University Press, 2003.

———. "Mountains, Land and Kin Networks: Burkes Garden, Virginia, in the 1840s and 1850s." *Journal of Southern History* 58, no. 3 (August 1992): 411–34.

Marler, Scott. "Rural Merchants and Consumers in a New South Louisiana, 1840–1940." Ph.D. diss., Rice University, 2006.

Marsden, Peter V., and Noah E. Friedkin. "Network Studies of Social Influence." In Stanley Wasserman and Joseph Galaskiewicz, eds., *Advances in Social Network Analysis: Research in the Social and Behavioral Sciences*, 2–26. Thousand Oaks, CA: Sage Publications, 1994.

Matthews, James M., ed. *Statutes at Large of the Provisional Government of the Confederate States of America, from the Institution of the Government February 8, 1861 to its Termination, February 18, 1862, Inclusive.* Richmond, VA: R. W. Smith, Printer to Congress, 1864.

Maurer, Noel. *The Power and the Money: The Mexican Financial System, 1876–1932.* Stanford, CA: Stanford University Press, 2002.

McCandless, Perry. *History of Missouri.* Vol. 2, *1820 to 1860.* Columbia: University of Missouri Press, 2000.

McGrath, Michael C. *State Almanac and Official Directory of Missouri.* St. Louis: John J. Daly, 1878–88 editions.

McPheeters, Dr. William M. *"I Acted from Principle": The Civil War Diary of Dr. William M. McPheeters, Confederate Surgeon in the Trans-Mississippi.* Edited by Cynthia Dehaven Pitcock and Bill J. Gurley. Fayetteville: University of Arkansas Press, 2002.

McPherson, James M. *Battle Cry of Freedom: The Civil War Era.* New York: Oxford University Press, 1988.

Meinig, D. W. *The Shaping of America.* Vol. 2, *Continental America, 1800–1867.* New Haven: Yale University Press, 1993.

Melton, E. J. *Melton's History of Cooper County, Missouri: An Account from Early Times to the Present.* Columbia: E. W. Stephens, 1937.

Meneely, Howard. *The War Department, 1861: A Study in Mobilization and Administration.* Columbia University Studies in History, Economics, and Public Law no. 300. New York: Columbia University, 1928.

Messages and Proclamations of the Governors of the State of Missouri. Columbia: State Historical Society of Missouri, 1922.

Miles, Kathleen White. *Bitter Ground: The Civil War in Missouri's Golden Valley — Benton, Henry and St. Clair Counties.* Warsaw, MO: The Printery, 1971.

Military Laws of the Confederate States, Embracing all the Legislation of Congress Appertaining to Military Affairs from the First to the Last Session Inclusive. Richmond, VA: J. W. Randolph, 1863.

Miller, Roger LeRoy, and David D. VanHoose. *Essentials of Money, Banking and Financial Markets.* New York: Addison-Wesley, 1997.

Miner, John B. *A Psychological Typology of Successful Entrepreneurs.* Westport, CT: Quorum Books, 1997.

Missouri Baptist Biography. Liberty, MO: Missouri Baptist Historical Association, 1914.

Missouri Biographical Dictionary: People of All Times and Places Who Have Been Important in the Life of the State. New York: Somerset Press, 1995.

Missouri State Gazetteer and Business Directory. . . . St. Louis: Sutherland & McEvoy, 1860.

Missouri Troops in Service During the Civil War. 57th Congress, 1st Session. Senate Document No. 412. Washington: Government Printing Office, 1902. LexisNexis Congressional. http://web.lexis-nexis.com (accessed October 27, 2009).

"Missouriana: Ballots from the Battlefields." *Missouri Historical Review* 37 (January 1943): 202–7.

Mitchell, Reid. *The Vacant Chair: The Northern Soldier Leaves Home*. New York: Oxford University Press, 1993.

Moneyhon, Carl H. "The Impact of the Civil War in Arkansas: The Mississippi River Plantation Counties." *Arkansas Historical Quarterly* 51, no. 2 (1992): 105–18.

Morrison-Fuller, Berenice. "Plantation Life in Missouri." *Glasgow (MO) Missourian*, June 2, 1938; June 9, 1938; June 23, 1938; June 30, 1938; July 7, 1938.

Morrow, Lynn. *John Sappington: Southern Patriarch in the New West*. N.p.: by the author, n.d.

Myers, Margaret G. *Financial History of the United States*. New York: Columbia University Press, 1970.

Napton, Hon. William Barclay. *Past and Present of Saline County, Missouri*. Indianapolis, IN: B. F. Bowen, 1910.

National Park Service. *Civil War Sites Advisory Commission Report on the Nation's Civil War Battlefields*. Washington, DC: U.S. Government Printing Office, 1994. LexisNexis Congressional. http://web.lexis-nexis.com (accessed October 27, 2009).

Neely, Mark E. Jr. *The Civil War and the Limits of Destruction*. Cambridge, MA: Harvard University Press, 2007.

———. "Was the Civil War a Total War?" *Civil War History* 50, no. 4 (December 2004): 434–57.

Nichols, Richard. "Thoroughly Bad Guy." *New York Times*, Sunday Book Review Section, October 27, 2002.

Ninth Census of the United States: Statistics of Population. Tables I to VIII Inclusive. Washington, DC: Government Printing Office, 1872.

Noe, Kenneth W. "Who Were the Bushwhackers? Age, Class, Kin, and Western Virginia's Confederate Guerrillas, 1861–1862." *Civil War History* 49, no. 1 (March 2003): 5–25.

Oakes, James. *The Ruling Race: A History of American Slaveholders*. New York: Alfred Knopf, 1982.

O'Flaherty, Daniel. *General Jo Shelby: Undefeated Rebel*. Chapel Hill: University of North Carolina Press, 1954.

Olpin, Larry. "Missouri and the Civil War Novel." *Missouri Historical Review* 85, no. 1 (October 1990): 1–20.

Ordinances in relation to Elections, Voters, and Civil Officers, Passed at the Called Session of the Missouri State Convention, Begun and Held at the City of Jefferson, on Monday, June 2nd, 1862. Jefferson City, MO: Joseph P. Ament, Public Printer, 1862.

Painter, Harold N., A. B., A. M. *Freemasons and Freemasonry in Pettis County, Missouri: 115 Years*. Sedalia, MO: by the author, 1963.

Paludan, Phillip. *A People's Contest: The Union and Civil War 1861–1865*. Lawrence: University Press of Kansas, 1996.

Parker, Nathan H. *Missouri as it is in 1867*. Philadelphia: J. B. Lippencott, 1867.

Parrish, William E. *History of Missouri*. Vol. 3, *1860–1875*. Columbia: University of Missouri Press, 2001.

———. *Turbulent Partnership: Missouri and the Union, 1861–1865*. Columbia: University of Missouri Press, 1963.

Past and Present Membership of the Missouri Supreme Court. Kirksville: Northeast Missouri State College, 1968.

Paxton, W. M. *Annals of Platte County, Missouri*. Kansas City: Hudson-Kimberly Publishing Company, 1897.

Peck, John Mason. *Forty Years of Pioneer Life*. Edited by Rufus Babcock. Philadelphia: American Baptist Publication Society, 1864.

Phillips, Christopher. "Calculated Confederate: Claiborne Fox Jackson and the Strategy for Secession in Missouri." *Missouri Historical Review* 94, no. 4 (July 2000): 389–414.

———. *Damned Yankee: The Life of General Nathaniel Lyon*. Baton Rouge: Louisiana State University Press, 1996.

———. "Judge Napton's Private War: Slavery, Personal Tragedy, and the Politics of Identity in Civil War-Era Missouri." *Missouri Historical Review* 99, no. 3 (April 2005): 212–37.

———. *Missouri's Confederate: Claiborne Fox Jackson and the Creation of Southern Identity in the Border West*. Columbia: University of Missouri Press, 2000.

A Pictorial Souvenir of Lexington, Missouri Containing History and Information Pertaining to the Best City in the West. Lexington, MO: Lexington Press, 1912.

Pinney, Thomas. *A History of Wine in America, from the Beginnings to Prohibition*. Berkeley: University of California Press, 1988.

Political History of Jackson County: Biographical Sketches of Men who have Helped to Make it. Kansas City: Marshall & Morrison, 1902.

Porter, Glenn, ed. *The Encyclopedia of American Economic History*. New York: Scribner and Sons, 1980.

Portrait and Biographical Record of Buchanan and Clinton Counties, Missouri. . . . Chicago: Chapman Brothers, 1893.

Portrait and Biographical Record of Clay, Ray, Carroll, Chariton and Linn Counties, Missouri. . . . Chicago: Chapman Brothers, 1893.

Portrait and Biographical Record of Johnson and Pettis Counties, Missouri. . . . Chicago: Chapman Brothers, 1895.

Portrait and Biographical Record of Lafayette and Saline Counties, Missouri. Chicago: Chapman Brothers, 1893.

Pratt, J. T. *Pen-Pictures of the Officers and Members of the House of Representatives of the Twenty-Sixth General Assembly of Missouri*. N.p.: by the author, 1872.

Previts, Gary John, and Barbara Dubis Merino. *A History of Accountancy in the United States: The Cultural Significance of Accounting*. Columbus: Ohio State University Press, 1998.

Primm, James Neal. *The Lion of the Valley: St. Louis, Missouri 1764–1980*. St. Louis: Missouri Historical Society Press, 1998.

Proceedings of the Missouri State Convention, Held at Jefferson City, July, 1861. St. Louis: George Knapp & Company, 1861.

"Proposed Adjustment of the Account of the State of South Carolina with the Secretary of the Treasury on Account of Bonds Held by Him as Custodian of the Indian Trust Fund, and Claims of that State for Moneys Expended in the Wars of 1812 and 1836" (March 20, 1900). Senate Document 232, 56th Congress, 1st session. LexisNexis Congressional. http://web.lexis-nexis.com (accessed October 27, 2009).

Public Laws of the State of Illinois, Passed by the Twenty-Second General Assembly, Convened January 7, 1861. Springfield, IL: Bailhache and Baker, Printers, 1861.

Public Laws of the State of North-Carolina, Passed by the General Assembly at its First Extra Session of [May] 1861. Raleigh, NC: John Spelman, Printer to the State, 1861.

Public Laws of the State of North-Carolina, Passed by the General Assembly, at its Second Extra Session, [August] 1861. Raleigh, NC: John Spelman, Printer to the State, 1861.

Rainey, T. C. *Along the Old Trail: Pioneer Sketches of Arrow Rock and Vicinity.* Marshall, MO: Marshall Chapter, Daughters of the American Revolution, 1914.

Rawick, George P., editor. *The American Slave: A Composite Autobiography; Contributions in Afro-American and African Studies.* Vol. 11, *Arkansas Narratives Part 7, and Missouri Narratives.* Westport, CT: Greenwood, 1972.

Reavis, L. U. *St. Louis: The Future Great City of the World.* St. Louis: Gray, Baker, 1875.

Register of Officers and Agents, Civil, Military, and Naval, in the Services of the United States on the Thirtieth September, 1859. Washington, DC: William A. Harris, Printer, 1859.

Report of the Committee Appointed by the Chamber of Commerce of St. Louis on "Trade, Commerce and Manufacturing." St. Louis: St. Louis Chamber of Commerce, 1852.

Reports of Cases Argued and Determined in the Supreme Court of the State of Missouri. Vol. 33. St. Louis: George Knapp, 1863.

Reports of Cases Argued and Determined in the Supreme Court of the State of Missouri. Vol. 35. St. Louis: George Knapp, 1865.

Reports of Cases Argued and Determined in the Supreme Court of the State of Missouri. Vol. 36. St. Louis: George Knapp, 1866.

Reports of Cases Argued and Determined in the Supreme Court of the State of Missouri. Vol. 37. St. Louis: George Knapp, 1866.

Reports of Cases Argued and Determined in the Supreme Court of the State of Missouri. Vol. 38. St. Louis: George Knapp, 1867.

Reports of Cases Argued and Determined in the Supreme Court of the State of Missouri. Vol. 39. St. Louis: George Knapp, 1867.

Reports of Cases Argued and Determined in the Supreme Court of the State of Missouri. Vol. 41. St. Louis: George Knapp, 1868.

Reports of Cases Argued and Determined in the Supreme Court of the State of Missouri. Vol. 43. St. Louis: St. Louis Democrat, 1869.

Reports of Cases Argued and Determined in the Supreme Court of the State of Missouri. Vol. 44. St. Louis: M'Kee, Fishback, 1870.

Report to the Committee of the House of Representatives of the Twenty-Second General Assembly of the State of Missouri Appointed to Investigate the Conduct and Management of the Militia. Jefferson City, MO: W. A. Curry, 1864. Reprint, Columbia, MO: State Historical Society of Missouri, 1998.

Revised Statutes of the State of Missouri, Revised and Digested by the Eighteenth General

Assembly, During the Session of One Thousand Eight Hundred and Fifty-Four and One Thousand Eight Hundred and Fifty-Five . . . Vol. 1. Jefferson City, MO: James Lusk, Public Printer, 1856.

Revised Statutes of the State of Missouri, Revised and Digested during the Thirteenth General Assembly of the State of Missouri, During the Session of Eighteen Hundred and Forty-Four and Eighteen Hundred and Forty Five. St. Louis: J. W. Dougherty, 1845.

The Revised Statutes of the State of Missouri Together with the Constitutions of Missouri and of the United States. 2nd ed. Saint Louis: Chambers, Knapp & Company, 1840.

Rios, Jose Arthur. "Assimilation of Emigrants from the Old South in Brazil." *Social Forces* 26, no. 2 (December 1947): 145–52.

Ritter, Charles F., and Jon L. Wakelyn. *American Legislative Leaders 1850–1910.* New York: Greenwood Press, 1989.

Rives, John C. *The Congressional Globe: Containing the Debates and Proceedings of the Second Session of the Thirty-Sixth Congress; also, of the Special Session of the Senate.* Washington, DC: Office of the Congressional Globe, 1861.

Rives, John C. *The Congressional Globe: Containing the Debates and Proceedings of the First Session of the Thirty-Seventh Congress.* Washington, DC: Office of the Congressional Globe, 1861.

Rives, John C. *The Congressional Globe: Containing the Debates and Proceedings of the Second Session of the Thirty-Seventh Congress.* Washington, DC: Office of the Congressional Globe, 1862.

Roark, James L. *Masters Without Slaves: Southern Planters in the Civil War and Reconstruction.* New York: W. W. Norton, 1977.

Robinson, J. H. *Mountain Max, or Nick Whiffles on the Border: A Tale of Bushwhackers in Missouri.* New York: Caldwell, 1861.

Rockoff, Hugh. "Varieties of Banking and Regional Economic Development in the United States, 1840–1860." *Journal of Economic History* 35, no. 1 (March, 1975): 160–77.

Rolle, Andrew F. *The Lost Cause: The Confederate Exodus to Mexico.* Norman: University of Oklahoma Press, 1965.

Rolnick, Arthur J., and Warren E. Weber. "Banking Instability and Regulation in the U.S. Free Banking Era." *Federal Reserve Bank of Minneapolis Quarterly Review* 9, no. 3 (summer 1985). http://www.minneapolisfed.org/publications_papers/qr/ (accessed October 27, 2009).

———. "Free Banking, Wildcat Banking, and Shinplasters." *Federal Reserve Bank of Minneapolis Quarterly Review* 6, no. 3 (fall 1982), 10–19. http://www.minneapolisfed.org/publications_papers/qr/ (accessed October 27, 2009).

———. "New Evidence on the Free Banking Era." *American Economic Review* 73, no. 5 (December, 1983): 1080–91.

Root, George A., and Russell K. Hickman. "Pike's Peak Express Companies, Part I: The Solomon and Republican Route." *Kansas Historical Quarterly* 13, no. 3 (August 1944): 163–95.

———. "Pike's Peak Express Companies, Part II: The Solomon and Republican Route—Concluded." *Kansas Historical Quarterly* 13, no. 4 (November 1944): 211–42.

Rothstein, Morton. "The Changing Social Networks and Investment Behavior of a Slaveholding Elite in the Ante-Bellum South: Some Natchez 'Nabobs,' 1800–1860." In Sidney M. Greenfield, et al., *Entrepreneurs in Cultural Context*. Albuquerque, NM: University of New Mexico Press, 1979.

Russell, Charles Wells, ed. *The Memoirs of John Singleton Mosby*. Boston: Little, Brown and Company, 1917. Electronic ed., University of North Carolina, Chapel Hill, "Documenting the American South, Beginnings to 1920." http://docsouth.unc.edu/fpn/mosby/mosby.html (accessed October 27, 2009).

Russell Trust Association. *Catalogue*. New Haven: Russell Trust Association, 1913.

Sageman, Marc. *Understanding Terrorist Networks*. Philadelphia: University of Pennsylvania Press, 2004.

Sampson, F. A. "The Honorable John Brooks Henderson." *Missouri Historical Review* 7, no. 4 (July 1913): 237–41.

Sandage, Scott A. *Born Losers: A History of Failure in America*. Cambridge, MA: Harvard University Press, 2005.

Sandy, Wilda, and Hal Sandy. *Here Lies Kansas City: A Collection of Our City's Notables and Their Final Resting Places*. Kansas City: B. Schneider, 1984.

Scarborough, William Kauffman. *Masters of the Big House: Elite Slaveholders of the Mid-Nineteenth Century South*. Baton Rouge: Louisiana State University Press, 2003.

Scharf, J. Thomas. *History of Saint Louis City and County*. Philadelphia: Louis H. Everts, 1883.

Schranz, Ward L. *Jasper County, Missouri in the Civil War*. Carthage, MO: Carthage Press, 1923. Reprint, Carthage, MO: Missouri Kiwanis Club, 1988.

Schumpeter, Joseph Alois. *Theory of Economic Development: An Inquiry into Profits, Capital, Credit, Interest, and the Business Cycle*. Cambridge, MA: Harvard University Press, 1934.

Schweikart, Larry. *Banking in the American South from the Age of Jackson to Reconstruction*. Baton Rouge: Louisiana State University Press, 1987.

Shackelford, Thomas H. "The Shackelford Amendment." *Missouri Historical Review* 1, no. 2 (January 1907): 121–28.

Shannon, Fred A. *The Organization and Administration of the Union Army*. Cleveland, OH: Arthur H. Clark Company, 1928.

Shoemaker, Floyd C. *Missouri and Missourians*. Chicago: Lewis Publishing Company, 1943.

———, ed. *Missouri Day by Day*. Columbia: Missouri State Historical Society, 1942–43.

———. *Missouri's Hall of Fame: Lives of Eminent Missourians*. Columbia: Missouri Book Company, 1918.

Shortfield, Luke [John Beauchamp Jones]. *The Western Merchant*. Philadelphia: Grigg, Elliot, 1849.

Sifakis, Stewart. *Who Was Who in the Civil War*. New York: Facts on File, 1988.

Sinisi, Kyle S. *Sacred Debts: State Civil War Claims and American Federalism, 1861–80*. New York: Fordham University Press, 2003.

Skocpol, Theda. *Protecting Soldiers and Mothers: The Political Origins of Social Policy in United States*. Cambridge, MA: Belknap Press of Harvard University Press, 1995.

Skowronek, Steven. *Building a New American State: The Expansion of National Administrative Capacities, 1877–1920.* New York: Cambridge University Press, 1982.

Smith, Mellcene Thurman, and Jessymin Thurman Lewis, comps. *History and Lineage Book, National Society Daughters of the American Colonists in Missouri.* St. Louis: St. Louis Law Printing, 1936.

Smith, W. Wayne. "An Experiment in Counterinsurgency: The Assessment of Confederate Sympathizers in Missouri." *Journal of Southern History* 35, no. 3 (1969): 361–80.

Smith, William R. *The history and debates of the Convention of the people of Alabama: begun and held in the city of Montgomery, on the seventh day of January, 1861; in which is preserved the speeches of the secret sessions, and many valuable state papers.* Montgomery, AL: White, Pfister & Company, 1861.

Snead, Thomas L. *The Fight For Missouri From the Election of Lincoln to the Death of Lyon.* New York: Charles Scribner & Sons, 1886.

Speare, Haseltine, Armstrong, Waddell, Schulz family tree. Rootsweb. http://wc.rootsweb .ancestry.com/cgi-bin/igm.cgi?db=:1944857 (accessed October 27, 2009).

Stamp, Kenneth. *And the War Came: The North and the Secession Crisis.* Baton Rouge: Louisiana State University Press, 1950.

Standard Atlas of Adair County, Missouri. Chicago: George A. Ogle, 1898.

Stanley, Lois, George F. Wilson, and Maryhelen Wilson. *Death Records from Missouri Newspapers: The Civil War Years, January 1, 1861 to December 31, 1865.* N.p.: by the authors, 1983. Reprint, n.p.: by the authors, 1985.

———. *Death Records from Missouri Newspapers: January 1, 1866–December 31, 1870.* Sedalia, MO: by the authors, n.d.

Statistics of the United States (including Mortality, Property, &c.,) in 1860. Washington, DC: Government Printing Office, 1866.

Stevens, Walter B. *Centennial History of Missouri (The Center State): One Hundred Years in the Union.* Chicago: S. J. Clarke Publishing Company, 1921.

———. *Missouri the Center State, 1821–1915.* Chicago and St. Louis: S. J. Clarke Publishing Company, 1915.

———. *St. Louis: The Fourth City, 1764–1909.* St. Louis: S. J. Clarke Publishing Company, 1909.

Stephens, Wilma Bruce, comp. *Bible Records of Saline County, Missouri.* Marshall, MO: Marshall Chapter, Daughters of the American Revolution, 1962.

Stern, Philip Van Doren. *Secret Missions of the Civil War: First-Hand Accounts by Men and Women Who Risked Their Lives in Underground Activities for the North and the South, Woven into a Continuous Narrative.* New York: Bonanza Books, 1959.

Steward, Dick. *Duels and the Roots of Violence in Missouri.* Columbia: University of Missouri Press, 2000.

Stewart, A. J. D. *History of the Bench and Bar of Missouri.* St. Louis: Legal Publishing, 1898.

Stiles, T. J. *Jesse James: Last Rebel of the Civil War.* New York: Alfred Knopf, 2002.

The St. Louis Directory, for the Years 1854–5, Containing a General Directory of the Citizens, and a Business Directory, with an Almanac, from July, 1854, to January, 1856. St. Louis: Chambers & Knapp, 1854.

Sturm, O. P. "The Great Chicago Conspiracy." *Marion County Magazine* 1, no. 6 (1904), 55–61.

Sutherland, Daniel E. "Guerrilla Warfare, Democracy, and the Fate of the Confederacy." *Journal of Southern History* 68, no. 2 (May 2002): 259–92.

———. "Former Confederates in the Post-Civil War North: An Unexplored Aspect of Reconstruction History." *Journal of Southern History* 47, no. 3 (August 1981): 393–410.

Tap, Bruce. "'Union Men to the Polls, and Rebels to their Holes': The Contested Election between John P. Bruce and Benjamin F. Loan, 1862." *Civil War History* 46, no. 1 (March 2000): 24–40.

Terrell, W. H. H., Adjutant General. *Indiana in the War of the Rebellion.* Vol. 1. Indianapolis, IN: Douglass & Conner, 1869.

Territorial Kansas Online. http://www.territorialkansasonline.org/cgiwrap/imlskto/index .php (accessed October 27, 2009).

Terry, Robert. "Dr. John Sappington: Pioneer in the Use of Quinine in the Mississippi Valley." In *Proceedings of the Tercenteniary Celebration of Cinchona.* N.p.: privately printed, 1931.

Thelen, David. *Paths of Resistance: Tradition and Dignity in Industrializing Missouri.* New York: Oxford University Press, 1986.

Thrapp, Daniel. *Encyclopedia of Frontier Biography.* Glendale, CA: Arthur H. Clark, 1988.

Timberlake, Richard H. *Monetary Policy in the United States: An Intellectual and Institutional History.* Chicago: University of Chicago Press, 1993.

Todd, Richard Cecil. *Confederate Finance.* Athens, GA: University of Georgia Press, 1954.

Tombstone Inscriptions. Kansas City: Union Cemetery Historical Society, 1986.

Townes, A. Jane. "The Effect of Emancipation on Large Landholdings, Nelson and Goochland Counties, Virginia." *Journal of Southern History* 45 (August 1979): 403–12.

Udovitch, Abraham L. "Reflections on the Institutions of Credits and Banking in the Medieval Islamic Near East." *Studia Islamica* 41 (1975): 5–21.

The Union Army: A History of Military Affairs in the Loyal States, 1861–65: Records of the Regiments in the Union Army, Cyclopedia of Battles, Memoirs of Commanders and Soldiers. Madison, WI: Federal Publishing, 1908. Reprint, Wilmington, NC: Broadfoot, 1997.

United Daughters of the Confederacy. *Minutes Book, 1999 General Meeting.* Richmond, VA: UDC, 1999.

United Daughters of the Confederacy, Missouri Division. *Reminiscences of the Women of Missouri During the Sixties.* Jefferson City, MO: Hugh Stephens, 1922.

United States Biographical Dictionary and Portrait Gallery of Eminent and Self-Made Men: Missouri Volume. New York: United States Biographical Publishing Company, 1878.

U.S. Census Bureau. *Statistical Abstract of the United States, 2004–2005.* http://www .census.gov/prod/2004pubs/04statab/income.pdf (accessed October 27, 2009).

U.S. Census (manuscript). Population schedules for the Seventh, Eighth, Ninth, Tenth, and Twelfth censuses, 1850, 1860, 1870, 1880, and 1900. National Archives Microfilm Series. Ancestry.com. http://search.ancestry.com/search/Default.aspx?cat=35 (accessed October 27, 2009).

U.S. Census (manuscript). Slave schedules for the Seventh and Eighth censuses, 1850 and 1860. National Archives Microfilm Series. Ancestry.com. http://search.ancestry.com/search/Default.aspx?cat=35 (accessed October 27, 2009).

U.S. Census (manuscript). Agricultural schedules for the Seventh, Eighth, and Ninth censuses, 1850, 1860, and 1870. Microform rolls. State Historical Society of Missouri, Columbia.

U.S. Department of Commerce, Bureau of the Census, *Historical Statistics of the United States, Bicentennial Edition.* Vol. 2. Washington, DC: U.S. Government Printing Office, 1975.

U.S. Department of Commerce, National Oceanic and Atmospheric Administration, and National Ocean Service. *Distances Between United States Ports.* Washington, DC: National Ocean Service, 2002.

U.S. Department of Labor, Bureau of Labor Statistics. "Table Containing History of CPI-U: U.S. All Items Indexes and Annual Percent Changes from 1913 to Present." Consumer Price Index webpage. http://www.bls.gov/cpi (accessed October 27, 2009).

U.S. Senate. *Biographical Directory of the U.S. Congress.* http://www.senate.gov/pagelayout/history/g_three_sections_with_teasers/people.htm (accessed October 27, 2009).

U.S. Statutes at Large. Hein Online, William S. Hein & Company, Inc. http://www.heinonline.org (accessed October 27, 2009).

Veblen, Thorstein. *The Theory of Business Enterprise.* New York: Mentor Books, 1932.

"Virginia Marriages, 1740–1850." Provo, UT: The Generations Network, Inc., 1999. Ancestry.com, http://www.ancestry.com/search/db.aspx?dbid=3723 (accessed October 27, 2009).

Walker, Francis W. *A Compendium of the Ninth Census (June 1, 1870), Compiled Pursuant to a Concurrent Resolution of Congress and Under the Direction of the Secretary of the Interior.* Washington, DC: Government Printing Office, 1872.

The War of the Rebellion: A Compilation of the Official Records of the Union and Confederate Armies. Washington, DC: United States Government Printing Office, 1880–1901. Making of America Collection, Cornell University Library, http://digital.library.cornell.edu/m/moa/index.html (accessed October 27, 2009).

Warfield, Joshua Dorsey. *The Founders of Anne Arundel and Howard Counties, Maryland: A Genealogical and Biographical Review from Wills, Deeds and Church Records.* Baltimore: Kohn & Pollock, 1905. Ancestry.com. http://search.ancestry.com/iexec/?htx=BookList&dbid=24819&offerid=0:7858:0 (accessed October 27, 2009).

Warner, Ezra J. *Generals in Gray: Lives of the Confederate Commanders.* Baton Rouge: Louisiana State University Press, 1959.

Watts, Hampton Boone. *The Babe of the Company.* Fayette, MO: Democrat-Leader Press, 1913.

White, Edgar. *General History of Macon County, Missouri.* Chicago: Henry Taylor & Company, 1910.

Wiener, Jonathan M. "Planter Persistence and Social Change: Alabama, 1850–1870." *Journal of Interdisciplinary History* 7, no. 2 (autumn 1976), 235–60.

———. *Social Origins of the New South.* Baton Rouge: Louisiana State University Press, 1978.

Wilken, Paul H. *Entrepreneurship: A Comparative and Historical Study.* Norwood, NJ: Ablex, 1979.

Willcox, James M. A *History of the Philadelphia Savings Fund Society.* Philadelphia: J. B. Lippencott Company, 1916.

Williams, Betty Harvey, comp. Henry and St. Clair County, Missouri, Marriage Records. http://www.rootsweb.ancestry.com/~mohenry/marriage.html (accessed October 27, 2009).

Williams, Greg H. *Civil War Suits in the U.S. Court of Claims: Cases Involving Compensation to Northerners and Southerners for Wartime Losses.* Jefferson, NC: McFarland & Company, Publishers, 2006.

Williams, Walter, and Floyd C. Shoemaker. *Missouri, Mother of the West.* Chicago: American Historical Society, 1930.

———. *History of Northwest Missouri.* Chicago: Lewis Publishing Company, 1915.

Wilson, Mark R. *The Business of Civil War: Military Mobilization and the State.* Baltimore: Johns Hopkins University Press, 2006.

Woodman, Harold D. *King Cotton and his Retainers: Financing and Marketing the Cotton Crop of the South, 1800–1925.* Lexington: University of Kentucky Press, 1968.

Woodward, C. Vann. *The Burden of Southern History.* Baton Rouge: Louisiana State University Press, 1960. Reprint, New York: Mentor Books, 1969.

———. *Origins of the New South, 1877–1913.* Baton Rouge: Louisiana State University Press, 1962.

Woodward, William S. *Annals of Methodism in Missouri.* Columbia: E. W. Stephens, Publisher, 1893.

Wright, Gavin. *Old South, New South.* New York: Basic Books, 1966.

Wyatt-Brown, Bertram. *Southern Honor: Ethics and Behavior in the Old South.* New York: Oxford University Press, 1986.

Yale University. *Catalogue of the Officers and Graduates of Yale University in New Haven, Connecticut, 1701–1924.* New Haven: Yale University, 1924.

Yamey, Basil S., ed. *The Historical Development of Accounting: A Selection of Papers.* New York: Arno Press, 1978.

Young, William. *Young's History of Lafayette County.* Indianapolis, IN: B. F. Bowen, 1910.

Younger, Cole. *The Story of Cole Younger by Himself.* St. Paul, MN: Minnesota Historical Society Press, 2000.

INDEX